The Sailor's Wind

A Manual of Sail Trim

Winning: The Psychology of Competition

Advanced Racing Tactics

The Tactics of Small Boat Racing

Positioning: The Logic of Sailboat Racing

The Techniques of Small Boat Racing

Performance Advances in Small Boat Racing

Wind and Strategy

The
Sailor's
Wind

STUART H. WALKER

Illustrated by the author and Thomas C. Price

W. W. Norton & Company, Inc. • New York • London

For information about permission to reproduce selections
from this book write to
Permissions, W. W. Norton & Company, Inc., 500 Fifth Avenue, New York, NY 10110

The text of this book is composed in Berkeley Book with the display set in Centaur
Manufacturing by Fairfield Graphics
Book design and desktop composition by Dana Sloan

Library of Congress Cataloging-in-Publication Data
Walker, Stuart H.
The sailor's wind / Stuart H. Walker : illustrated by the author and Thomas C. Price.
p. cm.
Includes bibliographical references and index.
ISBN 0-393-04555-2
1. Sailing. 2. Winds. 3. Sailboat racing.
GV811.W275   1998
797.1'24—dc21   97-39322 CIP

W. W. Norton & Company, Inc., 500 Fifth Avenue, New York, N.Y. 10110
http://www.wwnorton.com
W. W. Norton & Company Ltd., 10 Coptic Street, London WC1A 1PU

1 2 3 4 5 6 7 8 9 0

To my mother and my father,

Alice and Robert Walker,

who stimulated me to understand

and challenged me to explain

the world around me

Contents

Introduction

Alfred North Whitehead said that learning occurs only when knowledge is "needed," when it can be applied to a real situation, when it can be tested. The sailor learns in accord with this precept: he sails, he recognizes a distinctive event that affects his performance, he acts or reacts, his performance improves or deteriorates, he considers various explanations for the outcome, he discusses them with his peers and/or he reads about similar situations in the available literature, he races again and evaluates the correctness of his assumptions. He feels a need to know, he seeks understanding, and he tests that understanding during a subsequent sail. (Note: The masculine pronoun is used throughout to indicate either a male or a female sailor.)

I have organized *The Sailor's Wind* so as to introduce readers to low-level wind flow in the manner described above. Each section of the book begins with a chapter describing a particular aspect of wind behavior in a representative venue. The reader is challenged to analyze what is described, just as he is challenged on the water to analyze what he has observed. Subsequent chapters in each section complement his analysis, explain why the wind behaved as it did, and enunciate the principles that govern that behavior. I hope the reader will be so intrigued by the observations presented in the descriptive chapters that he will eagerly turn to the analytic chapters for an explanation.

This teaching technique works because it is both challenging and fun. I have used it in sailing, in medicine (it is the standard approach by which I taught medical students for 30 years), and in writing—in my columns in *Sailing World* magazine for 35 years and in my books.

The knowledge presented here is the result of 60-plus years of sailing in more than 6,000 races in all parts of the world and in a wide variety of conditions. A review of my records (kept on almost every race in which I sail) and an analysis of information gathered at many different venues in many different conditions provide a unique insight into the behavior of surface winds. To clarify the concepts derived from this experience, I have reviewed the recent meteorological literature, reports of instrumental observations, and studies of computer models. Although meteorologists have shown surprisingly little interest in low-level wind flow, what they have learned is fully incorporated in this presentation.

The first sections of the book introduce the fundamental physical principles that underlie wind behavior, the next discuss the behavior of the large-scale gradient winds, and the latter present the behavior of the small-scale thermal winds (the sea/lake breezes, the upslope winds, and the downslope winds). As the book is designed to satisfy the interests of coastal sailors, the subsections within these three major divisions are based on the orientation of winds to the coast: onshore winds, offshore winds, parallel-to-shore winds. This is, of course, appropriate because the behavior of wind near shore is largely determined by its transit of the coast.

At the beginning of each section is a list of venues characterized by the wind behavior under discussion. The lists indicate the dominant wind type at the venue—the one about which the local sailor needs the greatest insight. The lists also indicate other sites around the world at which winds similar to those of a sailor's home venue can be expected and where his local knowledge can be applied.

Although many will read the book in sequence, I suspect that most—desiring to understand a particular event or phenomenon—will refer to specific sections nonsequentially. Following a morning race in which a sea breeze backs and dies, a reader—with a "need to know"—will turn to those chapters that describe the primary sea breeze and then to those that explain its behavior. The book is designed, constructed, labeled, and indexed to facilitate this approach.

I have tried to adhere to the principle of KISS (Keep It Simple Stupid) and have thus included only the physics I thought essential. However, an appreciation of the sailor's wind requires a willingness to see physical relationships. To help the reader with the basic physical principles underlying meteorology, I have provided a simple summary in the prologue, and to help with the terminology, a glossary. As the reader considers a section of particular interest, I recommend that he occasionally revisit the prologue and/or the glossary. The more complex physics required to understand sea breeze fronts and upslope and downslope winds I have segregated into four appendices.

In the introduction to each of my books I have attempted to fix the presentation within the general structure that underlies successful sailing. In the introduction to my book on sail trim, I said that boat speed was the most important element of sailboat racing—because it permitted the beneficiary to succeed without an understanding of strategy, tactics, and boat handling! And in the introduction to my book on the psychology of competition, I said that psychology is the most important element of all—but subsequently admitted that "Nothing improves one's psyche as much as a fast boat."

I should like to say now that an understanding of low-level wind flow is even more important than an understanding of speed and psychology. But I can't. Many sailors succeed in racing and coastal cruising with very little understanding of low-level wind flow. To "start ahead and cover" in a fast boat solves the problems of most races. However, in concentrating on boat speed, many sailors miss the most intellectually challenging part of the game. There is much satisfaction to be had in predicting the wind's behavior, detecting means by which courses may be shortened or completed more rapidly, creating a Grand Strategy. Knowing what is "going on," which wind is present and which wind will develop, provides an enormous psychological advantage. And, as I said, psychology is the most important element of all!

Prologue

≈≈≈≈≈≈≈≈≈≈≈≈≈

The intent of this book is to explain *why* the air in which we sail behaves as it does. Understanding *why* will permit the prediction of *what* will happen. But in order to predict what *will* happen, it is first necessary to know what *can* happen, what *is* possible.

Weight and Pressure: The Physics Affecting Two Blocks of Air

Let's consider the state and behavior of two blocks of air at rest to either side of a coastline (as it is the near-shore air in which we are interested). The air in these blocks is a gas composed of sparsely distributed moving molecules. The air in the block has *density*—the number of molecules per unit volume—and *weight*—the total weight of all of its molecules.

Due to gravity this weight exerts pressure downward. The pressure at the top of the blocks is created by the weight of the molecules above the blocks. The *surface pressure*, the pressure at the surface beneath the blocks, is created by the weight of all the molecules above the blocks plus those within them. The surface pressure beneath the sparsely distributed molecules of the warm, light overland air is less than the surface pressure beneath the densely packed molecules of the cold, heavy overwater air.

The air in each block has not only weight, but also temperature, a measure of the kinetic energy (heat) of its moving molecules. Because the air is a gas, it can expand or contract. Boyle's law recognizes that there is a direct relationship between expansion or contraction, and temperature. If the pressure above and surrounding either block of air diminishes, the air within the block will expand and rise; as the density of its contained molecules is thereby diminished, the total kinetic energy of the molecules in the block and therefore their temperature will diminish. If the pressure above either block increases and the block contracts, the air within the block will *subside* (sink) and the density and temperature of its contained molecules will increase. The relationship works in reverse as well. If the temperature of the molecules in the overland block increases (as often occurs), the molecules will disperse and the volume will expand. If the temperature of the molecules in the overwater block decreases, the molecules will come closer together and the volume will contract.

Note the apparent paradox: When the pressure surrounding a block of air is reduced (when the block is elevated, for instance), the air in the block cools as it expands; but when the block of air is heated (when the underlying surface is heated, for instance), the air in the block expands as it heats—in both cases reaching the same volume at the same temperature.

Heating by the Sun

Now let's stir up—expand and contract—the air in these blocks and consider the results. When the surface of the land is heated by the sun, by *insolation,* the near-surface air is heated by *conduction* and, at some level of heating, parcels of the near-surface air separate, rise into, and heat and expand the cooler air above. This very important process is known as *convection.* The molecules in the heated, expanded, overland block are displaced upward and laterally: The original volume becomes less dense (lighter), whereas the air above and surrounding the block, to which molecules have been added, becomes more dense (heavier). The total weight of all the air above the surface (in the block and above it) is reduced and the pressure downward at the surface below it is diminished, but the pressure at the top of the block, where molecules have been added by being displaced upward, is increased. The surface pressure beneath the surrounding air (outside the block) is also increased by the addition of the displaced molecules and becomes greater than the surface pressure beneath the heated block.

The air in the overwater block is minimally affected by insolation (because the water beneath dissipates heat so readily) and therefore does not expand. Indeed, this air, remaining at rest above the cold water surface for a long period, will cool and contract. Molecules in the air above and surrounding the block will then subside into the newly available space and be added to the contracted air within the block. The total weight of the air in the block and the downward pressure at the surface increases, but the pressure at the top of the block, above which molecules have been removed, decreases. The surface pressure in the surrounding air (outside the block) is also decreased by the removal of molecules and becomes less than the surface pressure beneath the cooled block.

Local Circulation: Thermal Winds

The changes in pressure induced by the expansion and contraction of the air within the neighboring blocks create a disparity in pressure, a *pressure gradient,* between them. Due to gravity, this pressure gradient causes the air under higher pressure at the surface beneath the overwater block to move toward the surface beneath the overland block where the air is under lower pressure, and a horizontal surface flow is established. At the same time, the air under higher pressure above the overland block is forced toward the top of the overwater block, where the air is under lower pressure, and a horizontal upper-level flow is established. Air added to the top of the overwater block increases the surface pressure gradient, and air added to the top of the overland block increases the upper-level pressure gradient. A continuous circulation—in this case a sea breeze between the contracted overwater air and the expanded overland air—is established and will be maintained as long as heat is added (by insolation) to the overland air.

This circulation—the *atmospheric engine*—is fundamental to all horizontal air flow, global as well as local. Insolation heats a surface; the overlying air, heated by conduction and convection, expands and is displaced upward and laterally; the surface pressure at the heating site diminishes; the surface pressure in the surrounding air increases; a pressure gradient is established; and, in response to this *pressure gradient force,* air moves horizontally—*wind* blows—from the site of higher pressure toward the site of lower pressure.

Global Circulation: Gradient Winds

Upper-level air subsiding above cold, contracted near-surface air at the poles results in polar high pressure. Cold air flows from this higher pressure area equatorward at the surface until it reaches a latitude (between 40° and 60°) where the warmer surface causes it to expand and rise and where it converges with hot tropical air to produce a circumferential ring of low-pressure centers—*the polar front.* Heated air expanding and rising results in low pressure in a circumferential ring at the equator, known as the *Equatorial Convergence Zone.* From this low-pressure zone, air flows poleward aloft until it reaches a latitude (between 20° and 40°) at which the colder surface of the underlying water causes the air to subside and produce a circumferential ring of *subtropical highs.* The polar front and the subtropical highs move about 15° to 20° poleward in summer and equatorward in winter, in association with seasonal variations in insolation. This *global circulation* from the poles toward the equator at the surface and from the equator toward the poles aloft—analogous to the interblock circulation described previously—operates continuously and affects every part of the globe's surface.

Despite these large-scale movements, air tends to accumulate in segregated *air masses* and to acquire the more-or-less homogeneous characteristics of extensive, underlying surfaces such as water or tundra. Such air masses are named for their latitude—tropical or polar, underlying surface—continental or maritime, and/or specific locale. North American air masses are *continental polar (cP), maritime polar Pacific (mPp), maritime polar Atlantic (mPa), maritime tropical Gulf (of Mexico) (mTg), or maritime tropical Pacific (mTp).*

Within air masses above relatively homogeneous cold surfaces air subsides (adding more weight to the preexisting contracted surface air) so as to form huge high-pressure systems. Over Canada and Siberia, *continental polar highs* composed of cold, dry air accumulate and intermittently, as permitted by the midlatitude *jet stream* (a river of westerly flowing air at the level of the tropopause—see p. xvi), flow southward, pushing cold fronts ahead. Over the tropical oceans, *maritime tropical (subtropical) highs* composed of warm moist air accumulate and intermittently flow northward, pushing warm fronts ahead.

Heat and Moisture in the Near-Surface Air

The characteristics—the temperature, rate of change in temperature with height, moisture content, etc.—of the air in the blocks are primarily dependent on the blocks' latitude and the air mass from which the blocks derive. These characteristics, however, are modified by the surfaces over which they subsequently flow—over which they are *advected* (<u>ad</u>vection refers to horizontal flow, <u>con</u>vection to vertical flow). If the blocks are located far to the north or south of the polar front, these characteristics will vary little from day to day; but if they lie along the polar front, they will be modified cyclically at approximately weekly intervals.

Temperature is chiefly dependent on the season and the time of day (which determine the degree of insolation). Moisture content is greater in air overlying water than in air overlying land and is greater in warm air (which permits a larger portion of the water to be in its evaporated gaseous form—*water vapor*) than in cold air. Moisture content affects temperature in that water vapor and *water droplets* (water in its condensed liquid form) absorb heat directly from insolation, water droplets (cloud) reflect longwave radiation from the earth's surface (the *"greenhouse effect"*), and the process of *evaporation* (the transformation of water droplets into water vapor) absorbs heat whereas the reverse process of *condensation* releases heat (the *"latent heat of condensation"*).

Vertical Movement: Convection

When heated, a parcel of free air expands (becomes less dense) and rises until it reaches a level above which the surrounding air is less dense. When cooled, a parcel of air contracts and sinks to a level below which the surrounding air is more dense. But a parcel of air does not maintain its volume as it rises or sinks. As it rises, it is subjected to progressively less surrounding pressure and therefore expands. As it sinks, it is subjected to progressively more surrounding pressure and therefore contracts. When it expands or contracts, its density changes (and therefore the amount of energy contained within a given volume changes) and (in accordance with Boyle's law) its temperature changes. The temperature changes associated with vertical movement—the cooling that accompanies *expansion* during elevation and the heating that accompanies compression during subsidence— are called *adiabatic* changes.

All air, whenever and however it moves vertically—along a slope, within a rising or a sinking wind, within the free air as an updraft or a downdraft—changes its density and temperature adiabatically (at the *adiabatic lapse rate—ALR*), at approximately 0.6° Fahrenheit (F) per 100 feet (1° Celsius per 100 meters). These adiabatic changes tend to negate the influences that caused the air to move vertically in the first place and to halt its further movement. Air caused to subside (because it has become cooler and denser), heats as it subsides. Finding itself warmer and therefore less dense than its surroundings, it soon ceases to subside. Air caused to rise (because it has become warmer and less dense), cools as it rises. Finding itself cooler and therefore denser than its surroundings, it soon ceases to rise.

Air moving vertically changes in density and temperature as a consequence of that movement, but nonmoving air at differing levels in the atmosphere is also characterized by differing density and temperature. Typically, density and temperature decrease with altitude, because the atmosphere loses heat with distance from its heat source—the earth's surface.

If the temperature in the surrounding air falls rapidly with altitude (if the *surrounding air lapse rate [SLR]* is greater than the ALR), the air is said to be *unstable,* and vertical movement is facilitated. If the temperature falls slowly with altitude (if the SLR is less than the ALR), the air is said to be *stable,* and vertical movement is restricted. If the SLR becomes positive, if the temperature rises with altitude, there is said to be an *inversion* (or an *inversion layer*), and vertical movement is halted. Inversions isolate a warm layer above a cold layer, typically a turbulent layer above a calm surface layer, and often a layer isolating a gradient wind above a layer containing a thermal wind.

Turbulence

Turbulence is the movement of air in directions other than that of the general flow. *Mechanical turbulence* is due to friction, is random in all directions, and is proportional to the speed of the flow. In the blocks of air it is greatest at the surface and least at the top. It is greater over land (above irregular terrain) than over water. *Thermal turbulence* (convection) is induced by insolation and is entirely vertical—upward in updrafts, downward in downdrafts. Thermal turbulence is typically absent in the overwater block, but is the major source of turbulence in the overland block and proportional to insolation, i.e., maximal in early afternoon and absent at night.

Convection transmits heat to the *turbulent layer* (the layer between the surface and an overlying inversion within which thermal turbulence takes place) in *eddies, streams (updrafts),* and *sheets*. When updrafts of heated air rise to the top of the turbulent layer, they induce *replacement downdrafts* that rush parcels of upper air downward to the surface, where they impact as *gusts*. The air in (and near) the overland block (during insolation) is far more turbulent, and the air at its surface moves at a higher speed and is far more gusty than the air at the surface of the overwater block.

Horizontal Movement: Wind

Large-scale winds such as the global prevailing winds and the weather system winds of the midlatitudes are known as *gradient winds*. Smaller-scale winds resulting from the pressure differences associated with local differences in surface temperature (downslope and upslope winds, and sea and land breezes, for instance) are distinguished from gradient winds and are called *thermal winds*. Gradient winds extend over hundreds of miles, occupy or are associated with changes in the entire depth of the *troposphere* (the lowest portion of the atmosphere within which all weather conditions are manifest), often obliterate thermal winds in their path, and vary with the meanderings of the jet streams that flow along breaks in the *tropopause* (the top of the troposphere) at approximately 35,000 feet. Thermal winds extend over tens of miles, rarely occupy layers above 2,000 feet (and are usually confined to even lower strata), regularly displace (upward or laterally), but do not obliterate, gradient winds, and vary with diurnal temperature changes.

Because large-scale, or *synoptic*, pressure gradients between the highs, lows, and fronts of the global circulation usually exist, surface air is typically moving in a gradient wind. In order for the air in the blocks to be unmoving, an inversion must protect the low-level air from the effects of the synoptic pressure gradient and from the turbulence of the gradient wind. Light, expanded hot air—above an inversion—is unable to penetrate heavy, dense cold air below. Only a low-level, *thermal pressure gradient* created by a local change in surface heating will initiate air flow—a *thermal wind*—below an inversion.

Wind involving the near-surface air within the blocks may either be induced by a local difference in expansion or contraction—a thermal wind (induced by local differences in the heating of the underlying surface), or by entrainment within air moving in response to a *synoptic pressure gradient* (in the absence or following the dissipation of an inversion)—a *gradient wind.*

Once moving, the blocks of air acquire momentum, direction, and speed, and these characteristics will vary within the block, chiefly with height above the surface. Friction, which resists flow at all levels, is greatest at the surface and causes speed and momentum to be least at the surface and greatest at the top of the blocks.

Coriolis Force

Motion is initially in the direction of, and speed is proportional to, the pressure gradient force. Once initiated, however, movement is deviated (relative to the surface of the earth) by an effect known as the *Coriolis force.* Differences in the speed of rotation of the earth at different latitudes cause the trajectory of all flow to be deviated in proportion to its speed and to its vertical separation from the earth's surface. This force is increasingly active as one nears the poles (where small differences in latitude are associated with large differences in the speed of rotation) and absent at the equator.

In the Northern Hemisphere the Coriolis force causes all flow to appear (to an observer on the surface) to be deviated to the right *(veered).* Consequently, air flowing out from a center of high pressure is veered into a clockwise circulation, and air flowing into a center of low pressure is veered into a counterclockwise circulation. The faster the movement, the less it is affected by friction (which attaches near-surface flow to the rotating surface) and the more it is affected by the Coriolis force. Consequently, from the surface to the top of the blocks, the air, flowing at progressively higher speeds, is progressively more affected by the Coriolis force and becomes progressively more veered.

Deviation of Flow

The blocks of moving air (if their movement carries them parallel to shore) may demonstrate *divergence* and *convergence.* The air in the overwater block (because of reduced surface friction) will move at a higher speed and therefore will be veered to the flow of air in the overland block. If the blocks are moving with *water on their right,* the veering air in the overwater block will deviate away— *diverge* from—the air in the overland block; whereas if the blocks are moving *with water on their left,* the veering air in the overwater block will deviate toward—*converge* with—the air in the overland block. Divergence causes a reduction in pressure at the interface between the two blocks, subsidence from above, and an acceleration of air flow. Convergence causes an increase in pressure at the interface, elevation of the air below, condensation (cloud formation) above, and a slowing of flow.

The movement of the blocks of air is deviated by surface obstacles in their path. The cold, dense air in the overwater block resists elevation and is instead *channeled* (changed in direction and speed—slowed or accelerated—in the horizontal plane) so that it flows around and between obstacles. The lighter, less dense air in the overland block, already characterized by vertical motion (convection), readily rises (*orographic lift*) to surmount obstacles and, although slowed, changes direction minimally.

Upslope flow is enhanced by the progressively diminishing pressure and the ease of convective separation associated with higher altitude, but is resisted by gravity and the adiabatic cooling due to elevation. *Downslope flow* is aided by gravity and in some instances by wave formation, but diminished by the adiabatic heating due to compression.

Acknowledgments

≈≈≈≈≈≈≈≈≈≈≈

Sailboat racing is a grand meteorological laboratory to which few investigators have access. Experiments—with every possible variable varied—can be repeated again and again, until the observer "gets it right." My competitors have by their success and failure throughout the years demonstrated how the sailor's wind behaves and why. I thank them.

I extend particular thanks to Dr. Willard Standiford, who reviewed the entire manuscript and helped me to make it more readily understandable. The staff of the United States Naval Academy Library was extremely helpful in ensuring that I had access to all of the modern meteorological literature on low-level wind flow.

In addition to drawing on my own extensive experience in the venues discussed, I sought out local experts, compared their observations, and in many cases enlisted their help in recording typical wind patterns. I am particularly indebted to those who assisted me in my analyses of the winds of foreign venues: Alan Watts, the meteorologist-author whose pioneer investigations of the secondary sea breeze along England's south coast initiated the scientific study of low-level wind flow; Jean Pierre Marmier and Raymond Cardis, who collected locally published information on the winds of the Lake of Geneva, and Frederic Nicolaidis, who translated that information from the French; Gerold Worlitz-Wellspacher, who provided his extensive experience of the Wolfgangsee's Brunn wind and translated my analysis into German so that it could be critiqued by others; Franco Santoni, whose experience with the winds of Lago di Garda must be second to none; Willie Packer, who not only analyzed the Fremantle Doctor but also produced a video describing its intricacies; Erich Hirt, who grew up on the Starnbergersee and knows "the lake winds"; Hartley Watlington, who knew the vagaries of every gust that ever crossed Bermuda's Great Sound; and José Ramon Domenech, who provided special insights into the Levante at Cádiz.

Dick Besse and Ernest Hauser provided decades of observations of the winds of the Finger Lakes. Bob Bowden, in providing the report of the effects of the Lake Norman microburst, and John Lee, in recounting his experience sailing within it, were invaluable to my analysis of microburst behavior. Jim Roosevelt, by providing some of the early folklore concerning Long Island Sound, greatly assisted my analysis of its winds. For an entire summer Mildred Wright collected data on the winds of the Georgia coast that permitted me to make generalizations about the winds at Savannah. John Townsend helped me analyze the winds experienced during the 1995 Pre-Olympic Regatta and gave me his excellent study of the coastal winds at Charleston. Jerry Castle and Frank Shumway provided both knowledge and opportunities that were essential to my diagnosis of Rochester's southwester. Joe Ellis's extensive experience with the sea breeze of St. Petersburg clarified my observations and corrected some of my initial conclusions.

The Sailor's Wind

I. *Simple Onshore Winds*

1. The West Coast

Fair weather cometh out of the north.
—PSALMS 37:22

Th is presentation of the principles that determine and modify low-level air flow begins with a description of the summer winds of the U.S. West Coast. These winds are variants of *primary sea breezes,* the simplest of all air flows and the easiest to understand. Because they are simple winds, the manner in which they are modified by variations in insolation, by latitude, by shoreline topography, and by their interaction with other winds is easily recognizable. They represent an ideal introduction to the sailor's wind (Table 1).

Each day in summer along the West Coast, the surface air moves from the cool ocean toward the heating land. This movement, like all air movement, is in response to a difference in pressure, a pressure gradient. The major pressure gradient on the West Coast is a local (as distinguished from a large-scale, or synoptic) gradient created by a local difference in the expansion, density, weight, and therefore pressure of the air overlying the heating land relative to the air overlying

3

the cold ocean. The flow is a simple one because the thermal gradient is protected by an atmospheric lid, an inversion, from the effects of the ever-present synoptic pressure gradient and therefore operates in isolation. However, as we shall see, even a simple air flow is strengthened, diminished, deviated, lifted, and disturbed by a variety of forces associated with time, temperature, and topography.

Subtropical continental coasts lie beneath nearly permanent high-pressure air masses—subtropical highs. These form as upper-level air moving poleward from the Equatorial Convergence Zone subsides over the major oceans at 20° to 40° latitude. In summer the subtropical highs move farther poleward and bring their inversions and their typical wind patterns to the midlatitudes. Summer weather on the West Coast of the United States resembles that on the East Coast because a subtropical high, the East Pacific High, occupies the entire offshore ocean (as does the Bermuda High in the Atlantic), and provides a similar *subsidence inversion* all along the coast. (Figure 1.1)

TABLE 1: CLASSIFICATION OF THE SAILOR'S WINDS

AIR-MASS WINDS
    Trade winds under the subtropical highs

GRADIENT WINDS
    Outflow winds from high pressure
    Inflow winds toward low pressure

PRIMARY SEA/LAKE BREEZES UNDER INVERSIONS

SECONDARY SEA/LAKE BREEZES UNDER OFFSHORE GRADIENT WINDS

AMALGAMATED SEA BREEZES WITH ONSHORE GRADIENT WINDS

UPSLOPE WINDS
    Simple upslope winds
    Onslope winds
    Valley winds
    Expansion differential winds
    Gradient-induced upslope winds

DOWNSLOPE WINDS
    Nocturnal or shade-induced downslope winds
    Glacier (fall) winds
    Mountain winds
SMALL-LAKE WINDS
    Lake breeze/gradient wind combinations
    Lake breeze/upslope combinations
    Lake breeze/downslope ("translake") combinations
GRADIENT-INDUCED DOWNSLOPE WINDS
    Cold (Bora-like) winds
    Hot (Föhn-like) winds

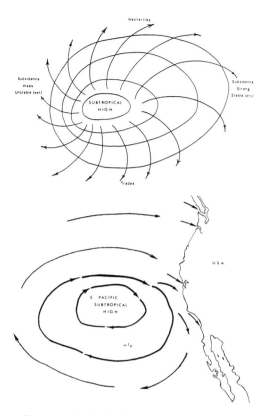

Figure 1.1. The East Pacific Subtropical High

Subsidence inversions form within the subtropical highs because the lower levels of the air mass, suprajacent to the cold sea, cool and contract, causing the upper-level air to subside, and because, over water, thermal turbulence (the vertical mixing of air heated at the surface) is minimal. As air subsides, it is compressed from above by an increasingly large mass of air and, under compression, gains heat. The upper (subsiding) air becomes progressively warmer, while the lower (contracting) air in contact with the sea becomes progressively colder—an "inversion" of the usual cold-air-over-warm relationship. As subsidence inversions are dependent on the coldness of the water that underlies them, they ordinarily do not extend far inland, but at the shoreline have a profound effect on sea breeze formation.

Above and isolated by these inversions from the cold, dense air below, large-scale (synoptic) pressure gradients produce warm gradient wind flows. Below the inversions, the heating of the surface of the land by the sun (insolation) generates thermal gradients that produce onshore flows of cool marine air and create the typically delightful climate of the subtropical coasts.

A wide band of cold contracted air that induces additional subsidence and results in higher surface pressure overlies the cold California Current, which (as it flows southward) warms the winter along the coasts of Washington and Oregon and cools the summer of California. From this band of high pressure, and beneath the subsidence inversion, primary sea breezes flow toward the heating continental interior through every low-level opening in the coastal wall created by the Cascade Range, particularly at Los Angeles, San Francisco, the Columbia River, and Puget Sound.

The eastern portions of subtropical highs that border continental west coasts (such as the East Pacific Subtropical High) overlie cold water in polar currents flowing equatorward and are therefore associated with far greater subsidence than are the western portions of subtropical highs along continental east coasts, which overlie warm currents flowing poleward. On west coasts the colder water causes greater contraction of the overlying air and therefore greater subsidence, a stronger subsidence inversion, and a far greater extension of the inversion inland. Consequently, the marine layer is far more isolated and the primary sea breeze far better protected (Figure 1.2).

On the West Coast the gradient wind rarely appears at the surface (whereas on the East Coast it typically appears at the surface). The sea breeze (without any gradient wind admixture) is typically the first and only wind of the day. Because steep near-shore mountains block its access to the heating interior, it is weak, except at a few narrow openings through which it flows at high velocity (see Table 1, p. 4).

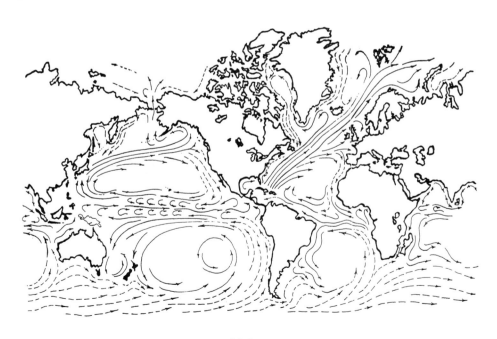

Figure 1.2. Global ocean currents

Los Angeles

The Primary Sea Breeze

The cool, moist marine layer that gives coastal Southern California its delightful climate is confined like a huge lake, 2,000 feet deep, by the subsidence inversion and the mountains that rise a few miles inland. Each morning the heating of the land initiates convection, heats and expands the marine layer, elevates the subsidence inversion, melts the subinversion layer of stratocumulus cloud, and reduces the inshore surface pressure. Within a mile of shore, the marine air begins to move toward the heating surfaces, and this movement gradually spreads both shoreward and seaward.

At Los Angeles the extensive near-shore plain facilitates the invasion of the sea breeze front, and the coastal mountain range adds a strong upslope flow (a combination that is regularly stronger in the mountain canyons than offshore). But no major river leads the marine air inland, and the subsidence inversion prevents the marine air from reaching and separating from the mountain peaks. Thermal turbulence over the offshore islands brings stronger flow to the inshore water surfaces, and where the flow is confined by elevated shores, a strong 16- to 18-knot sea breeze develops.

Newport Harbor

On most summer days the sea breeze appears out of morning calm by 0800 (in contrast to the much later onset of the sea breeze along the East Coast) and near the Balboa shore is usually a 4- to 6-knot south-southwesterly (range 185° to 230° magnetic; note that all bearings mentioned in this book are magnetic) with marked oscillations. The flow strengthens and becomes progressively more stable as heating ashore becomes more uniform. During the 1968 Olympic Trials the morning surface wind oscillated between a more westerly (230° to 250°) air flow, most evident at the surface inshore (to the west of the course), and a more south-westerly (at 220° to 230°) air flow, most evident offshore (to the southwest). This segregation was most evident in the morning, when races were often won by the boat that continued farthest offshore on starboard tack and then tacked to windward of the fleet in a progressively increasing back.

Later in the day the strategy was typically reversed. The stronger and veered (more westerly) near-shore flow spread farther offshore (to or beyond the weather mark), and the veering increased to and beyond the starboard layline. By tacking immediately from the starboard end of the starting line and short-tacking up the beach, we won (or nearly won) two races of the '68 trials and the right to represent the United States in the '68 Olympics (Figure 1.3).

A number of factors combine to produce the progressive veering in the sea breeze characteristic of the Southern California coast and serve to introduce this behavior. The upper portion of Figure 1.3 shows that over water a sea breeze is composed of an upper-level flow minimally affected by surface friction and therefore more veered by the Coriolis force, and a near-surface flow greatly affected by surface friction and minimally affected by the Coriolis force. As a sea breeze transits

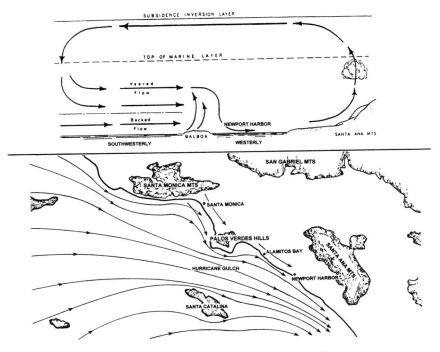

Figure 1.3. Progressive veering in the Southern California sea breeze

land, thermal turbulence—the creation of updrafts and downdrafts initiated by the separation and elevation of parcels of heated near-surface air—accelerates the surface flow and brings to the surface veered portions of the upper-level air flow. Any water surface to leeward of a segment of hot land (such as Newport Harbor, inland and to leeward of Balboa Island) receives a more veered, more northwesterly air flow. This alteration in direction entrains the near-shore portions of the offshore air flow and causes all the air flow along the coast to become more northwesterly.

In addition, as a sea breeze strengthens, its overwater portions accelerate and, in response to the Coriolis force, veer as they accelerate—an effect known as *velocity veer*. As the day progresses, the entire onshore flow becomes progressively more veered to its initial trajectory (approximately perpendicular to the coast), and progressively more northwesterly. The lower portion of Figure 1.3 shows the strong, fully veered sea breeze in late afternoon.

In Southern California this velocity veer is exaggerated by *channeling*, by deviation in the horizontal plane as a cold flow alters course and is slowed or accelerated when it meets a topographic obstacle. As the cold, dense marine air strikes the coastal mountains obliquely, it is deviated so that it flows more parallel to shore, from a more westerly direction. This deviation is particularly prominent in the vicinity of the

8

Santa Monica Mountains, which rise directly from the shore. A dramatic acceleration and alteration in the direction of the surface layers of the sea breeze is required by their confinement between the Palos Verdes Hills and Santa Catalina.

A fourth factor contributes to the progressive veering of the near-shore air flow. Because of the lessened friction, the segment of any parallel-to-shore flow that flows over water is accelerated and (to the extent that it is accelerated) veered, whereas the adjacent, slowed portion that flows over land is relatively backed. Consequently, along the Southern California shoreline, where the veered sea breeze flows nearly parallel to shore with water on its right, the overland and overwater segments of the sea breeze flow diverge from one another. Divergence (by diminishing lateral friction) causes acceleration. A band of overwater flow develops near shore that becomes stronger and more veered than the flow farther offshore.

The result of this divergence along the coast near Newport Harbor is a band of strong, veered (more westerly) flow inshore and a zone of unaffected, (relatively) light, backed (more southwesterly) flow offshore. Divergence (as well as thermal turbulence and the velocity veer) increases as insolation increases and the sea breeze flow strengthens. The veering of the Southern California sea breeze therefore increases with time and spreads progressively offshore as more and more of the flow is entrained.

Alamitos Bay and Marina del Rey

The strongest sea breeze of Southern California is created in "Hurricane Gulch" by the confinement of the onshore flow between the abruptly rising shores of Santa Catalina Island and the Palos Verdes Peninsula. Alamitos Bay, at the eastern end of Hurricane Gulch, is famous for the veering of its sea breeze and its requirement of an early port tack.

Alamitos Bay demonstrates the important difference between a static shift due to channeling, for instance, and a progressive shift due to a velocity veer or divergence. To the extent that a shift is due to channeling, it will be present constantly, but only in a particular portion of the course. To the extent that the shift is due to a change in velocity, it will be present only in association with a change in velocity, but will be present over the entire course. At Alamitos Bay the westerly shift is usually evident throughout the day and largely restricted to the right side of the course. It seems reasonable to presume that the veering is largely due to channeling around the Palos Verdes Peninsula, not to a velocity veer.

Farther north off Marina del Rey the westerly, as it flows near shore, is recovering from its deviation along the face of the Santa Monica Mountains. It backs with distance inshore, where it is maximally affected by the deviation induced by the mountains. Offshore the flow is progressively less affected by the mountains and remains northwesterly. A progressive veer as one goes offshore and a back near the beach result—the reverse of the situation at Newport Harbor. An early (but not immediate) port tack is still required, however; in the backed near-shore air, port tack is headed more offshore than elsewhere along the coast and leads most directly to the offshore channeled veer. South of Santa Monica late in the day the divergence of the overwater segment becomes increasingly evident, and a band of veered flow may develop near the beach.

The Columbia River Gorge

This, the North American mecca for boardsailors, is the quintessential site for heavy-air sailing. In one 30-mile stretch, as the Columbia River passes through the Cascade Range, all the elements required for creating strong surface air flow are assembled. It has all the attributes of the other West Coast sailing venues—the strong, protective subsidence inversion provided by the East Pacific High, cool marine air from over the near-shore upwelling produced by the diverging California Current, water-level access for the marine air to an extended shoreline, an extensive near-shore plain leading onto the slopes of high coastal mountains, producing a strong upslope flow—plus a major expansion differential (Figure 1.4).

The Expansion Differential

The temperature disparity between the cold near-shore water (brought from the depths to the surface by the upwelling) and the hot coastal plain creates a strong primary sea breeze. Under the usually clear skies created by subsidence in the East Pacific High, the dense marine air moves readily across the ocean beaches and up the Columbia River. After crossing the coastal plain the sea breeze front becomes imbedded in the general upslope flow of the Cascades and accelerates toward their peaks. Just to the north of the Columbia River are 8,000-foot Mt. St. Helens and 12,000-foot Mt. Adams, and just to the south is 11,000-foot Mt. Hood—mountains higher than at any other U.S. coastal site.

But the wind that whistles through the gorge, though confined by these peaks, is heading for the Columbia Plateau—a huge expanse of open rolling country to the east of the Cascades at an altitude 1,500 to 3,000 feet above the coastal plain. The upslope flow is blocked from rising to surmount the Cascade

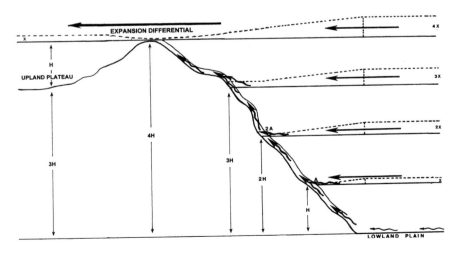

Figure 1.4. Flow toward an upland plateau due to an expansion differential

10

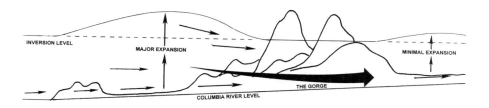

Figure 1.5. Acceleration of flow through the Columbia River Gorge in response to differential expansion

ridge by the subsidence inversion. The flow's only route to the low pressure overlying the Columbia Plateau is through the one gap below the inversion, the Columbia River Gorge (Figure 1.5).

The difference in altitude between the coastal plain and the Columbia Plateau results in a major difference in the atmospheric expansion produced by insolation. Above the coastal plain, to the west of the gorge, insolation expands the air between sea level and an altitude of 1,500 feet (as well as farther aloft). But above the high Columbia Plateau to the east of the gorge, there is no air at an altitude below 1,500 feet and no expansion. Consequently, as the plain and the plateau heat each day, the pressure levels in the expanding air above the coastal plain rise far higher than above the plateau, and a major pressure differential drives massive amounts of air through the gorge (see Chapter 35).

Channeling

En route from the coast to Portland the Columbia River runs for 80 miles through the coastal plain. Near Portland low hills appear and the riverbed begins to rise. Sixty miles east of Portland the steep granite walls of the gorge appear. Although at first (near Stephenson) they are but 100 feet high (allowing large amounts of subinversion air to escape laterally), the strength of the westerly wind increases dramatically. Whitecaps appear on wide expanses of the river. Farther east, below the Hood River Toll Bridge, at the Fish Hatchery (the "Hatch") and off Swell City, the walls of the gorge rise abruptly to 300 feet and the passage narrows. Now most of the subinversion marine layer, unable to rise above the cliff tops, is confined within the gorge, and the wind velocity increases to 30-plus knots. Thousands of boardsailors are attracted by the rolling waves produced as the accelerated westerly flowing current meets the strong west wind. At Rowena, 15 miles farther upriver, and at Maryhill State Park, 30 miles beyond, the gorge narrows and the river shallows, creating even stronger winds and bigger waves.

Diurnal and Seasonal Variations

Because the upland plateau and the mountains to the east heat (with the sun advancing from the east) before the gorge and the plains to the west, a westerly upslope flow begins in early morning, and the boardsailors are planing by 0700.

11

The strongest winds are delayed, however, until the sea breeze begins, the coastal plain heats, and the expansion differential enhances the upslope flow.

Flow through the gorge reaches its peak velocity in late spring and summer. The fifth of May is the traditional opening day of the boardsailing season, which extends through September. However, "frigid howlers" occasionally appear in October and on clear days throughout the winter—whenever insolation of the coastal plain expands the coastal air relative to that above the inland plateau.

Downriver (western) sites nearer the coast tend to have stronger winds in the spring, when the temperature disparity between the ocean and the coastal plain is greatest and the sea breeze is strongest. Upriver (eastern) sites nearer the upland plateau tend to have stronger winds in late summer, when the heating of the plain is greater—increasing the disparity between the expansion above the plain and the plateau—and the upslope flow is strongest.

The Synoptic Gradient

The synoptic gradient—the difference in pressure between the East Pacific High offshore and the typical summer *heat low* (low pressure persisting over the heated desert) of the interior valley—significantly modifies the total pressure differential and the resultant flow. As long as the clear subsidence skies of the subtropical high dominate the coast (as they typically do from May through September) a sea breeze and a westerly upslope flow will occur. But occasionally a central California heat low slips to the west over the Cascades, moves up the California coast, and displaces the offshore high.

When low pressure moves offshore, not only is the pressure gradient reduced (or reversed), but the subsidence inversion is eliminated. The thermal flow that develops is no longer confined to the low levels within the gorge, but flows far above its cold waters without disturbing them. However, within a few days the offshore low dissipates, a new low forms above the Columbia Plateau, and the East Pacific High, its inversion, and the "nuclear days" (as gorge sailors like to call them) return. The most renowned talents in the area are the computer whizzes whose programs predict the strength of the gorge's winds from the synoptic pressure data and the movements of the heat lows.

Puget Sound

In summer the East Pacific High covers a large portion of the ocean west of Puget Sound and provides the same subsidence inversion and protection for primary sea breeze development that it provides farther south. Here, however, the ocean and the marine air are far colder, the coastline and the area affected (within Puget Sound) far larger, and therefore the sea breeze, as it funnels through the Strait of Juan de Fuca, is far stronger. The strait is confined, though not nearly so narrowly, by high mountains similar to those lining the Columbia River Gorge. Beneath the inversion, all but small portions (which enter through gaps in the Olympic Mountains or between the mountains on Vancouver Island) of the marine air are carried inland through the strait. The huge shoreline of the sound, the relatively low-lying near-shore land, and the large mountains that contribute strong upslope flows combine to produce a strong and massive sea breeze (Figure 1.6).

Each morning, at a speed proportionate to the degree of insolation inland, a sea breeze front advances down the strait and spreads throughout the expanse of the sound toward the thousands of miles of heating shoreline. The 25- to 30-knot gale, when channeled through the narrow strait, becomes a 15-knot wind in the open sound and a mere 5- to 10-knot breeze as it spreads north toward Vancouver and south toward Seattle. The front arrives about noon as a westerly off Port Angeles in the strait, and appears at 1500 or later as a northerly off Seattle. It strengthens in the narrow channels approaching Mt. Rainier to the southeast, and to the north off Bellingham where, enhanced by upslope flow on its approach to Mt. Baker, it is a southerly.

Because Puget Sound is on the track of North Pacific depressions spawned by the Aleutian Low, a southerly gradient wind often opposes the northerly sea breeze at Shilshole (just north of Seattle). If there are breaks in the cloud cover, a *secondary sea breeze* may advance down the sound, pushing a zone of convergence calm and the southerly gradient wind ahead of it. Deprived of its protective subsidence inversion as it moves inland, the sea breeze may ebb and flow with variations in cloud cover and insolation. Late in the day the southerly is likely to reappear.

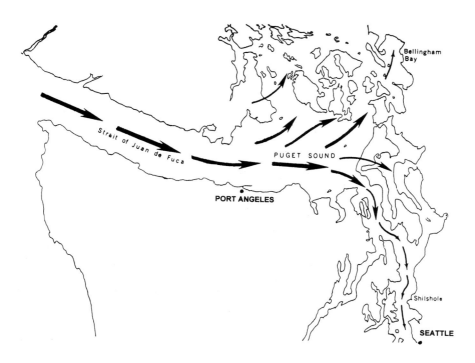

Figure 1.6. Channeling in the Puget Sound sea breeze

13

2. Insolation: The Atmospheric Engine

The sun was warm, but the wind was chill.
You know how it is with an April day.
　　　　　　　　　—ROBERT FROST

The preceding description of West Coast winds indicates that horizontal air flow results when portions of the surface of the earth respond to insolation and are heated disparately. On the West Coast, air flow is initiated by a rise in the temperature of the land in the absence of any significant change in the temperature of the ocean. Heating of the land during insolation results in convection and it is convection that drives the atmospheric engine (see prologue, p. xiii).

Convection (the separation from the surface, expansion, and elevation of heated air) reduces the density of the air in the turbulent layer above and, consequently, decreases the pressure at the surface below. The reduction in surface pressure, relative to an adjacent site, creates a pressure gradient down which air flows. The large-scale reduction in surface pressure associated with relatively constant heating at the equator initiates and maintains the great global air circulation, while near a shoreline the transient reduction in overland pressure associated with diurnal heating creates the local sea/lake breeze.

Horizontal air flow, typically the consequence of a local reduction in surface pressure, varies with the determinants of convection: the response of a surface to insolation, the transmission of heat to the near-surface air, bubble formation, separation, the vertical movement of parcels of heated air, expansion, and the formation of replacement downdrafts. Variations in convection are particularly important in determining the likelihood, time of onset, direction, and strength of thermal winds such as sea/lake breezes.

The Heating of the Atmosphere

The earth gains energy (is heated) almost entirely by shortwave (ultraviolet) radiation from the sun (insolation). The atmosphere absorbs some of this radiation, but 42 percent of it reaches the earth, where it either heats the surface or is reflected back. *The lower levels of the atmosphere gain heat almost entirely from the earth's surface,* chiefly by convection (the vertical movement of heated air), slightly by longwave (infrared) radiation (which is absorbed by water vapor and carbon dioxide in the air), and, within immediately adjacent layers, by conduction (Figure 2.1).

The lower portion of the atmosphere is characterized by a 500- to 15,000-foot-deep turbulent layer within which all horizontal air flow takes place, confined beneath the tropopause (the top of the troposphere where temperature ceases to fall with height), and by a near-surface, "smooth" or boundary layer a few inches to 300 feet deep. Heated air that separates from the surface rises rapidly through the near-surface layer, affecting it but minimally, and mixes with the air

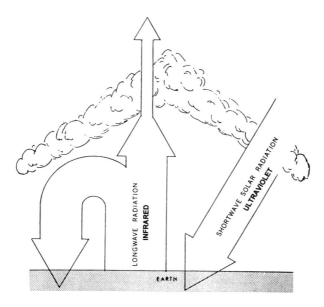

Figure 2.1. Insolation (ultraviolet) and reflection (infrared)

in the turbulent layer. Above the turbulent layer at the upper extreme of convection is a temperature inversion, a layer of varying thickness where the temperature ceases to fall with height—due to any of the following: the tropopause, the cessation of updraft movement and the accumulation of heated air, the compression and heating of air subsiding from above, or the cooling and contraction of air suprajacent to a cold surface.

The Response to Insolation

Land heats far more rapidly than water, not merely because its heat capacity is only one-third as great, but because all of the insolation is absorbed (or reflected) in the top few millimeters of the soil and because, due to the insulating effect of myriad tiny air pockets, heat is so poorly disseminated through the soil. On the other hand, in clear water 50 percent of insolation is immediately distributed throughout the top 30 feet and is rapidly disseminated into deeper water by turbulent mixing. The result is rapid warming and cooling of land surfaces and minimal changes in the temperature of water surfaces.

Flat, barren, and dry land absorbs heat best; hilly, forested surfaces least. Snow reflects almost all of the shortwave radiation received but absorbs almost none. By its obstruction of some portions of the shortwave (ultraviolet) input, cloud cover diminishes surface heating; but, by its far greater obstruction of longwave (infrared) output (the greenhouse effect), cloud cover markedly diminishes the cooling of the surface and of the lower atmosphere.

Separation

The daytime atmosphere over land is characterized by hot expanded air under (relatively) cold contracted air—*instability*. The slightest change in the equilibrium between gravity (the tendency of cold, dense air to sink) and buoyancy

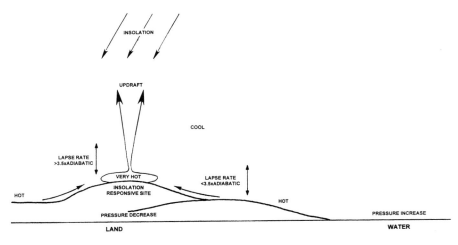

Figure 2.2. A bubble of heated air separating from the surface

(the tendency of warm, expanded air to rise) results in the vertical movement of free air. But at the surface, in the absence of any pressure from beneath, the lowest layer of air—even though expanded—is pinned down by dense suprajacent air and will not rise until it is heated (by longwave radiation and conduction) to a temperature far above its surroundings. Its buoyancy is insufficient to overcome gravity—until it separates (Figure 2.2).

The frequency of mirages over heated surfaces demonstrates that a layer of increased density often overlies a layer of lesser density. On a clear day in summer the land is often heated above 100°F while the overlying air is in the 80s. But the shimmering of those mirages indicates that separation is occurring and that heated air is rising in eddies and streams.

Bubble Formation

The first stage of separation is the formation (within the boundary layer) of tiny accumulations of heated air—"bubbles." Bubbles form (as they do at the bottom of a pot of water when the water begins to boil) because, unable to separate, heated air flows horizontally, attached to the surface, toward maximally heated surface areas called *nucleation sites*. Above such a site (in response to Boyle's law, which requires that the volume of a gas is proportional to its temperature) the heated air expands. An expanding bubble is unable to separate, is fixed to the surface, and continues to entrain additional heated air until its temperature rises to a level such that after it separates and rises, its temperature and density, altered at the rate regularly associated with vertical movement (the adiabatic lapse rate—0.6°F per 100 feet) are equal to or less than its surroundings at the higher level. *Separation will not occur until the rate of decrease in temperature with height (the lapse rate) between the bubble surface and the suprajacent air becomes 3.5 times as great as the adiabatic rate.*

The ease and rapidity with which this lapse rate is exceeded and separation occurs depends on the degree of, and the response of, the surface to insolation—how hot the surface becomes—and on the temperature of the overlying air—how cold the air in the near-surface layer was before insolation began. In very warm air large bubbles form before the lapse rate at the bubble surface rises sufficiently to permit separation. In very cold air the inherently high lapse rate permits separation of even small bubbles with minimal surface heating.

Updraft Formation

Once bubbles, large or small, begin to separate, two additional phenomena come into play. First, the sudden drop in pressure beneath the abruptly rising and expanding bubble forces surrounding air toward the evacuated site. If the surrounding air has been sufficiently heated and is less dense than the suprajacent air, it will entrain beneath the bubble, and a stream of heated air will flow upward. At any one site this process is always discontinuous; all the heated air accumulating in a given bubble separates, entrains the surrounding heated air, and roars aloft, leaving only cool air behind. A period of seconds or minutes then elapses before the surface air is again heated sufficiently to separate.

Second, as the bubble rises, its volume increases (due to expansion under the progressively diminishing pressure and entrainment) more rapidly than its surface area. As a result, buoyancy forces (associated with volume) increasingly exceed drag forces (associated with surface area), and its rate of rise constantly accelerates. The result is an ever-enlarging chimney of heated air (an updraft) rushing upward through the surrounding denser air and creating a "draft," into which surrounding parcels of heated air under higher pressure are forced.

Thermal Turbulence

As millions of bubbles separate and coalesce into updrafts (or other forms of vertically moving air), heated air is carried aloft until it reaches a level above which the air is less dense (more expanded). As the updraft rises, it displaces colder, denser air that, free of the impeding effects of surface friction, has been moving horizontally at a higher speed and, due to the Coriolis force, in a more veered direction relative to the near-surface air. In response to the decreased pressure beneath the expanding updraft, a downdraft of this upper-level air rushes to the surface. The result of this vertical movement, this thermal turbulence, is the strengthening and veering of the surface air flow, and a more uniform distribution of heat and speed throughout the turbulent layer. When the entire overlying air mass becomes so uniformly heated that its lapse rate approaches the adiabatic rate, separation ceases. Convection sows the seeds of its own destruction.

Rising air cools, both because it is surrounded by increasingly cold air and because its molecules, increasingly separated from one another in the expanding air, contribute less heat to a given volume. Inasmuch as, in a given air mass, all separation takes place at approximately the same temperature, all individual updrafts, cooling at a rate associated with distance risen, will cease to rise at approximately the same altitude—the inversion level—at which the rising air becomes colder than the air in the layer immediately above. The inversion (pre-existent, or formed where the updrafts cease to rise) confines the heating to and seals the turbulent layer from the air above.

3. Horizontal Air Flow

Whistle to your plough boys,
Sing to your ship.
—ENGLISH PROVERB

Air movement is due to gravity. Air flows horizontally from a site of higher weight/density/pressure toward a site of lower weight/density/pressure, down a pressure gradient. A synoptic pressure gradient is said to exist when the pressure disparity and movement affect the entire troposphere; a thermal pressure gradient is said to exist when only the lower layers of the troposphere are affected, move beneath, and are separated from the synoptic flow (Table 2).

Pressure Heads

The simplest example of horizontal air flow is the *glacier wind* (Figure 3.1). The increased density and weight of the icy air in contact with a glacier (as much as 5 percent greater than the surrounding air), will cause an increase in surface pressure and a 20- to 30-knot flow of air from the glacier's surface toward a nearby

TABLE 2: BASIC PRINCIPLES OF SURFACE FLOW OVER WATER

1. Near a coast two winds are almost always present at the surface—a large-scale gradient wind and a small-scale thermal wind such as a sea/lake breeze.
2. In stable conditions (e.g., over water) thermal and gradient air flows are separated by the layering of hot air above cold (by inversions). In unstable conditions (e.g., over insolated land) updrafts from the heated surface break through inversions, and downdrafts of upper-level flow penetrate and mix with cold surface air.
3. The Coriolis force causes a change in the direction of all moving air in proportion to its speed. With an increase in velocity it produces, in the Southern Hemisphere, backing; in the Northern Hemisphere, veering—and vice versa.
4. The prime factor in sea breeze generation is the difference in temperature between heated land and cold adjacent water.
5. Optimal sea/lake breeze generation is achieved in the presence of cold water, strongly heated land, cold air over land that becomes colder with altitude at a high lapse rate, an indented shoreline across which a low-level near-shore plain provides ready access to the heating sites, and a linear orientation between a narrow arm of a sea or lake and a steep-sided valley.
6. The speed and direction of an onshore sea breeze are determined by its ability to cross the beach, form a sea breeze front, and penetrate inland.
7. The local knowledge regarding sea/lake breezes that should be sought is their time of onset and offset and typical velocity, and whether that velocity varies with time and/or location on the course; their range and median direction; and whether that direction varies with time and/or location on the course.
8. Sea/lake breezes, because they are cold and dense, hug the surface and are channeled by the topography of the near-shore land.
9. The cold marine air in the sea/lake breeze front coming over land facilitates separation, thermal turbulence, and when it comes offshore onto inland waters, downdraft gusts.

warm vegetated surface. The pressure gradient created by the greater density of the contracted glacial air relative to the expanded air above the vegetated surface is increased by the difference in altitude between the denser air, on top of or within the glacier, and the altitude of the slope below. The resultant *pressure head* (the density difference times the altitude difference) maintains a constant air flow. (The relationship is comparable to the available pressure and the resultant flow when water is stored in an elevated water tank.)

Pressure heads are produced whenever a constant source of cold such as ice or evaporation from a waterfall, or a constant source of heat such as a smoldering volcano, is elevated above its surroundings. I have sailed around and around in the 6- to 8-knot outflow of cold air generated by the evaporative cooling of the Lake of Geneva's Jet d'Eau, a 300-foot fountain in the lake. Along the surface of every waterfall is a downdraft of cold air created by the evaporating spray. In front of and above Brazil's giant Iguassu Falls, paragliders ride updrafts induced by the constant downdraft.

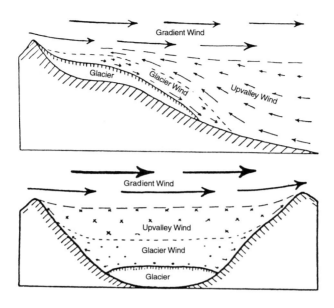

Figure 3.1. A cold glacier wind flows beneath a warm upslope wind (From Geiger, The Climate near the Ground; after E. Eckhart.)

Pressure Gradients

Persistent pressure heads are unusual. Air flow ordinarily results from a temporary change in the weight (due to the expansion or contraction) of the air overlying a particular site. Expansion may be due to the heating of an underlying surface or of the moisture contained within an overlying column of air, or to the condensation of contained water vapor (releasing the "heat of condensation"), or to the elevation of air to a level of reduced pressure. Contraction may be due to the cooling (or coldness) of an underlying surface, or to the evaporation of contained water droplets, or to the sinking of air to a level of increased pressure. Such changes produce proportionate changes in the weight/density/pressure above and below the affected mass of air relative to the unaffected surrounding air—i.e., pressure gradients (Figure 3.2).

It is useful to think of pressure gradients in terms of levels of equal pressure in the vertical plane. When a column (with finite dimensions) of air is heated, its expansion causes some molecules of air to escape beyond the original confines of the column, and those remaining spread farther apart. The expanded column weighs less and exerts a reduced pressure downward, but the unaffected air above the column does not expand, does not become lighter. Therefore, although the surface pressure at the bottom of the heated column and the pressure at levels within the column diminish, the level above the heated column of any given pressure (the force downward [due to gravity] of any given amount of air) is raised *relative to its surroundings.* At the surface an inward pressure gradient is created toward the reduced pressure at the base of the column, but aloft a reverse outward pressure gradient is created away from the increased pressure above the column!

When a column of air is cooled and contracts, surrounding air is drawn into the column and the air within the column becomes denser and heavier, but the unaffected air above the column, although it subsides in response to the contraction below, does not contract, does not become heavier. Therefore, within the cooled column the level of any given pressure is raised relative to its surroundings, but in the subsiding air above, the level of any given pressure is lowered. At the surface a pressure gradient is created outward from the increased pressure at the base of the column, and aloft a pressure gradient is created inward toward the reduced pressure above the column.

The development of the primary sea/lake breeze epitomizes the formation of a pressure gradient. Expansion of the air above insolated land and contraction of the air above cold water result in differences in the pressures overlying them at the surface and aloft, an onshore pressure gradient and an offshore flow of air aloft (Figure 3.3).

A pressure gradient (synoptic or thermal) is established when the level of a given pressure above a particular site is raised by expansion or lowered by contraction (relative to the pressure in the surrounding air). Gravity then causes the air under greater pressure to slide down the pressure gradient toward the site of lower pressure.

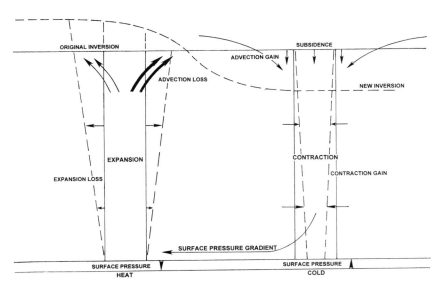

Figure 3.2. *Surface heating produces a thermal pressure gradient. The expansion of a column of air above a heated surface results in a loss of mass and a decrease in surface pressure; contraction has the opposite effect.*

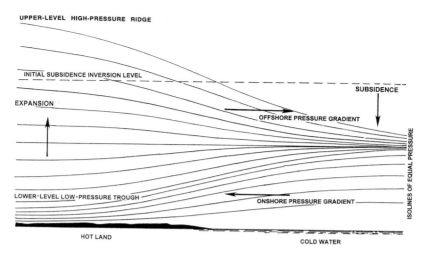

Figure 3.3. Thermal pressure gradients creating a primary sea/lake breeze

Resistance to Horizontal Flow

The result of a pressure gradient is horizontal flow, a flow that will persist as long as the pressure gradient persists and exceeds the effects of the *adiabatic changes in density induced by vertical movement and frictional resistance. The greater the vertical component to the flow, as in downslope and upslope winds, the greater are the restricting effects of adiabatic changes in density (which increase density with elevation and decrease density with subsidence, and thereby oppose gravity or buoyancy*—vide ut infra). *The greater the horizontal component, as in sea breezes and gradient winds, the greater are the restricting effects of friction (which oppose all motion).*

In free air the resistance occasioned by friction operates maximally at the surface and diminishes progressively to an altitude of 2,000 feet (above which atmospheric density is so reduced that friction becomes negligible). Friction engendered by a stream of air moving through other air is directly proportional to its viscosity and to the density of the surrounding air and its turbulence. Although density is proportional to temperature, viscosity is inversely proportional. And although the molecules are more closely packed in a cooler, denser gas, they are less active, less inclined to impinge on one another, less viscous. Cool air sinks, not merely because it is heavier, but because it is less viscous.

The Underlying Surface

As we shall see, wind is markedly affected by the surfaces over which it flows. Friction induced by passage over the earth's surface is typically greater than that induced by passage through free air and is directly proportional to the irregularity of the surface. The reduced friction associated with passage over water doubles the velocity of a flow coming offshore from forested land.

During the day, the temperature of the land is typically higher than the temperature of the water (and vice versa at night), so that in daytime thermal turbulence induced by convection is typically greater over land. But convection depends on the temperature of the overflowing air as well as the temperature of the surface, so that when the water is warmer than the air, convection may develop over water.

In an offshore wind the sailor experiences the effects of the mechanical and thermal influences imparted during its passage over land. In an onshore wind (particularly a sea/lake breeze) a sailor experiences the effects of the thermal influences that will be imparted during the overland passage to come and that are transmitted backward in the entrained flow. He also experiences the direct effects on the surface air flow of the mechanical and thermal influences of the water itself.

The Forces Determining Horizontal Flow

The force resulting from a difference in pressure, causing a horizontal movement of air, is known as the pressure gradient force. Once initiated, motion in response to a pressure gradient force is modified by the earth's rotation: a layer of moving air, to the extent that it is separated from the friction of the earth's surface, tends to continue its initial trajectory while the earth rotates out from under it. As a consequence, all moving air in the Northern Hemisphere appears to an observer

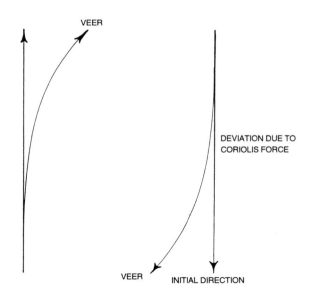

Figure 3.4. Veering due to the Coriolis force

on the earth's surface to veer, all in the Southern Hemisphere to back. This deviation is proportional to the speed of the flow; the more rapid the flow, the less able it is to adhere to the earth's rotating surface (Figure 3.4).

The force causing this alteration in direction, which does not begin to operate until motion begins, is known as the geostrophic, or Coriolis, force. *All flow (gaseous or liquid) deviates in response to the Coriolis force so as to approach a perpendicular to the pressure gradient, so as to flow nearly parallel to the* isobars *(the lines, approximately perpendicular to the pressure gradient, of equal pressure). But because the pressure gradient force always exceeds the Coriolis force, flow is always oblique to the isobars, away from the center of high pressure and toward the center of low pressure (in response to a third [theoretical] force known as the* centripetal force*).*

A near-surface air flow slowed by friction is (almost) unaffected by the Coriolis force and flows in the direction of the pressure gradient force. But with increasing height, as friction diminishes and the flow accelerates, the Coriolis force operates with increasing effect, until above 2,000 feet flow typically follows the isobars. In the Northern Hemisphere each successive layer of an air flow is accelerated and veered relative to the layer below.

Laminar and Turbulent Flow

Air moving at less than approximately 5 knots flows without mechanical turbulence, in *laminar flow* (with all of its molecules streaming in the direction of flow). Air moving at higher speed becomes turbulent. Laminar flow is characterized by marked friction and slowing in the near-surface layer, and minimal friction in the smoothly flowing layers above. The result is a marked variation in the speed of flow with height—*wind shear;* the lower few feet hardly moves; the next layer, 6 to 20 feet above the surface, flows rapidly and aligns with the pressure gradient; the next, 20 to 30 feet above the surface, accelerates and veers in response to the Coriolis force.

Laminar flow is typical of the early development of a sea/lake breeze or of the initial appearance of a gradient wind above a relatively warm water surface. Once established, such flow develops pulsations—periodic variations in velocity. With increasing speed the pulsations disappear, the flow becomes steady, and oscillations in direction develop. As a laminar flow dies, the oscillations become larger.

When the water is warmer than the overflowing air, flow is typically laminar. Warm water may initiate convection, the separation and elevation of parcels of heated air. Variations in velocity and direction are typically associated with such convective formations. In laminar flow, such variations tend to persist at their site of origin (in contrast to those developing in turbulent flow, which move downwind at the speed of the flow). Consequently, a boat sailing in light air must move to an area of shifted flow or increased velocity; she cannot expect it to come to her.

Laminar flow disappears abruptly at speeds greater than 5 knots because the viscosity of air (in the usual temperature range) is insufficient to prevent turbulence (eddies, swirls, and random movements equally distributed in all directions). With increasing speed this random turbulence produces homogeneity. The speed and direction of the flow become everywhere the same. The near-surface wind shear disappears.

25

Velocity and Trajectory

The velocity of a moving mass of air is proportional to the pressure gradient and inversely proportional to the friction occasioned by its movement. As is true of all mass, it has inertia, resists being set in motion, and once in motion it has momentum, a tendency to continue the motion. Once set in motion, momentum requires air to continue its trajectory, despite gravity, density, and opposing pressure differences—up a mountain slope, through a denser air mass, into a zone of increased pressure. A flow of less dense air may invade a more dense mass and continue its trajectory for a considerable distance (as does the Santa Ana wind when it meets the cool sea breeze of Southern California, for instance).

The direction of a flow in a vertical plane may be "deformed" by frontal influences (the lifting of a warm air mass by a colder one) or by orographic influences (mountainous terrain). The direction of a flow in a horizontal plane may be "deviated" by topographic features (channeling, frictional refraction, or barrier effects).

Because the movement of an entire mass of air must be reasonably constant, changes in the speed of a portion of a moving mass must be compensated by reciprocal changes in its local cross-sectional area and vice versa. Alterations in the speed of a segment of air (due to variations in the pressure gradient, for instance) result in corresponding alterations in the frontal area (chiefly the height) of that segment. Alterations in the frontal area of the segment (due to confinement by topography—i.e., channeling—for instance) result in corresponding alterations in speed. When a mass of air accelerates into an area of low pressure (as when a sea/lake breeze crosses a shoreline), the height of the segment at that site is reduced. When a sea breeze front is slowed by an opposing air flow, the height of the segment at that site increases. When the cross-sectional area of a northwesterly flow is confined by its entrance into San Francisco Bay or an upslope flow is confined within the Columbia River Gorge, the confined segment accelerates. When the sea breeze emerges from the Strait of Juan de Fuca into the wide expanse of Puget Sound, the spreading segment slows.

Convergence and Divergence

Air flows of different origin, or segments of a single air flow, may interact so that they converge toward and slow one another, or so that they diverge from and accelerate one another. Convergence occurs in the horizontal plane when two flows move toward one another at the same level. Convergence occurs in the vertical plane when a faster-moving flow (or segment of a flow) overtakes a slower-moving flow (or segment).

Convergence results in deceleration, an increase in pressure at the level of the slowing, upward convection (associated with adiabatically induced condensation), mechanical turbulence, and as the rising air loses density, a fall in surface pressure. Doppler radar (the standard meteorological means of demonstrating convergence and divergence) shows a zone of increased density due to condensation and cumulus cloud formation.

26

Divergence occurs in the horizontal plane when two flows move away from one another at the same level. Divergence occurs in the vertical plane when a fast-moving flow (or segment of a flow) accelerates away from a slower-moving flow (or segment).

Divergence results in acceleration, decreased lateral (or vertical) pressure (the "Bernoulli effect"), sinking (associated with adiabatically induced heating and evaporation) due to the decrease in pressure at the surface of the accelerated layer, decreased turbulence, and as the sinking air gains density, a rise in surface pressure. Doppler radar shows a zone of decreased density due to the evaporation of water droplets and cumulus cloud.

Divergence and convergence are regularly evident at shorelines, where the abrupt change in underlying surface friction causes a change in the speed of movement of the surface layer, and whenever an obstacle such as a terrain feature or a front is encountered. In winds flowing parallel to shore, the overland and overwater segments, moving at different velocities, will converge or diverge. Turning in the horizontal plane (around a mountain range or a ridge of high pressure) induces divergence or convergence depending on whether the turn (in the Northern Hemisphere) is clockwise and aligned with the Coriolis force, which accelerates the adjacent segment of flow (the "corner effect"), or counterclockwise and opposed, which slows it.

Expansion and Subsidence

Expansion and subsidence produce vertical movement of entire layers of the atmosphere (as distinguished from convection, in which segments of air move through various layers). Layer movements occur when the temperature/density/weight of a large mass of air at a particular level changes or when the altered speed of a layer of subjacent or suprajacent air results in divergence or convergence and a level of altered pressure.

Expansion of a surface layer (by conduction and convection above a heating surface) causes the elevation of a suprajacent layer. Convergence (when a layer encounters increased surface friction, moves upslope, is exposed to another, laterally converging, flow; where a localized thermal gradient ceases to operate; where a cold frontal movement lifts warm ambient air; and where [in the Northern Hemisphere] a horizontal flow turns counterclockwise in opposition to the Coriolis force) at any level causes expansion and the elevation of the suprajacent layer. Expansion lifts pressure levels above an affected layer, dissipates inversions, and promotes the transmission of gradient flow to the surface.

Contraction of a surface layer (above a cold surface) causes the subsidence of a suprajacent layer. Divergence (when a layer encounters decreased surface friction, moves downslope, is exposed to another laterally diverging flow; where a localized thermal gradient begins to operate; and where [in the Northern Hemisphere] a horizontal flow turns clockwise in alignment with the Coriolis force [the corner effect]) at any level causes contraction and the subsidence of the suprajacent layer. Subsidence lowers pressure levels in layers above, creates or enhances inversions, and promotes the development of thermal flow at the surface.

Over water, the lower layers of the atmosphere typically contract and subside and induce the subsidence of suprajacent layers. Subsidence (which contributes to sea/lake breeze development and to the formation of the great subtropical high-pressure systems) is due both to the contraction of the near-surface layers and to the decreased viscosity of cold air in contact with cold water. In strong air flows, subsidence over water is significantly aided by the divergence associated with the decrease in friction and the acceleration of the surface air flow. An airplane experiences a sudden drop in buoyancy on the transition from flying over land to over a lake, primarily because, as the lower layers of the air flow accelerate, suprajacent pressure falls and suprajacent air subsides. An airplane experiences an abrupt elevation on the transition from flying over water to flying over land primarily because, as the lower layers of the air flow decelerate, suprajacent pressure increases and suprajacent air rises.

4. The Interaction between the Gradient and the Thermal Wind

I am a feather for each wind that blows.
—SHAKESPEARE

At all times near shore, two winds are potentially present. A synoptic pressure gradient—a difference in atmospheric pressure that gradually changes over a span of hundreds of miles—is constantly present, and a local thermal pressure gradient—instigated by diurnal variations in the temperature of one surface site relative to another—is also constantly present. Each gradient produces wind: the synoptic gradient, a gradient wind; the thermal gradient, a thermal wind. Therefore, two winds are "always" present simultaneously.

Of course, experience belies this assertion because ordinarily only one wind occupies the surface layer where we can detect it (while the other has been displaced upward where we cannot detect it), and thermal winds arise, die, and sometimes reverse their direction with variations in insolation. In addition, one wind may be the consequence of such a large pressure gradient that the other is swept away by it. Hurricanes and tornadoes accommodate no rival flows.

The spectrum of interaction between the two winds includes at one end the gradient wind alone: If the advected air in the gradient wind is cold and the synoptic pressure gradient is strong, no thermal wind will be evident. At the other end of the spectrum is the thermal wind alone: If a surface, unusually cold in comparison with its surroundings, creates a strong thermal pressure gradient (and the synoptic pressure gradient is weak), no gradient wind will be evident. Between these extremes are various mixtures of the two winds. The gradient wind may persist but be altered in strength and direction, or the thermal wind may develop but be similarly altered. Both winds may be present simultaneously at different locations or both may appear recurrently at the same location. They may be aligned and amalgamate to produce a single stronger wind; they may converge and displace one another; they may diverge from and accelerate one another; or they may flow perpendicularly to and diminish one another (Table 3).

TABLE 3: GRADIENT WIND—SEA/LAKE BREEZE (SLB) INTERACTIONS

Air Temperature	Near-Shore Wind	Offshore Wind	Shifts
GRADIENT WIND: OFFSHORE			
Cold	Gusty gradient wind	Gradient wind	Osc.
Warmer	Two winds simultaneously	Secondary SLB	Pers.
Hot	Secondary SLB	Secondary SLB	Osc.
GRADIENT WIND: ONSHORE			
Cold	Amalgamated SLB	Amalgamated SLB	Pers.
Warm	Layered SLB	Gradient wind	Osc.
GRADIENT WIND—PARALLEL TO SHORE—BACKED TO THE SEA BREEZE			
Cold	Gradient wind	Light SLB	Pers.
Warm	Overland gradient wind	Overwater gradient wind convergence	Pers.
GRADIENT WIND—PARALLEL TO SHORE—VEERED TO THE SEA BREEZE			
Cold	Amalgamated SLB	Amalgamated SLB	Pers.
Warm	Primary SLB—veered	Primary SLB—backed divergence	Pers.
Pers. = Persistent Shift	Osc. = Oscillating Shift		

The Direction of the Two Winds

The direction of the gradient wind is primarily determinative of the outcome: If the thermal wind is aligned, a stronger amalgamated wind is likely to result (e.g., an amalgamated sea/lake breeze). If approximately perpendicular to one another, each will be diminished, oscillating shifts may develop between the two, or the colder or stronger may progressively or intermittently displace the other from the surface. If opposed, the colder will undermine the warmer, or if of similar temperature, they will converge and at the surface be limited to appearing to either side of an intermediary zone of calm (Figure 4.1).

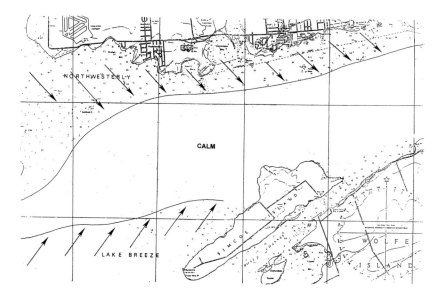

Figure 4.1. The secondary lake breeze—two winds simultaneously

The Temperature of the Air in Each Wind

The temperature of the flows determines which will occupy the surface. In order to be evident at the surface, the thermal wind must be (and almost always is) colder than the gradient wind. When a gradient flow (aligned or opposed) is (or becomes) warmer than the thermal, it will be undermined and displaced upward by the thermal wind.

If the temperature of two opposing flows is approximately the same, convergence may lead to hours of midday calm over an entire near-shore racecourse. If the temperature disparity is sufficiently great, the two flows may be separated above and below an inversion—an *advection inversion*—formed as the cold thermal wind lifts the warm gradient wind to an upper level. Except at the inversion interface, where friction will slow both, the two winds flow essentially unopposed at their gradient velocity. This mechanism commonly supports sea/lake breeze generation and is of major importance along continental coasts. With or without the aid of a preexisting inversion, an onshore flow of cool marine air will, once established, lift a warmer gradient flow from the surface and create a protective inversion.

The Pressure Gradient of Each Wind

Whether aligned or opposed, the wind with the stronger gradient will usually occupy the surface, particularly if its temperature is colder. When the two flows are of approximately the same temperature and approximately aligned, a vector analysis of their respective gradients will indicate the composite direction of the surface flow.

In an amalgamated sea/lake breeze, however, the temperature of one flow (the marine air) is typically less than the temperature of the other. Consequently the gradient wind is increasingly displaced from the surface so that at the peak of the thermal gradient, the surface flow is (almost) entirely sea/lake breeze from the sea/lake breeze direction. In this case the surface shift, rather than being toward an intermediate direction proportionate to the strength of each flow (and derivable by vector analysis), is toward (and typically reaches) the direction of the primary sea breeze.

Diurnal, Weekly, and Seasonal Variations in Insolation

The sea/lake breeze appears after sunrise (typically after many hours of sunlight), strengthens to a peak velocity (with maximum insolation) in late afternoon

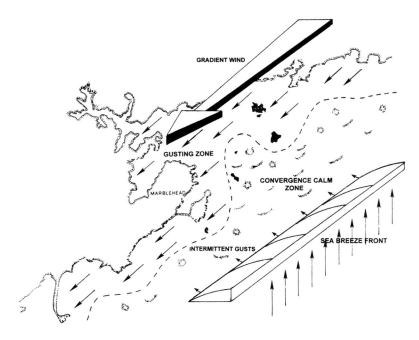

Figure 4.2. The gusting zone. Gusts appearing in the convergence calm zone are elements of gradient wind.

or evening, and then dies away completely in early to late evening. In the midlatitudes weekly variations in sea/lake breeze generation are induced by the changing orientation of the gradient wind to the coast. In early summer increased insolation associated with a maximum disparity between the temperatures of the land and the water, and a decrease in the strength of the synoptic pressure gradient, combine to facilitate sea/lake breeze generation. In winter decreased insolation due to the reduced duration of daylight, the lower inclination of the sun, and increased cloud cover, and an increase in the synoptic pressure gradient, combine to diminish sea/lake breeze generation. Other thermal winds show similar diurnal and seasonal variations.

The Presence of Gusting

During insolation over land and within 2 or 3 miles of shore (within the "gusting zone"), thermal turbulence produces downdrafts that, accelerated by gravity, bring higher-velocity veered upper-level air to the surface. Gusts, the splashes induced by the impact of downdrafts, sweep the ambient air upward and away. This behavior is typical of (even hot) unstable offshore gradient and downslope winds, particularly during periods of maximum insolation. Near shore, within the gusting zone, gusts sweep away a sea/lake breeze and occupy the surface; farther offshore, beyond a zone of calm, in the absence of gusting the colder sea/lake breeze often displaces them (Figure 4.2).

5. The Varieties of Sea/Lake Breeze Circulation

Awake O north wind; and come thou south;
Blow upon my garden.
—SONG OF SOLMON 4:16

An onshore flow from cool water toward heated land that develops during insolation is best called a sea/lake breeze (the nature of the water body is immaterial). The sea/lake breeze circulation is classically described as closed: a shallow, rapid onshore flow at the surface accompanied by a deep, slow return flow aloft. This conception assumes that aloft over land, as heated air accumulates above surface low pressure, high pressure develops and that aloft over water, as cooling air subsides above surface high pressure, low pressure develops. The upper-level *trough* (area of low pressure) over the water receives flow from the upper-level *ridge* (area of high pressure) over the heated land, just as the surface trough over the heated land receives flow from the surface ridge over the water (see Figure 3.3, p.23). In the midlatitudes, however (except in midsummer), most sea/lake breezes do not have such a simple circulation.

The components of a sea/lake breeze that are common to all varieties are

- a mass of cold, contracted air over water, creating a surface pressure higher than over land
- continuous subsidence—from an upper-level outflow of heated air below an inversion or from an offshore or onshore gradient wind—onto the cold, contracted mass of overwater air
- separation and convection(induced by insolation) over land that expand and reduce the surface pressure
- a surface flow from the overwater high pressure toward the low pressure at the surface of the heating shore, and commonly but not necessarily . . .
- a sea breeze front that, as it crosses the shoreline and invades inland, greatly enhances the onshore flow

Two elements of this circulation are essential:

1. Air must flow out from above the heating sites as fast as it accumulates, and air must flow into the high-pressure ridge over the water as fast as it is depleted.
2. Cold air must flow continuously over the heating land—in a cold, unstable gradient wind or in a sea breeze front—so as to maintain the high near-surface lapse rate on which separation depends.

The Three Types of Sea/Lake Breezes (see Table 4, p.36)

Primary (or pure) sea/lake breezes (Figure 5.1): Primary sea/lake breezes (the classic variety) develop full, autonomous circulations under the protection of pre-existing inversions. Their thermal gradient depends on the development of a sea breeze front that "crosses the shoreline." The high lapse rate and dramatic increase in separation as the cold leading edge of the marine air invades the heating land creates a low-pressure trough into which the dense marine air rushes. These moderate to strong winds are characterized by persistent shifts (induced by variations in velocity), smooth water, and minimal oscillations.

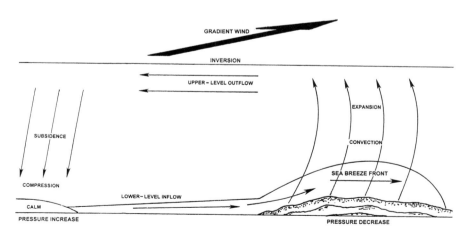

Figure 5.1. The primary sea/lake breeze

Secondary (or "pure") sea/lake breezes (Figure 5.2): Secondary sea/lake breezes rely on an unstable offshore gradient wind for their upper-level outflow and the replenishment of their depleting overwater high-pressure ridge. The thermal gradient is induced and maintained by the high lapse rate, deep turbulence, and a major fall in overland pressure associated with the gradient wind's overland passage. They occur in two major forms: in association with cool, unstable northerlies that warm with the daily increase in insolation, and with hot, unstable gradient flows.

Because (relatively) cold air is brought in over the hot land by the gradient flow, secondary sea/lake breezes do not depend on (though they are greatly enhanced by) the crossing of the shoreline by a sea breeze front and frequently halt short of the shoreline. They often produce the pattern of "two winds simultaneously": a steady, moderate sea/lake breeze in smooth water offshore, separated by a zone of calm from the near-shore gusting zone of the gradient wind.

TABLE 4: CLASSIFICATION OF SEA/LAKE BREEZES

I. Primary Sea/Lake Breezes (developing a sea breeze front under an inversion)

- Morning to afternoon—persistent
  Under a subsidence inversion (typically on the eastern periphery of a subtropical high)
- Morning—transient
  Under a radiation inversion near shore on lakes and coasts
- Midday—persistent
  Under an advection inversion on a steep-sided water body—lake, fjord, or bay

II. Secondary Sea/Lake Breezes (developing under offshore gradient winds)

- Limited to over water
  Under a "cool" offshore gradient wind
- Developing a sea breeze front over land
  Under a "warm" offshore gradient wind

III. Amalgamated Sea/Lake Breezes (combined with onshore gradient winds)

- Partially amalgamated
  Under warm, aligned, onshore gradient winds
- Fully amalgamated
  With cool, aligned, onshore gradient winds

IV. Offshore Sea/Lake Breezes (coming offshore onto bays, lakes, and rivers after transiting land)

- Primary and secondary, under subsidence inversions and warm offshore gradient winds
- Amalgamated (partial or complete)

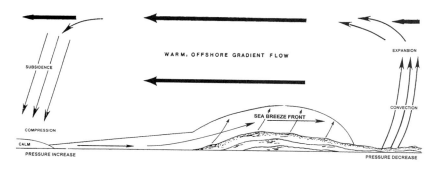

Figure 5.2. The secondary sea/lake breeze

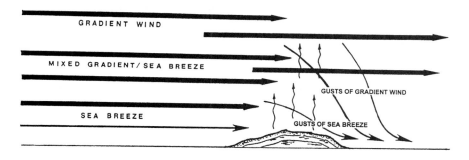

Figure 5.3. The amalgamated sea/lake breeze

Amalgamated sea/lake breezes (Figure 5.3): Amalgamated sea/lake breezes add a thermal gradient to a preexisting onshore gradient wind, which is then characterized (during periods of insolation) by high velocity, big waves, and oscillating shifts between the two winds, toward and away from the thermal gradient.

The Primary Sea/Lake Breeze under an Inversion

Primary sea/lake breezes, ones that conform to the classic concept described above, establish their sea breeze fronts and develop only under preexisting inversions—inversions due to subsidence, radiation, or advection (see chapter 8). The strongest inversions occur under the great subtropical highs, where huge masses of stable air heat by compression as they subside above the cold oceans. On the west coasts of the continents (on the eastern periphery of the subtropical highs) near which cold ocean currents flow equatorward, subsidence is most pronounced, and there the proximity of strong inversions, cold oceans, and hot deserts (created by the drying effects of subsidence) provides optimal conditions for sea breeze generation.

The primary sea/lake breeze is distinct from the secondary sea/lake breeze because it develops in very different settings, but the latter is an imitation of the former, and in many instances (for example when the supra-inversion flow is hot and offshore) the primary becomes the secondary. *The primary sea/lake breeze requires a protective inversion during its initial development (Phase I) and the establishment of a sea breeze front thereafter (Phase II). By contrast, the secondary sea/lake breeze relies on the warmth of, and the high near-surface lapse rate in, the preexistent gradient flow to create an inversion and to produce an overland pressure drop, and requires no sea breeze front.*

When a primary sea breeze develops under the subsidence inversion of a subtropical high, three distinct layers form in the atmosphere along the coast. Cold, moist air in the low-level onshore sea breeze flows inland at the surface; warmer, dried marine air in the upper sea breeze circulation flows seaward at the intermediate level; and confining the two layers below and thus protecting the sea breeze circulation from the gradient wind, hot, dry subtropical air subsides onto the inversion. These are the conditions of the world's best sailing areas—on the west coasts of continents near which cold ocean currents flow adjacent to hot deserts—off Fremantle, in Western Australia; off Southern California; and off the west coast of Africa. Similar, but weaker and less certain, primary sea breezes develop along subtropical continental east coasts and in the midlatitudes in summer.

A second type of primary sea breeze is the transient flow (common in the midlatitudes) that develops in early morning under the protection of a persisting nocturnal radiation inversion. Because these sea/lake breezes develop only minimal fronts and rarely invade more than a few hundred to a few thousand yards beyond the shoreline, they are only a few tens of yards deep, extend but a few hundreds or thousands of yards offshore, and rarely reach more than 5 to 6 knots in velocity. They disintegrate in late morning when the subinversion air becomes sufficiently heated to destroy the inversion.

A third type of complete primary sea/lake breeze circulation often develops where cold marine air is trapped between the steep shores of mountain lakes, fjords, and coastal bays. Warm air advected in a summertime gradient wind often flows from ridge to ridge without disturbing the cold marine air. Below this advection inversion a moderate midday low-level primary sea/lake breeze often develops and may provide the only decent summertime sailing.

The Secondary Sea/Lake Breeze and Offshore Gradient Flow

In the midlatitudes the gradient flow most supportive of sea/lake breeze generation is offshore, cold, and unstable: The offshore element provides the upper arm of the sea/lake breeze circulation; the coldness facilitates separation over land; and the deep instability induces a major fall in overland surface pressure. This symbiotic relationship is so important that Alan Watts, discussing England's South Coast, considers it essential.

Variations in the temperature, strength, and gustiness of the gradient wind block, limit, or facilitate the invasion of the secondary sea/lake breeze, resulting in a diminution of offshore flow, two winds simultaneously (the gradient wind in its gusting zone along the shoreline, separated from the sea breeze offshore by a zone of convergence calm), or a complete sea breeze front crossing the shoreline and invading far into the land. The sea breeze front established in the latter situation is indistinguishable from that of a primary sea breeze.

When hot gradient winds flow across and offshore from a major landmass, as they do in summer along the U.S. East Coast, they are regularly lifted from the surface in early afternoon by the onshore flow of a sea/lake breeze. These dry gradient flows, although relatively stable, permit separation and convection under intense mid-day insolation, facilitate the creation of a cross-shore thermal gradient, and when lifted to an upper level, establish a protective inversion for the onshore flow of marine air and a means of replenishing the overwater subsidence.

The crossing of the shoreline and the establishment of a sea breeze front add significantly to the strength of the secondary sea/lake breeze, but the height of turbulence is typically greater ahead of the front than within it. Whereas in a primary sea/lake breeze the most waterward line of cumulus forms where turbulence begins within the sea breeze front, in a secondary sea/lake breeze the most waterward line of cumulus forms in the gradient flow and indicates the cessation of deep turbulence rather than its beginning.

The Amalgamated Sea/Lake Breeze and Onshore Gradient Flow

A cool onshore gradient flow also replaces heated air with cold air, facilitates the maintenance of a high near-surface lapse rate, replenishes near-shore high pressure, and sweeps away upper-level outflow from over the heating land. If the temperatures of the gradient wind and the sea/lake breeze (the marine air) are markedly disparate, the colder will displace the warmer and will occupy the surface alone. However, if the gradient wind has had a prolonged fetch over the water, its temperature will be similar to the marine air, and the sea/lake breeze and the gradient wind will amalgamate. On north-facing shores northerly gradient winds, typically colder than the water and its marine air, are likely to dominate the surface; on south-facing shores amalgamated sea/lake breezes composed of marine air that is colder than the southerly gradient winds are likely to dominate the surface.

Amalgamations of the sea breeze with onshore gradient flows result in the strongest onshore flows of the midlatitudes. Maximum strengthening occurs on shores that in summertime (when sea/lake breeze generation is at its height) face the typical gradient wind direction. The combination of an onshore gradient southwesterly and the lake breeze at Kingston, Ontario; the combination of an onshore gradient southwesterly and the sea breeze at Buzzards Bay; and the combination of an onshore gradient northwesterly and the sea breeze at San Francisco are examples.

The Sea Breeze of the Forecasters

Despite their ubiquity sea/lake breezes, because they occupy only the lowest levels of the atmosphere and are so limited in extent, are typically ignored by weather forecasters. In the midlatitudes some forecasts may predict "winds becoming onshore," but only along subtropical coasts (where, under persistent subtropical highs, they are a major and regular feature of the daily weather) are they reported as sea or lake breezes.

Forecasts of sea/lake breeze speed and direction are often misleading because they typically derive from a measuring site subject to frictional and velocity variation, channeling, and gradient wind admixture differing from that at the surface of the sailing venue. Data regarding a sea/lake breeze that are derived from a 60-foot mast inland or a buoy 7 miles offshore bear an inexact relationship to the wind on a near-shore racecourse.

Amalgamated sea/lake breezes are usually reported as vector resolutions of the predicted strengths of the two winds. This may be appropriate for the mixture that occurs over land amidst thermal turbulence but is inappropriate for sailors, who sail at the water's surface in a layer that is (almost) pure marine air. A primary sea/lake breeze developing under an inversion flows in its "true" direction (over a range varying with its velocity). Amalgamated sea/lake breezes of similar velocity occurring at the site may be presumed to be deviated relative to the primary sea/lake breeze direction and may be expected to shift toward that direction.

II. *Gradient Winds: Diurnal Variations*

Midlatitudes: Coasts

Lakes

Rivers

6. The Winds of Savannah

Small showers last long,
But sudden storms are short.
— SHAKESPEARE

In the preceding section we discovered how simple onshore flows—primary sea breezes—behave along a western continental coast, how their frequency and strength are proportionate to coastal insolation, how they are enhanced by upslope flows and expansion differentials, how they are deviated by shorelines, how they are accelerated by confinement in narrow channels. We learned how pressure gradients are created and how air flows are deviated in the horizontal plane by the Coriolis force and the underlying topography, and in the vertical plane by convergence and divergence and by expansion and subsidence. We found that two winds—a local thermal wind and a large-scale gradient wind—are typically present together during daylight hours along a coast. We recognized three types of sea/lake breezes and learned how they interact with gradient winds.

Now let us investigate the typical summer winds at Savannah, Georgia, on the U.S. East Coast. Here we will see that the strength of the typical sea breeze and its interaction with the gradient wind depend on the time of day, the stability of the air, the strength of the overlying inversion, and the turbulence—mechanical and thermal—induced by each wind. We will learn why strong air flows reach the surface and why sometimes, with convergence or beneath an inversion, they are excluded.

Savannah's Three Summertime Surface Wind Regimes

At Savannah, under the subsidence inversion in the northwest quadrant of the Bermuda High, the ready access of the marine air to the vast coastal lowlands often induces a strong primary sea breeze. Because the near-shore water off Savannah is far warmer than at a similar latitude on the West Coast, however, the subsidence inversion is not nearly as strong and the sea breeze not nearly as dependable, and it is more likely to be of the secondary variety. And there is the problem of getting to the wind—10 to 12 miles through the marshes from the launching sites. But offshore, in the afternoon of three out of five summer days, one finds a lovely 14- to 16-knot onshore breeze.

The presence or absence of factors conducive to sea breeze generation results in three distinct wind regimes:

Regime 1: On the 12 days out of 30 that the gradient wind is from between west and south, a strong primary or secondary southeast sea breeze develops.

Regime 2: On the 10 days out of 30 that the gradient wind is from between south and east, a variable amalgamation of gradient wind and southeast sea breeze (associated with thunderstorms) develops.

Regime 3: On the 8 days out of 30 that the gradient wind is from between northwest and east (associated with frontal passage or nearby low pressure), the gradient wind appears alone.

The weather patterns and wind systems typical of a particular coastal locale depend on its latitude; its position relative to semipermanent high-pressure systems (such as subtropical highs), the polar front, and the ocean currents; and the orientation of the coast to the prevailing gradient wind.

Subsidence, Subsidence Inversions, and Sea Breezes

Subsidence results from the contraction of air suprajacent to a cold surface and increases in proportion to the coldness of that water. At Savannah a band of cool water lies between the coast and the Gulf Stream. Above the cool water, contraction is pronounced and the surrounding air (chiefly from over the heated land to the west but also from over the warm Gulf Stream to the east) subsides, compresses, heats, and forms a moderately strong inversion. The result is an upper-level trough of low pressure—into which the typical hot southwest gradient flow subsides above a surface band of high pressure—within which the marine air cools and contracts. The preexistent subsidence inversion is reinforced, permitting the marine air to flow toward the heating land while protected from the interference of the gradient wind.

At Savannah, as in Maine and Finland, the sea penetrates into the land in long reaches, and the land penetrates into the sea in numerous low-lying islands. From 10 to 20 miles inland of the "coast" there is nearly an equal amount of sea and land. This permits the subsidence inversion to move farther inland during the day and to overlap the nocturnal radiation inversion throughout the night. Even 10 miles from open water along such coasts on summer mornings the surface is often calm —protected from the gradient wind by the two inversions (Figure 6.1).

The many coastal inlets permit marine air to flow at sea level far into the heating interior, and at high tide particularly, the low-lying marsh land permits it to come ashore readily. In early morning the nascent sea breeze front is usually protected by a radiation inversion that extends far out into the marshes. When (at about 1000) updrafts break through this inversion, they often bring the hot gradient flow to the near-shore surface. If, however, subsidence is intense in a particularly hot southwesterly, updrafts will halt at the upper, subsidence inversion, the sea breeze front will continue its invasion, the cool marine air will continue to facilitate separation, and with increasing insolation the local low-level sea breeze will expand into a full-scale ocean sea breeze. Even when the inversions are weak, intense midday insolation will generate a sea breeze that will lift the hot, dry southwesterly from the surface by creating a protective advection inversion.

The disparity between sea surface temperature and land surface temperature is greatest at the beginning of the flood tide when the cold offshore water is

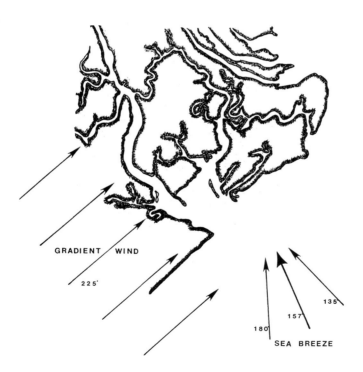

Figure 6.1. The secondary sea breeze at Savannah

45

brought into direct contact with the drying, low-level land. The cold air elevated by the rising water more readily surmounts the low banks of Savannah's many inshore channels and spreads rapidly across its hot marshes. If the flood occurs in the morning so as to coincide with the diurnal increase in insolation, subsidence offshore increases in concert with heating inshore, and the thermal pressure gradient is enhanced. Mark Powell, in a study of sea breeze development in the summers preceding the 1996 Olympics, demonstrated a direct correlation between sea breeze strength and morning low tide.

The generation of a primary sea breeze depends on the presence of cold water and subsidence offshore and of an inversion that protects the beginning sea breeze front from the interference of the gradient wind.

Regime 1

In summer the Atlantic (or Bermuda) Subtropical High occupies almost the whole of the North Atlantic and typically prevents the polar front from moving south of Savannah. For periods of three to seven days the southwest flow on the western periphery of this high (which usually forms an elongated center, a "ridge," of high pressure paralleling the coast) brings hot, clear, relatively dry air (from across the southern states) to Savannah. A newspaper or TV forecast of "wind—west to southwest at 10 to 15 knots" is the best assurance that the Bermuda High and its subsidence inversion are present and that the southeast sea breeze will appear in late morning and be strong (Figure 6.2)

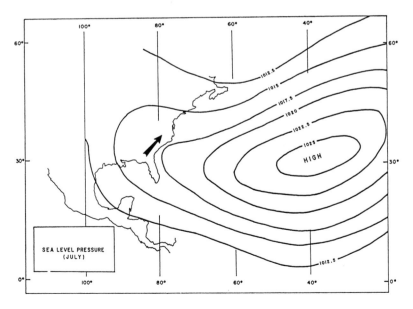

Figure 6.2. The Bermuda High (From Essenwanger, World Survey of Climatology.*)*

In summer an occluded front (that may drift a little south or a little north, but crosses Georgia only once in a summer month) typically forms across the mid-North American continent between the polar air and the subtropical high. If the weather map shows the front nearby to the northwest, one can be even more confident that (with the Bermuda High pressed southward) the gradient wind will be southwesterly and hot, that subsidence over the near-shore water will be prominent, that the subsidence inversion will be strong, and that a primary sea breeze will develop.

However, the subsidence inversion developing over the relatively warm water of the Gulf Stream is not nearly as strong as that beneath the East Pacific and Indian Ocean Highs. Nocturnal longwave radiation from the cooling land is inhibited by the moist air (brought ashore by the daily sea breeze), and consequently the radiation inversion is also often weak (or absent). Over the near-coast land the gradient flow of the Bermuda High regularly penetrates the weak radiation inversion, the morning wind is typically the southwesterly, and the primary sea breeze is commonly delayed until insolation is strong (at midday).

The sea breeze should be expected whenever
1. The gradient wind is forecast to be west to southwest
2. The morning surface wind is blowing from the forecast (gradient wind) direction or the sea surface is calm
3. In late morning the gradient wind, if present at the surface, dies
4. Visibility (from offshore) is high
5. The cumulus give way to completely clear skies as one moves downriver and offshore

Subsiding air heats by compression and thereby melts mid- and low-level cloud. Completely clear skies (except for occasional high cirrus) indicate subsidence and a strong, protective subsidence inversion.

The Sea Breeze Flow

If in the morning the radiation inversion is strong, and the inshore surface is calm, the primary sea breeze appears at about 1000 to 1100 off the outer islands. Within a mile or two of shore its initial direction is from 160° to 180° at 2 to 4 knots. As it increases in velocity, it spreads offshore and inshore and by noon, or shortly thereafter, up the rivers. By 1130 it will usually be blowing at 8 knots from approximately 160° to 175°. It will strengthen rapidly thereafter and by late afternoon may reach 18 knots and veer to 195° (Figure 6.3).

A weak radiation inversion will diminish the near-surface lapse rate, will delay separation, will provide little upper-level outflow to increase subsidence offshore, and as a result, the southwest gradient wind will occupy the surface inland and over near-shore waters. In these (the usual) circumstances the sea breeze becomes evident offshore at about noon as a diminution in the gradient wind to less than 5 knots, associated with a gradual back (from approximately 230° to 210°). After 20 to 40 minutes of light shifty air the surface flow strengthens and the wind backs farther left.

By 1230 the surface wind on the offshore racecourses backs to approximately 180° to 185° at 8 knots, and on the inland rivers shifts abruptly to the sea breeze

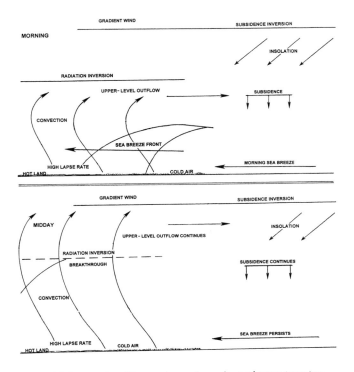

Figure 6.3. Preservation of the morning sea breeze by overlapping inversions

direction. The marine air lifts the warm gradient wind from the surface and flows across the shoreline as a secondary sea breeze. While the breeze is building and spreading (both offshore and inshore), patches of diminished velocity persist in the racing areas, requiring "a hunt for pressure." By 1330 to 1400 the wind offshore becomes homogeneous at approximately 12 knots and backs to 175°. By 1500 its strength increases to 15 knots and it backs to 170°, by 1600 to 165°, and by 1700 to occasionally as far left as 160°. The late-onset secondary sea breeze, which develops by lifting the gradient wind from the surface, is never as strong as the early-onset primary sea breeze, which develops out of calm beneath a radiation inversion.

The general rule is that if the sea breeze begins as a backing from the southwesterly (200° to 240°) gradient flow, it will continue to back as it increases in speed to 16 (or more) knots, to approximately 165° (the median sea breeze direction). If it develops out of calm at 165° to 185°, it will veer (not back) in proportion to its velocity to as far right as 190°. Medium oscillations at 8- to 12-minute intervals over a range of 10° to 15° are characteristic of both winds, overwhelm the effect of the persistent backing (or in strong winds, the veering), and require keeping to the lifted tack.

The strongest sea breezes develop in spring or early summer out of early-morning calm. They follow a low tide at 1000 to 1100 and heavy cumulus formation ashore, and appear offshore by 1130. They rapidly increase in velocity from 8 knots at 1130 to 14 knots by noon, and veer (as subsidence clears the offshore skies) with their increase in velocity from 170° to 185°. At peak velocity (18 to 20 knots), at 1600, they are oscillating over a range of 10°—between 180° and 190°.

The primary sea breeze develops most readily and reaches its greatest strength after a clear, cool night, with a morning flood tide, when subsidence is evidenced by completely clear skies, and the subsidence inversion is strengthened by a hot, dry gradient air flow. The more common secondary sea breeze develops between noon and 1300 by lifting the southwesterly from the surface, and as it strengthens, backs the surface flow toward the sea breeze median.

Regime 2

The second regime, the next most common, is the consequence of the Bermuda High moving north so that the gradient wind is from the south or southeast. Southerly and southeasterly winds advect warm, moist air from the Gulf of Mexico or the South Atlantic onto the coast. The increased cloud cover impairs the separation and thermal liftoff necessary to sea breeze formation and encourages the development of thunderstorms. In this second regime the relatively cool gradient southeaster blows at the surface throughout the night and into the morning, and the sea breeze develops later in the day, is weaker, is likely to be backed to the usual sea breeze, and in late afternoon near shore (in Wassaw Sound and within a few miles of the outer islands) may be dissipated by the cold downflow from thunderstorms.

The moist air of this regime absorbs infrared radiation and impairs the formation of the nocturnal radiation inversion. This greenhouse effect prevents the land from cooling (making for hot nights and hot mornings inland), obviates the high near-surface lapse rate that permits early-morning separation and subinversion flow waterward, impairs sea breeze generation, and permits the relatively cool gradient wind to occupy the surface.

By midday the relatively cool water between the Gulf Stream and the beach as well as the insolation ashore are usually sufficient to generate a weak sea breeze, but this low-level flow is only slightly cooler than the gradient southeasterly. Despite this temperature similarity, amalgamation is incomplete; both winds are evident at the surface, and the resultant flow is a mixture of the two winds oscillating between the gradient wind direction and 160°.

When gradient winds come from the sea and advect warm, moist air to the coast, sea breeze generation is impaired and associated with large oscillating shifts between the two winds.

Regime 3

The northward movement of the polar front in summer is the consequence of the increased heating of the Northern Hemisphere oceans and the northward displacement of their overlying zones of subsidence. Across North America the polar front phases continue their march down the chain of the Great Lakes, and the front itself intermittently shifts to the south or to the north of that line. However, centers of low pressure (or troughs) occasionally form over the Gulf of Mexico, and when hot moist air is drawn across Texas and Louisiana, may fuse with the polar front and drag it as far south as Alabama.

In summer the Bermuda High is usually strong enough to block the access of such systems to the Atlantic coast, but when a particularly strong surge of continental polar air is drawn into the circulation, a cold front may advance as far south as North Carolina—and, rarely, cross Savannah and move offshore. Although the cold front almost immediately dissipates within the subtropical high and the gradient wind veers from west through north to east in a matter of hours, the subsidence inversion is eliminated. Cold (rather than warm) air occupies the upper layers over the sea and stimulates vertical convection over the land. During the several days required for the subsidence inversion to re-form, no sea breeze appears and light gradient winds from the eastern quadrants occupy the surface both day and night.

Tropical storms developing in the warm ocean southeast of Savannah may displace the Bermuda High to the north and create a persistent (day and night) easterly air flow that advects air from cool central Atlantic sites across the Gulf Stream. Except for the thermal turbulence and small oscillations introduced during this passage, the cool gradient flow is steady (remains within 10° to 15° of its morning direction), sweeps the warmer local marine air inland, and prevents sea breeze generation.

When gradient winds flow from the north or east and advect cold air to the coast, the gradient flow occupies the surface, the inversion is eliminated, and the sea breeze fails to appear.

7. Stability and Instability

When the glass falls low, prepare for a blow.
—ENGLISH PROVERB

There is a spectrum of near-surface wind behavior, based on and proportionate to a quality called stability—the tendency of air above a cold surface to form a cold surface layer that resists vertical mixing and is separated by an inversion from a warmer overflow. This spectrum ranges from complete calm in a cold surface layer beneath a warm, nonturbulent overflow, to patches of wind of varying strength in a cold surface layer intermittently penetrated by a warm, turbulent overflow, to frequent oscillations in speed and direction in a surface layer warmer than the overflow. Because the sailor must adjust his sail trim as well as his strategy to these variations in stability, he should assess the temperature of the water surface in areas where he expects to sail.

Stability (or instability) is the measure of the ease with which air moves vertically. Because, as it moves vertically, the pressure surrounding it varies, it expands or contracts and responds to Boyle's Law, which specifies a fixed relationship between volume/density and temperature. Because the change in pressure with change in altitude is essentially fixed, the change in temperature with change in altitude—the lapse rate—is also essentially fixed and is known as the adiabatic lapse rate (the *ALR*)—0.6°F per 100 feet (1.0°C per 100 meters). Because the same change in pressure occurs regardless of the means of vertical movement—thermal or mechanical turbulence, orographic or frontal lift, upslope or downslope flow—the adiabatic lapse rate applies to all vertical movement (see prologue).

Vertical movement (on which horizontal air flow depends) is limited by the rate of change in the temperature/density of the surrounding atmosphere, i.e., the lapse rate in the surrounding air (the *SLR*). Because the earth's surface is the primary source of heat, the temperature of the troposphere (ordinarily) decreases with height. The average rate of change (the average SLR) is 0.4°F per 100 feet (0.66°C per 100 meters) of vertical distance.

The Surrounding Air Lapse Rate

Because the SLR determines the facility of vertical movement in a given segment of air (its buoyancy), it is known as a measure of "stability." When, as is usual, the lapse rate in the surrounding air (the SLR) is less than the fixed rate associated with vertical movement (the ALR), lifting air rapidly becomes cooler and denser than the surrounding air and sinks back, and sinking air rapidly becomes warmer and lighter than the surrounding air and ceases to sink. Air in which lifting (and sinking) is limited by a low SLR is said to be stable. The atmosphere is stable when its lowest levels are cool and its midlevels are warm and become rapidly warmer with height.

When the SLR is greater than the ALR, lifting air remains warmer and less dense than the surrounding air and continues to lift, and sinking air remains cooler and denser and continues to sink. Air in which lifting (and sinking) is facilitated by a high SLR is said to be unstable. The atmosphere is unstable when its lower layers are hot and its midlevels are cold and become rapidly colder with height.

Because the height of displacement of air moving upward (an updraft) and air moving downward (a downdraft) determines the height of the column of air of altered density/weight that it creates, it also determines the extent of the change in pressure at the surface below, the velocity of the vertical motion induced, and the character of the replacement downdraft. If the surrounding air is stable, heated air—cooling and gaining density at a higher adiabatic rate—rises only a short distance before it reaches a level of equal density. The change in surface pressure is slight, the velocity of vertical motion low, and the horizontal flow resulting from the impact of a replacement downdraft minimal. If the surrounding air is unstable, heated air will rise and persist in that rise to a great height, until a level (the top of the turbulent layer) characterized by a major decrease in the SLR is reached. The change in surface pressure is great, the velocity of vertical motion high, and the horizontal flow resulting from a replacement downdraft strong and veered.

Stability

In stable conditions a warm layer lies above a cold surface layer (creating an inversion) and below a cold upper layer (at some usually distant height). Stability characterizes the lower atmosphere at night and over water. When colder than the overlying air, water initiates no thermal turbulence. Stability increases with cloud cover, with rain, and with the advection of warm air. Stability is characterized by reduced surface air flow, a cessation of separation, and an absence of thermal turbulence—typified by the calm at the cold surface of the Chesapeake and Long

Island Sound when a southerly gradient wind advects warm air in springtime.

Low pressure results in stability. Cold, dense air moves toward surface low pressure; forces warm, less dense air to rise; and results in a layer of warm air above cold. Condensation associated with the lifting reduces insolation and surface heating and releases heat aloft, thereby perpetuating stability. Rain diminishes surface wind velocity as movement of air laden with heavy droplets dissipates more energy, and because evaporation cools the surface and halts thermal turbulence. The least surface wind (and the worst sailing) occurs in rain in winter, when the near-surface air lies in a cold, stagnant pool above cold water.

Stable air resists lifting or sinking, whatever the genesis of the displacement. Stable air will "channel," will deviate and compress laterally and accelerate through a gap, rather than rise to surmount an obstacle. The stable onshore portion of a sea/lake breeze behaves like water, channeling into gaps and around obstacles, resisting lift. However, a stable surface flow may result from overland instability—downdrafts, created in unstable air, splash a thin, cold, stable layer across a near-shore surface (Figure 7.1).

Unstable air facilitates vertical motion and is characterized by thermal turbulence. Stable air limits vertical motion and diminishes thermal turbulence. Adjacent layers rubbing against each other or the surface of the earth will, however, create mechanical turbulence that—after a long delay and a long fetch—will transmit motion from one stable layer to another, sometimes in the form of waves along the interface. Separated by an inversion, adjacent layers of stable air can flow in opposite directions with little interference.

Instability

In unstable or buoyant conditions, a cold layer (that may extend to the tropopause) lies above a warm surface layer. Instability is typical of the lower atmosphere over land during the day and increases in proportion to the degree of insolation and the amount of surface heating. Instability is characterized by the enhancement of vertical movement, thermal turbulence, buoyancy, and a strong, gusty surface flow.

High pressure produces instability. The associated subsidence melts cloud, facilitates insolation and surface heating, results in a near-surface layer of warm air below cold, and stimulates convection. The strongest surface wind and the best sailing occur in sunshine in summer when thermal turbulence brings elements of friction-free upper-level air flow to the near-shore surface.

Instability facilitates lifting or sinking, whatever the genesis of displacement. In unstable air any impetus (orographic, frontal, or convective) will cause a parcel to move vertically, and once set in motion to progressively accelerate as, relative to its surroundings, it becomes progressively heavier when falling and progressively lighter when rising. In unstable air, insolation initiates updrafts and (subsequently) downdrafts, cylinders of rising and sinking air that progressively enlarge as they entrain surrounding air. Updrafts rush to the top of the turbulent layer, where they slow to a halt; downdrafts rush to the bottom of the turbulent layer where, because they do not reach a level where the SLR is lesser, they accelerate onto the surface as gusts (Figure 7.2).

Downdrafts, induced by the decrease in surface pressure beneath an updraft, reach a volume, projected area, and velocity comparable to the volume, projected

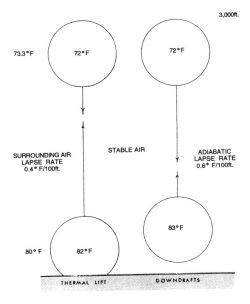

Figure 7.1. Thermal turbulence in stable air

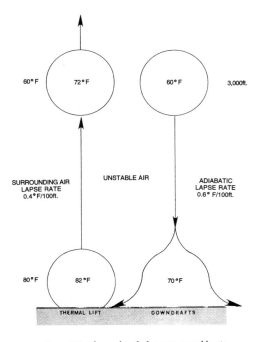

Figure 7.2. Thermal turbulence in unstable air

area, and velocity of the updrafts they replace. The higher the level to which the updrafts rise (the deeper the turbulent layer), the more dramatic is the reduction in surface pressure and the more violent are the downdrafts that accompany them. The intermittent appearance at the surface over land and near shore (within the gusting zone) of downdrafts creates the dramatic variations in wind speed and direction characteristic of unstable air.

Condensation and Evaporation

At some altitude and some degree of cooling, lifted air reaches its dew point and condenses its contained water vapor. When condensation occurs in an updraft, cumulus cloud forms. When it occurs aloft in frontal lift (associated with the invasion of an air mass of a dramatically different density), cirrus cloud forms. When it occurs in orographic lift (consequent to rising above terrain features), stratus cloud forms. When it occurs at the surface, fog forms.

Condensation, the transformation of water vapor (a gas) into water droplets (a liquid), regularly occurs in rising air and is associated with the release of heat. This addition of energy causes the rising air to become warmer and less dense and facilitates its continued rise. Evaporation, the transformation of water droplets into water vapor, occurs in sinking or heated air and is associated with the absorption of heat. The extraction of energy causes the sinking or heated air to become cooler and denser and facilitates its continued sinking. Condensation accelerates updrafts; evaporation accelerates downdrafts (Figure 7.3).

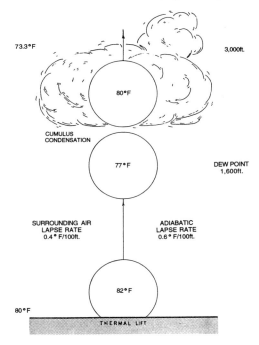

Figure 7.3. Cumulus cloud formation in an updraft

55

The strongest vertical movements—thunderstorms, tornadoes, microbursts, hurricanes—are associated with the condensation of water vapor at great heights. Liftoff in dry, unstable air may result in the ascent of a massive updraft to 6,000 to 8,000 feet. But liftoff in warm, moist, unstable air in which condensation is occurring may result in an updraft capped by a towering altocumulus castellanus cloud at 11,000 to 15,000 feet. Convergence of the surface air flow en route to separation over a preferential liftoff site, combined with condensation, may result in a giant cumulonimbus cloud at 20,000 feet that will convert the energy of condensation into a thunderstorm. The massive release of energy associated with over-ocean hurricanes and typhoons is consequent to the condensation of huge masses of warm water vapor at 30,000 feet.

The evaporation of condensed water droplets or ice crystals, by cooling and increasing the relative density of a large downdraft, accounts for the hurricane force with which a microburst strikes the surface.

The greater is the moisture content of a given mass of unstable air, the greater will be the height of its contained updrafts, the greater will be the drop in surface pressure beneath, and the greater will be the violence of the replacement downflow.

Cumulus Cloud Formation

Cumulus cloud formation is important to the sailor, as it is often reflected in shifts or alterations in the speed of surface flow. The bottom of every cumulus cloud is a furnace. The heat production associated with condensation results in a dramatic expansion of the surrounding air and an abrupt fall in the local pressure. This abrupt fall in pressure attracts all upward-moving air in the vicinity. A particular cumulus cloud can be observed to persist for long periods; it maintains itself because it attracts updrafts. Cumuli grow to a certain size (dependent on the character of the airstream) and there reach an equilibrium, gathering new updrafts at a rate equal to the rate of dissipation. Rather than creating their own cumuli, new updrafts are drawn into existing ones.

The upper portion of every cumulus cloud is a refrigerator. Here the water droplets—borne upward by the heated, expanding air into a cooler air mass—are evaporating. The cooling results in a contraction of the surrounding air, an increase in density, a decrease in viscosity, and a ring of cold, sinking air around the cumulus core. This subsidence increases the surface pressure in patches adjacent to sites of separation, updraft formation, and lowered surface pressure.

Frank Bethwaite, the famous Australian investigator of sailing winds, has noted that after the initial appearance of random cumuli, increased surface heating causes such clouds to assemble into an interlocked hexagonal pattern. This formation apparently represents the efficient coalescence of all updrafts within a limited area into the least possible number of cumuli. With further increases in heating (particularly over warm water in winter and within particularly cold air flows overriding hot land), the hexagonal pattern shifts to a longitudinal one—strings, or *streets,* of cumuli arranged in closely packed rows aligned with the wind flow. It is the gathering of updrafts into cumulus clouds at the condensation level that creates these patterns, not the number or distribution or mode or shape of the convective parcels.

8. Inversions: Daily Formation and Breakthrough

*The winds of the daytime wrestle and fight longer
and stronger than the winds of the night.*
—ENGLISH PROVERB

The temperature of the lower layers of the atmosphere ordinarily diminishes with distance from the source of heating, the earth's surface. A reversal of that condition, the presence of warm air above cold, is termed an inversion. Inversions may occur due to

- the loss of heat by the earth's surface through radiation and the cooling of the surface air—a radiation inversion
- the drainage of cold air from above a cold surface onto a lower-lying surface—a conduction inversion
- the advection (in a horizontal flow) of heated air from above a heated site—an advection inversion
- the compression and gain in heat (due to that compression) of air subsiding onto the cold contracted air above a cold surface—a subsidence inversion (Figure 8.1)

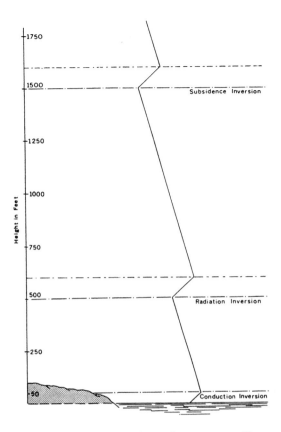

Figure 8.1. Inversions—layers of warm air over cold

Diurnal variations in the creation and dissipation of inversions determine the major diurnal variations in surface air flow. Inversions may exclude all wind from the surface or exclude the gradient wind from the surface and facilitate the development of a thermal wind in the protected surface layer.

Radiation, Conduction, and Advection Inversions

Morning

In most latitudes (except for the polar regions), during the night (particularly on clear nights) the loss of heat from the land by longwave radiation lowers the surface temperature below that of the air. The lowest layers of air become cooled by conduction, and the cooled air flows downslope to accumulate over low-lying land and water. Inversions—a radiation inversion over the land and a conduction inversion over the water—form between the warmer upper air and the cold near-surface air. The gradient wind is displaced above these inversions, and the surface becomes calm.

The surface will usually remain calm until morning, when insolation heats the surface of the land and induces thermal turbulence. Updrafts of heated air then rise to and eventually (with increased surface heating) break through the radiation inversion. Replacement downdrafts bring the supra-inversion air and the gradient wind to the land and to the near-shore surfaces. Cloud cover and high humidity during the night absorb the outgoing longwave radiation from the cooling earth, diminish surface cooling, and negate the formation of a radiation inversion. During the day rain, snow, or ice or extensive cloud cover reduce thermal turbulence and permit a conduction inversion to persist or to develop over water, the lowest and coolest available surface. Only with the aid of mechanical turbulence (eddies and waves) will gradient winds penetrate through such inversions to the surface of large water bodies, while small water bodies will remain completely calm.

Wind present at the surface of near-shore waters in early morning means that mechanical turbulence or cloud cover has been sufficient to prevent a nocturnal radiation inversion from forming. Any early-morning gradient wind is likely to persist because the thermal turbulence associated with the diurnal insolation to come will bring even stronger upper-level flow to the surface. However, if the gradient flow is warm, clear, and relatively dry, insolation may facilitate separation and convection, and at midday or thereafter diminish overland surface pressure sufficiently to generate a secondary sea/lake breeze.

Calm in early morning indicates that the gradient wind is weak and/or warm and confined above a radiation inversion, and that (if insolation is effective) thermal winds are likely to develop. The accumulation of cold air at the surface associated with nocturnal radiation produces a high near-surface lapse rate that in early morning facilitates separation. In spring and fall (or in summer if the water is particularly cold, as it is along the New England coast or in Swiss lakes) local primary sea/lake breezes frequently develop after clear nights within harbors or other shoreline indentations that facilitate the access of the marine air to the heating sites ashore.

Midday

By 1000 to 1100, insolation typically increases thermal turbulence sufficiently to permit updrafts to break through the radiation inversion. The local primary sea/lake breeze (if any) begins to back and die. The backing and dying may be interspersed with periods of strengthening and shifting as the inversion is alternately broken through and re-formed, and is usually succeeded by a brief period of calm (Figure 8.2).

If the gradient wind flowing above the inversion is strong and its advected air cool, it may now be brought to the surface by the thermal turbulence. If the gradient wind is weak and its advected air hot or the water very cold (typical of ocean coasts and mountain lakes in summer), an advection inversion will maintain the protection provided by the nocturnal radiation inversion. The gradient wind will be unable to penetrate to the surface, and surface flow at midday or in early afternoon will depend on the presence of insolation, surface heating, and the onshore movement of the marine air in a primary sea/lake breeze. Even if the gradient

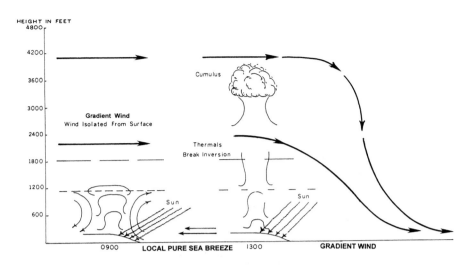

Figure 8.2. Inversion breakthrough

wind is strong but hot, as it is along the U.S. East Coast at Savannah and on the Chesapeake, the onshore flow of marine air may lift it from the surface and form a strong, protective inversion at the interface.

Evening

All afternoon winds—gradient winds and primary, secondary, and amalgamated sea/lake breezes—diminish in late afternoon or evening as thermal turbulence diminishes, and all back as they diminish. One must be alert to decreases in velocity and expect them to be accompanied by backing. If racing at 1700 on a summer day in a secondary sea breeze—a wind that typically veers markedly during its development, and backs markedly during its dying—one should keep to the left of the competition.

Along coasts where the near-shore surface is vegetated or interspersed with water, the nocturnal radiation inversion re-forms readily, and a warm gradient wind is typically lifted from the surface and replaced by evening calm. A cooler gradient wind will persist longer (at least until thermal turbulence ceases). Primary sea breezes ordinarily die by 1900 (or earlier), but on coasts where they extend over deserts far into the interior, their peak velocity may not be reached until 2100.

In late afternoon, as it loses its sea breeze element, an amalgamated sea breeze shifts toward its component gradient wind. The dying of the secondary sea breeze as insolation diminishes may permit the gradient wind, if strong and gusty, to regain the surface. In these situations the sailor should position himself upwind or at an improved sailing angle in the gradient wind as it reappears. Because any sea/lake breeze persists longest near shore, and the gradient wind reappears first near shore, "in a dying secondary sea/lake breeze, go for the shore."

Four Common Midday Wind Regimes

1. In the absence of effective insolation and thermal turbulence (complete cloud cover, rain, excessive heat and/or humidity), the radiation inversion (if any) shifts imperceptibly into a persistent advection inversion. The marine air sits in a stagnant pool at the bottom of the atmosphere. No gradient wind will disturb the leaves; no fall in overland pressure will draw the marine air ashore; the surface of the water will languish in an all-day calm (Figure 8.3).

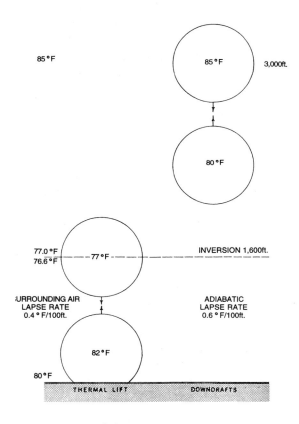

Figure 8.3. The limitation of movement by an inversion

2. Despite the presence of effective insolation and thermal turbulence over land, if the advected air is very hot and dry or the water surface very cold, as it is in winter and spring, the radiation inversion will shift imperceptibly into a persistent overwater advection inversion. Despite strong air flow ashore (where thermal turbulence brings downdrafts of upper-level flow to the surface), the gradient wind will be excluded from the water surface. If the shoreline is steep, the lake

or bay may remain calm all day. In mountainous terrain, moderate to strong lake breezes downslope or upslope flows may accompany such conditions.

3. In the presence of effective insolation and thermal turbulence, if the advected air is warmer than the marine air, mechanical and thermal turbulence will dissipate the morning radiation inversion, and the gradient wind will reach the surface. Secondary sea/lake breezes may develop in these conditions if: (*a*) separation and liftoff of heated air in an unstable air flow result in a major fall in overland surface pressure and the gradient flow becomes warmer than the marine air, or if (*b*) separation and liftoff are induced by intense midday insolation in a hot and dry, even though, stable, air flow and the strong advection inversion created at the interface protects the onshore flow. If the near-shore topography facilitates invasion, the secondary sea/lake breeze will cross the shoreline, and the overwater surface flow will strengthen. If the gradient wind is blowing onshore, an amalgamated sea breeze may develop.

4. In the presence of effective insolation and thermal turbulence, if the advected air is colder than the marine air (as it typically is in winter), the gradient wind will be present at the surface in early morning. Separation and liftoff of heated air will occur over land, thermal turbulence will rise to great heights, and downdrafts of the cold gradient wind will sweep away the marine air. No sea/lake breeze will develop.

9. Calm

In a calm sea, every man is a pilot.
—ENGLISH PROVERB

Calm is rarely the absence of wind. Nocturnal calm and calm persisting into the morning or all-day calm are due to the displacement of the gradient wind above an inversion and of the absence beneath that inversion of any stimulus to thermal wind generation. Calm developing after a period of surface air flow, usually at midday, is due to the convergence of two flows—of similar strength and temperature—and the vertical displacement of each.

Inversion Calm

All motion mechanically or thermally induced—horizontal or vertical—takes place in the turbulent layer, and if it is to reach the surface, must be transmitted across an interface into the stagnant boundary layer. Each night cold air accumulating at the surface merges with and thickens the boundary layer, creates a low-level conduction inversion, and blocks the transmission of mechanical turbulence. The dissipation of such a low-level inversion and the initiation of surface air flow depends on the development of thermal turbulence which, because it is entirely vertical, readily transmits motion through an inversion. Over water, where thermal turbulence is absent and the transmission of motion depends entirely on mechanical turbulence, even strong air flows may be unable to break through a low-level inversion (Figure 9.1).

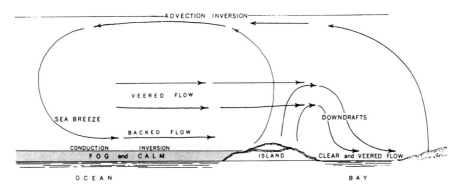

Figure 9.1. The offshore sea/lake breeze

The typical nocturnal near-coast and inland calm is due to loss of heat from the land by radiation, the chilling and sliding downslope of air in contact with the cooling surfaces, and the elevation of the boundary layer as cold air accumulates above the lowest nearby surfaces. Pools of cold air form and become trapped above confined water bodies. The coldest, densest layers of such pools are at the bottom; the warmest at the top. Their lapse rate is typically negative; air lifted within them sinks back immediately. Even after dawn, when downdrafts induced by thermal turbulence begin to penetrate to and splash at the surface, the near-surface air, lifted and compressed against the bank, slides back to re-form the unmoving surface pool. Not until late morning, following downdraft after downdraft, is the cold surface air finally swept away and replaced by upper-level flow.

An onshore wind that is even slightly warmer than the marine air will lift from the surface beginning at a site nine times higher than the altitude of terrain features on a leeward shore. The minimal mechanical turbulence of such a flow, unable to penetrate the pool of stagnant marine air trapped against a bank, often leaves leeward near-shore segments of even large water bodies in calm. At Rochester, New York, in the morning following the passage of a cold front, a zone of calm regularly extends a half mile from shore despite the surface presence, farther out, of a 20-knot onshore northerly. Several hours will elapse before the purely mechanical turbulence of even a strong onshore flow drags the cold, dense near-shore air, parcel by parcel, over the bluffs and penetrates to the near-shore surface.

All-day calm is usually due to the merging of the nocturnal radiation inversion with an advection inversion created by a warm gradient air flow or the absence of thermal turbulence under dense cloud cover. Such an inversion is typical of spring along the U.S. East Coast, when southerly gradient winds are composed of particularly warm air and the waters over which they flow are particularly cold.

Convergence Calm

Calm that develops during daylight hours—calm appearing during a race—is usually consequent to the development and convergence of a second wind.

For calm to result from convergence, the two winds must

- derive from equivalent pressure gradients (if one is far stronger, it will dominate)
- be of similar temperature (if one is far colder, it will occupy the surface and displace the other aloft)
- be directed in opposition or approximately perpendicular to one another (if aligned, they will amalgamate into a single flow)

Typically, one of the two winds is a gradient wind, the other a thermal wind. Typically, the calm appears in late morning as insolation is increasing and the thermal wind gradient reaches a strength equal to that of the gradient wind, or in late afternoon as insolation is decreasing and the thermal wind gradient diminishes to a strength equal to that of the gradient wind.

Convergence can also occur within a gradient wind when two segments oppose one another. At Rochester, along the southern shore of Lake Ontario, the overland and overwater portions of the parallel-to-shore southwester converge over the lake to produce a late-morning calm. Two portions of a thermal wind may also oppose one another. After channeling through separate mountain passes, two portions of the general upslope flow toward Austria's Dachstein massif converge over the Wolfgangsee from its opposite ends. Wherever downslope and upslope winds appear alternately, a period of calm precedes each turnover. On Italy's Lago di Garda the downslope Peler, which blows all night, is succeeded after dying in late morning by a 2-hour period of calm before being replaced at about 1300 by the upslope Ora. On the Swiss lakes of the Bernese Oberland, the south Föhn coming over and down the north face of the Alps is opposed by the upslope thermal wind. The result may be an entire day of alternating light thermal wind, calm, light Föhn, calm, light thermal wind—and never a completed race. The outflow from a thunderstorm characteristically produces a zone of calm as it converges with a sea/lake breeze—"the calm before the storm" (Figure 9.2).

At most coastal sites the typical cause of calm is the convergence accompanying the development of a secondary sea/lake breeze (Figure 9.3). As the thermal gradient increases in late morning, the marine air begins to move toward shore, lifting the warming offshore gradient wind, until it reaches the near-shore gusting zone. Here the far greater penetration, lower temperature, and higher velocity of downdrafts from the gradient flow block the further encroachment of the marine air. At the surface, between the near-shore gusting zone and the offshore sea/lake breeze zone, the two flows, at approximately equal strength and temperature, meet. Each is forced upward, leaving calm (the absence of horizontal flow) at the surface. The combined upflow rises above the sea/lake breeze front, is swept seaward

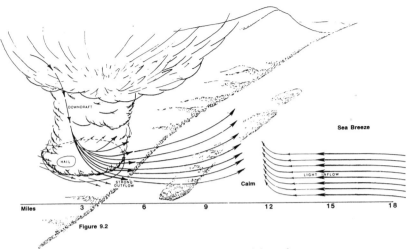

Figure 9.2. The thunderstorm and the sea breeze

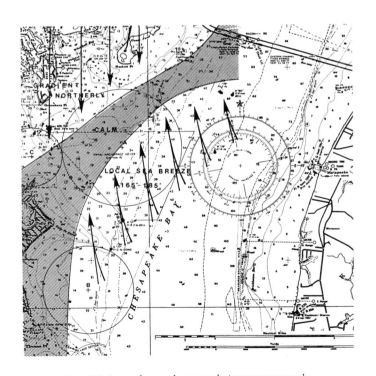

Figure 9.3. A secondary sea breeze producing convergence calm

in the upper levels of the gradient flow, subsides as it cools over the water, and increases the surface onshore thermal pressure gradient.

The secondary sea/lake breeze may not be strong enough to push away the near-shore gusting zone—and a persistent state of "two winds simultaneously" may result. This interaction may repeat itself in the opposite order late in the day: as the thermal wind dies (and backs), the gradient wind strengthens and the gusting zone spreads offshore, pushing the zone of calm ahead.

If insolation is occurring, advection and subsidence protect the development of thermal winds. Although morning calm is typical of coastal areas under subsidence inversions—Savannah, San Diego, and Fremantle, for instance—midday calm is rare. Strong sea breezes develop in the cool marine layer because they are separated from the gradient wind in the warm air above—i.e., because convergence is prevented. Only when the subsidence inversions are weakened by the invasion of a cold or warm front do secondary sea breezes converge with gradient winds in the marine layer and does midday calm appear.

Calm is temporary ("Be a long ca'm spell, if it ain't," says the Maine fisherman). Management of calm requires the recognition that it is transient and that (unless it has been present under an inversion since early morning) it is due to the convergence of two winds. One must identify the wind that has been present and assume that the other of the pair common to the site is strengthening and about to appear. If racing, one must decide which of the two will be present when the boats arrive at the next mark, and if necessary move within one wind to a position that will be advantaged in the other. If the mark will be in the old wind, one must remain in it or return to it as directly as possible; if the mark will be in the new wind, one must escape from the old, crossing the intervening zone of calm into the new, as directly as possible.

10. Sailing beneath the Waves

Who has seen the Wind?
Neither you nor I;
But when the trees bow down their heads,
The wind is passing by.
—Christina Rossetti

In spring, warm 15- to 20-knot southerlies may shake the treetops ashore but flow unnoticed above the surface calm of even large water bodies such as Chesapeake Bay and Long Island Sound. Near shore, the downdrafts of thermal turbulence carry their momentum through the inversions, but farther offshore penetration is dependent on mechanical turbulence—"natural airstream oscillations"—the disturbance of flow induced by friction between parcels of air of varying density and/or with the surface. Stable air flows flowing over wet or snow-covered land induce no thermal turbulence and bring no downdrafts/gusts to the near-shore surface. Penetration of the accompanying overwater conduction inversion can be achieved only by mechanical turbulence operating over a fetch of hundreds of yards.

Mechanical Turbulence

Whereas thermal turbulence is vertical (half operating downward), mechanical turbulence is random; only a small portion of it moves downward and is capable of penetrating through an inversion into a subjacent layer (Figure 10.1). In the absence of thermal turbulence, the regular flow at the surface requires the cumulative effect of an air flow's prolonged overwater transit (see prologue).

In the absence of thermal turbulence, mechanical turbulence associated with even strong air flows ordinarily produces little flow at the surface of small lakes and rivers. For a warm, stable wind to penetrate the deep pool of cold, dense marine air during its short transit from shore to shore, some special impetus, some influence in addition to mechanical turbulence, is required.

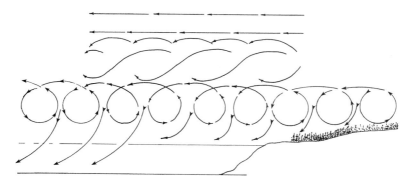

Figure 10.1. Mechanical turbulence penetrating a conduction inversion

A Race beneath a Conduction Inversion

The 1994 Ice Bowl Race up the narrow (300- to 400-yard-wide) Severn River in Maryland was sailed in a stable southerly. The water temperature was 32°F, the air temperature was approximately 45°F, and the gradient wind (predicted to flow at 15 to 20 knots) was flowing over snow-covered land. We presumed that above the snow there would be no thermal turbulence and that the warm air flow would have difficulty penetrating the pool of cold marine air trapped between the high (50- to 80-foot) banks of the Severn. The southerly, which blew at 10 to 15 knots across the surface of the open Chesapeake, never exceeded 10 knots at the surface of the river, and then only in patches and intermittently (see Figure 36.1, p.267, for a map of the river—in different conditions).

We reckoned that the warm flow coming obliquely off the southwestern shore of the river would reach the surface most readily along the leeward (northeastern) shore. Pre-race observations confirmed these presumptions and disclosed large areas of minimal flow (or complete calm) immediately to leeward of bluffs along the left (southwestern) shore. We determined to jibe immediately after the downwind start toward the right (northeastern) side of the river.

As the gun fired, a localized streak of stronger wind appeared and three boats roared across the middle of the line. They were 100 feet down the course before we crossed at the starboard end and jibed. As we limped along to their right in minimal air, the rest of the fleet pulled ahead. But 300 hundred yards down the course the leaders stopped—and we moved up in an 8-knot streak. We soon ran out of wind and stopped in turn. Following a brief period of total calm, a new breeze appeared ahead of the fleet, and the leaders once again raced away. When we arrived to leeward of where they had been, we picked up their breeze, they slowed, and we recovered what we had just lost. But before we could overtake them, the wind died, and, when it reappeared once again, they were the first to receive it.

Cyclic Variations in Air Flow

This cycle—near calm, new breeze appearing ahead of the fleet, the leaders surging away and then running out of wind, the followers picking up their wind and nearly catching them, the wind dying generally, and the leaders sailing into a fresh breeze once again—was repeated five times in about 45 minutes as we moved up the narrow river. But after the first two cycles the net gain was ours. Each time the wind died we had been able to come up from our leeward position on a faster course. By the time we reached the site where the river widens into Round Bay, we were fourth and closing fast. In a prolonged lull with the three leaders barely moving, we surged up and across, ahead of the two to leeward, and in an abrupt increase in wind velocity, drove over the third and into the lead.

As we emerged into Round Bay, we could see that a mile from the windward shore the upper-level flow was continuously reaching the surface. But between the high banks of the narrow river, the cold air had not been so readily displaced. Only in the river's center, far from the windward bank, had turbulence in the warm air flow penetrated the inversion (forced less dense air through more dense) and reached the surface. And throughout our passage up the river the surface flow had been intermittent, disappearing completely at regular intervals. Despite these fluctuations in velocity, the flow had shown little change in direction, which seemed to indicate that penetration, not the upper-level wind velocity, had been varying.

This penetration appeared to have been cyclic. Following a lull affecting all boats, the leaders had regularly entered a zone of increased wind and had sailed away for several minutes, gaining 200 to 300 feet. Then, as the leaders sailed out of the breeze, the tailenders entered it and caught up—typically recovering all they had lost—until they in turn ran out of wind. After approximately the same interval, the leaders entered a new patch and pulled away to their former lead.

Waves

Cyclic fluctuations suggest wave activity. A *wave* is a circular movement of a medium (upward on the after side, forward on top, downward on the forward side, and backward at the bottom) that propagates an elevated crest and a depressed trough along the surface of an interface in the direction of the initiating force.

The near-surface turbulent layer—a few hundred to a few thousand feet thick—is typically confined by an inversion. If so, a warmer gradient wind typically flows above colder, denser air at and below the inversion interface, much as a surface wind blows across a water surface. The gradient wind creates waves along the inversion surface just as a surface wind creates water waves. If the turbulent layer is very thick, these waves are unlikely to influence the near-surface air flow. But if the inversion is but a few hundred feet above the surface, wind waves (like water waves) may be transmitted to the bottom.

Frank Bethwaite has demonstrated the influence of such waves in a variety of conditions associated with low-level inversions and believes that they often cause sequential oscillations in the direction and strength of the near-surface wind flow. He points out that very shallow flows such as sea/lake breezes can develop only shallow waves (low-amplitude oscillations), whereas deeper layers such as the outflows from polar air masses typically produce high-amplitude oscillations. Bethwaite correlated days of unusually regular oscillations in the Kingston, Ontario, lake breeze with high pressure and a strengthening of the marine air inversion by subsidence.

On the day of the race described, the Severn lay beneath a conduction inversion; very cold air was trapped between the high banks of the river, above which the warm gradient wind was flowing. A wave of upper-level flow may have been progressing along the surface of the inversion, and its penetrating trough may have been intermittently transmitting motion to the surface of the water (Figure 10.2).

Lee waves, stationary oscillations of the atmosphere, occur when stable airstreams pass over or around obstructions. The flow reaching the surface of the Severn had traversed low hills before coming offshore above the river. Although these low obstructions are not comparable to those that have been demonstrated to produce the dangerous lee waves associated with aircraft disasters, the transit of a series of minor obstacles could set low-amplitude waves into motion. The resonance of such wave trains, periodically interfering with and reinforcing the wave amplitude, could have contributed to the fluctuations in wind penetration we witnessed (Figure 10.3).

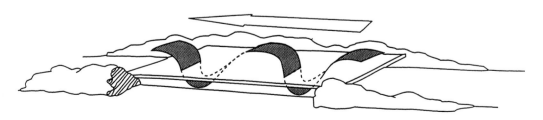

Figure 10.2. Waves induced by mechanical turbulence

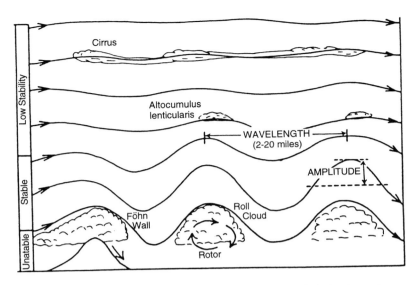

Figure 10.3. Lee waves to leeward of a mountain range (From Barry and Chorley, Atmosphere, Weather and Climate; *after Wallington, 1960.)*

Cyclic Phenomena

In the atmosphere cyclic phenomena are common. Medium oscillations in unstable air flows produce shifts alternating in direction that benefit first boats on one side of the fleet and then those on the other. Around-the-World racers experience cyclic fluctuations in air flow and in their positions as successive fronts overtake them in the Southern Ocean. Water waves permit the members of a fleet to surf down successive wave faces. Exposure to multiple cycles of a cyclic event should ultimately result in equal outcomes for those exposed. Unequal outcomes derive from differences in experience, typically from differences in exposure to the first and last event of the cycle (which are difficult or impossible to manipulate).

However, outcome may be improved—whether of the oscillating shifts of large-scale convection, of the recurrent frontal passages of the Southern Ocean, or of waves propagating along an inversion interface—if each phase of a cycle is used to attain the best possible position for entry into the next. When the cyclic phenomenon is velocity variation, optimal positioning is to leeward—the boat should be headed off in the gusts so that it can be brought back up on the fastest possible course in the lulls.

III. *Gradient Winds: Weekly and Seasonal Variations*

Midlatitudes: Coasts
                              Lakes
                              Rivers

11. Miami: The Polar Front in the Subtropics

March comes in like a lion,
Goes out like a lamb.
—AMERICAN PROVERB

In the preceding section we learned that gradient winds and sea/lake breezes vary each day with variations in insolation, that stability and instability modify surface air flow, that inversions form and confine winds to layers above or below them, that calms are caused by convergence or by the exclusion of wind by an inversion, and that mechanical turbulence can be manifest in waves.

We have examined the character of low-level winds. Now let us learn something about their weekly and seasonal variations in the midlatitudes. We shall see that these variations are chiefly consequent to the west-to-east movement of the polar front and result in a sequence of regularly repeated, standard patterns. I have selected Miami as the site that best illustrates the phases of the polar front because in winter, when the front reaches this far south, its phases are dramatic and distinctive. Here, in winter, the centers of successive highs pass to the north, as they do at most sites in the United States in summer. The phase sequence described below is dependent on this orientation. When a high-pressure center passes to the south, the phase sequence is abbreviated. (See chapter 20, "Rochester.")

Phase I: The Northwesterly

By the time the northwest air flow behind a cold front reaches South Florida, much of its strength has been dissipated (in thermal and mechanical turbulence). If it arrives during daylight hours, the flow rapidly reaches its peak surface velocity and during the next two days, in association with a progressive but very gradual veer, weakens progressively. Its surface velocity and gustiness fluctuate each day with variations in insolation and thermal turbulence, typically peaking at about 1400.

On Biscayne Bay, one regularly sees a difference between "inshore" and "offshore" (near the mainland shore and near the Key Biscayne shore). On the second day after cold front passage, and when the northwesterly drops below 15 knots, it is strongest and relatively backed near the mainland shore and becomes weaker and veered, presumably by an abortive inflow of marine air, near the key. As the weather mark is typically near the mainland shore, a course to the left usually provides both stronger wind and a relative back. A Biscayne Bay rule that applies in these conditions is "If the wind is to the left of 360° (320° to 360°), go left."

Occasionally on Biscayne Bay, on the second day (rarely the first) after a cold front passage, the advected air becomes so warmed by its passage over heated land that the cool marine air is able to undermine it, lift it from the surface (at least offshore), and replace it with a secondary local sea breeze. The result is one of the common conditions at Miami in which two winds are present simultaneously. In midbay, where the race committee often sets the course, is a zone of calm where the two winds converge and the struggling sea breeze is displaced upward and swept offshore in the gradient flow.

Even at a site as far from its polar origins as Miami, the northwesterly is a strong, cold, and unstable flow, usually strong enough to prevent sea breeze generation and unstable enough to produce violent downdraft gusts and large oscillations.

Phase II: The Northerly/Northeasterly

At Biscayne Bay a strong (greater than 15-knot) northerly or northeasterly, appearing between two and four days after a cold front passage, is likely to persist throughout the day and be characterized by large and protracted oscillations (30° or more) lasting 20 to 30 minutes; relative to the time spent on an average windward leg, these constitute persistent shifts.

The Local Sea Breeze

A weak, warmed northerly or northeasterly typically dies and disappears by midmorning, and is replaced by a secondary sea breeze. Racing commences in a steady 6- to 12-knot sea breeze that begins at approximately 100° and gradually veers with time. The intrusion of Key Biscayne channels the water-level layer of the onshore flow around the tip of the key and along its shoreline into the northern reaches of the bay. This causes the wind to back with distance to windward; near the Rickenbacker Causeway the median wind direction is 140°; near the southern tip of the key its median direction is 110°, with a range of 100° to 120° (Figure 11.1).

Frequently the secondary sea breeze is able to invade only the outer areas of the bay. Near the mainland shore and near the key the gradient northeasterly is brought to the surface in a gusting zone, and for much of the afternoon "two winds simultaneously" occupy the surface.

Northerly and northeasterly gradient flows are often sufficiently unstable to induce a secondary sea breeze and sufficiently cold to prevent the developing onshore flow from reaching the mainland shore.

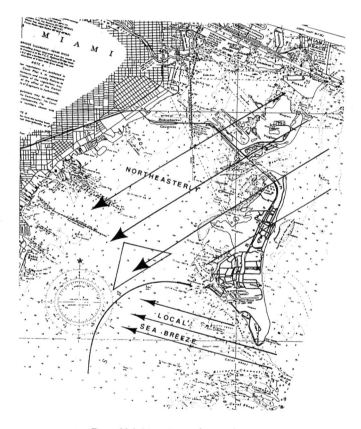

Figure 11.1. Miami's secondary sea breeze

Phase III: The Easterly

The gradient easterly usually breaks through the radiation inversion over Key Biscayne and reaches the surface along the bay shore at about 0900. But around 1100 the local secondary sea breeze appears off the tip of the key, lifts the warmer

77

easterly from the surface and spreads westward and northward into the bay. By midday the sea breeze flow usually dominates the entire bay, gradually veering with time and with distance north into the bay (Figure 11.2).

In midafternoon—sometimes sooner—the channeled backing most evident near the key shore may increase abruptly and be associated with a zone of dying sea breeze or near calm extending parallel to the key and about a mile offshore. The backed wind is the gradient easterly (or northeasterly) that has been flowing aloft above the sea breeze and is brought to the near-key surface by the increasing thermal turbulence of midafternoon. When the weather mark is near the key shore, races are often won by the boat first able to cross the zone of calm and enter this backed flow. By late afternoon, with the diminution of thermal turbulence, the overflowing air disappears from the surface and the low-level around-the-key sea breeze spreads across the entire course.

These phenomena account for another Biscayne rule (applicable only to courses near the key): "When the wind (the gradient wind) is to the left of 100°, go left (expecting the gradient wind to be brought to the surface by thermal turbulence)." Later in the afternoon an equally good rule is: "When the wind is to the

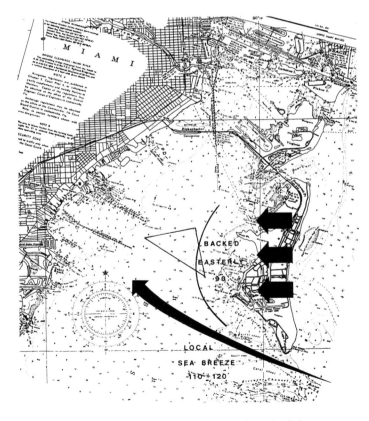

Figure 11.2. Gradient flow brought to the surface by thermal turbulence

right of 100° (which means that it is the sea breeze), go right (expecting it to veer as it increases in velocity)."

If the sea breeze is going to dominate, expect it to be evident by 1030 (before the first start). If the easterly dies during the race, expect the sea breeze to appear and persist only in the right corner. Frequently, only the boats that reach that corner receive its benefits—a most distressing sight for the sailors who watch them march across the horizon in a huge and inaccessible starboard tack lift.

Thermal turbulence, created as a sea breeze flows over land, may produce a near-shore zone in which gusts of upper-level gradient wind (as well as sea breeze) reach the surface.

Phase IV: The Southeasterly/Southerly

In South Florida the southeaster is directly aligned with the local portion of the East Coast ocean sea breeze. At Biscayne Bay gradient winds so aligned (southeasterly and southerly) have traversed long stretches of ocean prior to reaching South Florida, have acquired the temperature of the marine air, amalgamate readily with the sea breeze, and create the best possible sailing conditions.

The Ocean Sea Breeze

Along the southern Florida shore the southeasterly breaks through the radiation inversion and appears at the surface by 1030. Its initial direction is close to that predicted for the gradient wind. The late-morning shift will be toward the large-scale amalgamated ocean sea breeze, whose median direction is 166°. Gradient winds veered (up to 20°) to 166° will back to that direction and winds backed (up

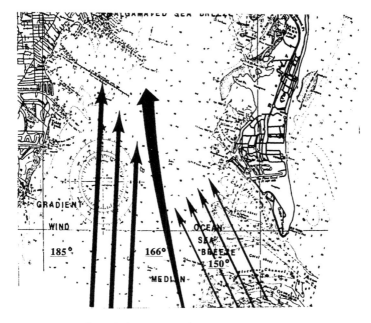

Figure 11.3. Miami's amalgamated ocean sea breeze

79

to 20°) will veer to that direction. Gradient winds between 155° and 175° will be maximally strengthened and will show only the inherent velocity veer. Most fully developed, strong (15- to 18-knot) veered ocean sea breezes will flow (in midafternoon) from about 165° to 175° (Figure 11.3).

These flows come across small islands and heated shoal water, and develop thermal turbulence, downdraft gusts, and oscillating shifts (10° to 12°). In the morning it is wise to keep to the sea breeze median (165°) side of the rhumb line, but to avoid the layline until late in the leg. In early afternoon the sea breeze should strengthen to 16 to 18 knots—and with the acceleration, veer to 170° or even 175°. Then, while the breeze is building, one should keep to the right of the rhumb line. Late in the day as insolation diminishes and the sea breeze component dies, the surface flow shifts toward the original gradient wind direction.

With increasing insolation the surface flow of an amalgamated sea/lake breeze becomes chiefly composed of and flows in the direction of the sea/lake breeze component.

Phase V: The Southwester

In South Florida the southwester is rarely seen: In summer the center of the Bermuda High is to the northeast and the flow is southeasterly; in winter the Continental Polar (cP) High usually displaces the Bermuda High farther south, and at its most southern position provides southeast flow.

Phase VI: The Warm-Sector Westerly

In winter in South Florida a warm front may overtake the cP air that has invaded behind a cold front and restore the sway of maritime tropical Gulf of Mexico (mTg) air (within the Bermuda High) to the region immediately south of the polar front.

Thunderstorms are common as the warm, moist air is lifted by both frontal and thermal influences. Because their upper-level steering winds are westerly and Key Biscayne entices them eastward, thunderstorms (originating over central Florida) are likely to come offshore onto Biscayne Bay. One should expect a shift toward the dark cloud, a major increase in velocity as the roll cloud approaches, a dramatic drop in velocity as the storm passes overhead, and a gradual return to the original wind's strength and direction. If the original wind was the sea breeze, however, it may never regenerate.

On South Florida's "east-facing" coast a westerly may be lifted from the surface by the onshore movement of cool marine air in a secondary sea breeze and produce "two winds simultaneously." In winter and spring, when the coastal water and the marine air are still very cold but the land and the westerly are hot, a zone of gusty westerly flow may persist along shores and within harbors (in the gusting zone) while the sea breeze develops offshore.

If they are sufficiently strong, even hot offshore flows may maintain near-shore gusting zones in opposition to invading sea breezes.

12. Weekly Alterations in Wind Patterns

Long foretold, long last, short notice, soon past.
—ENGLISH PROVERB

In the midlatitudes the position, movements, and deviations of the polar front are the major determinants of local weather and wind patterns. Movements of polar front features from east to west determine the daily and weekly alterations in low-level wind flow. Movements north and south determine the seasonal alterations. Daily weather maps, which diagram the location and conformation of the polar front, indicate the origin of the conditions extant and predict the winds to come.

The polar front separates masses of cold polar (typically continental—cP) air to the north from masses of warm tropical (typically *maritime—mT*) air to the south (Figure 12.1). To each side these masses of air subside over and assume the

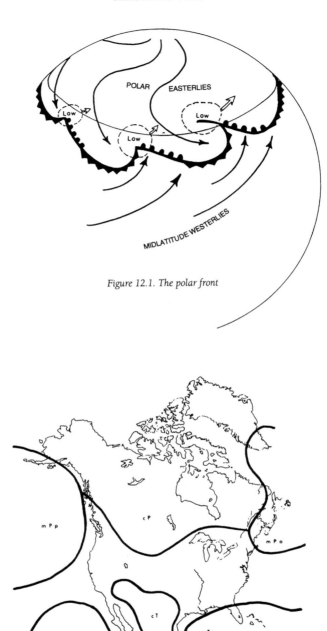

Figure 12.1. The polar front

Figure 12.2. The air masses of North America

character of the cold, homogeneous surfaces beneath. Continental polar air becomes cold and dry over central Canada, and maritime tropical gulf air becomes cooler, but still hot and moist, over the Gulf of Mexico. The subsidence and increase in density in such air masses (over cold Canadian tundra and "cold" ocean water) result in a rise in surface pressure and the formation of two persistent "highs"—a cP High to the north and an mT High to the south (Figure 12.2).

Air flows out from these centers of high pressure and in toward centers of low pressure. Because in the Northern Hemisphere the rotation of the earth (Coriolis force) causes all moving air to veer, gradient winds flowing outward from a center of high pressure develop a clockwise circulation, and gradient winds flowing inward toward a center of low pressure develop a counterclockwise circulation.

Interactions between the two air masses—the cold burrowing under the warm as a cold front, the warm lifting above the cold as a warm front—occur in association with north/south dips of the polar front. Where sharp kinks form, the lifting of one air mass by the other results in such expansion of the lifted air that surface pressure falls, a "low" forms, and air is drawn in from surrounding surfaces.

The Jet Stream

The general westerly trend of the upper-level air in the midlatitudes, due to the earth's rotation and the direction of flow on the poleward sides of the subtropical highs, is responsible for the inexorable movement to the east of the entire polar front, its kinks included, at about 300 to 500 miles per day. We now know that the track of this easterly movement is chiefly determined by waves in an upper-level, rapidly moving river of air known as the *midlatitude jet stream,* which periodically causes polar air to invade the Tropics, or tropical air to invade the Subarctic. Because water provides the fuel and heated land the energy required for convection, the polar front and its low-pressure systems tend to migrate along the chain of Great Lakes or along the Gulf of Mexico/Atlantic seaboard, where both fuel and energy are available.

The jet stream moves north/south with seasonal changes in the proximity of the sun and the inclination of the earth. In summer the jet stream and its accompanying polar front move north, and for weeks on end the polar front may never move south of the Great Lakes, which means that almost the entire United States lies trapped in the hot, humid tropical air advected by the Bermuda High. The reverse may be true in winter, when for weeks on end the jet stream and the polar front may never move north of the Mason-Dixon Line and much of the United States shivers in cold, dry continental polar air.

The Sequential Phases of the Polar Front

Guided by the jet stream the features of the polar front migrate from west to east, and for sites across which the front migrates (most of the United States and Europe), a reasonably standard set of six to eight gradient wind phases emerges. With myriad minor variations, an invasion of tropical air to the north alternates with an invasion of polar air to the south, and the six to eight standard phases reappear in cycles. The frequency with which polar or tropical air reappears, of course, depends on the season and the latitude of the site. In spring and fall over the northern United States, the sequence repeats itself at approximately weekly intervals, each phase lasting approximately one or two days. In summer or winter, with the front displaced to the north or south, one or two of the phases may persist for a week or more.

If we select a site somewhere along the U.S. East Coast and take the passage of a cold front as the initial event, the series begins with a northwesterly flow of cold polar air on the eastern side of the circulation around a center of cP high pressure. The second phase appears as the center of the cP High—passing to the north, as is typical in summer—moves eastward and the flow on its eastern side veers to the north and northeast. When the center of the high is close and due north, the gradient flow is from the east and the advected air comes from the Atlantic Ocean. The fourth phase develops when the high moves to the east and gradient flow from the southeast or south advects air from the southern North Atlantic or the gulf over the hot southern states. If the high moves offshore and fuses with the North Atlantic Subtropical High (the Bermuda High), the next (the fifth) phase will be the "southwester"—the prevailing gradient wind of East Coast summers—which brings mTg air across the southern states and to the Atlantic seaboard (Figure 12.3).

Ahead of a low that may follow the movement of a cP High along the polar front, the gradient wind will also be south or southwest (strengthening the southwest flow behind the center of high pressure), accompanied by increasing cloud and thunderstorms. As the low migrates along the polar front, the next phase over a site to its south is a warm front passage. Tropical air rides up over polar air, accompanied by varying amounts of cloud and rain. The warm front is followed

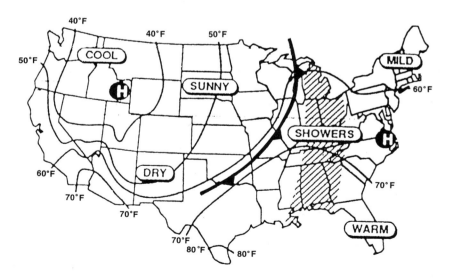

Figure 12.3. A cold front moving eastward across the United States

by the "warm sector"—the zone to the south of a low between a warm front and a following cold front. Here the gradient wind is from the west and may be strong, as both the high to the south and the low to the north create a westerly gradient that is accelerated by the frontal convection.

After the warm sector the sequence begins again with a cold front passage. If, of course, the center of the low passes directly over the site or to its south, no warm sector is experienced and the sixth phase is the often strong easterly or northeasterly (the New England coast's "three-day nor'easter") gradient flow to the north of the low. The cool, moist advected air drawn in from the northern North Atlantic produces thick layers of cloud (stratus and nimbostratus) and rain (or snow).

The sequence is abbreviated if the center of the high passes to the south, as it often does in the northern United States, Canada, and Europe. The phases of northerly to southeasterly flow are eliminated, and the gradient wind shifts from northwesterly ahead of the high to westerly as it passes, and to southwesterly behind it. If the center of the high is a north-south ridge (as it typically is in summer), even the westerly phase may be eliminated, and the gradient wind shifts abruptly from the northwest to the southwest. The final phase is typically prolonged as the cP High slides off the Atlantic Coast toward heated water farther south and merges with the Bermuda High.

Local Weather

These cyclically recurring patterns of gradient flow interact with four important additional factors:
1. The characteristics of the advected air brought to the site (temperature, stability, and moisture content)
2. The rate at which air qualities change
3. The orientation of the coast over which the gradient wind flows (east-, south-, west-, or north-"facing")
4. The inherent capability of the coast to generate a sea/lake breeze

Advected Air

The precise qualities of local weather, the day-to-day variations, are largely determined by the temperature and moisture content of the surfaces over which the gradient wind has flown recently. The colder and denser the advected air is, the more likely is the gradient wind to sink to and flow at the surface, strong and turbulent. The warmer the advected air, the more likely it is that the gradient wind will be excluded from the surface—particularly from the surface of cold water—by an inversion above the cold, dense surface air. Dry air facilitates insolation of the surface and the development of a high lapse rate (buoyancy), thereby enhancing sea/lake breeze (particularly secondary sea/lake breeze) generation. Moist air has the opposite effect.

Air Movement

Alterations in the qualities of advected air always lag behind changes in pressure. Just as the initial gusts of a sea breeze appearing at the head of an estuary are composed largely of air that has lain in and been warmed by the land surrounding the estuary, so the air that appears immediately behind a cold front is far warmer than the air that appears the following day.

Air may move either because it is responding directly to a pressure gradient (a difference in pressure between two widely separated sites) that causes all the air between the two sites to move simultaneously, or because it is entrained in air already moving. The former is typical of large-scale movements, the latter of gusts, downflow winds, and thunderstorms.

In gradient winds that advect major alterations in temperature, stability, and moisture, all the air over a span of 500 or more miles begins to move as soon as the pressure gradient changes. Thus at a given site the air that moves first is the air that was present previously at the site and retains its qualities. On the Atlantic coast during the first 12 hours after the appearance of a cold front, the air received is largely derived from sites in the middle Atlantic and midwest regions of the United States. Only on the second day (after 24 hours of flow) will air derived from Canada arrive.

The Orientation of the Coast

The orientation of a coast to the gradient flow determines the influence of the flow on the near-shore water-surface wind and the interaction of that flow with a potential sea/lake breeze (see Table 5). An onshore wind that acquires the temperature of the marine air will usually penetrate to the water surface and provide a strong sailing breeze. An offshore flow will penetrate to the near-shore water surface only if insolation is effective and produces thermal turbulence; then, if warmer than the marine air, it may be replaced by a secondary sea/lake breeze. Because of marked differences in the friction induced by land and water, parallel-to-shore flows split into overwater and overland segments that (depending on whether they flow with water on their right or their left) will either interfere with or reinforce one another.

If, for instance, the gradient flow is onshore, a southerly flow on a "south"-facing coast (a coast facing the south quadrant—southeast to southwest), the potential for an amalgamated sea/lake breeze is high. If the gradient flow is offshore, a northerly flow across a "south"-facing coast, a secondary sea/lake breeze may develop by lifting the offshore flow from the surface.

The Character of the Coast

Finally, the coast itself has inherent properties that make it more or less likely to propagate a sea/lake breeze and that determine whether, on a day of supportive gradient wind flow, one or another of the three sea/lake breeze types will appear. A strong sea/lake breeze is far more likely to be generated when there is a narrowing topographic funnel leading the marine air inshore or a low shoreline along which islands and peninsulas alternate with numerous inlets rather than an unindented coast, or when there is a river providing water-level access to the interior rather than a straight line of bluffs, or when there is a low-lying barren near-shore plain rather than the buildings of a large city.

TABLE 5:
CLASSIFICATION OF WIND BY ORIENTATION TO THE COAST

The direction of flow of a gradient wind may be 1) onshore—veered to a perpendicular to the shore, 2) onshore—backed to a perpendicular to the shore, or 3) offshore. The direction faced by a coast determines the frequency of these three orientations and the likelihood of the generation of one or another of the three sea/lake breeze types.

ORIENTATION	STABILITY	SEA/LAKE BREEZE	SURFACE FLOW
Onshore—backed to the sea breeze or Parallel-to-shore— water on the left	Stable	Obstructed	Calm Two split segments simultaneously or alternately
Onshore—veered to the sea breeze or Parallel-to-shore— water on the right	Stable	Enhanced	Amalgamated sea/lake breeze
Offshore	Stable and hot inversion	Impeded	Calm Primary sea/lake breeze
	Stable and cool		Intermittent flow • Oscillations • Lee waves, rotors
	Unstable	Enhanced	Secondary sea/lake breeze • Two winds simultaneously

13. Seasonal Alterations in Wind Patterns

The trumpet of a prophecy! O wind,
If winter comes, can spring be far behind?
—PERCY BYSSHE SHELLEY

The varying inclination of the earth's axis (during its annual orbit of the sun) determines the seasons and results, in summer, in greater insolation and a displacement of the polar front, the subtropical highs, and their related weather features poleward and, in winter, in lesser insolation and a displacement of all typical weather patterns equatorward. In association with obvious changes in average daily temperature and duration of daylight, these shifts result in characteristic alterations in wind patterns (Figure 13.1).

Shifts in the position of the polar front and the great subtropical highs are of major interest to the racing sailor. They determine not only the gradient winds that will be extant in a given locale, but also the likelihood that thermal winds will displace them. The latter ultimately depend on the relationship between the temperature of the earth's surface and the temperature, speed, and direction of the gradient wind flow, all of which vary with the seasons.

Global Wind Patterns

The Subtropical Highs

In summer, the North Atlantic Subtropical High (the Bermuda High) extends over most of the North Atlantic Ocean, and the East Pacific High (the Aleutian High) extends over most of the North Pacific Ocean. The clockwise circulation around these subtropical highs creates the prevailing wind patterns of the northern oceans—westerly on their poleward sides, easterly on their equatorward sides. The smaller landmasses and larger oceans of the Southern Hemisphere produce three high-pressure air masses—the South Pacific, South Atlantic, and Indian Ocean Highs—about which the circulation is counterclockwise, but again westerly on their poleward sides, easterly on their equatorward sides.

The air within the subtropical highs sinks toward the cool ocean surface, heats by compression as it sinks, and produces the great subsidence inversions that determine primary sea breeze generation along the continental coasts. The circulation around each of the subtropical highs (in both hemispheres) brings cold air and a wind-driven cold current from the poles to the west coasts of the continents, and warm air and a wind-driven warm current from the equator to the east coasts of continents. The result is a stronger subsidence inversion and a stronger sea breeze on the west coasts of continents than on the east.

Interaction with the cold polar air masses that lie poleward of these high-pressure systems creates the polar front, resulting in cyclic variations in wind

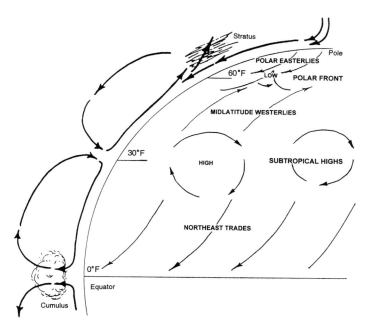

Figure 13.1. The global circulation of the atmosphere

89

direction along that front. The westerly near-surface air flow along the northern peripheries of the subtropical highs combines with the westerly midlatitude jet stream to move the sequential phases of the polar front to the east at about 15 to 20 knots. But in the warm air on their southern peripheries no such interaction disturbs the continuous easterly flow of those winds known (because of their persistence throughout the year) as the Trades—northeasterly in the North Atlantic and Pacific, southeasterly in the South Atlantic, South Pacific, and Indian Oceans.

Seasonal Movements

In summer the subtropical highs, reinforced by the subsidence into their hemisphere of additional upper-level outflow from the Equatorial Convergence Zone, shift poleward, push the polar front poleward, and shift the typical weather patterns poleward. In winter, as subsidence diminishes, the subtropical highs shift equatorward, draw the polar front equatorward, and shift the typical weather patterns equatorward.

In winter on the east coast of North America the subsidence inversion associated with the Bermuda High barely extends as far north as Miami. In summer the subsidence inversion moves to New England, where primary sea breezes blow over Martha's Vineyard and into Buzzards Bay. In winter in Europe the subsidence inversion associated with the Azores High only rarely reaches as far north as Portugal. In summer it moves as far north as Scandinavia and may persist for weeks at a time. During the Soling World Championship at Helsinki in July 1994, beneath that inversion primary sea breezes developed on every racing day.

Summer Heat Lows

In addition to the poleward movements of the subtropical highs and the polar front, a third major summertime climatological event is the formation of *heat lows*. The increased duration and intensity of insolation on the major continental landmasses, particularly on those that are barren and insolation-responsive, results in an almost continuous heating and expansion of their overlying air. The resultant fall in surface pressure produces a persistent heat low, an area hundreds or thousands of miles in diameter toward the center of which surrounding surface air is moving and being deviated into a counterclockwise circulation in the Northern Hemisphere. In the Northern Hemisphere, huge heat lows form over central Asia and North Africa and smaller ones over Mexico and the Iberian Peninsula. In the Southern Hemisphere, heat lows form over southern Africa, Argentina, and Australia (Figure 13.2).

The development and disappearance of these heat lows affect seasonal wind patterns. On the Iberian Peninsula the strong heat low creates the dominant winds of summer: northerlies on Portugal's west coast, southerlies on Spain's east coast, easterlies along Spain's south coast. In summer in the Algarve (the south coast of Portugal) the offshore northerlies are often strong enough to block sea breeze development, whereas at Málaga (on Spain's southeast coast) the onshore southerlies produce strong amalgamated sea breezes. In Western Australia in summer the hot easterlies coming offshore from the poleward side of the heat low oppose the sea breeze, but because they are so hot, are readily lifted from the near-shore surface.

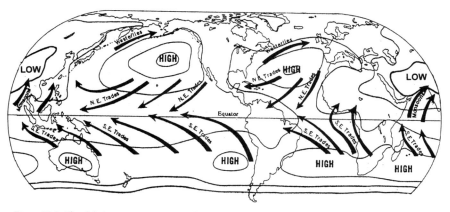

Figure 13.2. *The global synoptic pressure gradients—July* (From the Hammond Universal World Atlas.)

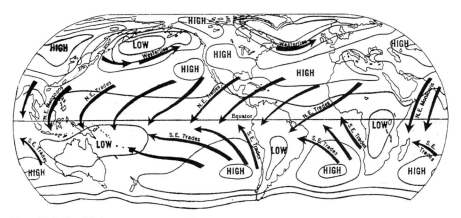

Figure 13.3. *The global synoptic pressure gradients—January* (From the Hammond Universal World Atlas.)

In spring and fall, sea breeze frequency and strength diminish in part because the offshore flow from the heat low is no longer available to maintain overwater subsidence.

Winter Patterns

In winter in the Northern Hemisphere the polar lows move south behind the polar front and occupy much of the North Pacific and the North Atlantic. Continental Polar Highs strengthen over the uniformly snow-covered expanses of Canada and Siberia. The Atlantic and Pacific Subtropical Highs shrink and move southward. Heat lows disappear and high pressure shifts toward the landmasses. But over the relatively homogeneous southern oceans the change is modest: Between the roaring forties and the shrieking sixties the strong westerlies rush on unabated (Figure 13.3).

U.S. East Coast Seasonal Wind Patterns

At a given coastal site in the midlatitudes the seasonal movement of weather features could mean, in winter, the presence of the polar front with its attendant frequent passage of fronts and lows; in spring, the lessened frequency of frontal passage, and with increasing insolation, the development of strong secondary and amalgamated sea breezes; in summer, the presence of the periphery of a subtropical high and a subsidence inversion facilitating the generation of primary sea breezes (or the presence of a heat low whose strong gradient winds may negate sea breeze generation); and, in fall, the return of the polar front and—due to the diminution of the water/land temperature disparity—a reduction in thermal wind generation.

Summer

Subsidence occurs throughout the subtropical highs, but the resulting inversion varies in intensity with the coldness of the underlying water and the warmness of the overflowing air. The strength of the inversion is least in midocean, where the air and the water are of similar temperature (allowing the gradient wind to regularly reach the surface); greater along the continental coasts, where the air is hottest; and greatest along the west coasts, where the water is coldest (isolating the gradient wind above the marine layer) (Figure 13.4).

The position of the Bermuda High (which usually forms a ridge parallel to the coast) and its subsidence inversion determine the pattern of summertime wind along the U.S. East Coast. In the Caribbean, over the Virgin Islands and Puerto Rico, the gradient flow (in the southwest quadrant of the high) is easterly and, in "midocean," where the subsidence inversion is weak, readily penetrates to the surface. At Ponce, Puerto Rico, where I sailed in the 1979 Pan-American Games, the wind direction is printed on the chart of the racing area—120°! Every day (and every night) the Trades bring the marine air ashore in a 20-knot flow from 120°.

Farther north, at Miami, the gradient flow on the western periphery of the Bermuda High is southeasterly and provides a light to moderate amalgamated sea breeze flow at 160° to 180°. Over the southeastern states, from Georgia to New Jersey, the gradient flow is southerly to southwesterly. But because throughout most of the year this flow comes over land, it advects dry, hot air across the coast and offshore. The result is a strengthening of the subsidence inversion along the coast, and in proportion to the disparity between the temperature of the ocean water and the heating land, a primary sea breeze—weak in Florida and Georgia, where the ocean is warm; strong in New Jersey, where it is cold.

When in summer the Bermuda High extends to New England, its southwest flow approaches the coast over water. The cool gradient flow amalgamates readily with the marine air and, where the coastline protrudes to the east along the south coasts of Long Island and Cape Cod, creates the strongest sea breezes of the East Coast.

Winter, Spring, and Fall

On the Chesapeake Bay (along the mid-Atlantic coast of the United States) winter is characterized by strong northerly gradient flows and secondary local sea

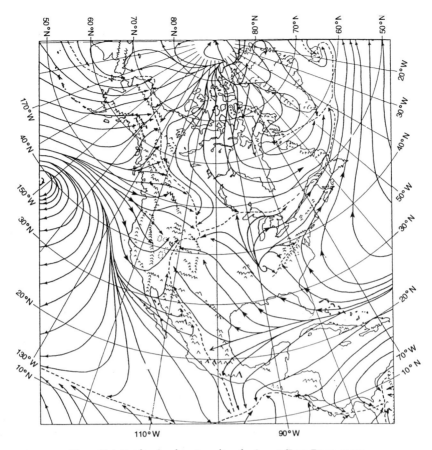

Figure 13.4. Resultant surface streamlines for August (From Essenwanger, World Survey of Climatology; after Navair, 1966.)

breezes facilitated by the high lapse rates in the cold, dry polar air.

Spring and early summer produce both secondary local sea breezes under cold offshore gradient winds and the strongest of all amalgamated sea breezes. Although the northward shift of the Bermuda High provides a protective subsidence inversion along the ocean coast, as the near-shore water becomes warmer and the advected air hotter and moister, sea breezes become weaker. On the Chesapeake in midsummer the ocean sea breeze, crossing the 30-mile width of the Eastern Shore, may appear in late afternoon as the only significant wind of the day (the "anchor breeze").

In fall, with the inshore water as warm as the land, both local and ocean sea breezes become weak. As winter approaches, the inshore water becomes cold but the ocean remains relatively warm; local sea breezes become stronger and more frequent, but ocean sea breezes remain weak and infrequent.

14. Polar Front Phases: The U.S. Atlantic Coast

Red sky at morning, sailors take warning.
Red sky at night, sailor's delight.
—ENGLISH PROVERB

Phase I: The Northwesterly (see Table 6, p. 96)

A cold front is the leading edge of a cP air mass burrowing south and eastward. In response to a strong gradient the air in the periphery of the cP air mass runs outward from its center toward the front. The advected air, depending on its distance from its central Canadian source and on the time since cold front passage, becomes increasingly dry, cold, unstable, and buoyant (distinguished by a higher than adiabatic lapse rate) to thousands of feet above the surface. As the clear, cold air passes over well-insolated land, separation occurs readily and results in the continuous liftoff of convective streams, cumulus cloud formation at 3,000 to 10,000 feet, and strong replacement downdrafts of veered upper-level flow (Figure 14.1, p. 100).

The most dramatic wind shift occurring regularly along the U.S. East Coast is that induced by the acceleration of the northwesterly flow as a cold front moves offshore. During insolation look for deepening of the billowing cumulus in the west, clearing of the stratus overhead, and then a hard, dark line of ruffled water racing off a western shore. Keep to the right when beating in the preceding westerly winds. The northwesterly, if it arrives during daylight hours, will reach its peak surface velocity almost immediately. In winter the northwester's velocity may exceed 30 knots, but in summer, composed of the relatively warm air advected from sites immediately behind the front, it may be unable to prevent a secondary sea breeze from developing. On the second day after cold front passage the flow, though weaker, will often be colder and therefore more likely to block sea/lake breeze development and to dominate a near-shore racecourse. For the next one or two days the flow will weaken in association with a progressive but very gradual veer.

Over near-shore waters on south- and east-facing coasts, the northwesterly produces classic oscillating wind conditions (Category 1; see Table 7, p. 130) as the surface flow alternates between the backed friction-slowed low-level flows and the veered high-velocity upper-level flows. Near shore it is punctuated by gust impacts. Amalgamated sea/lake breezes are rarely generated as the marine air is swept away by the colder, denser flow, but some enhancement of near-shore flow may be recognized on north-facing coasts such as the south shore of Lake Ontario.

The northwesterlies are the strongest of the regular, cyclically recurring winds of the midlatitudes. As gusts composed of higher-velocity veered upper-level air flow occur with increasing frequency on approach to shore, a progressive veer is often evident as progress is made to windward. The flow becomes lighter and more homogeneous with distance offshore.

Medium oscillations that persist for 5 to 7 minutes and produce both backed and veered oscillating shifts in the air flow occur in addition to gusts. Although the outflow from a gust splash is the high-velocity veered air of a downdraft, variations in the boat's position relative to the splash will cause some gusts to appear to be backed. Until the sailor is close to the weather mark, the basic tenets of oscillating wind strategy apply: "Keep to the tack lifted to the median wind," "Tack in significant headers" (whether due to evanescent gusts or more durable medium oscillations), "Avoid the laylines," etc.

Each day, the northwester's surface velocity and gustiness fluctuate with variations in insolation, typically reaching a peak at about 1300 in winter and 1500 in summer. But, particularly in summer and on the second day of northwesterly flow (as the center of the high approaches and the gradient decreases), surface velocity diminishes (over time) after the cold front passage and may sometimes decrease during early afternoon.

Occasionally on the second (in summer often the first) day of northwesterly flow the advected air may be (or become) so warmed by its passage over heated land that the cool marine air is able to undermine it, lift it from the surface (at least offshore), and replace it with a secondary sea breeze. The northwester is likely to persist in the near-shore gusting zone, while the sea breeze, whose coldest, heaviest elements accumulate over the deepest water, develops offshore and lifts the gradient flow from the surface.

TABLE 6: POLAR FRONT PHASES (U.S. EAST COAST)

PHASE I: THE NORTHWESTERLY

Gradient	strong
Advected air	cold, dry, polar
Stability	unstable
Sea/lake breeze	unlikely; occasionally in summer, second day

PHASE II: NORTHERLY/NORTHEASTERLY

Gradient	moderate
Advected air	cool, dry, polar
Stability	unstable
Sea/lake breeze	likely as secondary

PHASE III: THE EASTERLY

Gradient	weak, transient
Advected air	cool, moist, maritime
Stability	stable
Sea/lake breeze	likely but weak

PHASE IV: THE SOUTHEASTERLY/SOUTHERLY

Gradient	weak, above inversion
Advected air	warm, moist, maritime
Stability	stable
Sea/lake breeze	likely as amalgamated

PHASE V: THE SOUTHWESTERLY

Gradient	strong
Advected air	warm, tropical
Stability	stable
Sea/lake breeze	likely as amalgamated; often strong

PHASE VI: THE WARM-SECTOR WESTERLY

Gradient	strong
Advected air	warm, moist, tropical
Stability	stable
Sea/lake breeze	likely as amalgamated; strongest sea/lake breezes

PHASE VII: THE LOW-PRESSURE SOUTHERLY/WESTERLY

Gradient	moderate
Advected air	warm, moist, tropical
Stability	upper instability
Sea/lake breeze	none

PHASE VIII: THE LOW-PRESSURE EASTERLY/NORTHEASTERLY

Gradient	strong
Advected air	cool, moist, maritime
Stability	moderately unstable
Sea/lake breeze	none

Phase II: The Northerly/Northeasterly

A day or two after the passage of a cold front the high has usually moved sufficiently to the east and north that the gradient flow has veered to the north or northeast. Because the gradient that resulted in the initial surge of polar air has dissipated, these winds are not as strong as the northwesterlies; and because the advected air has had longer contact with warm surfaces, they are warmer.

Along the U.S. East Coast, northeasterlies flow parallel to shore with water on their left and suffer from the typical consequences of such flows. The segment of the northeasterly flowing over land is slowed by friction and therefore backed relative to the segment flowing over water. The resultant convergence between the two adjacent flows over near-shore waters diminishes the net surface velocity (to less than forecast) and results in a confused mixture of winds at the surface. In the morning this mixture is chiefly composed of gusts of the cold, dense upper-level portions of the backed (more northerly) overland segment (brought to the near-shore surface by thermal turbulence). In summer, around midday, a period of calm followed by a sudden veer often heralds the appearance of the cooler, veered (more easterly) overwater flow, which undermines the warmed overland flow and lifts it from the surface.

Because by early afternoon both segments of the advected air may become warmer than the marine air, northeasterlies on south-facing coasts are often replaced by secondary sea/lake breezes. Three flows—the upper levels of the overland gradient flow, the overwater gradient flow, and the marine air in the sea/lake breeze—may be present sequentially. Because their temperatures are often so similar, it is difficult to predict which will dominate (though it is possible that one will) and best to conclude that oscillations among the three will continue throughout the day.

In most locales (the Chesapeake and Long Island Sound, for instance) each shift should be treated as an oscillation to a wind that will soon be replaced by one of the other two. One should move to the side of the course from which the next oscillation is likely to appear—keep to the right in a gradient northerly, to the left in a sea breeze. Keep to the right in a midday easterly, expecting the sea breeze; to the left in a late-afternoon easterly, expecting a return to the overland northerly. But recognize that a reverse shift is a likely precursor to a progression in either direction!

Phase III: The Easterly

The gradient flow is easterly when high pressure is centered directly to the north. Along the U.S. East Coast this means that a polar high has moved a long way from its site of origin in central Canada, that its pressure gradient has dissipated, and that the easterly gradient flow will be weak. In addition, on north- and south-facing coasts, because it is perpendicular to the thermal gradient, easterly gradient flow interferes with sea/lake breeze generation. Convergence between the overland and overwater portions of the easterly flowing parallel to a south-facing coast, such as along the north shore of Lake Ontario or along many segments of the Atlantic coast, is particularly detrimental.

At most sites along the U.S. East Coast the easterly produces the worst possible sailing conditions. The moist, nonbuoyant, thermostable ocean air (warmer than the continental air in winter, colder in summer) drawn in by the easterly diminishes insolation and blocks convection. Regardless of the orientation of the coast, the local sea breeze (if it develops at all) flows weakly, veers minimally, and dies early. Big shifts between portions of the light gradient wind and a weak, transient sea breeze are typical. The dying of either wind may be followed by a series of protracted oscillations toward one and away from the other.

Phase IV: The Southeasterly/Southerly

As the center of high pressure moves eastward, the pressure gradient and the gradient flow become progressively weaker. Once the polar high is off the coast, strong surface air flow depends on the development of a sea/lake breeze. But the advected air coming off the ocean is warm, moist, and stable and provides a poor substrate for sea/lake breeze generation.

Don't expect a sea/lake breeze on the hot, muggy days of summer unless the coast is "south"-facing. The high water-vapor content of the easterly and southeasterly absorbs shortwave radiation and diminishes insolation. But the major deterrent to sea/lake breeze generation is the low near-surface lapse rate. Despite even intense heating, the surface temperature rarely rises sufficiently above the low-level air temperature to permit separation.

Phase V: The Southwester

In summer, once the polar high is swept offshore the Bermuda High regains its coastal position and advects warm mTg air from the southwest. Along the U.S. East Coast the southwester is the prevailing wind of summer and may persist for many days in succession. It produces three different surface wind patterns depending on the presence or absence of the subsidence inversion and the orientation of the coast.

Pattern 1: Along much of the east-facing Atlantic coast (Georgia, the Carolinas, Virginia, and New Jersey), the subsidence inversion is reinforced by the advection of hot air across the southern United States and extends inland. Along these coasts the strong inversion facilitates the generation of a strong, dependable primary or secondary sea breeze.

Pattern 2: Over south- and southwest-facing portions of the coast, where the southwester approaches land from over water, a single reasonably uniform flow, an amalgamated sea breeze, develops as the cool, overflowing gradient wind and the marine air become homogeneously interspersed. In bays open to the southwest, such as Buzzards in Massachusetts and Kingston in Ontario, the southwester brings cool marine air far into the land and produces a strong amalgamated sea/lake breeze—the "smoky southwester."

Pattern 3: Inland, far from the oceanic subsidence inversion, the warm, moist advected air provides a low lapse rate that inhibits sea/lake breeze generation. On the north and west interior-facing coasts of the Great Lakes, the southwester's parallel-to-shore segments, with water on their left, converge and destroy the organized circulation of the sea/lake breeze.

Phase VI: The Warm-Sector Westerly

A warm front eventually catches up with the coastal high pressure and brings stratus cloud and showers to the region immediately south of the polar front. Its passage is followed by the appearance of the warm sector, a triangular region whose apex is a "low" located somewhere along the chain of the Great Lakes, whose eastern limit is the warm front and whose western limit is another cold front leading another invasion of cP air. The counterclockwise circulation around the low pressure to the north and the clockwise circulation around the high pressure to the south reinforce one another to produce a particularly strong westerly gradient wind (Figure 14.2).

Between two fronts providing frontal lift, the warm sector is characterized by convection and condensation—the creation of cumulus, altocumulus castellanus, and cumulonimbus (thunderstorm) clouds—in the moist tropical air. The sailor must be on the lookout for counterclockwise surface inflow induced by 5- to 10-mile-diameter cells beneath the cumulonimbus clouds.

In the presence of the cold water of June (before the Bermuda High moves its subsidence inversion to New England), when an approaching cold front compresses the mTg air in the warm sector, a strong southwesterly-westerly gradient produces the best amalgamated sea breezes of the year. At Kingston, Ontario, and Buzzards Bay, on Long Island Sound, and in portions of the Chesapeake marine air flows onto south-facing coasts and into inlets, lifts the hot, dry westerly gradient flow from the surface, and protected by the advection inversion, races inland.

In the spring, if the offshore westerly is sufficiently strong and sufficiently cool, thermal turbulence over land will continue to bring (often strong) gusts of the westerly to the surface inshore of a band of calm and/or confused shifting produced by convergence with a secondary sea breeze ("two winds simultaneously").

Phase VII: The Low-Pressure Southwester

To the east of a low-pressure center tracking along the Great Lakes and to either side of a warm front trailing its warm sector, the gradient flow will also be southwest (from west to south). Far from the low the gradient is created by the center of high pressure, and the gradient wind behaves as in Phase V above. Close to the low, cloud cover becomes complete, humidity high, and rain frequent. Under these circumstances a sea/lake breeze will not develop. Surface flow is then the consequence of the gradient flow alone or of the frequent thunderstorms that develop in the rising air (Figure 14.3).

As long as the cloud cover remains complete, the concern is for protracted oscillations associated with and emanating from cumulonimbus formations. Look for and head toward "black clouds" (the darkest ones around) and their accom-

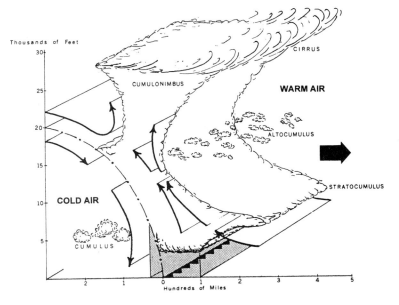

Figure 14.1. A cold front

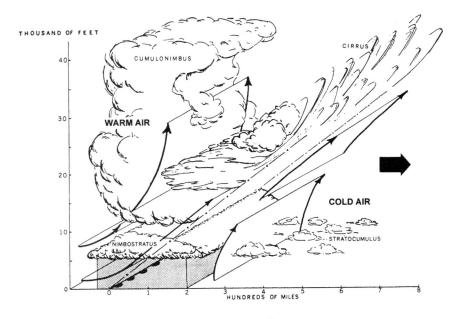

Figure 14.2. A warm front

100

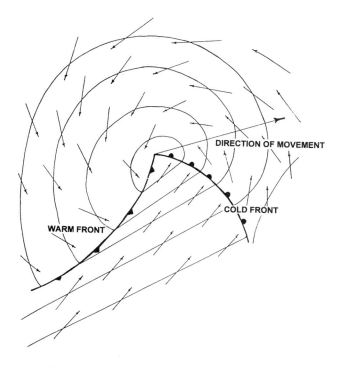

Figure 14.3. Circulation around a center of low pressure

panying downdrafts which, although they converge with and diminish the gradient flow initially, will cause a shift toward the black cloud (followed by an oscillation back toward the southwester).

The low-pressure southerly-southwesterly is also seen in association with an *occluded* (stationary) front. Then after a period of calm, if convection is occurring over land and downdrafts of upper-level flow intermittently melt the stratus and stratocumulus formations, a secondary sea/lake breeze may develop.

Phase VIII: The Low-Pressure Easterly/Northeasterly

A center of low pressure, often elongated into a trough (Figure 14.4), developing in the Gulf of Mexico typically crosses northern Florida and migrates up (and lingers off) the East Coast. Flow to the north of such a low comes onshore from the east or northeast and accounts for the name given to this weather along the New England coast—"a three-day nor'easter." Such flows occur once or twice each summer and are occasionally seen in association with hurricanes. The gradient is often strong; winds along the coast are commonly at 20 or more knots. The advected air from the ocean feels cold and damp. The dense cloud cover, heavy moisture, and frequent rain block insolation, separation, and sea/lake breeze generation.

Because the advected air is cold, thunderstorm production is unlikely. To leeward of peninsulas and on lakes, medium oscillations are prominent as the strong, cool overland flow induces mechanical and thermal turbulence, but gusting (in the absence of insolation) is minimal.

These flows are insufficiently buoyant to demonstrate an increase in velocity or veering near the weather shore. Blanketing is prominent; the warm air continues to flow at land height and does not sink to the water surface until it reaches a considerable distance offshore. Velocity offshore in open water is greater than near shore.

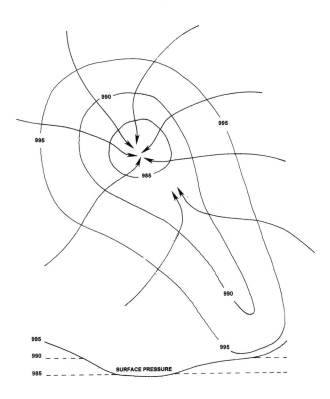

Figure 14.4. Streamlines representing surface flow into a trough of low pressure (in millibars)

102

IV. *Gradient Winds: Offshore Flow*

Delaware River	Lake Pontchartrain	Bermuda
Eufaula Lake	Lake Ray Hubbard	Chiemsee
Hingham Bay	Lake St. Clair	Edersee
Hudson River	Lake Toccoa	Ijsselmeer
Kentucky Lake	Lake Wheeler	Kiel
Mississippi River	Lake Winnebago	Lake Balaton
Lake Champlain	Lake Winnipesaukee	Neusiedlersee
Lake Minnetonka	St. Lawrence River	Punta Ala
Lake Murray	Saratoga Lake	Ronneby
Lake Oahe	Sarnia	Travemunde
Lake of the Ozarks	Toledo	Wannsee

15. Bermuda

A veering wind, fair weather
A backing wind, foul weather.
—AMERICAN PROVERB

In the preceding three sections we have recognized that variations in pressure, temperature, and density determine low-level wind flow and that these variations are chiefly related to variations (diurnal, weekly, and seasonal) in insolation. We have investigated the relationship of these factors to the production of sea/lake breezes, stability and instability, inversions, and the movements of the polar front.

We can now shift our attention from the general—wind of any origin at any site—to the specific—wind along a coast. The most important determinant of the behavior of coastal winds is the orientation of the wind to the coast. We will first investigate gradient winds (in sections IV and V)—as their orientation to the coast determines the behavior of the thermal winds—and then proceed to an investigation of thermal winds. We have already discussed simple onshore winds and should now turn to offshore winds. Their transit of land introduces instability, thermal turbulence, downdrafts, downbursts, gusts, and medium oscillations. We will now look at Bermuda, where on the Great Sound all winds are offshore.

Bermuda's Great Sound is like a lake—but a lake surrounded by water rather than by land. The surface wind variations are determined by four factors: the season, the relationship of the small island to the sea, the presence of the Gulf Stream, and the thermal turbulence (Figure 15.1).

The Season

In winter and spring the polar front, straddling Bermuda, brings steep gradients, recurrent low pressure, and high-velocity upper air flow to the island. Cold air flowing over the warm Gulf Stream and the warm island (where the air temperature almost never falls below 40°F) results in the typical vertical instability and gusting. In summer, when Bermuda lies immersed in its own (the "Bermuda") subtropical high beneath a strong subsidence inversion, warm air flow over the only slightly less warm surrounding waters produces vertical stability, separates the surface air from the already weak gradient flow aloft, and because the small island is unable to generate a significant sea breeze, results in light air or calm at the surface—the "horse latitudes." International Race Week is scheduled in the spring.

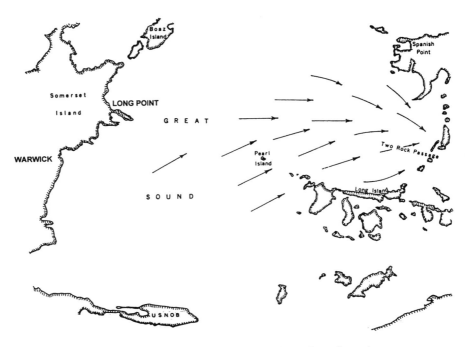

Figure 15.1. Bermuda's Great Sound—channeling in the southwesterly

The Relationship of a Small Island to the Sea

Gradient winds come to Bermuda across the relatively smooth surface of the sea and therefore at velocities considerably in excess of those created by similar gradients over land. The island acts as an abrupt barrier, deviating the otherwise smooth flow from its previous trajectory. Recent photographs of the earth from orbiting satellites have revealed turbulent cloud formations above obstacles in the sea and for the first time have shown the presence of huge Von Karman vortices, 10 times the diameter of an island, swirling off its lee quarter. Mechanical turbulence, introduced by the interposition of the island in the ocean airstream, adds significantly to the turbulence of Bermuda's winds.

All air flow approaching Bermuda is heavily laden with moisture, and as it approaches over the Gulf Stream it contains streets of cumulus or stratocumulus clouds often accompanied by showers. When subjected to elevation (due to mechanical or thermal turbulence over the island), this moisture condenses into additional cloud. Bermuda Race navigators often locate the island by its overlying cloud concentration.

In summer, within the island's many harbors the subsidence inversion may permit light local primary sea breezes to develop within a few hundred yards of shore. In calm conditions during winter a light land breeze from the cooling land to the warm sea may appear. But the surrounding sea is relatively warm, often warmer than the land, and whatever weak sea breeze develops perpendicular to a segment of shoreline converges with another from the opposite shore before it invades more than a few hundred yards inland.

Thermal Turbulence

Because the water temperature of the Gulf Stream is minimally altered by the seasons and because water is extremely thermostable, the temperature of the island's air rarely falls below 40°F and rarely rises above 80°F day or night. Air derived from the continent and air derived from the eastern and, to some extent the southeastern, Atlantic as well as the North Atlantic is cooler than the Gulf Stream. After traversing the Gulf Stream, the warm shallow water over the northern reefs, and the heated land, the cool marine air typically develops a high near-surface lapse rate. Updrafts of warm air from over the shallow near-shore water and the island itself rise through the cold air—often to great heights—and alongside them downdrafts rush to the surface.

In Bermuda, all winds are onshore, flowing at the velocity of the gradient, minimally impeded by surface friction over the relatively smooth ocean. Cloud streets indicate the development of medium oscillations, generated as horizontal convective rolls form over the Gulf Stream. The result, when added to the mechanical turbulence created by the island itself, is the characteristic gusty, shifty air flow of Bermuda. Northerlies and easterlies are the most unstable as they derive from over the cold Atlantic, and southwesterlies the most stable as they derive from over the warm Gulf Stream. Because the greatest amount of thermolabile land lies to the east, easterlies are even more turbulent on the Great Sound (at the western end of the island) than would be predicted from their inherent instability.

Oscillating Shifts

The result on the racecourses of the Great Sound is a strong wind (much stronger than that which would derive from a similar gradient over an inshore lake) and oscillating wind conditions: the intermittent presence at the surface of lulls (low-velocity backed surface flow), gusts (high-velocity veered upper-level flow), and medium oscillations that periodically veer or back the surface air flow. Oscillating shifts are more pronounced when the air is cooler and the land warmer—i.e., maximally evident in north winds on clear days, least evident in south winds on rainy days—but they are always present.

Oscillating shifts in an unstable air flow are due both to brief downdraft gusts induced by the passage of the air flow over nearby heated land and to more prolonged medium oscillations introduced by passage over more distant insolation-responsive surfaces (such as the Gulf Stream).

Shoreline Effects

Two aspects of low-level wind flow are related to proximity to shore: the gusting zone in offshore winds and divergence/convergence in parallel-to-shore winds.

1. Although the near-shore gusting zone encompasses the entire surface of the Great Sound, the closer one approaches the windward shore, the greater the proportion of gusts—downdraft-derived upper-level strong veered flow—one encounters (Figure 15.2).

2. When an air flow comes down the long axis of a water body, its overwater segment accelerates and veers relative to its overland segments to either side. The flow coming down the right side of a water body (looking to windward) therefore diverges from its neighboring overland segment and produces a band of enhanced near-shore flow, whereas the flow coming down the left side converges with and diminishes near-shore flow (see Figure 28.3, p. 209)

These two effects create a condition in which one side of the course, the one to the right of the weather mark, is obviously advantaged. The difference is most pronounced in light air and along the Somerset shore, but is almost always evident in Bermuda and constitutes the most important determinant of Bermuda strategy. "Go right, expecting a veer and a strengthening off the shore to the right." The Bermudans say, "When the wind is in the south go west, and when the wind is in the north go east."

The additional advantage of the two basic rules, according to the Bermudans, is that in complying one comes back to the fleet on starboard.

On lakes and other small bodies of water such as the Great Sound, the shore is favored, not the middle, and because of veering in the gusting zone and strengthening associated with divergence, the favored shore is usually the one to the right (looking upwind).

Channeling

Blanketing and leeward barrier effects are scarcely evident in the typically unstable, gusty winds. Unstable air lifts and sinks readily close to barriers. However,

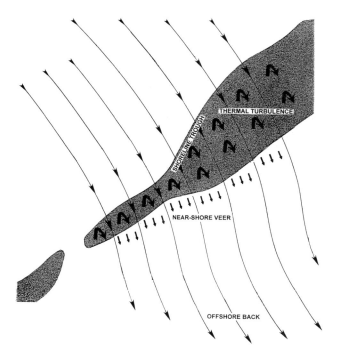

Figure 15.2. Acceleration into the shoreline trough and thermal turbulence producing near-shore veering

the surface layer, composed largely of the cold, dense upper-level air from within downdrafts, is stable and flows like water around topographical obstacles. In the center of the Great Sound the wind follows its intended path—veered in the gusts, backed in the lulls. Along each shore the air flow tends to follow the shoreline, deviating outward from its trajectory as the sound widens and inward as the sound narrows.

For a boat sailing upwind, a diverging (from the wind flow) shoreline provides a progressive lift with approach to shore and requires a course "up the middle," whereas a converging shoreline provides a progressive header and requires a course up one shore or the other. The optimal management of a channeled shift is to approach the shore to windward of its deepest indentation (where the shoreline is diverging with distance to windward)—in a lift on the way in—and to leave the shore just short of a point or headland (where the shoreline is converging)—in a lift on the way out (Figures 15.3 and 15.4).

The course to windward may be shortened by sailing in the channeled shifts created as a cold, dense air flow deviates to pass promontories along a shore.

Strategy

During Race Week 1990 in four races (12 beats) in southeasterlies, a net advantage to boats moving right—early toward the western USNOB shore and

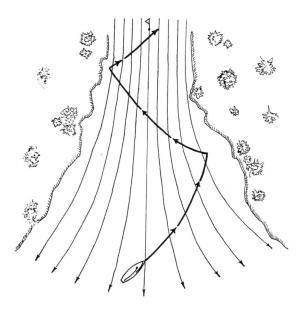

Figure 15.3. Near-shore lifts in a diverging wind flow

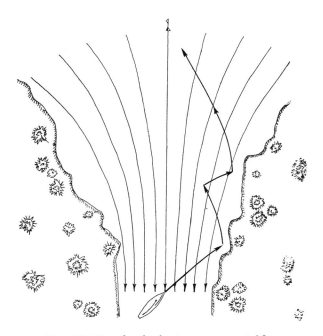

Figure 15.4. Near-shore headers in a converging wind flow

frequently, in addition, in the "clear" water beyond the naval base—was evident. In the only race to be held in a northwester, veered gusts off the Somerset shore advantaged the right side dramatically on the first beat. In a northerly wind on the final day the right paid below Pearl Island (lesser chop, plus some veering off the islands), but beyond it, in a wind flow coming through the open sound entrance, the shifts were pure oscillations. This was the only wind direction and the only area of the sound in which the advantage to the right was not evident.

In southwest winds the channeled veer beyond Long Point requires a move to the right (so as to be inside at the point), and additional veered gusts in the bay beyond usually benefit the boat that goes farthest right. West winds as they flow off the Warwick shore split into separate surface flows to either side of Long Point, so that the competitor meets a backed flow to the left of the rhumb line and a veered flow to the right. Because the weather mark is to the right of Long Point in the veered flow, one must avoid being trapped to the left, unable to return without a major loss. The boats that go right initially (almost) always win.

Within a few hundred yards of the windward mark, which is always set close to a weather shore, additional veered gusts almost always favor boats coming in on, or above, the starboard layline. Often, a boat that has led all the way up the beat is overtaken close to the mark by a competitor who has gone just a little farther right.

In Bermuda one must use the oscillating shifts to move right. The air flow along the right shore is stronger and contains more frequent and more veered gusts; sometimes the entire air flow is veering with distance to windward. Until close to the weather mark, one should play the shifts and the competition on the right side of the beat—but should, almost always, seek the starboard layline 100 to 200 yards from the mark. Conservative "digging back in," "avoiding the laylines," is usually disastrous.

16. A Meltemi at Santorini

Lord, ifen I'd knowed ye was sellin' wind so cheap,
I'd only asked for a penny's worth!
                    —NEW ENGLAND FOLKLORE

It is difficult when sailing near shore in the gusting zone of an unstable north-westerly or an offshore sea breeze to make sense of what seems to be haphazard violence. One needs to look down from above to recognize the organization, the patterns, and the timing of the gusts. I spent eight days in the Aegean on the volcanic island of Santorini, four of them in a Meltemi, and had such an opportunity to observe, from a vantage point 1,000 feet above the flooded caldera, the behavior of gusts. The Meltemi, a strong, dry, unstable northerly flow, induced mechanical and thermal turbulence as it struck the outer slopes of the semicircular island, rose gradually to the volcano's rim, and spilled down its near-vertical inner walls to the sea. Upslope flow induced along the outer slopes and on the inner cliff face coalesced into massive updrafts at the rim. The distinctive, regularly repeated, and easily visible impact patterns on the protected interior waters of the caldera created by the replacement downdrafts provide insights into the character of gusts, their postimpact spread, and their interactions with the ambient surface air flow (Figure 16.1).

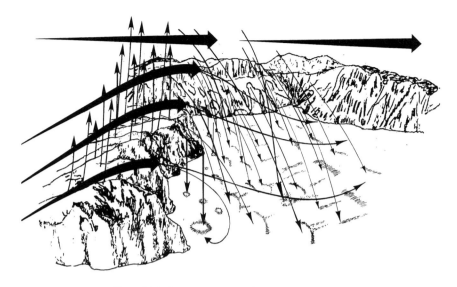

Figure 16.1. Gust patterns in a Meltimi at Santorini

Gust Patterns within the Gusting Zone

At Santorini in a 40- to 50-knot Meltemi, from midmorning until late afternoon (during maximum insolation), four zones in which downdraft impacts produced distinctive patterns of disturbed water were noticeable:

• CIRCLE ZONE

Near shore (within 10 to 300 yards of the cliffs), with the ambient wind almost eliminated by blanketing, downdrafts were first evidenced as spots of ruffled water 5 to 10 yards in diameter. These spots spread rapidly (in all directions), cleared centrally to form circles up to 200 yards in diameter, and persisted for 20 to 30 seconds. On a racecourse one rarely sees downdrafts descending into a completely protected zone, unaffected by the ambient surface air flow. But at Santorini—where the windward shore rises abruptly 700 to 1,000 feet above the water and only vertically descending air could reach the surface within 300 yards of shore—one could see the impact patterns of pure downdrafts. That they were circular demonstrates that a downdraft is a vertical cylinder with its most rapidly descending air in its external walls (Figure 16.2).

• ARC ZONE

Slightly farther offshore (100 to 1,000 yards), but overlapping the near-shore zone, downdrafts produced arcs 50 to 500 yards long and perpendicular to the ambient wind direction. From the arcs, streaks of ruffled water spread rapidly downwind and persisted for 20 to 30 seconds. Occasionally the momentum of a downdraft was so great that a full but extremely transient circular pattern of violently

113

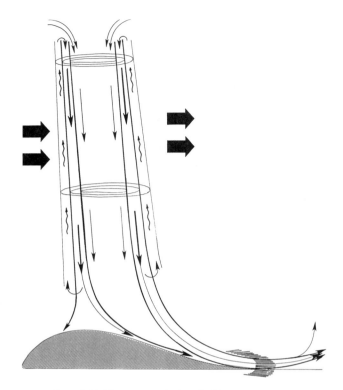

Figure 16.2. The anatomy of a downdraft/gust

disturbed water formed. Typically the downdrafts were swept laterally during descent, and the result of their oblique impact was a semicircle that soon became a broad arc of disturbed water spreading laterally and moving downwind from the point of impact. A boat moving upwind at 5 to 6 knots would traverse such an arc, moving downwind from its impact site at 20 to 30 knots, in a second or two.

In this zone, *mososcale downbursts* (Fujita terminology—coined by the University of Chicago research meteorologist), 10- to 100-yard-diameter areas of intensely disturbed water suddenly appeared, and persisted for 10 to 40 seconds. Columns of spray, the lower portions of which were blown violently downwind, rose 10 to 100 yards above the surface. The disturbed water and the shower, which often continued to rise for many seconds and in some cases could be seen (before it evaporated) several hundred feet above the surface, swept rapidly downwind. This dramatic elevation demonstrates that downdrafts develop an internal circulation that includes an external shell of rising air.

• STREAK ZONE

Farther offshore (500 to 2,000 yards), downdrafts produced long streaks (10 to 100 yards across and 100 to 1,000 yards long) with or without evident arcs or bars of darkened, ruffled water. These streaks, evident for 2 to 3 minutes, either remained in place or progressed downwind only slightly. They were the result, presumably, of downdrafts incorporated into large segments of the free-flowing upper air that was itself descending obliquely.

The concentration of these downdraft forms in a line directly downwind from a ridge or promontory on the shore implies that they are initiated in response to almost continuous liftoff at particularly insolation-responsive sites. Their persistence implies that a pressure drop at the surface of the land upwind creates a prolonged updraft and an oblique downdraft corridor, down which upper-level flow is directed.

• PATCH ZONE

Farther offshore (1,500 to 10,000 yards) relatively homogeneous patches and bands of dark ruffled water with whitecaps and persisting bars and streaks of darker, even more agitated water (extending 100 to 200 yards along and 1,000 to 2,000 yards across the air flow) could be seen. As these persisted for 3 to 7 minutes, they were presumably the result of oblique additions of upper air flow (whose descent may have been facilitated by medium oscillations in the unstable flow).

Five thousand yards to leeward, the surface flow became more homogeneous, but large bands and streaks of darkened water recurrently appeared and persisted. Occasionally an advancing arc of darkened water (with or without some rising spray) demonstrated gusting far to leeward of the land. At other times one could recognize very large areas of change, water more or less darkened than previously, presumably representing medium oscillations, rather than gusts, inserted into the air flow at some distant upwind site.

In lighter winds the patterns of downdraft impact were evident only at midday (during the period of maximal surface heating) and only off headlands (which extended the heating surfaces farther "offshore"). The typical pattern was an arc of darkened water accompanied by several streaks of similar darkness radiating downwind, outward from the arc. Arcs and streaks appeared abruptly 100 to 2,000 yards to leeward of the shore, reached full intensity within a few seconds, persisted with little change in position and with little reduction in intensity for about 15 to 25 seconds, and then faded rapidly and disappeared. Gusts of the same size, intensity, and shape (arc, streak, or a combination thereof) tended to reappear every 20 to 30 seconds at the same site, and their patterns varied primarily with distance from shore. In the absence of significant thermal turbulence in early morning and evening, only near-shore circular splashes were evident.

On the final day of the Meltemi, cumulus cloud formation was sufficient to demonstrate that updrafts rose 1,000 feet above the island prior to condensation (and another 1,000 feet within the clouds) so that downdrafts were dropping 2,000 or 3,000 feet. The close association of downdrafts with updrafts was evident along the steep cliffs of the caldera. The 20 to 30 feet of air nearest the cliff face could often be seen (by its contained dust, mist, or plastic bags) to be moving upward (following the slope contours) while strong downdrafts were striking the water surface just offshore.

17. Unstable Air Flows: Gusts

Quick rise after low, sure sign of stronger blow.
—AMERICAN PROVERB

Unstable air flows are characterized by vertical movement (convection), which occurs in at least four forms:

1. As eddies—discontinuous small wisps that rotate (as do "dust devils") while rising through (but not disturbing) the ambient air
2. As updrafts—persistent cylindrical columns that are fed by streams of separating surface air and entrain smaller updrafts as they rise
3. As *horizontal convective rolls (HCRs)*—long helices that produce vertical sheets of rising air
4. As other, as yet undefined large-scale vertical movements

Eddies (as defined above) have little effect on horizontal air flow and do not influence the overwater wind. Downdrafts accompany columnar updrafts and modify overland and near-shore surface wind flow by introducing gusts and intergust lulls that cause marked variations in velocity and direction. HCRs, which presumably account for the medium oscillations in speed and direction that characterize unstable air flows and create "oscillating wind conditions," and other as yet undefined forms of large-scale convection are also accompanied by compensating downflows.

In unstable (buoyant) air flows the surface wind over land and near shore (in the gusting zone) is a mixture of parcels of air of differing speed and direction—parcels of whatever horizontal surface flow is extant and parcels of higher-velocity upper-level flow brought to the surface in various types of downflow. Variations in surface wind speed and direction also result from the varying friction between ascending and descending parcels and from variations in the angle and velocity of downdraft impacts. Superimposed upon these abrupt variations are medium oscillations lasting between 3 and 20 minutes. The speed and direction of the residual surface air flow over land and in the near-shore gusting zone obey the laws of probability but are largely unpredictable. Farther offshore, beyond the gusting zone, where medium oscillations are the sole cause of oscillating shifts, their frequency and direction are predictable.

Thermal Turbulence

When cold air flows over a warm surface (typically heated land) the atmosphere becomes unstable (develops a high lapse rate). Heated air begins to rise from the surface in eddies and soon thereafter in cylindrical parcels (updrafts) that separate from the surface and rush to the top of the turbulent layer. In response to the change in surface pressure induced by their separation and expansion, falling parcels of air (downdrafts) rush toward and slam into the surface as gusts. Updrafts and downdrafts are local phenomena, evident only over and immediately to leeward of heated surfaces. The sailor encounters them only in the near-shore gusting zone (Figure 17.1).

Updrafts

Convection is characterized by the intermittence of separation. At a given site a bubble of heated air periodically reaches a sufficiently high lapse rate that it bursts. At preferentially heated sites bubbles re-form and burst again. Soon columns of heated air are streaming upward through the turbulent layer, creating a venturi effect, and "drawing in" smaller parcels. Several thousand feet above the surface, updrafts—amalgamating all of the nearby rising air—become large columnar parcels, their volume and effect on surface pressure chiefly determined by the height to which they rise.

As air rises, it cools and loses density (expands) adiabatically. If it cools to a temperature below the condensation level, a cumulus cloud forms that, by the release of the heat of condensation, heats and expands the surrounding air and supports further elevation.

In unstable air with a high lapse rate (SLR), rising air—despite cooling at the adiabatic rate (ALR)—becomes with expansion progressively lighter than its surroundings. Because its surface area increases less rapidly than its volume, buoyancy forces increasingly exceed drag forces. Consequently, a rising column accelerates

117

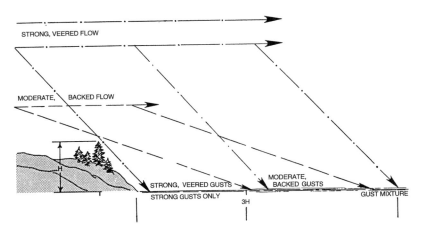

STRONG, VEERED FLOW

MODERATE, BACKED FLOW

STRONG, VEERED GUSTS

STRONG GUSTS ONLY

MODERATE, BACKED GUSTS

GUST MIXTURE

3H

Figure 17.1. The gusting zone

progressively until it reaches an inversion level, where it is halted abruptly by a layer of lighter air. A replacement downdraft, despite heating at the adiabatic rate, becomes (with compression) progressively denser and heavier than its surroundings and falls faster and faster until it slams into the surface. Consequently, the speed of the updraft as it reaches the inversion and the speed of the downdraft as it reaches the surface are determined by the height to which the updraft has risen.

The effect of an updraft is to reduce the total weight of the air in the column through which it rises both by expansion and, when it reaches the inversion, by the escape through lateral spread of a portion of the rising mass. The pressure upon the surface below is determined by the height of the column of reduced density. The higher the updraft rises, the greater is the volume/mass of the air that has been displaced and the greater is the drop in surface pressure. Inasmuch as the updraft is halted by an inversion, the height of the inversion determines the fall in surface pressure and the strength of the thermal pressure gradient that it induces.

Downdrafts

Within the turbulent layer alongside intermittent streams of rising heated air, downdrafts (cylindrical segments of cold air) fall with the acceleration due to gravity, their impact velocity dependent on the height from which they fall. They are initiated by the sudden drop in surface pressure resulting from the expansion and dissipation of the air in a heated column (by the arrival of an updraft at the top of the turbulent layer).

Any falling object, including a mass of air, accelerates as it falls at 32 feet per second. Although after falling 2,000 feet such a mass could theoretically be moving at 180 knots, friction slows it markedly. Downdrafts in the northwesterly gradient flows behind cold fronts, falling 3,000 to 10,000 feet, may on impact spew water high into the air. Although much of their vertical velocity is thereby dissipated, the inherent horizontal speed of the air they contain and through which they have descended, plus their residual vertical velocity, is often translated into a horizontal flow in excess of 40 knots.

Each parcel of vertically moving air, ascending or descending above and to leeward of a heated site, becomes a progressively expanding cylinder, a segment of a column. Friction drags the vertical surfaces of the rising or falling cylinder in the reverse direction. In response the air in the cylinder's center is pulled outward and forward, resulting in an interior circulation whose maximum forward (and reverse) flow is in its circular wall. The air within the cylinder retains the horizontal momentum of its origin, and the entire cylinder moves laterally at the speed of the ambient wind. Although the height from which the air falls determines its impact velocity, its cylindrical structure and the angle at which it impacts determine its impact pattern.

The cumulus cloud at the top of an updraft and the impact site at the bottom of an accompanying downdraft appear in a line to leeward of a liftoff site. As the cumulus move out over water, where no additional updrafts are available, they dissolve into the cooling air flow. The front line of clouds indicates the termination of updraft turbulence and predicts, a few thousand yards beyond, the termination of downdraft turbulence, the periphery of the gusting zone.

Gusts

Gusts are the manifestations of the impact of downdrafts. They vary in size, speed, and direction in proportion to the height from which they fall, the volume of air that they entrain, the velocity of the air flow through which they fall, and the velocity of the air flow at the surface. Typically, gusts are the result of downdrafts 10 to 100 yards in diameter, composed of upper-level air flow moving at a speed 30 to 50 percent in excess of the surface flow and accelerating as they fall from less than a few thousand feet. Although they dissipate much of their energy on impact, a concentrated segment of outflow, as it sweeps downwind, typically doubles the velocity of surface flow. Sometimes downdrafts are far larger, as great as a thousand yards in diameter ("microbursts"). They may reach velocities in excess of 100 knots while falling and 50 knots after impact, and may totally overwhelm the ambient surface air flow.

As the most rapidly descending air in the circular wall of a downdraft strikes the surface, it disturbs the water in a circle or an arc pattern and moves rapidly downwind. The intense disturbance of the surface water at the site persists until the full height of the cylinder has impacted. However, prolonged exposure to thermal and mechanical turbulence during descent may so disorganize the cylindrical structure that the classical impact pattern is not evident.

T. T. Fujita at the University of Chicago and others have shown by various means (including computer modeling) that a downdraft impact results in a standard pattern of horizontal outflow. Just outside the edge of the circular impact, at the bottom of an upturning eddy, a zone of extreme wind speed develops in the spreading air. Beneath this eddy a stagnant cushion of cold air accumulates and within a few seconds lifts the extreme wind from the surface. But if the impact is oblique, the cushion of cold air accumulates only on the upwind side, behind the impact, and by blocking the spread of outflow in that direction, holds the extreme wind to the surface and confines and prolongs its effects to the advancing downwind side.

Barrier Effects

Barrier effects—blanketing induced by an elevation to windward or lifting induced by an elevation to leeward—are most evident in stable air flows, which lack preexistent turbulence and buoyancy. In stable conditions a barrier produces a reduction in surface air flow for a distance 20 times the height of a windward barrier and 9 times the height of a leeward barrier. The vertically moving portions of unstable air flows lift over or sink beyond such barriers and minimize these effects. However, gust splashes (after impact) consist of cold, dense air flowing at the surface and are consequently extremely stable and markedly affected by barriers. Barrier effects are prominent near shores (on small lakes, in rivers, and harbors) in the gusting zones of unstable offshore air flows (Figures 17.2a and 17.2b). (See chapter 10, "Sailing beneath the Waves.")

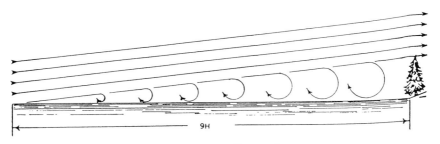

Figure 17.2a. Leeward barrier effects

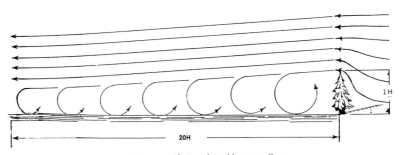

Figure 17.2b. Windward barrier effects

The Gusting Zone

In an unstable offshore wind, downdrafts derived from the thermal turbulence over the land continue to impact the surface for a variable distance to leeward of the shore. The extent of this gusting zone is increased by the height of the instability and by the velocity of the air flow. A downdraft (slowed by friction) falling 2,000 feet can be swept downwind during its descent as much as 1,000 or 2,000 feet by a 30-knot air flow. Instability may extend to 10 to 12,000 feet and velocity may reach 40 knots in the outflows from cold, cP air masses. The resulting gusting zone may extend 5 miles offshore and contain gusts that increase the median surface wind speed by 10 to 15 knots and veer its direction by 15° to 20°. The closer that a boat approaches the shore (and the sites of thermal turbulence), the greater will be the velocity, veering, and chaos of the surface air flow she encounters.

Gusts, which periodically bring high-velocity and therefore veered upper-level flow to the surface, are swept downwind within a segment of an operative medium oscillation. Depending on the position of the boat relative to the gust splash, the abrupt increase in wind speed may cause an additional header or lift as it modifies the medium oscillation extant. Near shore in the circle or arc zones, the shift induced by the gust, because it is so evanescent, infrequently warrants a tack. Each gust persists for only 20 to 40 seconds, and an additional one typically appears within 20 to 40 seconds of the first. Farther offshore, where oscillating shifts derive chiefly from medium oscillations and occur less frequently, tacks are often warranted.

It is sometimes suggested that the acceleration of an offshore flow as surface friction diminishes with its crossing of a shoreline will result in a progressive veer with distance to leeward and that, consequently, a sailor should expect to experience a progressive back with approach to shore. Such a progression is rarely evident except in stable offshore flows such as those advecting very hot air or overflowing very cold or snow-covered land. In all my years of sailing throughout the world, I have been confident of experiencing it only early in the day in the summer, in light, hot southwesterly winds coming offshore above the cold lake at Rochester, New York.

Usually the divergence associated with the abrupt reduction in friction at a shoreline produces a near-shore overwater trough that accelerates and veers the oncoming overland flow before it reaches the coast and leaves little additional veering to take place over the water. And during daylight hours in most offshore winds (gradient or thermal), the downdrafts of veered upper-level flow brought to the near-shore surface by the overland thermal turbulence completely obscure any "acceleration back."

Gust Patterns in the Gusting Zone

The gust patterns I witnessed at Santorini (see chapter 16) are now readily understandable. Near shore in the Circle Zone, cylindrical downdrafts were blanketed by the 700- to 1,000-foot cliffs and so had little horizontal velocity, impacted the surface vertically, and spread in a circle from the cylinder's perimeter. Their impact pattern was evanescent as a cushion of cold air formed and displaced the extreme air flow from the surface. Farther from the shore in the Arc Zone, the cylinders were displaced laterally by the ambient air flow, struck obliquely, and were limited by the surface air flow and the cold air cushion from spreading in any direction other than as an arc downwind. But here the gusts were strongest both because the downdraft cylinders from which they derived were intact and because their impact focused extreme winds on the surface downwind. They often showered spray in a narrow streak high into the air.

The Streak and Patch Zones presumably provide classic oscillating wind conditions—the mixture of gusts and medium oscillations expected by competitors sailing in unstable air flows on typical racecourses within a mile or so of shore. Here downdrafts appear about every 30 to 60 seconds and medium oscillations appear about every 4 to 8 minutes, and both are accompanied by speed and directional variations. The result is a mixture of medium oscillating shifts and downdraft gusts, usually veered, that obscure the exact periodicity of the shifts. The preponderance of gusts in the Streak Zone (and farther inshore) causes the median wind to be veered relative to the wind farther offshore. This difference may not be evident over the 1 or 2 miles of a near-shore racecourse, all of which may be within the gusting zone, but will be evident to a boat approaching from several miles out.

Farther offshore beyond the Patch Zone, beyond the reach of the overland updraft-downdraft turbulence, only medium oscillations are present. Here large bands or patches, 500 to 3,000 yards in diameter, of shifted (stronger or lighter) air flow move downwind at the speed of the general surface flow. Whereas in gusts an increase in strength is associated with veering, medium oscillations produce patches of strong (or light) wind that may be either backed or veered. These are the shifts that require tacking and that must be awaited—that demand a strategy based on the recognition of a median wind and the withholding of a tack until a heading shift beyond that median wind has appeared.

Management of Unstable Air Flows

Dramatic differences in velocity occur near shore in the Circle Zone (as those who frostbite in small harbors know) when gusts intrude on an ambient wind markedly reduced by barriers. These conditions require highly twisted flat sails set well off the centerline to avoid overpowering and/or capsize. Farther out in the Arc Zone, the short duration of a gust permits fuller sails to accommodate the intermediate air flow, but requires easing the sheets and a sharp luff—"Ease, luff, trim, bear away." In the Streak Zone (and farther offshore), velocity variations are sufficiently prolonged that trim can be altered to accommodate them—"shifting gears."

In the Patch Zone, downdraft gusts and medium oscillations appear as patches and produce predictable oscillating shifts as well as variations in velocity. Here strategy becomes all-important: Upwind, the course can be shortened by a proper utilization of the shifts; downwind, average speed can be increased by a proper utilization of the velocity variations. "Upwind—go for the shifts (take the lifted tack toward the next header); downwind—go for the velocity variations (jibe toward the dark streaks)."

122

18. Unstable Air Flows: Medium Oscillations

It's an ill wind that blows no good.
—ENGLISH PROVERB

As discussed in the preceding chapter, unstable air flows—cool winds flowing over heated land or warm water—are characterized by numerous variations in the direction and strength of the near-surface air flow. In offshore winds (the typical unstable winds of round-the-buoys sailing), the near-shore gusting zone is characterized by gust/lull sequences and other larger and lesser fluctuations. Gusts produce velocity variations of about 35 percent of the average wind speed, persist for from 30 seconds to 4 minutes, and appear at approximately the same site after the previous gust has moved 200 to 1,000 yards downwind. Lesser fluctuations produce velocity variations of about 15 percent of the average wind speed, persist for about 10 to 15 seconds, and appear about 40 to 100 yards apart. In the gusting zone no "ambient wind" appears; variations are continuous. No regular association is evident between these variations in wind speed and variations in direction; i.e., the gust/lull sequence does not account for oscillating shifts. A third form of variation, the medium oscillation, does.

Oscillating shifts in offshore wind flows, the major determinants of outcome in races in all unstable air flows, are associated with *medium oscillations*—sequential variations in wind direction to either side of a median. They appear in strong north-westerlies as large and abrupt shifts in the wind flow, acting over half- to 2-mile-wide areas of the racecourse. They are typically heralded by a marked change in the ruffling of the surface water. They may also appear as more gradual but extremely regular shifts in lower-velocity offshore winds.

Within the near-shore gusting zone, shifts in the erratic surface air flow are unpredictable. The outflow patterns produced as gusts impact the surface in various positions so distort the regular pattern of oscillations that a boat sailing to windward can respond only to the shifts and the alterations in wind speed as they arrive. But farther offshore, beyond the gusting zone, where directional changes are primarily due to medium oscillations (shifts of 10° to 20°, occurring at predictable intervals), a boat can be positioned so as to gain in each of them.

A Race on Tampa Bay

Unstable northerly and northeasterly air flows are typical of wintertime on Tampa Bay, and because the racecourse (off St. Petersburg) is 3 to 5 miles from the windward shore, gusts are absent but medium oscillations are often evident. In January of 1996, on the second day after a cold front passage, the wind had shifted from northwest to northeast and had diminished to an average of 10 to 12 knots. We started the final race of the day in a 10- to 12-knot air flow that had been oscillating over a range of 10° to 12° and was in its backed phase at about 35°.

In a weather-going current we were able to squeeze in at the pin, emerge in clear air, and pull away on starboard. During the first 4 minutes after the start, as a large portion of the fleet tacked to port, the wind gradually veered to 45°. We were initially unable to tack because of the proximity of boats on our weather quarter and subsequently, in the veer during which those boats—including that of Bruce Savage, *RSA 47*—lifted away, preferred to continue on starboard. After approximately 4 minutes the wind backed to 40°, Savage tacked, and we tacked on his hip. We were both able to cross all those remaining on starboard, and as the back progressed to 35°, looked "up" relative to the early port tackers. As we lifted off Savage, I had delusions of victory.

At about 8 minutes after the start, the wind began to veer again, and Savage began to pull out from under us. I toyed with the idea of tacking but felt that because I was the farthest left of the entire fleet, I should comply with the old adage, "Don't tack until boats to leeward on the same tack, tack." At about 11 to 12 minutes we saw *Norway 116*, Hermann Johannessen, approaching to cross us (and everyone else) on starboard. As a large portion of the boats from the right corner were now on starboard in the veer, we decided to tack under Johannessen while Savage continued on port. Within a minute of our tack we were headed, the back had returned, and we tacked again behind Johannessen. We were now close to the port layline; the final shift would be a veer, and 3 minutes later (at 16 minutes after the start) we were headed down, looking to cross astern of eight boats on the starboard layline, including Savage, who rounded in fifth.

We had had a good start and clear air, and that had kept us in the top 10—but we had thrown away a position in the top 5 or better. We had sailed the first minute or two on starboard in a back, and given an advantage to all those (including Johannessen) who had tacked to port immediately. On starboard we had gained in 4 minutes of veer, and by positioning ourselves farthest to the side of the course from which the next shift, a back, had appeared, had gained more than anyone else during the first 4 minutes we sailed on port.

Our big mistake had come when the wind began once again to veer. Had we tacked immediately we would not have lost to all the boats crossing on starboard from the right, but we would have positioned ourselves even closer to the port layline, farther from the final veer. Savage had done the correct thing: continued on port through that veer and on into the next back, so that in the final veer he was to the right. We had compounded our error by tacking after most of the veer had elapsed. We had positioned ourselves farther away from the final shift and had been forced to sail the wrong tack (port, in the veer) for the final 3 minutes.

Oscillating Shifts

An unstable air flow is characterized by medium oscillations—alternating shifts in wind direction that recur at regular intervals every 3 to 20 minutes, that are typically less abrupt than gusts, and that may be evident many miles to sea.

Offshore in an unstable air flow, medium oscillations appear as large patches (between 1,500 and 3,000 yards in diameter) of deviated air—sometimes stronger, sometimes lighter—that move downwind at the speed of the general surface air flow. If the air flow is moving at 15 to 20 knots, a boat sailing to windward will cross a patch of shifted air 2,000 yards wide in approximately 3 to 4 minutes; at 8 to 12 knots, in approximately 6 to 8 minutes (the typical frequency of medium oscillations).

Medium oscillations in direction appear in patches of strong or light wind that may be either backed or veered. The magnitude of the accompanying shifts is proportional to the general wind velocity. In an 8- to 12-knot air flow they are typically about 10° to 15°; in a 20-knot air flow, 30° to 40°. The range of the shifts is relatively fixed, and therefore a median direction can be calculated; but the degree of deviation of the wind in a particular patch to either side of that median is highly variable.

Horizontal Convective Rolls (HCRs)

It has recently been recognized that one of the most common forms of large-scale, boundary-layer convection (of which a variety probably exist) is the horizontal convective roll. HCRs develop when *wind shear* (the progressive veering of wind with height) causes a rising column of heated air to twist into a horizontal helix. Continued rotation entrains additional air so that such helices, approximately aligned with the surface air flow, ultimately extend downwind for miles. Because adjacent rolls counterrotate, persistent bands of vertical flow (alternately upward and downward) develop in the regions between them; bands of altered surface flow, backed or veered and strengthened or diminished by the direction of the adjacent vertical flow, develop beneath them (Figure 18.1).

Cumulus Cloud Streets

Where HCRs form over land or over water that is warmer than the overflowing air, chains of cumuli—*cumulus cloud streets*—aligned "like pearls on a string," stream downwind at the condensation level above the upflow band between them. Cumulus cloud streets are characterized by separated segments of strong upflow—ridden to great heights and for long distances by gulls and sailplanes—and to either side of the clouds and between them by segments of turbulent downflow. Over land in the cool, unstable winds that produce medium oscillations, multiple lines of cumulus clouds appear to an observer in an airplane above them to be streaming precisely along the wind flow. But to an observer on the surface offshore, waves of flat-bottomed cumuli (that may coalesce laterally) appear to be marching toward him across the wind flow, and he may have difficulty in distinguishing the "streets" that are flowing downwind toward him (Figure 18.2).

Each cumulus cloud overlies a segment of the helical circulation producing upflow. Each gap between cumuli overlies a segment of the helical circulation producing downflow and subsidence (thereby melting the cloud). The formation of separated cumuli along a street indicates the intermittence of upflow and downflow within the helix, and implies abrupt variations in the direction and strength of the surface flow beneath the street.

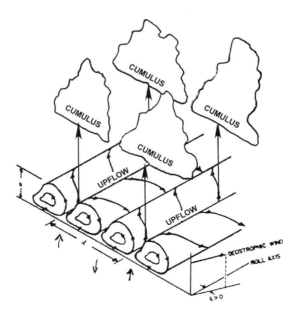

Figure 18.1. Horizontal convective roll circulation (From Kelly, "Horizontal Roll and Boundary-Layer Interrelationships Observed over Lake Michigan," Journal of the Atmospheric Sciences; after Brown, 1980.)

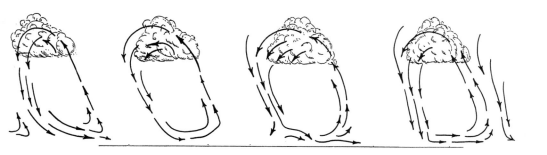

Figure 18.2. Medium oscillations under a cumulus cloud street

O. M. Johannessen, at Norway's Nansen Institute, has demonstrated by the use of synthetic aperture radar (SAR) that as a cold air flow comes off the Greenland ice cap and flows out over the warmer ocean—from a surface producing no convection to a surface characterized by convection—streaks of increased wave activity that are precisely aligned with the cloud streets above form on the warm sea surface. This indicates that turbulent mixing eliminates wind shear; the wind direction aloft along which the cloud streets are streaming is the same as the wind direction below in which the HCRs are forming.

But as an air flow comes offshore over cool water—from a surface producing convection to one that is not—convection, condensation, and cloud formation cease. The bands of helically circulating air and the cumuli persist for many miles and continue to alter the surface flow, but the precision of the helical patterns and the regularity and distribution of the shifts they produce presumably deteriorate.

Sailboats sailing to windward in an offshore wind are presumably sailing along a particular HCR (or parallel to and between a pair of HCRs). The oscillating shifts they encounter (typically associated with cumulus cloud streets) are presumably due to the intermittence of upflow and downflow within the helical circulation along an HCR. The medium oscillations perceived by the sailor occur as the helices stream downwind over water and their variably directed segments cross above a given site. The shifts induced derive from the differing directions of flow at the bottom of the helix, where alternately the flow is upward and backed and downward and veered (Figure 18.3).

These alternating phases of backed and veered flow at the surface—medium oscillations—should be expected whenever there is insolation in cool offshore winds of greater than 8 knots. Their frequency and range is proportional to the instability and strength of the air flow—from every 10 minutes and over a range of 10° in moderate air, to every 3 minutes and over a range of 40° in heavy air. Although within the gusting zone oscillating shifts are often so disturbed by concomitant updrafts and downdrafts that they seem to occur randomly, farther offshore, in the absence of gusts, their periodicity is evident. There, strategic decisions can and should be made based on that periodicity.

Low-Level Cumuli

As the survival of cumulus clouds depends on continuous convection, they typically disintegrate as they leave the shore, and persist only on inland waters or for a few miles off a coast. Each cloud represents an atmospheric engine: Condensation taking place within the updraft is heating the surrounding air, lowering the surrounding pressure, and inducing additional inflow from below and from alongside. Although the power of the engine diminishes with distance from the heated surface (the land), the condensation, pressure drop, and inflow continue for some distance offshore.

When cumulus clouds appear close to the surface—at less than 1,200 feet or closer than half their height—they affect the surface air flow directly. If they are white, which indicates that they contain fine water droplets too small to fall as rain, they are characterized by a relatively strong, confined updraft that causes an inflow of air along the surface from all directions. As the cloud is moving downwind with the ambient air flow, the effect of this inflow is to decrease the air flow where it opposes the ambient flow—downwind of the cloud—to strengthen the air flow where it aligns with the ambient wind—upwind of the cloud—and to deviate the air flow along both sides toward the cloud. When cumulus clouds

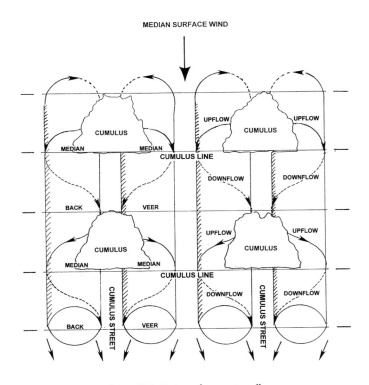

Figure 18.3. Horizontal convective rolls

appear in streets, however, the helical convection produces medium oscillations that completely obscure this inflow effect.

Cumuli that have become black contain large, heavy water droplets that are falling within the cloud. These droplets are enlarging by coalescence with others and will soon fall to the surface as rain. Black clouds, some of which will become thunderstorms, are characterized by the strong downflow along their leading edge. The increased velocity in the direction of the cloud's movement should be sought: "Head for the blackest cloud!"

Management of Medium Oscillations

A wind shift permits a properly positioned boat to shorten her course to the windward mark. In any and all shifts, success in shortening the course depends on
- *Spending an amount of time to each side of the fleet—essentially to each side of the rhumb line—equal to and temporally correlated with the amount of time that the shift is to the corresponding side of the median wind direction.*
- *Being positioned in the final shift, inside and farthest (without overstanding) to the side of the course from which that final shift develops. (The optimal position is precisely on the "new layline" in the shifted wind.)*

When sailing offshore (beyond the gusting zone) in moderate to strong unstable offshore winds, expect medium oscillations. Prior to starting, determine the frequency and regularity of the shifts, the shift phase (veer or back) extant, and the portion of that phase that will have elapsed at the time of the start. Start so as to be able to tack to the lifted tack as soon as possible.

Watch the leading boats in clear air at the extremities of the course (their tacking probably indicates the beginning of a shift to their side) and tack (assume their tack) when they tack, if
- *the predetermined interval has elapsed (approximately) and*
- *the compass shows at least the beginning of a header*

Try to predict (6 to 8 minutes in advance) the shift that will be extant when you approach the windward mark, and be on the side of the course from which that final shift will emanate. Be willing to sail through a heading phase without tacking in order to do so. Recognize that the direction of the air flow in the downflow patches associated with medium oscillations (as in some gusts) is revealed by the shiny streaks of smooth water imbedded in and surrounded by the faster-moving air.

Management of the Varieties of Oscillating Wind Conditions

The management of classic oscillating wind conditions (shifts occurring every 3 to 20 minutes and/or over a range from 10° to 40°) is dependent on principle 1: The boat should be positioned so as to be on the same side of the rhumb line and for the same period of time as the shifts. (The maxims of Category I [Classic Oscillating Wind Conditions] apply.) (See Table 7, p. 130.)

The management of less frequent, smaller shifts (occurring every 10 to 15 minutes and/or over a range of less than 10°) on usual-length racecourses should be in accordance with conservative ("Keep to the rhumb line, cross 'em when you have gained") principles. (The maxims of Category III [Conservative] apply.)

The management of protracted or large shifts (occurring every 20 to 60 minutes and/or over a range from 25° to 50°), including those that are persistent, is dependent on principle 2: The boat should be positioned farthest to the side of the course from which the final shift will develop. (The maxims of Category II [One Side Obviously Advantaged] apply.)

TABLE 7: HIERARCHY OF SHIFT EXPERIENCE

1. MEDIUM OSCILLATIONS   •Frequent shifts (every 3–20 min., 10°–40°)
(Classic Oscillating Wind Conditions)

Typical conditions:	Cold, offshore flows
	North-northwesterly gradient winds
	Offshore sea/lake breezes
	Downslope winds

| Management: | Category I (Classic Oscillation Shifts) |

2. MINIMAL OSCILLATIONS   •Infrequent shifts (every 10–15 min., less than 10°)

| Typical conditions: | Veered to onshore gradient winds |
| | Primary and secondary sea/lake breezes |

| Management: | Category III (Conservative) |

3. PROTRACTED OSCILLATIONS   •Infrequent shifts (every 20–60 min., 20°–50°)

| Typical conditions: | Backed to onshore or parallel-to-shore winds with convergence between segments |
| | Amalgamated sea/lake breezes |

| Management: | Category II (One Side Obviously Advantaged) |
| | Advantaged side is the side of the final shift |

4. LARGE OSCILLATIONS   •Frequent shifts (every 5–30 min., >25°+)

Typical conditions:	Intermittent offshore flows
	Downslope winds
	Offshore gradient winds altered by near-shore topography

| Management: | Category II (One Side Obviously Advantaged) |
| | Advantaged side is the side of the final shift |

---

19. Thunderstorms and Downbursts

Yet Freedom! Yet thy banner torn, but flying,
Streams like the thunderstorm against the wind…
—LORD BYRON

A thunderstorm is created when convection develops in an airstream, the lower levels of which are moist and the upper levels of which are unstable. Inasmuch as thunderstorms require a hot surface (usually land, which they will not leave in the absence of additional heated land to leeward) to initiate and maintain convection, and water to add moisture and the heat of condensation to the rising air, they typically occur near ocean coasts. Along the U.S. East Coast they develop from 10 to 20 miles inland and, guided by the upper-level westerlies, move eastward toward the water. Sea/lake breezes facilitate thunderstorms because they bring moisture ashore over heated land and stimulate thermal liftoff (Figure 19.1).

Unstable air aloft permits a column of heated air to rise and to retain its moisture until it reaches great heights—15,000 to 30,000 feet. As the heat released in condensation lowers its density and facilitates further elevation, additional updrafts

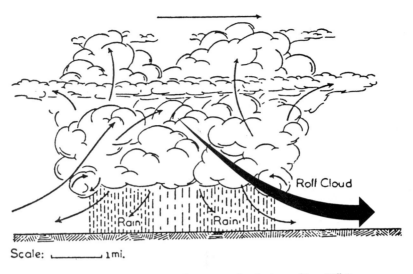

Roll Cloud

Scale: |_____| 1 mi.

Figure 19.1. Circulation of a thermal, convective thundershower (From Willett and Sanders, Descriptive Meteorology.)

entrain beneath and alongside the rising column of heated air. Soon the massive surge of rising air coalesces its moisture into water droplets and becomes visible as black cloud—the cumulonimbus. Entrainment into and expansion within the updraft diminish surface pressure sufficiently to cause the convergence (toward the base of the primary updraft) of surface air from an area 12 to 20 miles in diameter.

Structure

When updrafts aided by upper-level instability and condensation reach these great heights, downdrafts hurtle downward alongside them to splash against the surface at speeds in excess of 50 to 70 knots. As the downdrafts descend, the water droplets they contain evaporate and cool the lower air. In dry air over the desert, evaporation may be complete; in moist air near a coast, a drenching downpour usually reaches the surface.

Downdrafts spreading out from the base of the storm form a cold front that advances ahead and in the direction of the storm's upper-level steering winds. Where peripheral updrafts slide alongside the centrally located downdrafts, vortices form the *roll*, or *squall*, cloud. Rotating around a horizontal axis, these vortices, or *rotors*, accelerate the outflow along the storm's leading edge. In the early stages of thunderstorm development, rain and/or hail accompany the cold downflow; later, in more mature storms, the rain lags behind the outflow, which spreads progressively farther ahead. As the downflow cools the land ahead of the advancing storm, the inflow of heated air is diminished and the storm weakens (Figure 19.2).

The upper levels of the thunderstorm—the cumulonimbus cloud—respond

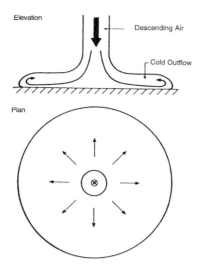

Figure 19.2. Descent of cold air in a thunderstorm (From Linden and Simpson, "Microbursts: A Hazard to Aircraft," Nature.)

to the westerly air flow aloft and move at about 15 knots from west to east toward heated surfaces and moisture. Surface pressure and surface air flow follow this movement, so that inflow is directed toward a center a few miles behind the upper-level cloud and outflow is recognized at progressively greater distances ahead. An observer in the path of a storm will first experience (from as much as 10 miles away) a shift in the ambient surface air flow as air is drawn into the low pressure. A period of dramatically diminished flow and/or calm due to convergence usually follows. This phase is succeeded abruptly by the cold front passage: a sudden increase in wind velocity, a shift to a wind direction outward from the center of the storm cloud, a sudden drop in temperature, and early in a storm's development, rain (or hail). The cold outflow may be as much as 5,000 feet deep and its velocity, at an altitude of 1,000 feet, may exceed 75 knots.

Downflow surrounds a central zone of rapid upflow (and is in turn surrounded by a far larger zone of gradual inflow). As this ring of downflow reaches and spreads across the surface, it is deviated around the central low pressure into a counterclockwise (in the Northern Hemisphere) circulation. If the storm passes overhead, the cold front will be followed by a zone of central calm and then the reappearance of the markedly backed downflow on its far side. If the storm passes to the right, an observer will experience a strong wind (whose velocity is increased by the storm's forward progress) along the left margin of the storm that is initially backed to the storm's trajectory and veers with time. If the storm passes to the left, an observer will experience a lesser wind (whose velocity is diminished by the storm's forward progress) along the right margin of the storm that is even further backed to its trajectory and backs with time.

Offshore Thunderstorms

On ocean coasts a thunderstorm, opposed by the sea breeze and seeking the low pressure above heated land, will migrate parallel to the shore. But on inland waters (lakes and enclosed bays such as the Chesapeake) the relatively weak sea breeze and the low pressure provided by the heating land on the far shore may combine to bring a thunderstorm offshore. The initial outflow will then shift the ambient wind (usually after a period of calm) toward the storm and the sailor (if he wishes to continue racing) should maneuver so as to be "upstorm" ("Head for the blackest cloud").

Because the outflow is deviated into a counterclockwise circulation around the storm center, if the storm's trajectory is to the right of one's position, a port tack approach will provide a progressive header followed by a beneficial starboard tack lift. If the storm's trajectory is to the left of one's position, a starboard tack approach will provide a progressive header and a beneficial port tack lift.

Interaction with the Sea Breeze

Along ocean coasts under subsidence inversions the strong, deep onshore sea breeze flow is usually sufficient to keep thunderstorms onshore. Only in late evening after the sea breeze dies will the storms drift out to sea. In the afternoon, from a position offshore at Savannah, one can observe huge cumulonimbus formations as they develop inland, move shoreward, and then in the southwest gradient wind slide to the northeast, parallel to shore. Rain and 40-knot winds can be seen to slash across the upper marshes, but 3 to 5 miles offshore, where the tops of the giant cumulonimbus clouds seem to billow overhead, the sun still shines and the sea breeze continues unaffected (see Figure 9.2, p. 66).

At Savannah in the sea breeze regimes thunderstorm rain rarely comes within 3 to 5 miles of the sea, and low-level outflow is infrequently evident beyond the outer islands. However, within those 3 to 5 miles cold downdrafts, deflected along the surface, sweep the warmer sea breeze away. Beyond the periphery of this outflow and a narrow band of calm lies another zone, approximately 3 miles across, typically including Wassaw Sound and the near-shore racecourses, in which the sea breeze survives as a 2-knot patchy residue from a backed direction (120° to 150°). Farther offshore the sea breeze is stronger, but some diminution in velocity and backing is evident 3 to 4 miles out.

The alterations in the sea/lake breeze by the thunderstorm's outflow are due to convergence and depend on the relative strength and temperature of the two flows. Close to the thunderstorm icy cold high-velocity downdraft air occupies the surface; several miles away, after the downdraft air has become warmed and slowed by mechanical and thermal turbulence, the colder higher-velocity sea breeze occupies the surface. In the intervening zone, convergence produces eddying, upward displacement of both winds, and a dramatic reduction in the surface flow.

Later in the day, in proportion to the magnitude and number of thunderstorms extant, the entire sea/lake breeze flow is depressed. Cloud cover from the cumulonimbus reduces insolation and surface heating. Rain directly (by blocking insolation) and indirectly (through evaporative cooling after its cessation) cools the surface, reduces the near-surface lapse rate, and blocks separation.

If along an ocean coast a thunderstorm appears inshore when a fleet is racing in a sea breeze, its effect is most likely to be felt as the boats approach the most inshore (leeward) mark. If the area around the leeward mark appears to be in a zone of reduced wind (or calm), one should make the final approach on the course most perpendicular to the shore—so as to spend the least possible time within that zone—and jibe so as to enter the final, most diminished wind flow at the highest possible sailing angle.

Microbursts

Lake Norman (1989)

At 1300 hours on May 6, 1989, out of a "clear sky," a microburst struck 93 boats sailing in a regatta on Lake Norman, North Carolina: 19 crewmembers were swept overboard, two drowned; 4 boats sank, 62 were damaged. Within 10 minutes of the appearance of a "small area of dark sky to the west of the lake," "a wall of white water" hit the fleet. Many felt that the initial blast (variously recorded as 64 to 78 knots) was the strongest, knocking boats flat in the water, filling those with open companionways, preventing the lowering of sails, rolling two J-22s in a succession of 360s! For 5 to 8 minutes "the lake itself seemed to be lifted from its bed," a mixture of "lake water, rain, and hail" blew "like a fire hose" in a layer 10 feet deep across its surface, and 7-foot waves broke over its banks and flooded ashore.

John Lee, sailing on a J-29 in a southwest wind at 20 to 25 knots, had just rounded the leeward mark. Distressed by the blackness of the bottoms of the scattered (throughout a blue sky) cumulus, he decided to switch to a small jib. Two minutes later, looking to windward, he saw a "wall of gray, 30 feet above the water, obscuring the horizon" roaring toward them and called, "Let's get the sails down." Within 30 seconds—with the halyards released but the sails still up—the mast was horizontal. For 5 minutes they sailed at a 60° or greater angle, only intermittently able to wrestle the sails down in 3-foot increments. And then, suddenly, the wind decreased to its former strength and under bare poles the boat righted.

On the lake prior to the start of the race, at shortly after 1200, the wind had been from the southwest at 12 to 18 knots with higher gusts (some said 20 to 25). A few sailors were aware that "to the northeast" thunderstorms (ahead of a rapidly advancing cold front) had been predicted, but no one expected any form of severe weather (only 10 percent had checked their weather radios and none were aware that at 1230 NOAA had issued a microburst warning for the area).

National Weather Service reports from the Charlotte Station (15 miles away) show that between 1100 and 1500 the surface pressure fell from 29.090 to 28.960 inches, that at 1207 the peak wind speed was from 215° at 34 knots, and that at approximately 1300, under scattered cumulus cloud in the warm sector ahead of a rapidly advancing cold front, the wind was from 230° to 280° at 13 knots (Figure 19.3).

Those involved were too busy to take notes, but the disparity of their stories is impressive. John Lee reported no rain and said that no one got wet ashore; others were sure that not only rain, but also hail was mixing with the lake water; others

135

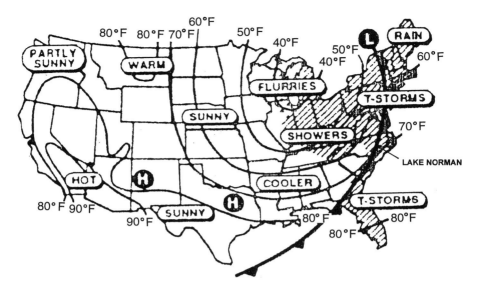

Figure 19.3. Forecast map for noon on May 6, 1989

thought that the rain followed the wind, others the reverse. Some reported the strong wind to have come from a "clear sky," others from huge black clouds with trailing *virga* (the vertical streams of water droplets trailing beneath a cumulonimbus cloud, indicating rain that evaporates before reaching the earth). Some said the wind was from the west, some the southwest, some the southeast, and some the north. The downburst that hit the lake must have come from nearly overhead, must have impacted a relatively small area, and as it splashed across the surface must have affected even boats in close proximity to one another quite differently.

The Pride of Baltimore (1986)

North of the Bahamas on May 11, 1986, a similar severe wind struck and sank the *Pride of Baltimore*, a replica Baltimore clipper, as she was heading northwest in a 28-knot easterly. She was making 8 knots with a double-reefed main, foresail, and staysail when at 1100 the wind increased to 30 knots and it was decided to take in the foresail. Shortly thereafter, at 1150, when she was "sailing comfortably," an intense blast of wind, "building to hurricane velocity in seconds" and sounding "like a freight train," struck her abeam. A horizontal "wall of cold air and water" laid her over until her boom struck the water. Despite the release of her mainsheet and her tiller being held hard to starboard, she would not bear away. As her masts reached the horizontal, water poured down her companionway, and her crew scrambled to escape. Minutes later, as the wind subsided, the *Pride* was gone, her upright mast tip momentarily visible and her masthead pennant fluttering a final farewell.

Violent Convection

Microbursts are extreme examples of common downdrafts. They are not uncommon; 13,000 are estimated to occur each year in the United States. Most of us have probably witnessed the impact of small variants. On a clear day with 15-knot westerly winds (just ahead of a rapidly advancing cold front), I remember seeing, from the 80-foot-high Severn River Bridge, the sudden appearance of a 200-foot-diameter patch of whitecaps from which spray was being blown high into the air (Figure 19.4).

A microburst (or misoburst, in Fujita terminology), a form of downburst between 0.5 mile and 2.5 miles in diameter, requires many of the same preconditions as does a thunderstorm and other forms of violent vertical atmospheric motion, but is distinguished by its association with high-pressure conditions. Lesser forms of high-pressure convection occur in dry, unstable air; but microbursts, like thunderstorms, hurricanes, and tornadoes, require moisture, the condensation and evaporation of which add tremendous amounts of energy to the vertical motion.

Optimal circumstances for microburst development include the approach of a rapidly advancing cold front that contributes frontal lift to the upper-level instability of the warm sector; springtime weather with its characteristic temperature contrasts; scattered cumulus and/or altocumulus at 10,000 feet, producing scattered rain showers

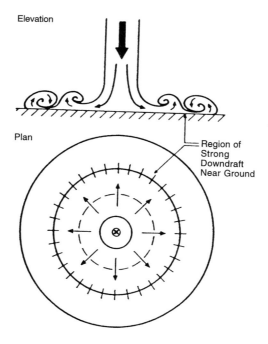

Figure 19.4. Leading-edge vortices in a microburst (From Linden and Simpson, "Microbursts: A Hazard to Aircraft," Nature.)

137

and virga (sometimes accompanied by thunderstorms and waterspouts); and warm, very dry (a large temperature/dewpoint spread) surface conditions.

Evolution

Investigators now believe (from direct observations and from modeling) that a series of events changes an ordinary downdraft (a 100-yard-diameter cylinder descending at 30 knots) into a giant microburst (a 0.5- to 2-mile-diameter cylinder descending at 70 knots):

1. A strong updraft forming in hot, dry surface conditions must entrain a huge volume of rising air; accelerate through highly unstable, moist air; become moisture laden; and condense its water vapor at a great height.
2. The downdraft that responds to this updraft, fueled by the energy released in condensation, must commence its descent from 30,000 feet or more in order to have sufficient time to entrain enough smaller downdrafts to create the large volume involved in the formation of a microburst.
3. The downdraft must fall through very dry, very unstable air en route to the surface (to facilitate evaporation). Warm sectors ahead of cold fronts provide just such conditions: a layer of moist tropical air lifted from the surface by the dry, cold air behind the front.
4. It is now presumed that the downdraft is accelerated by the melting of the ice crystals (in which form the moisture exists at the beginning of its descent) and by the subsequent evaporation of the melted crystals. Both melting and evaporation extract heat from the surrounding air, diminish the adiabatic heating associated with descent, and by increasing the density and weight of the downdraft air, accelerate its fall.

Structure

Microbursts are now recognized to be massive cylinders of descending air, the outer shells of which are dragged by friction with the surrounding air into a reverse, upward flow. A layer beneath this outer shell, entrained in this motion, is accelerated downward. When the cylinder strikes the surface, the more rapidly descending inner shell impacts with the greatest force and produces the circular or arcuate disturbance of surface water that is characteristic of a downdraft impact (Figure 19.5).

Fujita has demonstrated that when a downburst (like an ordinary downdraft) strikes obliquely, as it is almost certain to do, air compressed by its descent forms a cushion on the upwind side of its site of impact and directs "extreme winds" outward and downwind along the surface. Aloft in an aircraft (that relies on a unidirectional air flow), it is the wind shear—the abrupt transition from air moving in one direction to air moving in another—that causes a microburst to be so dangerous. At the surface it is the extreme wind itself (Figure 19.6).

In 1985 in *Nature*, P. F. Linden and J. E. Simpson reported the results of experiments analyzing the pattern of the outflow from a downburst impact. They showed that when a descending column of fluid reaches the ground and begins to spread out horizontally, an intense vortex with a horizontal axis forms at the leading edge of the outflow (sometimes a second vortex forms beyond the first). They asserted

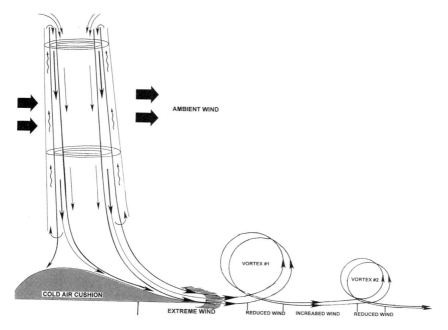

Figure 19.5. Anatomy of a microburst

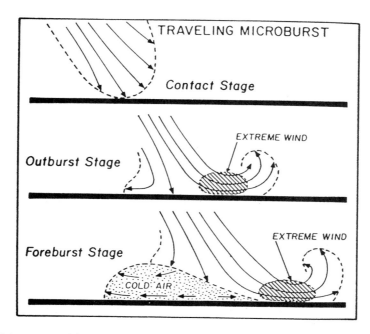

Figure 19.6. Extreme wind formation in a microburst (From Fujita, "Tornadoes and Downbursts in the Context of Generalized Planetary Scales," Journal of the Atmospheric Sciences.)

that the intensity of this vortex results from the rapid stretching of the length of the leading edge as the radius of the arc grows larger. Observers positioned on one or the other side of this leading-edge vortex would perceive a wind reduced or accelerated and a wind either aligned with or directly opposed to the ambient wind.

Analysis

The appearance of a microburst out of a "clear, blue sky" is now understandable. Ice crystals forming at 30,000 feet are either invisible or produce such a thin layer of cirrus that they go unrecognized. Small black clouds seen at lower levels are the consequence of the melting of the falling ice into water droplets. The frequently seen virga are streaks of water droplets descending in downdrafts. Their disappearance is the consequence of the complete evaporation achieved before the downdraft reaches the surface. A "wall of white water" is, of course, the effect of a microburst's impact on the surface of a lake or sea.

The downburst of May 1989 was presumably several kilometers in diameter when it obliquely impacted the surface of the lake in the vicinity of the Lake Norman Sailing Club and produced extreme winds that roared across the lake's surface at 70 miles an hour. The leading edge of this outflow was directed downwind (in the ambient wind), but presumably spread in an arc radiating outward from the site of impact. The lower tens of feet of the atmosphere were composed chiefly of lake water, but in some areas may have included rain and hail from within the downburst. That observers on the lake experienced winds of widely varied speeds, emanating from a variety of directions, is consistent with the presumption that horizontal vortices, or rotors, were forming and that on opposite sides of these rotors the wind was of dramatically differing speed and direction. The extreme winds continued for approximately 5 to 8 minutes until the entire downburst cylinder had completed its impact, and the rotors and other manifestations of its spread had dissipated.

V. Gradient Winds: Parallel-to-Shore Flow

20. Rochester

For every cloud engenders not a storm.
—Shakespeare

Near Rochester a 50- to 100-foot strip of pebble or sand beach separates Lake Ontario from the abrupt shoreline bluffs. During the night, cold contracting air sinks from the bluffs to the beach and onto the adjacent lake surface. The puddle of cold air that accumulates produces a conduction inversion above which both onshore and offshore gradient flows slide and into which they penetrate with difficulty. Such a shoreline is a great inhibitor of lake breeze generation, as it provides but a narrow strip of heated land at lake level to propagate a sea breeze front, and a high barrier to block the penetration of the dense marine air. The Genesee River provides a narrow low-level window through the 20- to 60-foot bluffs, and the lake breeze is at its strongest as it funnels past the Rochester Yacht Club on the river's right bank.

Rochester highlights the significance of the position of a coast relative to the polar front, and the orientation of a coast to the prevailing gradient wind direction.

In summertime its location close to the polar front causes successive highs to pass to the south and results in an abbreviated sequence of polar front phases. Its gradient winds are limited typically to three phases—a northwesterly ahead of the high (following a cold front passage), an evanescent (or absent) westerly as the high passes, and a southwesterly thereafter.

The gradient wind may gradually back to the west as the center of the high passes to the south or, more typically, when the high is a north-south ridge, may shift abruptly from northwest to southwest as the ridge passes overhead. The typical sequence at Rochester is a brief phase (one to two days) of northwesterly gradient flow, a day or two of lake breeze while the high-pressure ridge is overhead, a prolonged period (many days to weeks, if a strong Bermuda High holds the polar front to the north) of southwesterly flow.

The Northwesterly

Although in summer in midlake the northwesterly gradient flow may be strong, close to the southern shore it is weakened by the shoreline bluffs, which resist the elevation of the cold marine air. Because the gradient flow has transited 80 miles of cool lake en route to Rochester, it is devoid of the usual gusts and medium oscillations. If it is weak but cool, it may veer into a weak, patchy secondary lake breeze and lead to infrequent large shifts between the gradient flow at 300° to 360° and the lake breeze at 25° to 45°. If it is weak but warm (close to the ridge), it will be displaced aloft sometime after midday, and the lake breeze at 45° to 55° will occupy the entire near-shore surface.

The Lake Breeze

Once the high-pressure ridge is overhead or nearby to the east, the gradient flow aloft shifts gradually or abruptly to the west or southwest. A weak southwesterly (from 220° to 240°) may occupy the surface nocturnally and early in the morning (or appear during the day as a shift from the lake breeze). The weak synoptic gradient, the relatively cool, dry cP air (brought south in the preceding northerly flow), and the now offshore gradient flow combine at midday to facilitate secondary lake breeze generation. If the early-morning surface flow dies in mid- to late morning, expect a strengthening lake breeze from 45° to 65°.

But lake breeze generation at Rochester is impaired by the minimal amount of low-level land in front of the abrupt bluffs, the homogeneous topography with few significant hills, and the unindented shoreline. Except in springtime, when the southwesterly air flow is cool (providing a high lapse rate that facilitates thermal liftoff above the heated land), the lake breeze is rarely stronger than 10 knots. The developing flow demonstrates the "fan effect" (backing with distance offshore). Fully established, it is characterized by 8° to 10° oscillating shifts and by a gradual velocity veer to 75°.

If the southwesterly is predicted to appear during the day, expect it to arrive—following the dying of the lake breeze and a period of convergence calm—as a band of dark ruffled water along the shore. For the first 30 to 60 minutes thereafter, the hot southwesterly may be able to penetrate only the cold marine air in the near-shore gusting zone. If a race is started in a lake breeze and it begins to die, keep to the shore (on both beats and runs) so as to be positioned closer than the competition to the developing wind as it spreads gradually offshore.

The Southerly/Southwesterly

Early in the day the hot southwesterly accelerates and veers progressively as it leaves the friction of the land to slide over the cold lake and the cold marine air. A boat sailing to windward finds a back with distance toward shore. Presumably this back is due to the stable flow diverging, accelerating, and veering as it moves from the friction of the land out over the lake. Rochester is one of the few places in the world where this phenomenon (considered by some to be common) is recognizable—and even here it is evident only in stable conditions early in the morning or in light air, when thermal turbulence is minimal. But on the first beat of the day—particularly in light air—a long starboard tack held far into the left corner will reach a zone of near-shore, backed, and stronger air and may win the race.

Even when the weather-system gradient is predicted to produce a southwesterly wind at 15 to 20 knots—and is reported to be at this velocity over the airport about 15 miles inland—it rarely reaches more than 12 to 15 knots over the lake. Opposed by the thermal gradient and obstructed by the dense marine air, it is never as strong as predicted. At night and offshore as the warm air sinks to the cool (60° to 70°F) lake surface, the flow is even less and increases only gradually as the day dawns. With heating of the land above the temperature of the warm air, thermal turbulence begins and upper, more rapidly flowing veered air is brought to the surface over the land and in the gusting zone over the near-shore waters. But farther offshore, the pool of cold air, stagnant at the lake's surface creates an inversion above which the hot southwesterly slides.

The Westerly Southwesterly

As the cP High merges with the mTg (Bermuda) High, the southwesterly veers to 240°, 250°, 260°, or even 270°, the advected air becomes hotter and moister (less conducive of lake breeze generation), and the surface gradient wind becomes increasingly parallel to the southern shore of Lake Ontario.

Once established (until another cold front or a low-pressure system crosses the area), the southwesterly (at 240° to 270°) persists—aloft. However, at the surface any one (or a combination) of three different patterns may emerge:
1. The gradient flow—coming across the continent in the northwest quadrant of the Bermuda High—may persist.
2. The gradient flow, one segment of which is transiting land and another transiting water from west to east along Ontario's south shore, may split—the cooler overwater segment displacing (persistently or intermittently) the warm overland segment.
3. The overland flow, coming offshore, may induce a secondary lake breeze.
Over the land, the Bermuda High produces no subsidence inversion, and therefore,

along the southern shores of the Great Lakes the southwester fights the local lake breeze in the surface layer. If the lake breeze appears, it will do so in stages: The gradient wind will die; a zone of convergence calm will appear within a few miles of shore, spreading shoreward; the lake breeze will appear offshore and to the north and east as a zone of dark ruffled water, spreading southwestward toward shore ("two winds simultaneously"); and, finally, the lake breeze will strengthen and dominate the entire near-shore surface.

The factors that determine the three outcomes are the strength, direction, and temperature of the gradient flow; the coldness of the lake; and the strength of the lake breeze generating factors (particularly the temperature and instability of the advected air). The farther west, the more parallel to shore (veered to 240°) the gradient flow is or becomes, the more likely it is to split into overland and overwater segments. The more southerly, the more perpendicular to shore (backed to 240°) the gradient flow is or becomes, the more likely the lake breeze is to appear. The latter is also more likely in the spring, when the water is colder, or within a few days of the passage of a cold front, when the advected air, derived from a cP air mass, is cooler, drier, and clearer. In early spring, when the southwesterly is strong and cool, it is likely to persist alone; in midsummer, when the southwesterly is weak and hot (and moist), it is likely to split or be displaced.

Both splitting and lake breeze development require insolation and ordinarily do not diminish the overland southwesterly before 1000. If the southwesterly has been veered to 240° and the surface flow diminishes and veers further, expect the split segment at 300° to 330°. If the southwesterly has been backed to 240° and/or backs further as it dies and the lake breeze generating factors are supportive, expect the lake breeze. However, even if the southwesterly has been backed to 240°, if the lake breeze generating factors are weak, the lake breeze may be greatly delayed and sometimes, despite the evidence of convergence, may never appear at all.

The Westerly "Southwester" and Convergence

A Northwesterly in a Westerly

On two days of the 1991 Soling Worlds, between 1210 and 1240, the morning wind, which had been oscillating to the west of southwest, suddenly diminished to near calm and then abruptly reappeared as a 12- to 14-knot flow from 320° to 325°. On one of these days, a Wednesday, the morning wind had been the usual southwester from 240° to 255°. At about 1045, as the fleet came down the first run, the surface wind diminished, and following some 15° oscillations, died almost completely. Masthead instruments 50 feet above the lake were showing 5 to 6 knots at 260° to 270° while a glassy calm spread across the surface. Bugs were swarming annoyingly—onto vertical surfaces, about faces, and into hair (Figure 20.1).

Suddenly, just before noon, a dark patch appeared to the west, and within a few minutes a 4-knot wind at 290° to 300° was ruffling the surface. The flow increased and gradually veered so that by 1245 its speed had increased to 7 knots and its direction was steady at 320° to 325°. The afternoon race was started at 1400 in a wind from that direction that had increased to 10 to 12 knots. Thereafter, it gradually died and backed—down to 8 knots and 310° by 1530, to 7 knots and

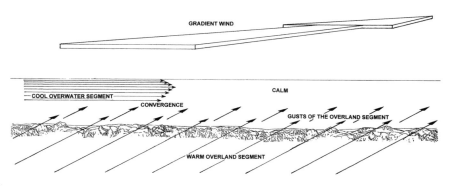

Figure 20.1. Calm and persistent shift due to convergence

300° by 1600. After a brief strengthening to 10 knots, by 1700 the wind was down to 7 knots and had backed to 285°. Before resuming its gradual backing and dying, it again veered abruptly to 325° for about 10 minutes (as the race finished). All the while that this 300° to 325° wind was blowing at the surface of the lake, the airport 10 miles inland was recording the wind at 260° to 270° and the 150-foot smokestacks near the beach were showing a wind from about 275°.

The next day, following a very light morning southwesterly, a similar calm persisted and required the cancellation of racing. Two days later the morning wind was again 240° to 255°, but between 1030 and 1130 veered to 260° to 270° and strengthened before dying to about 6 knots and backing. Bugs accumulated once again, but with a stronger air flow were less of a nuisance than they had been on Wednesday. At 1245 the wind speed again increased abruptly to about 10 knots and veered dramatically to 310° and then 320° and briefly 330°. Thereafter, until about 1400, this wind blew homogeneously with only small oscillations (between 320° and 325°) at 7 to 10 knots. By 1600 it had diminished to about 5 knots at 310°. Again throughout the afternoon the flow ashore remained to the left of 270°.

Two Portions of the Same Wind

The characteristics of this 315° to 330° wind that appeared on three successive days while the usual "southwester" was blowing ashore were as follows:

- It blew only at the surface of the lake—and was probably limited to a zone 1 to 5 miles off the beach.
- It developed at midday after the offshore "southwester" had become established at the surface.
- It was preceded by the accumulation of bugs—millions of them—indicating that two winds—two masses of air—were converging, catching the insects between them.
- It was veered to and steadier, with far fewer oscillations and velocity variations, than the morning offshore "southwester."
- It diminished (or obliterated) the morning offshore flow and then swept it aside until late afternoon, when the offshore flow reappeared.

When a hot, stable gradient wind flows parallel to a shoreline, the segment flowing near the surface over the water is less retarded by friction, accelerates, and, in the Northern Hemisphere due to the Coriolis force, veers. If the wind flows parallel to shore with water on its left, the relatively backed flow from over the land and the veered flow from over the water converge (Figure 20.2). When convergence occurs, surface flow is diminished (the only escape for the air is up) and the contents of the two air flows—bugs—accumulate.

If, of course, one flow is colder than the other, the colder flow will undermine and displace (rather than converge with) the warmer. In the morning in the racing area, when the gradient wind is predicted to be from 235° to 270°, the coldest air flow—and the only air flow strong and turbulent enough to penetrate the cold, dense, stagnant pool of lake air—is the higher-velocity upper-level flow brought to the surface by thermal turbulence in the southwesterly's overland segment.

By midday after the stagnant lake air has been swept away by the near-shore downdrafts and the overland air has become sufficiently heated, the nonturbulent air of the cooler overlake segment (which has been isolated above the pool of cold marine air) is able to subside to the surface. The overlake segment comes over 100 miles of water en route to Rochester, and by midday its lower levels are considerably colder than those of its overland counterpart. The dense overlake segment is then able to undermine the offshore flow and block the penetration of its downdrafts, and becomes the dominant surface wind of the afternoon.

If a southwesterly is predicted and by race time the surface wind on the lake is 300° to 360°, the overlake flow is already present. More typically it appears at about noon and persists until late afternoon. Free of thermal turbulence, of gusts and holes, it comes down the lake in medium oscillations about 12 to 20 minutes apart. It may veer progressively (as it fills in and increases in velocity) to as far right as 360° to 010°.

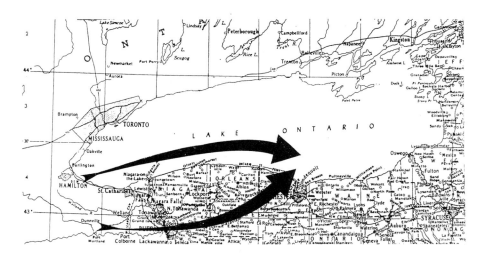

Figure 20.2. Splitting of a parallel-to-shore flow at Rochester

Without the help of the turbulent overland flow, the overlake flow is often unable to sweep away the cold lake air and unable to reach the surface. On the Thursday when, with no overland flow reaching the surface in the morning and the only wind recognized, a minimal overlake flow from 320°, no satisfactory sailing breeze ever developed.

When a gradient wind is flowing parallel to shore, its overwater and overland segments separate from one another, flow at differing speeds, and either diverge from or converge with one another. When they converge, their average speed of flow is diminished and a large shift (of 30° to 50°) occurs in the surface wind as one segment displaces the other.

Strategy

In a light southerly "southwester" and in a light westerly "southwester," go left, expecting the backed gusts of the overland segment to appear near shore. After the overlake flow is fully established and blowing from 320° to 345°, in early to midafternoon, treat shifts as oscillations, go right in the backed lulls, expecting the next shift (with an increase in strength) to be an oscillating veer, sweeping in from the right.

The convergence between the segments of a southwester flowing parallel to shore creates "large oscillations" (see Table 7, "Hierarchy of Shift Experience," page 130). At midday, while the overland flow is dying and the overlake flow developing, and late in the day, when the overland flow is returning to the surface, it is necessary to seek one layline or the other. On each beat the boat that is inside and to windward in the final shift (which comes from one corner or the other) will "get it right." Around midday, when the overland flow is dying, seek the right corner, looking for the overlake flow to appear. Late in the day, when the overlake flow is dying, seek the left corner, looking for the overlake flow to be replaced once again by the overland flow.

21. The Split Segments of a Gradient Wind: The Algarve and Andalucía

If the sun sets clear as a bell,
It's going to blow, sure as hell.
—ENGLISH PROVERB

When a gradient wind flows parallel to a coast, the near-surface elements of its overland segment are slowed and backed, whereas the near-surface elements of its overwater segment are accelerated and veered. Segmentation is pronounced in hot, stable gradient winds, which induce no thermal turbulence. When such winds flow in the quadrant veered to a perpendicular to the coast with water on their right, the divergence between the segments facilitates and strengthens sea/lake breeze flow.

However, when gradient winds flow in the quadrant backed to a perpendicular to the coast, convergence between the segments results in a diminution of flow and the undermining of one segment by the other, and disorganizes and delays the appearance of sea/lake breeze flow. Usually, as in the Levante at Cádiz in southern Spain (and the southwesterly at Rochester), one segment of the split flow gradually undermines the other and produces two persistent shifts several hours apart. Sometimes, however, the two segments appear alternately every 10 to 30 minutes in a series of oscillating shifts.

This latter pattern is frequently seen in late summer and early fall in the Algarve on the south coast of Portugal. Three-time gold medalist Jochen Schumann, in winning the 1994 Soling European Championship at Vilamoura with amazingly consistent finishes (2-4-1-2-2-2), demonstrated the proper management of this common situation.

Summer and Fall Winds in the Algarve

The typical summer wind pattern along the eastern Algarve coast is a strong, hot, and gusty northerly (the gradient wind on the western side of the Iberian Heat Low) in the morning, a brief period of calm in early afternoon, and then the sea breeze rolling in from offshore and rapidly building to 16 to 18 knots. In the western Algarve the northerly, cooled by its overwater passage along the Atlantic coast, often persists.

In late summer and fall, however, as insolation and local daytime temperatures diminish, the ridge of high pressure associated with the Azores High displaces the Iberian and Northwest African Heat Lows to the north. Along the Algarve coast the result is an easterly or southeasterly flow (on the northern periphery of the Northwest African Heat Low) parallel to the southern Portuguese coast.

A Day of Racing in a Southeasterly Gradient Wind

In the morning on each of the first two days of the championship, the gradient wind was southeasterly, and each day the fleet had been told to expect the westerly sea breeze (ranging between 240° and 280°). Prior to the 1300 start of the first race, the 12- to 14-knot wind at 110° had gradually veered to 140° (Figure 21.1).

Midday

During the first starting sequence, the wind diminished and shifted abruptly to 160° to 170°. After a postponement and a further diminution of wind strength to about 10 knots, the committee set a new course at 150°. Schumann started one-third of the way down the line with two-thirds of the fleet to his right, and one-third, including Mario Celon and the Dutchman Rudy den Outer, alone at the pin, to his left. Most of the former group, apparently believing that the advertised shift toward the sea breeze was in progress, tacked immediately to port. Schumann and most of those to his left continued on starboard in a slight veer to 160°; den Outer, the farthest left, looked lifted and desperate.

But one-third of the way to the mark, with the wind dying, den Outer and Celon entered a near-shore zone of increased velocity and experienced a big back.

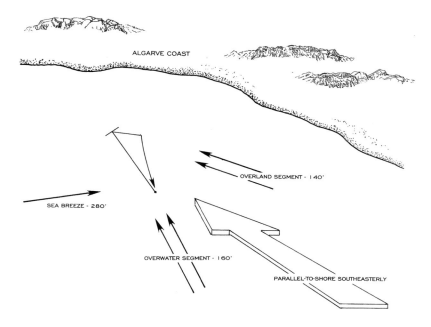

Figure 21.1. Splitting of a parallel-to-shore flow in the Algarve

At 1345, while the boats to the right and offshore floundered in a diminished 6- to 8-knot flow from 160°, den Outer and Celon tacked in a 14-knot flow from 140° and looked down at the entire fleet. As soon as Schumann reached the backed wind, he tacked to port on the leebow of the boats coming out of the left corner. He could cross everyone to his right and was within 100 yards of the leaders to his left.

The stronger air, now increased to 16 knots, gradually spread across the course, and the back progressed to 135°. Celon and den Outer were now over-standing and Schumann was close to the port layline. The first reach was extremely tight and when den Outer, having difficulty with his chute, fell to leeward, Celon took the lead. Once again the wind began to veer, and by the time the leaders reached the leeward mark it was 145° and diminishing. At the start of the second beat Celon headed right while Schumann, now fourth, took a short hitch on starboard. When the wind veered another 10°, Celon looked to have gained. But Schumann was now to his left and in the big back that followed, again accompanied by stronger air, passed the third-place Australians.

Midafternoon

For the third beat the race committee shifted the weather mark to the backed direction, and Schumann took the lifted port tack to the right. Halfway to the mark, when the wind diminished and veered, he tacked and crossed the second-place Danes. Thereafter, Celon was careful to sail the lifted tack and on the final beat, in a big back that permitted both boats to almost lay the mark, forced Schumann to settle for second.

Between races another back and an increase in velocity occurred, but at the start of the second race at 1610, the wind was from 165° at 8 knots. The Hungarian, Georgy Wossala, repeated den Outer's gambit and result, crossing the fleet from the left corner in a big back to 140° and strong air. Again Schumann was in the middle and able to cross the fleet to his right. But this time the wind was dying everywhere, and its strengthening along the port layline was evanescent. Shortly after the Dutchman Ned Potma, on the starboard layline in a slightly stronger residue, crossed Wossala and started down the reach, the wind died completely.

Late Afternoon

At 1725, with the fleet becalmed along that reach, a line of dark ruffled water appeared across the southwest horizon: the sea breeze at 260°! Potma and the other leaders, including Schumann, now 7th, to leeward of a large patch of calm, picked up their own 6-knot streak from 280° and came into the "jibe mark" well ahead. As the sea breeze became homogeneous and strengthened (and the race committee moved the second weather mark to a heading of 280°, continuing the beat that had begun at the "jibe mark"), the surface flow backed to the median sea breeze direction (260° to 270°). At the finish at 1830, with the wind at 11 knots and 280°, Schumann was fourth.

Convergence in the Split Segments of the Southeasterly

Three separate air flows had been present. During the 5-hour period between 1200 and 1700, the surface wind within 5 miles of shore had oscillated between the original gradient wind flow at 130° and a second flow from 165°. These oscillations had occurred at approximately 20-minute intervals. The backed flow had appeared in early morning and was more evident near shore on the left side of the course. The veered flow had appeared at about 1300 and was more evident offshore on the right side of the course (about 3 to 4 miles out). Shifts between the two flows persisted throughout the period of maximum insolation until replaced by calm, and at 1730, by the third flow, the sea breeze.

The two midday flows were the split segments of the southeasterly gradient wind flowing parallel to the coast with water on its left. The backed flow was the overland segment—brought to the surface near shore in early morning as thermal turbulence developed over the land. The veered flow was the overwater segment—evident offshore after the overland segment had become warmed and could be lifted from the surface (see Table 8, p. 154).

At Rochester the split segments are sufficiently different in temperature that one supplants the other (almost) completely. In the Algarve, over warmer water, the temperature of the two flows is sufficiently alike that they alternately displace one another in a series of oscillating shifts.

The first shift in such a series—a veer from the backed (more parallel-to-shore) flow to the veered (more onshore) flow—develops at about noon, after insolation has warmed the overland segment and within a few miles of shore where racecourses are often set. The

153

TABLE 8: PARALLEL-TO-SHORE FLOWS

Convergence (Water on the Left)

LOCATION	WIND VARIETY	DIRECTION
Rochester	Gradient wind	Southwesterly (Bermuda High)
Algarve	Gradient wind	Easterly (African Heat Low)
Long Island Sound	Gradient wind	Northeasterly (cP High)
Lake of Geneva	Downslope wind	Easterly (La Bise)

Divergence (Water on the Right)

LOCATION	WIND VARIETY	DIRECTION
Southern California	Amalgamated sea breeze	Primary sea breeze/northwesterly
Chesapeake	Amalgamated sea breeze	Bay sea breeze/southerly

next shift is an oscillation back to the initial direction of the overland segment (rather than a progressive veer toward the sea breeze). Shifts between these two directions may continue at medium (15- to 25-minute) intervals until late afternoon. Only when both segments die completely and a flow from the sea breeze direction appears beyond a zone of calm should one presume that the subsequent shift (to the sea breeze) will be persistent.

Strategy

Schumann, assuming that the veer prior to each start would be followed by a back to the initial direction, took a position in the middle of the line (from which he would lose little regardless of the direction of the next shift) and sailed the lifted tack until a big header (the expected back) appeared. When it did he was able to tack ahead and to leeward of the "corner-shooters," who could cross the entire fleet while gaining on the majority who had believed the veer would be persistent.

Subsequently Schumann played each of the protracted shifts as oscillations and discovered that a return shift always appeared during the 25 minutes required to complete a weather leg. He assumed each shift of the weather mark to be an indicator of a temporary shift in wind direction, took the lifted tack away from the direction of the mark shift, and was regularly rewarded by an oscillation to his side of the course.

It is interesting that Schumann—in the same kind of converging, parallel-to-shore gradient wind—failed (by one point!) to win the 1991 Soling World Championship at Rochester—because there he treated the shifts between the two segments as persistent. He was leading the series (by a huge margin) until, in two successive races (described in chapter 20, on Rochester), he dared to start at the port end of the line, headed left (toward what he thought would be a single persistent back) and found himself in a progressive veer to the overwater segment. He clearly profited by that experience. (See Table 7, "Hierarchy of Shift Experience," p. 130.)

The interaction between the split segments of a gradient wind flowing with water on its left may result in the sequential displacement of one segment by the other, creating a series of oscillating shifts.

The Levantes

The Levantes of southern Spain are stable air flows that develop whenever a synoptic gradient induces easterly flow in the western Mediterranean (usually in association with a low-pressure system over North Africa and a high-pressure system over northern Europe). The Sea of Almoran (the westernmost portion of the Mediterranean), confined by the 6,000- to 10,000-foot peaks of Spain's Sierra Morena to the north and the 6,000- to 7,000-foot ridges of Morocco's Rif and Atlas Mountains to the south, acts as a giant corral to focus the lower layers of such winds toward the Strait of Gibraltar. Continuous, strong easterly flow through the strait, into the neighboring Atlantic, and along the African coast may persist for three to five days (Figure 21.2).

But along the Spanish coast beyond the Strait of Gibraltar, the Levantes, with water on their left, divide into overwater and overland segments that converge

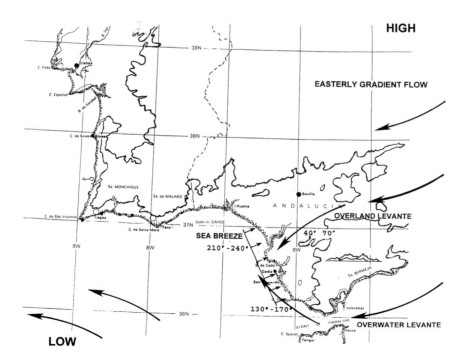

Figure 21.2. The Levante at Cádiz

and ultimately undermine one another, resulting in a characteristic diurnal pattern. Near-shore surface flow, isolated aloft by the radiation inversion, is weak or absent during the night, appears first during the morning as thermal turbulence breaks through the inversion and brings down the overland segment, and reaches full strength during the afternoon as the overwater segment lifts the overland segment from the near-shore surface.

In the Bay of Cádiz the backed overland segment coming over, around, and through the Serrania de Ronda and brought to the surface by thermal turbulence appears in mid- to late morning as a light, warm offshore wind at 40° to 70°. The veered overwater segment, cooled by its passage over the Sea of Almoran and accelerated by its channeling through the strait, appears in early afternoon as a moderate to strong, relatively cool wind at 130° to 170°.

Local lore describes the Levante as "turning with the sun," veering progressively each day. Strong Levantes, which may reach hurricane force in the strait and continue at 50 knots as they spread into the Atlantic and into the Bay of Cádiz (60 miles to the northwest of the strait), do veer progressively from the overland to the overwater segment during daylight hours. But weak ones tend to do so in a series of jumps sometimes punctuated by short periods of near calm as the warmer wind segment is lifted from the surface by the cooler one. Usually the morning nor'easter (the warm, overland flow) dies at midday, a progressively strengthening and veering southeasterly (the cool, overwater flow) replaces it during the afternoon, and finally in late afternoon the latter dies as it is lifted from the surface by the 210° to 240° sea breeze composed of even colder air from the Atlantic Ocean.

VI. *Thermal Winds: The Primary Sea/Lake Breeze*

Chesapeake	Pamlico Sound	Acapulco
Hyannis	Portland, Maine	Bergen
Lake Hopatcong	Portsmouth	Fremantle
Lake Lanier	San Diego	Helsinki
Lake Norman	San Francisco	Ireland
Long Island Sound	Santa Cruz	Lake Balaton
Marblehead	Savannah	Port Lincoln
Martha's Vineyard	Stuart/Melbourne	Starnbergersee
Mobjack Bay	Wrightsville Beach	Tegernsee
Newport		

22. The Primary Sea Breezes of the Atlantic Coast: Marblehead and Long Island Sound

Gray-eyed Athena sent them a favorable breeze,
a fresh west wind,
singing over the wine dark sea.

—HOMER

We have now explored the entire range of gradient wind behavior from its basic determinants to the specific modifications induced by orientation to a coast. We have seen how the phase of the polar front and the gradient wind direction modify the development of sea/lake breezes. We can now look at the thermal winds themselves. We shall see that they are governed by the same laws that govern gradient wind flows. They are distinctive in that they are confined to the near-surface layers of the troposphere and are usually colder than the gradient flow extant.

First we should investigate the primary sea/lake breeze—a sea/lake breeze that develops a complete, autonomous circulation under a preexistent inversion and develops in three forms:

1. As a local morning wind that appears along midlatitude coasts after clear nights

that developed a radiation inversion, or on clear, cold days in winter (see this chapter)
2. As a large-scale coastal sea breeze that appears under a subsidence inversion (see chapter 23, "Fremantle")
3. As a local lake breeze that appears above cold, steep-sided lakes under an advection inversion in summer (see chapter 25, "Small Lake Winds")

In summer primary sea breezes develop all along the Atlantic coast of the United States, but vary in frequency and strength depending on three major factors:
1. The strength and overlap of the radiation and subsidence inversions
2. The disparity between the temperature of the water and the midday air
3. The topography of the coastline (see appendix 1, "The Differences between Primary and Secondary Sea/Lake Breezes")

Morning Primary Sea/Lake Breeze Generation

A radiation inversion associated with a clear night causes the near-surface air to be cold and the near-surface lapse rate to be high at dawn, when insolation is beginning and the surface of the land is heating rapidly. A radiation inversion protects the nascent sea/lake breeze from the gradient wind, and most importantly provides a lid to guide an upper-level flow of heated air waterward to increase overwater subsidence and overwater pressure. It is this increase in pressure that starts the marine air moving shoreward and across the shoreline.

Under a strong radiation inversion the morning primary sea/lake breeze is the first wind of the day, starts early, persists until mid- or late morning, and unless a higher subsidence inversion exists, dies with inversion breakthrough. If a higher subsidence inversion does exist and overlaps the shore, the local sea/lake breeze will shift without a major reduction in wind speed toward the direction of a large-scale primary sea/lake breeze. If the subsidence inversion exists but overlaps poorly, the morning sea/lake breeze will die before being replaced by the larger-scale flow. In the absence of a radiation inversion, no morning sea/lake breeze will develop, and only if a strong subsidence or advection inversion and/or optimal shoreline topography are present will a large-scale sea/lake breeze develop later in the day.

The subsidence inversion necessary to the development of the strong afternoon Atlantic coast ocean sea breeze is typically stronger farther south where the air is relatively hot. The radiation inversion is typically stronger farther north where the air is more likely to be clear and dry (more likely to be derived from a cP air mass).

The topography of the coastline ultimately determines whether or not a large-scale sea/lake breeze will develop, as well as its time of onset and strength. Where sea and land are interspersed (many islands, bays, and rivers), the subsidence inversion overlaps the radiation inversion and the morning local sea breeze merges imperceptibly into the afternoon ocean sea breeze. Where the sea and land are abruptly divided, the radiation inversion disintegrates before insolation is sufficient to maintain an unprotected sea breeze front, and the morning local sea breeze dies before the afternoon sea breeze develops. Low-level near-shore land facilitates the initial entry of the sea breeze front and, as the radiation inversion dissipates, its maintenance. Rivers and harbors provide a long shoreline across which the marine air can invade to reach the heating sites. Primary sea breezes appear first and persist longest in such deep indentations (Figure 22.1).

Barren, low-lying land interposed between the ocean and inland water introduces thermal turbulence into a sea breeze flow, brings stronger upper-level elements to the inshore surface, and facilitates the invasion of the *sea breeze front* and its initial crossing of the shoreline. The ultimate ocean sea breeze is stronger where the shore is low lying and strongest where low-lying islands or peninsulas are interposed, weaker where bluffs and hills block its sea-level entry or where no offshore land is interposed.

The Primary Ocean Sea Breeze of the Atlantic Coast

In Maine the cold water and the interposed islands create a strong onshore surface flow in the inshore "reaches." Elsewhere along the New England coast the abrupt and relatively high shoreline interferes with the entry of the primary sea breeze except where inlets and interposed islands extend the radiation inversion waterward. Where alignment is appropriate—Buzzards Bay, Marblehead Harbor, Great South Bay—strong amalgamated sea breezes develop.

Along the New Jersey (Barnegat Bay), Delaware (Rehoboth and Indian River Bays), and Maryland and Virginia (Chincoteague Bay) coasts, the ocean sea breeze comes onto inshore waters over low, barren barrier islands under a subsidence inversion and provides great smooth-water sailing on almost every summer afternoon. As the subsidence inversion does not extend into Long Island Sound and the Chesapeake, their local morning primary sea breezes (dependent on radiation inversions) die before being replaced in the afternoon by overland or overwater (as in the lower Chesapeake) ocean sea breezes. Long Island Sound, because Long Island is oriented across the summer southwesterly flow, and the Chesapeake, because its upper portion is aligned with the southwesterly, often profit from the amalgamation of the ocean sea breeze with the gradient flow. But usually once the ocean sea breeze front has come ashore on the ocean beaches, these inland waters will be its beneficiaries regardless of the gradient wind direction.

Farther south along the Carolina and Georgia coasts, although the ocean is progressively warmer, the low-lying barren or marshy land facilitates the entry of the sea breeze front. Here the subsidence inversion overlaps the radiation, and the local primary sea breeze, developing in late morning, flows across the marshland, lifts the hot gradient flow from the surface, and fuses with the afternoon ocean sea breeze. No break in the inversions and no late-morning break in the onshore flow is apparent. Along the straight, unindented Florida coast the ocean water is warmed by the Gulf Stream, and the sea breeze front is less able to invade. Except where the sea breeze amalgamates with the gradient wind and flows into appropriately oriented waters such as Biscayne Bay, the onshore flow is weak.

Marblehead

Racing at Marblehead is conducted in open water to the southeast of Cat Island, where the sea breeze (coming directly from the Atlantic Ocean in the absence of

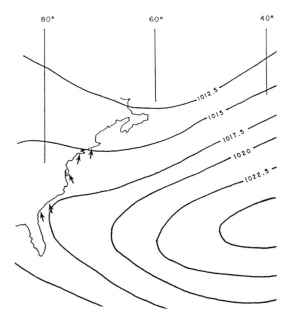

Figure 22.1. Strong primary sea breezes develop under the subsidence inversion where inlets, marshes, and barrier islands lead the marine air inland.

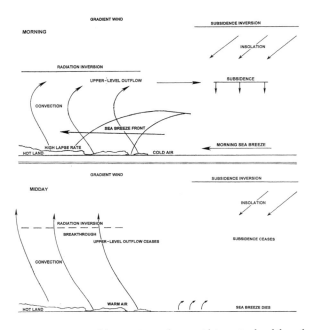

Figure 22.2. Disruption of the morning sea breeze with inversion breakthrough

interposed land) is weaker, backed, and far more erratic than it is in the harbor. On a typical summer day, with the gradient wind predicted to be "southwest 10 to 15 knots," the first evidence of wind is the local primary sea breeze disrupting the morning calm within the harbor. At about 0700 off Cat Island it is weaker, blowing at about 4 knots from 140° to 160°. However, by the time of a race start at 1000 it has usually increased to 6 to 8 knots, has become incorporated in the large-scale ocean sea breeze oriented to the general trend of the coastline, and has veered significantly.

Within the harbor, the incorporation of upper-level flow—introduced by thermal turbulence over the causeway—forces the sea breeze to steadily increase in velocity and progressively veer to about 200° to 210°. Not so in the racing area. There the first sea breeze is a teaser on which one cannot rely. Typically, after a 1000 start, the breeze dies and those who have tacked to port, hoping for a progressive velocity veer, often find that they are on the outside of a huge back. I once salvaged a second place at the weather mark when a 40° back lifted us to the weather mark by the great circle route!

At about 1100 to 1130, after about 30 minutes of very light air from 100° to 120°, a "new" onshore breeze fills in from 140° to 150°. By the end of a morning race at 1200 to 1230, this wind has built to 8 to 10 knots and has veered to 155° to 165°. During the break preceding a second race at 1400 it typically strengthens to 10 to 12 knots and veers further, to 165° to 175°. During the first beats of an afternoon race, gradual oscillations partially obscure a progressive velocity veer. At approximately 1600 the wind often veers abruptly to 185° or even 195°. Thereafter the veered flow continues to strengthen, and on the fleet's return is often gusting to 18 knots within the harbor.

Two Inversions

At Marblehead in early morning the land surface heats rapidly. Inland, in the cool air beneath the radiation inversion, the near-surface lapse rate rapidly rises to exceed the critical level. Heated air separates, updrafts lower surface pressure, and a primary sea breeze flows in beneath the radiation inversion. But by late morning the air beneath the inversion becomes uniformly heated, and the temperature disparity between the hot land and the hot air is no longer sufficient to permit separation. The inland low pressure dissipates and the onshore flow sputters and dies (Figure 22.2).

However, as insolation becomes progressively more intense over the land, separation begins again; warmed air flows offshore aloft, and subsides onto the subsidence inversion. The thermal gradient redevelops, and at optimal low-level entry sites the marine air flows across the shoreline once again. Soon a sea breeze front is again carrying cool air inland over large areas of heated land.

The sea breeze front now deepens, extends aloft to fuse with the subsidence inversion, and restores the high near-surface lapse rate to an ever larger area. The onshore flow strengthens progressively and veers to become the classic ocean sea breeze.

Long Island Sound

Two different sea breezes occur on Long Island Sound: a local morning primary or an afternoon secondary sea breeze blowing onshore from midsound onto the Connecticut shore (and occasionally onto the Long Island shore) and an ocean sea breeze that crosses Long Island and comes offshore onto the sound.

The North Shore Primary Sea Breezes

The local sea breezes on Long Island Sound are stronger than on the Chesapeake because the sound is deeper and the water is, for any season of the year, colder and because it exchanges with the ocean at each tidal change far more water than does the Chesapeake and consequently, with each flood tide, adds a far greater increment of coldness. The local Connecticut-shore primary sea breezes are stronger and more persistent with a flood tide and weaker and less persistent with an ebb tide.

The local primary (and secondary) sea breezes reach their maximum velocity in the spring—when the temperature disparity between the land and the inshore water is at its maximum—weaken in the summer, and are often absent in the fall. The ocean sea breeze reaches its maximum strength in summer—when the temperature disparity between the land and the ocean is at its maximum—diminishes in the fall, is absent in the winter, and reappears in spring.

The Local Primary Sea Breezes

The harbors and rivers along the Connecticut shore provide low-level access to a large expanse of heated surface, and in addition provide high confining banks that accelerate inflow. Therefore, the local primary sea breezes are separate flows, prominent at the mouths of harbors and rivers and absent where long stretches of bluffs block the access of the dense marine air to the inland heating sites. The basic direction of each local sea breeze is the local up-harbor or upriver direction. These are smooth, homogeneous flows with few oscillations, rarely exceeding 8 knots in velocity, providing excellent smooth-water sailing, and rarely veering more than 5° to 8° from their basic up-harbor direction.

On clear days in early morning as the land surface is heated by insolation, separation into the cold near-surface air occurs readily. Heated air in updrafts, halted by the radiation inversion, flows offshore to increase the overwater subsidence. By 0700, the cold marine air is moving along the surface toward the overland low pressure. The first ruffling of the water is seen a few hundred yards offshore, but within a few minutes the disturbance has spread farther offshore and throughout the near-shore area.

The radiation inversion persists over near-shore land and inshore water until, in late morning, updrafts and downdrafts, induced by insolation, distribute the surface heat throughout the subinversion layer and the inversion breaks through. Separation ceases and by 1100 onshore flow typically ceases. If the gradient wind is relatively cool, thermal turbulence may now bring it to the surface.

The Consolidated North Shore Primary Sea Breeze

If the sound is cold and/or the gradient flow hot, however, an advection inversion may permit the development of a larger-scale sea breeze. Radiation inversion breakthrough typically destroys the local sea breeze circulation at about 1000 to 1100 and results in a 30- to 60-minute period of calm. Heated air now rises to the higher inversion, spreads waterward, and once again, subsides over the sound. A new sea breeze (primary or secondary), associated with a greater height of turbulence and a greater fall in pressure, accelerates to a greater strength and veers progressively beyond the direction of the earlier flow. This flow extends farther offshore and consolidates all the local, in-harbor sea breezes into a single north-shore flow.

If a race along Long Island Sound's north shore is started in a light local sea breeze before 1100 and the wind begins to die, go left, expecting a progressive back with its diminution. Following a period of partial or complete calm, when a new sea breeze appears and strengthens, go right, expecting a "velocity veer."

The north-shore sea breeze, if it persists until afternoon, may be strengthened in midafternoon by the ocean sea breeze coming across the sound and amalgamating with the onshore flow. Depending on the orientation of the local coast, the ocean sea breeze may be either backed or veered to the north-shore sea breeze, and the shift that occurs with amalgamation may be in either direction (the stuff of local knowledge).

23. Fremantle: The Primary Subtropical Sea Breeze

*I was born in the breezes, and I had studied the sea as
perhaps few men have studied it, neglecting all else.*
—JOSHUA SLOCUM

Fremantle, on the southern coast of Western Australia, may provide the world's best sailing. The air is warm and bright, the water is cool and green, the latitude is optimal for sea breeze generation, and the strong subsidence inversion provides both clear skies and complete protection for a 20- to 25-knot afternoon onshore flow.

The Western Australian Doctors

The strong sea breezes of the Western Australian coasts are called "Doctors" because they provide relief from the heat. Their thermal gradients and their resultant velocity are directly proportional to the distance they penetrate inland, and their penetration is directly proportional to their opportunity to invade at near sea level (up a river valley or across a low coastline), and to the heat, aridity, and flatness of the terrain over which they flow.

Traveling over hot land, these sea breezes accelerate into the low pressure ahead, their bulging fronts sweeping away the stagnant desert air. The farther they extend inland, the more rapidly they flow and the more rapidly they drag the overwater flow ashore. The peak overwater velocity of the Doctors is reached in late evening simultaneously with the greatest penetration of their leading edges. (See appendix 2, "The Sea/Lake Breeze Front.")

The Fremantle Doctor, because it is able to invade the Swan River Valley through a narrow, sea-level opening in the shoreline hills, extends farther inland than does the sea breeze at any other west coast site. However, the south coast Esperance Doctor holds the penetration record. It races, steadily accelerating, across low, flat land from the south shore all the way to Kalgoorlie—200 miles in 6 to 8 hours—at a speed of greater than 25 knots (Figure 23.1).

Because the desert inland from Geraldton to the north of Perth is hotter and more barren than it is near Bunbury to the south of Perth and because the obstructive Darling Escarpment is lower, the Geraldton Doctor is stronger than the Bunbury Doctor and extends twice as far inland. The velocity of the sea breeze along the southern west coast is also reduced by the presence, only 60 miles from that coast, of land cooled by the south coast Esperance Doctor, which arrives earlier. In late evening in the remote desert at the extremities of sea breeze invasion, only a few dramatic "pulses" of wind may be felt, but they are accompanied by a most welcome 15° to 18°F drop in temperature.

The time and velocity of peak onshore flow correlate with the depth and time of maximum penetration of a sea breeze front.

The Fremantle Doctor

Fremantle and Perth lie on the Swan River near 30° south, a latitude that optimizes the alignment of the thermal gradient with the Coriolis force, on a rapidly heating, slightly elevated near-shore plain that extends from the coast to the Darling Escarpment 15 to 20 miles inland. Each afternoon the adjacency of contraction and subsidence in the air overlying the cold Western Australian Current and expansion in the air overlying the hot near-shore desert (a desert created by the hot, dry, subsiding air in the Southeast Indian Ocean Subtropical High) creates a dramatic thermal pressure gradient across the Western Australian coast. Because the consequent onshore flow of marine air has access to vast desert surfaces as it overflows the banks of the winding Swan and races inland, it draws one of the world's strongest sea breezes behind it.

The Gradient Wind Circulation

Because Fremantle lies in the circumferential subtropical high-pressure belt, the gradient wind of summer derives from the circulation around the Southeast Indian Ocean Subtropical High. In midsummer (January and February) the center of this high pressure lies persistently to the southwest of Fremantle. The strong and persistent Northwestern Australian Heat Low, which develops in the Equatorial Convergence Zone over the Western Australian desert, forces the high-pressure system to remain over water south of the Australian landmass. Between these stable

167

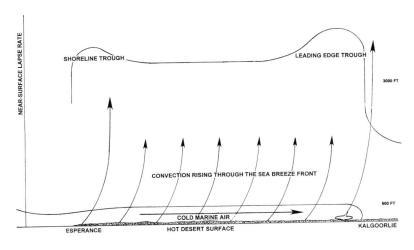

Figure 23.1. *The Esperance Doctor—speed of advance, 25 knots*

pressure systems flow the Indian Ocean's Southeast Trade Winds (counterclock-wise around the Subtropical High and clockwise around the Equatorial Low). Over land this "southeasterly" flow is more easterly, over water (offshore, nearer the center of the high) more southerly (Figure 23.2).

Centers of high pressure pass to the south of Fremantle in summer, and when they move are rapidly replaced so that gradient westerlies and northerlies are (almost) never seen. Except when the center of high pressure is directly to the west (and the gradient wind southerly), gradient flow is from the east (between northeast and southeast).

In summer, over water and along the coast, beneath the persistent subtropical high the upper levels of the atmosphere are subsiding and heating by compression. A subsidence inversion forms at a height of approximately 3,000 feet and separates the lower atmosphere into a hot upper and a cold lower (marine) layer. The strength of the Western Australian sea breezes is directly related to and varies with the strength of the subsidence inversion and the protection from the gradient easterlies that it provides.

The Western Australian Trough

The sea breeze at Fremantle is usually strongest in January (in early summer) and is typically weaker in March (in late summer). But even in midsummer its strength varies cyclically. After several days of 20- to 25-knot blows, its velocity gradually diminishes and for a day or two it may even fail to appear. These fluctuations are primarily associated with movements of the Western Australian Trough. (A *trough* is a dip in the isobars along a track extending away from a center of low pressure, a locus of sites at which the pressure is lower than at adjacent sites to either side.)

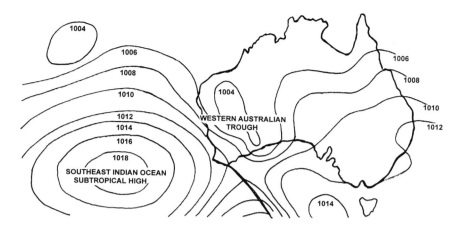

Figure 23.2. The trough of the Western Australian Heat Low

The Western Australian Trough forms as the easterly flow on the southern periphery of the heat low traverses the intensely hot Western Australian desert. When the trough first forms inland, the transcoastal thermal gradient—high pressure offshore to low pressure inshore—is enhanced, and the easterly-southeasterly gradient flow is hot and easily lifted from the surface by the invading marine air. A strong sea breeze develops early in the day, extends well inland, and cools the coastal zone.

However, because the heat and the trough are gradually carried west by the easterly gradient flow, after a few days the trough moves to the coast and eventually offshore. In this position the trough diminishes the diurnal transcoastal thermal gradient and produces a gradient northeasterly that flows in direct opposition to the southwesterly sea breeze. But most importantly, in the coastal zone there is uplift above the surface low pressure rather than subsidence. The inversion disappears and the offshore gradient flow meets the onshore sea breeze in the surface layers. The sea breeze progressively diminishes in strength and fails to penetrate inland. A heat wave develops along the coast, and thunderstorms appear inland.

Primary sea breezes depend on the strength, persistence, and height of the overlying inversion. When the inversion is dissipated by surface low pressure or thermal turbulence, the sea breeze disintegrates or is weakened.

Forecasting

Forecasts of sea breeze development and velocity rely heavily on observed alterations in the depth and position of the trough, but it is not clear which is cause and which effect. A strong sea breeze, by raising the near-coast surface pressure and by carrying cool marine air as far as 200 miles from the coast, keeps the trough inland. A weak sea breeze permits the heat and the low pressure to move west and the trough to move offshore. However, a recent study by J. D. Kepert and R. K. Smith indicates that sea breeze cooling is as important as inland heating in determining the trough's behavior. The movement of a heat trough from the inland California Valley to the Oregon coast similarly determines the strength of upslope flow in the Columbia River Gorge.

An overland near-coast trough enhances the transcoastal thermal gradient and is an important supporter of sea breeze generation. Its depth and movements therefore become important predictors of sea breeze strength.

The Development of the Onshore Flow

Over land each morning, updrafts of heated air break through the radiation inversion, and downdrafts bring easterly gradient flow to the overland and near-shore surfaces. But farther offshore there is no vertical mixing; the easterly—advecting hot air from the desert—lifts above the cold, dense marine air, reinforces the subsidence inversion, and isolates the marine air from the gradient flow. As the land surface becomes hotter and hotter (and the overlying air temperature increases to 105°F or more), thermal turbulence and expansion become marked, overland surface pressure falls, and heated air, rising into the easterly, flows seaward above and below the subsidence inversion to subside onto and increase the pressure over the sea.

At some time between 1300 and 1600, a dark line of ruffled water appears offshore beyond a zone of calm. The cool marine air begins to move across the ocean surface toward the low pressure beyond the beach, lifting the offshore easterly as it progresses shoreward. Oscillations in the easterly's surface flow, over a range of 20° (or more) toward the sea breeze and back, become prominent. Farther offshore, where the two flows converge, both are forced upward, and the surface becomes calm and hot. After 15 to 30 minutes of diminution and veering, the near-shore flow often strengthens and backs (for 10 to 15 minutes) before dying completely. In such a situation Peter Gilmour, by correctly moving left in the dying but temporarily reviving northeasterly (which never did give way to the sea breeze), won a race of the 1982 Soling Worlds.

Sometimes the sea breeze's rate of advance is delayed, and for up to an hour the two winds may persist simultaneously, the sea breeze offshore separated by a zone of calm from the near-shore gusts of the gradient wind. Occasionally, even after the sea breeze has occupied the entire surface, its flow is sporadically interrupted as much as 3 to 5 miles offshore by downdraft gusts of the easterly. This behavior is reminiscent of California's hot, gusty Santa Ana and of the Föhn's tendency to erratically interrupt the lake breeze along the surface of a Swiss lake.

Finally, in early afternoon, the sea breeze front (the Fremantle Doctor—"good for the heat that ails ya") breaks through the near-shore gusting zone, moves across the shoreline, and races up the Swan River. Within a few minutes the wind from the south-southwest accelerates to 18 to 20 knots and the temperature drops to 85°F. Following the initial upriver invasion vast quantities of ocean air surmount the coastal hills and are transported into the desert across the hundreds of miles of Western Australian coastline (Figure 23.3).

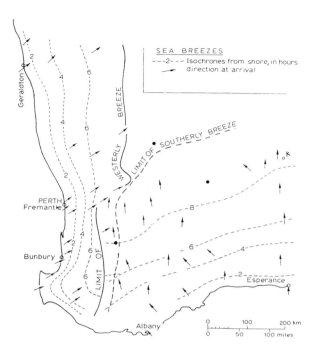

Figure 23.3. Rate of inversion of the Western Australian sea breezes
(From Essenwanger, World Survey of Climatology.)

Offshore at Fremantle the initial direction (between 1300 and 1600) of a typical primary sea breeze is 230° (range 220° to 240°). Its initial speed may be from 3 to 12 knots. It gradually strengthens until by evening (range 1840 to 2230) it has reached its peak velocity, which varies between 12 and 28 knots. As it increases in velocity it backs (due to the Coriolis force) from approximately 230° to 200° to 180° or even 170° and flows parallel to the coast with water on its left. Divergence between its overwater and overland segments further enhances its strength. When the sun sets, liftoff ceases, the sea breeze dies, and a radiation inversion forms overland. By 2300 the gradient easterly, now cool and steady, is blowing above the inversion ashore and at the surface offshore.

A study by C. E. Hounam showed that in summer at Fremantle, with an average temperature differential between land and sea air of 15°F, a 12- to 30-knot sea breeze appeared on more than 20 days each month. December sea breezes tended to be deep (approximately 2,000 feet) as they crossed the coastline, their fronts slowed by the opposing easterly. January and February sea breezes were shallower and stronger; the hotter opposing gradient wind lifted and slid seaward above the onshore flow more readily. In November and March with a 10°F differential, a 1,600-foot-deep, 10-knot sea breeze appeared on 15 days per month. In April, September, and October, with a 4° to 7°F differential, a 1,200-foot-deep, 5-knot sea breeze appeared on 8 to 10 days per month. Even in May, June, July, and

August, when the land was only transiently warmer than the sea, a 5-knot sea breeze appeared on 5 days per month.

Strong sea breezes result from strong thermal gradients in the presence of protective inversions.

The Opposition of the Gradient Wind

Early in sea breeze development, high-velocity downdrafts from the opposing gradient wind regularly break through the overwater marine layer and block the encroaching sea breeze. Strong gradient easterlies producing greater mechanical turbulence, and more unstable easterlies producing greater thermal turbulence, may so disrupt the frontal invasion that the marine air is never able to cross the shoreline.

Studies done by R. A. Wyatt at Hobart revealed that among offshore winds of approximately the same temperature, those directly opposed to the sea breeze exerted the maximum retarding effect. He also demonstrated a direct relationship between the time of onset of the sea breeze and the strength of the offshore gradient "head" wind. If at 0300 the gradient wind was 10 knots or less, the sea breeze appeared between 0900 and noon. If the gradient wind was 10 to 20 knots, the sea breeze appeared between noon and 1500. If the gradient wind was 20 to 30 knots, the sea breeze appeared after 1500 or not at all. My own records from Fremantle indicate that (with rare exceptions) if in early morning the easterly exceeded 15 knots, the accompanying sea breeze was weak, and that if it was less than 15 knots, the sea breeze was strong.

The Sea Breeze Front

If and when the sea breeze front comes ashore to form a Western Australian Doctor, one of the world's strongest sea breezes is entrained in its wake, and this strength is consequent to the character of the front. The cold marine air in the front is dramatically colder than the hot desert over which it flows and the hot ambient air under which it flows. The high near-surface lapse rate within the front causes the liftoff of air from the hot desert surface at a temperature far higher than that of the marine air. Consequently, despite adiabatic cooling, updrafts of this heated air rise clear through the front into the hot suprafrontal air *without heating or expanding the marine air within the front.* Because the sea breeze front remains at its original temperature, the abrupt temperature contrast between the frontal air and the hot surface (which ordinarily elicits a dramatic pressure drop only at the shoreline, where the cold marine air first comes ashore) persists, and because the frontal air mass remains shallow, the marine air is able to race ahead into a leading-edge trough that advances with the front. The dramatic inversion, caused by the continued coldness of the frontal air, at the top of the invading front protects it from the opposing gradient easterly.

The initiation of a subtropical primary sea breeze is dependent on the strength of the subsidence inversion. But once the inversion separates it from the opposition of the offshore gradient flow and the sea breeze front comes ashore, the strength of the overwater flow is dependent on the temperature and character of the surfaces over which the front flows. If (as in Western Australia) the temperature of the surface is extremely hot, the overflowing, relatively cool marine air will readily induce separation and updrafts will rise through the front without expanding it. If not obstructed by the topography, the shallow layer of marine air will flow both over water and over land at high speed. In the midlatitudes, where the temperature of the surface is relatively cool, accumulating bubbles must become relatively hotter before separating. Consequently, they rise minimally before reaching a warmer level, halt within and expand the sea breeze front, and slow the entrained overwater flow.

24. The Sea/Lake Breeze: Initiation

If I take the wings of the morning
And dwell in the uttermost parts of the sea
        —Psalms 139: 7–10

The sea/lake breeze is the most important example of a common group of winds initiated by the heating or cooling of a particular portion of the land surface to a temperature different from its surroundings. Included in the group are the land breeze, the forest wind, the valley and other upslope winds, and some downslope and cross-lake flows. They result from the creation of a thermal pressure gradient between a mass of cold, dense air accumulating above a poorly heated surface, and a nearby mass of heated, expanded air accumulating above a readily heated surface.

A primary sea/lake breeze develops in two phases:

- Phase I: Insolation (by heating the land) raises the overland near-surface lapse rate; causes the separation from the surface of bubbles of heated air; heats, expands, and reduces the pressure in the overland air; and establishes a pressure gradient from the colder, denser overwater air toward the warmer, less dense overland air that forces the marine air across the shoreline.

- Phase II: The overland flow of marine air, the "sea/lake breeze front" (by cooling the near-surface air) maintains the high near-surface lapse rate, the separation, the fall in overland surface pressure, and the pressure gradient necessary to the continuance and strengthening of the onshore flow. (See appendix 2, "The Sea/Lake Breeze Front.")

(Other sea/lake breezes—secondary and amalgamated—develop in Phase I by the same process, but may not [in the secondary type] or do not [in the amalgamated type] develop a sea/breeze front and proceed into Phase II.)

Phase I: The Generation of Onshore Flow

The Development of High Pressure over the Water

Because all land heats under insolation, it is the presence of a body of water that is responsible for the generation of a sea/lake breeze. The persistent coldness of water results in the cooling, contraction, and increase in density of the close suprajacent air, the subsidence and accumulation of additional air from farther aloft and from the surroundings, and an increase in surface pressure. The relative change in surface pressure and the resultant thermal gradient are proportional to the degree of coldness of the water. Coldness is most persistent in a large water body, such as an ocean, through which heat is rapidly dissipated, or in a smaller water body advantaged by the continuous inflow of a large volume of cold water. Deep mountain lakes are usually colder than shallow ones and develop stronger lake breezes.

Tidal changes significantly alter the cross-shore thermal gradient and the strength of generated sea breezes. The ebb tide from an estuary or an inlet spreads heated water over the near-shore ocean surface, whereas the flood tide brings cold ocean water into close proximity with the heating shore. The cross-shore dip in the near-surface pressure associated with the enhanced temperature disparity of a flood tide dramatically enhances the "smoky southwester" at the best sailing site on the U.S. East Coast, Buzzards Bay.

Water changes temperature with the seasons, but at a much slower rate than land. Large bodies of water demonstrate the greatest lag. In general, the sea/lake breeze is strongest in late spring when the water remains cold while the land has become hot. The disparity persists but diminishes in summer, particularly on small or shallow bodies of water. In the fall, because the water has remained warm while the land has become cool, sea/lake breezes are at their weakest. In winter in many parts of the world, water bodies develop temperature inversions, the coldest portion accumulating at the surface (where it exposes the marine air to even greater coldness). On clear winter days when the land surface becomes hot, the local sea/lake breeze may become quite strong.

The Development of Low Pressure over the Land

The initial event in sea/lake breeze generation is the insolation-induced rise in the temperature of the land surface and the consequent increase in the near-surface lapse rate to the level required for separation. As bubbles of heated air begin to separate from the surface, rise through, heat, and expand the overlying turbulent layer, the overland surface pressure begins to fall. A thermal pressure gradient develops between the reduced pressure at the surface of the heated land and the unchanged pressure at the surface of nearby unheated surfaces such as water. The critical change is the increase in the near-surface lapse rate: The overlying air must be or become so cold, or the underlying land must become so hot, that separation and convection become continuous. (See chapter 2, "Insolation: The Atmospheric Engine.")

The Radiation Inversion
Because the land surface is heated by shortwave radiation, which passes through the overlying air without heating it, and cooled by longwave radiation, which, if not blocked by cloud cover or high humidity, passes through the overlying air without altering it, the temperature of the land rises far more rapidly during the day and falls far more rapidly during the night than the temperature of the overlying air.

At night (particularly on clear nights) the near-surface air cooled by conduction from the cooling land accumulates beneath warmer air to create a radiation inversion. The cooled air runs downhill to collect over the lowest available sites. A radiation inversion provides three essentials to sea/lake breeze generation: cold near-surface air and, consequently, a high near-surface lapse rate; protection from the gradient wind; and a guide—after insolation begins—for an upper-level waterward flow that maintains or increases overwater subsidence and pressure (Figure 24.1).

At night the coldest air runs downhill to accumulate over the water and along its low-lying shores. In early morning the contrast between the temperature of the land surface when it begins to heat and the temperature of the cold overlying air is greatest at the shoreline, and here separation begins. Bubbles of heated air rise in eddies and subsequently in columns through the cold air to the radiation inversion. Halted by the inversion, the heated air spreads laterally down an upper-level pressure gradient toward the lowest pressure at that level—typically toward a nearby body of cold water, where contraction and subsidence have reduced upper-level pressure. This movement adds air to the overwater subsidence, increases overwater surface pressure, and initiates a flow of air along the surface from the cool water toward the heated land.

If the near-shore land is low lying, the cold, dense air overlying the adjacent water will respond to the thermal pressure gradient and flow toward shore in an overwater sea/lake breeze, cross the shoreline, and establish a sea breeze front. But because the early-morning onshore flow is composed of particularly cold, dense air, it is unable to rise above elevated shores and is typically limited to harbors, river mouths, and marshes, where the shoreline is low.

Radiation inversions are essential to morning sea breeze development. Afternoon sea/lake breezes regularly develop in their absence, but other generating factors, particularly the response of the land surface to insolation, must be far more intense.

The Initial Appearance of the Onshore Flow
A primary sea/lake breeze appears out of calm in early or late morning. Because the dense marine air clinging to the surface resists being set in motion,

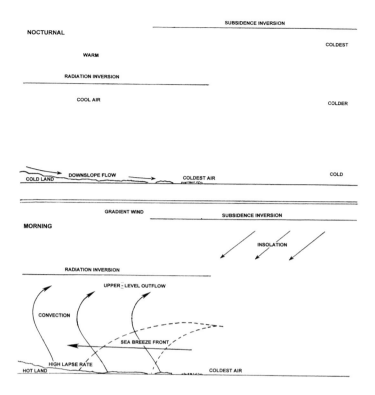

Figure 24.1. The effect of the radiation inversion on the developing primary sea/lake breeze

the first air to move—recognizable in the sails of a sailboat—is in a layer a few yards above the surface at the level of the heating sites ashore. Flow over a low-lying shoreline may be evident hundreds of yards inshore before the first ruffling of the offshore water is evident. Only after 10 to 20 minutes of gradually increasing velocity does the sliding air begin to drag the overwater surface air into motion and produce a dark line of disturbed water a few hundred meters to a few kilometers offshore.

Within minutes of its appearance the line widens and spreads laterally to fill in gaps between patches. Additional air to windward is drawn in, and the disturbance extends progressively offshore and shoreward. Ahead of the line in the near-shore zone, gusts of the moving suprajacent air sporadically penetrate to the surface. The first few gusts, downdrafts of upper air "free" of friction, are often stronger than the subsequently developing flow.

At first the depth of the moving air is but a few yards, its velocity but a few knots, and its direction approximately perpendicular to the shoreline. As additional marine air from the offshore surface and from the inversion layer above are entrained, the onshore flow gradually deepens, accelerates, and veers.

177

Evolution of the Morning Sea/Lake Breeze

Morning primary sea/lake breezes are evanescent because the relatively small volume of air beneath a radiation inversion is so quickly heated by convection that within a few hours the near-surface lapse rate falls below the level critical to separation. By late morning at most inland sites, and wherever no higher inversion exists, the temperature of the subinversion air rises to the level of the suprainversion air, the inversion dissipates, convection ceases, the unprotected sea breeze dies, and the upper-level gradient wind appears at the surface.

However, where the suprainversion gradient flow is very hot (forming an advection inversion) and/or where along continental coasts a higher subsidence inversion exists, the primary sea breeze, still protected from the gradient wind, continues or, after dying, returns. Once the radiation inversion dissipates, the subinversion heat is distributed throughout a larger volume, thereby diminishing the rate of rise of the temperature of the near-surface air. By midday or early afternoon the increasing insolation and heating of the land surface restores the lapse rate to a level permitting separation and again lowers overland surface pressure, the thermal gradient is reestablished, and the marine air flows onshore again in a large-scale sea/lake breeze.

Phase II: The Sea Breeze Front over Land

On the west coasts of continents where (due to cold ocean currents) near-shore subsidence is high, the overlying air hot, and the subsidence inversion strong and extensive, the sea breeze appears offshore in early morning and strengthens progressively, the sea breeze front comes ashore early, invades rapidly, and extends far inland, and the gradient wind is seen only at the surface nocturnally. Despite the dissipation of the radiation inversion in midmorning, the subsidence inversion maintains the waterward return flow of heated air above the sea breeze front but below the inversion. No break between the early-morning local primary sea breeze and the fully developed large-scale ocean sea breeze is evident (Figure 24.2).

On the east coasts of continents where (due to warm ocean currents) near-shore subsidence is diminished and the subsidence inversion weak and limited, the primary sea breeze appears late and is likely to be interrupted, the sea breeze front often comes ashore belatedly, invades slowly, and extends inland minimally, and the gradient wind often occupies the surface in early morning and returns in late afternoon (Figure 24.3).

If the shoreline is abrupt as it is at Marblehead, the overland radiation inversion and the overwater subsidence inversion meet, but barely overlap, at the shore. When the radiation inversion dissipates in late morning, no higher inversion exists over near-shore land to protect the sea breeze front and restore the necessarily high lapse rate. The morning primary sea breeze dies and is not replaced until insolation peaks at midday or in early afternoon and a larger-scale sea breeze front is able to carry its own inversion inland.

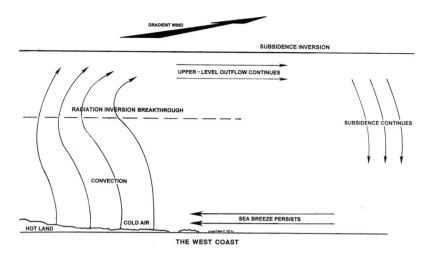

Figure 24.2. The strong subsidence inversion sustains the morning primary sea breeze.

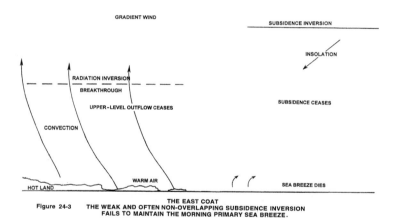

Figure 24.3. The weak and often nonoverlapping subsidence inversion fails to maintain the morning primary sea breeze.

However, if the shoreline is indented by numerous channels between low-lying islands and peninsulas, as it is at Savannah, the overland radiation inversion and the overwater subsidence inversion overlap (as they do on the West Coast). When the radiation inversion dissipates over near-shore land in late morning, a higher inversion exists to protect the sea breeze front and restore the necessarily high lapse rate. The morning primary sea breeze merges imperceptibly into a progressively strengthening ocean sea breeze.

25. Small Lake Winds

Rain before seven, clear before eleven.
—ENGLISH PROVERB

Although both a thermal wind and a gradient wind are potentially present at all times, lakes may be classified in a spectrum from those demonstrating primarily thermal winds to those demonstrating primarily gradient winds. Most demonstrate both, the thermal winds being either occasional (weak, transient, and dependent on the absence of a significant synoptic gradient or the presence of an advection inversion), recurrent (present whenever the gradient flow, either onshore or offshore, supports the lake breeze), or regular (present daily, usually due to upslope or downslope induction, but sometimes obscured by gradient flow).

Thermal Winds

The best sailing is found on lakes blessed by thermal winds, which in summer are far more dependable and typically far stronger than gradient winds. Lakes so blessed are either large, on certain portions of which strong lake breezes are induced, or narrow, the long axes of which, oriented toward large mountains, combine a lake breeze with an upslope flow or receive a downslope flow. The quintessential sailing lake is Garda, in Italy—large, deep, and cold with one end in the hot plains and the other, surrounded by towering cliffs, aimed toward the 10,000-foot Brenta massif—which generates a strong downslope wind toward the hot plains each morning and a strong lake breeze/upslope flow toward the high mountains each afternoon.

Small lakes produce primary lake breezes typically under advection inversions. The likelihood, pattern, and strength of lake breezes depend primarily on the elevation and shape of the shoreline as well as the more distant surrounding topography. A breeze of thermal origin suitable for sailing develops only where the surroundings organize lake breeze flow in one or possibly two directions, where there is low-level access to the inshore heating sites, and/or where nearby mountains induce upslope or downslope flows. Very large lakes, because their overflowing gradient winds acquire the temperature of the marine air, often produce on their leeward shores strong amalgamated lake breezes that provide good sailing (Figure 25.1 and Table 9, p. 182).

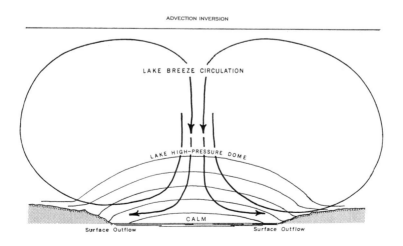

Figure 25.1. Idealized lake breeze circulation

181

TABLE 9: CLASSIFICATION OF LAKE WINDS

1. GRADIENT WINDS ONLY (MINIMAL LAKE BREEZES)	Lake Balaton
Typical Geography	Lake Norman
• Low, homogeneous surrounding topography	Wannsee
	Frisian lakes
	Midwestern lakes
• Very small or winding river/lakes	Prairie lakes
Typical Winds	
• Gusty offshore winds characterized by barrier effects	Kentucky Lake
2. GRADIENT WINDS AND OCCASIONAL THERMAL WINDS	Finger Lakes
Typical Geography	Chiemsee
• Distant mountains beyond near-shore plains	
• Small to moderate-size lake	New England lakes
	Thunerse
Typical Winds	
• Light onshore and upslope flows characterized by channeling	
3. GRADIENT WINDS AND RECURRENT THERMAL WINDS	Great Lakes
Typical Geography	Lake Champlain
• Large or deep lakes	Lake Pontchartrain
	Bodensee
	Lake of Geneva
	Ijsselmeer
Typical Winds	
• Strong amalgamated lake breezes in segments of the lake where the gradient wind is onshore	
• Secondary lake breezes in segments of the lake where the gradient wind is offshore	
4. GRADIENT WINDS AND REGULAR THERMAL WINDS	Alpine lakes
Typical Geography	Starnbergersee
• Nearby high mountains	Tegernsee
	Sierra lakes
• Small to large lakes	Jura lakes
	Italian lakes
Typical Winds	
• Combined upslope/lake breeze and downslope flows predictable as to time and direction	
5. REGULAR THERMAL WINDS AND OCCASIONAL GRADIENT WINDS	Lago di Garda
Typical Geography	
• Nearby high mountains	Wolfgangsee
• Steep-walled lakes within the mountains	Huntington Lake
	Maloja Pass
Typical Winds	
• Alternating, predictable upslope and downslope flow	

The Lake Breeze of the Small Lake

The likelihood of the appearance and distribution of one or the other of the two typical winds—the lake breeze (or some thermal wind of other origin) or the gradient wind—as well as the strength and direction of those winds depends on five major factors:

1. The time of day and the season
2. The temperature, strength, and direction of the gradient wind
3. The geographical characteristics of the lake and its surroundings
4. The location of the racecourse relative to the shore
5. The pattern of wind distribution

In summer in the midlatitudes, because the synoptic pressure gradient is minimal and gradient winds are weak or warm and often isolated above an inversion (radiation or advection), and because the temperature contrast between the heating land and the thermostable lake is maximal, thermal winds are strong and cool and therefore more likely to occupy the surface. Deep lakes (or ones through which water flows rapidly) are most thermostable and therefore provide the greatest summer temperature contrast and the best lake breezes. In winter, because the synoptic pressure gradient is strong, low pressure and its attendant cloud cover negate thermal wind generation, and the advected air is often colder than the water (better able than the marine air to occupy the surface), gradient winds dominate the surface.

The typical thermal wind of a small lake is a primary lake breeze that appears in late morning under a radiation inversion and persists and strengthens into a sailing breeze under an advection inversion. Secondary lake breezes may also develop along the side of a lake from which a warm and unstable gradient wind is flowing.

An advection inversion will persist throughout the day (or at least for prolonged periods of the day) when either the advected air is very hot or the surrounding land is irregularly elevated and forested (is relatively unresponsive to insolation). If the air advected by the gradient flow is sufficiently warm, the inversion will resist the thermal turbulence that threatens to dissipate it. Sometimes, as at Garda, at one end of the lake barren land produces sufficient thermal turbulence to dissipate the inversion while at the other forested land preserves it. Then the marine air moves beneath the preserved advection inversion across the lake toward the reduced surface pressure associated with thermal turbulence.

Lakes (and other bodies of water) in or near mountains develop thermal winds of greater velocity than do lakes in the plains. The height of a column of air of altered density largely determines its effect on surface pressure and the thermal pressure gradient. High mountains provide tall "chimneys," near-slope inclined planes of heated air under lesser pressure than their surroundings, up which heated air can rise to high altitudes.

The best sailing lakes are characterized by the combination of a low-level near-shore plain that facilitates the invasion of a lake breeze front and topographical elevations that generate upslope flow. A linear correlation between a valley lake and the upland extension of the valley aligns a segment of the lake breeze with the upslope flow of the valley. Steep cliffs within a narrow valley channel and accelerate whatever flow develops.

Primary Lake Breeze Generation

Clear nights and clear mornings are essential to primary lake breeze generation. On a clear night, as a result of the radiational cooling of the land, cold air flows downslope to accumulate over the lowest available surface—the lake and its surrounding lowlands—and forms a strong radiation inversion. On a clear morning the suprajacence of cold air to the strongly insolated land surface produces a high near-surface lapse rate that facilitates the separation and liftoff of heated bubbles. These bubbles, unable to rise beyond the radiation inversion (a few hundred yards above the surface), spread laterally beneath the inversion toward the lowest pressure at that level—above the nearby cold water. Here the heated air accumulates, sinks, and increases the pressure at the lake surface, and in response to the higher pressure, the marine air begins to move along the water surface toward the heating sites ashore.

Primary lake breezes develop when the advected air in the gradient wind is hot enough to maintain an advection inversion yet sufficiently buoyant to facilitate separation and liftoff. Secondary lake breezes develop when the advected air is but slightly warmer than the marine air, and highly buoyant. Excessively high temperature in the advected air blocks the development of either type of lake breeze as it prevents the near-surface lapse rate from reaching the level critical to separation. The worst summer condition is high temperature and rain; but high temperature, cloud cover, and high humidity—a hot and stable air mass extending to high altitude—will negate most lake breezes.

Offshore Gradient Winds

Relative to a small lake, all gradient winds and downslope flows are offshore. Those that advect air colder than the lake water will occupy the surface. Those that advect air warmer than the lake will be isolated above an advection inversion and will facilitate the generation of a primary lake breeze (Figure 25.2).

Gradient winds that are but slightly warmer and buoyant will induce a secondary lake breeze along the "windward" shore of the lake where the gradient wind is directly opposed to the lake breeze. A weak primary lake breeze may persist along other shores, but the major onshore movement will be in the secondary lake breeze, from the central zone of calm toward the "windward" shore. Only if the lake is large (when the onshore gradient flow may, by prolonged passage over the water, acquire the temperature of the marine air) will the gradient wind amalgamate with the lake breeze and produce a strong combined flow on the "lee" shore.

The Secondary Lake Breeze

On the side of the lake off which a but-slightly-warmer, buoyant gradient wind is blowing, thermal turbulence over the land will bring its stronger, colder

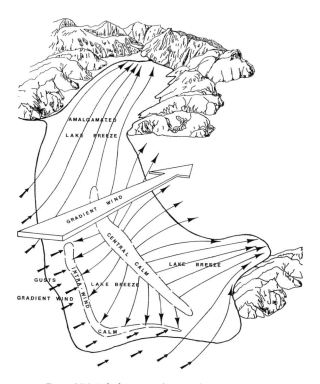

Figure 25.2. Lake breeze/gradient wind interactions

elements to the surface. If this flow is not strong or cold enough to prevent the development of a lake breeze and to dominate the entire lake, its upper-level flow brought to the surface by thermal turbulence may still dominate a "windward"-shore gusting zone.

Under these circumstances the lake breeze circulation is complete but shortened: heated air rising from the land is swept lakeward by the gradient wind, sinks into the upper-level trough over the cold lake, and is drawn along the surface toward the low pressure ashore. But before it can reach the shore, it is lifted from the surface and above a zone of calm, swept offshore again amidst the converging gradient wind. Tongues of the lake breeze, flowing shoreward, will intermittently extend across the calm and into the gradient wind, and downdrafts of the gradient wind will periodically appear in the intermediary zone or within the lake breeze itself.

Wind Patterns on the Lake

In early morning a primary lake breeze flows onshore from the center of a lake, toward the shore, in all directions. The movement of the near-shore air toward and across the shoreline progressively entrains additional air to windward. As the lake breeze front extends inland and its cold leading edge adds progressively more rising air to the circulation, the surface flow entrains air from farther and farther offshore—as far offshore as the sinking in the upper-level flow extends. Over a small lake, sinking (from all sides) will be maximal at its center, where the water is deepest and coldest and where the overlying air is therefore coldest and densest. Consequently, surface flow typically radiates shoreward from a calm central zone and gradually increases in velocity until close to the shoreline, where the maximal pressure drop coexists with the least friction.

This idealized lake breeze circulation develops only on a perfectly circular lake in which the deepest, coldest water is centrally located, the surrounding topography is uniform, and the synoptic gradient is minimal. Because every lake has indentations (across the longer shorelines of which the marine air can more readily reach the heating sites inshore) or is associated with topographical elevations that facilitate upslope flow, the primary lake breeze pattern is typically skewed.

Instead of forming a homogeneous pattern radiating from the center, the primary lake breeze is likely to be a set of distinct flows from the center, directly into the major indentations of the shoreline. On long, narrow lakes the lake breeze may flow in but two directions, onshore at each end or, on a lake with topographical elevations at only one end, it may be drawn into an upslope circulation and flow in but one direction. Large lakes, bays, and sounds may have sea/lake breezes blowing onshore on both sides. Usually topography, or in the case of secondary lake breezes, the prevalence of a particular direction for warm offshore gradient winds, results in the predominance of a single flow, and a particular shore is characterized by having "a good sailing breeze."

A secondary lake breeze creates a series of bands along the "windward" shore; nearest shore a band of gusty gradient flow, next a band of calm, then a band of secondary lake breeze, and farthest offshore the central zone of calm. Sometimes beyond the calm and extending all the way to the far shore is an amalgamated flow, occasionally the strongest on the lake, where the gradient wind again reaches the surface and combines with the lake breeze of the opposite shore. This flow is typically variable in both strength and direction as elements of each wind intermittently occupy the surface.

26. Light Air on a Lake

Straws tell which way the wind blows.
—ENGLISH PROVERB

Sailing in light air on a lake requires finding the side of the lake with the stronger wind. All lakes have two winds—a thermal wind (typically a lake breeze) and a gradient wind. Some have special thermal winds—upslope or downslope winds—that for certain periods of the day, often during racing hours, channel along their shores and require special management. In addition to acquiring local knowledge concerning that special management, the racing sailor needs to understand a few general principles common to the behavior of winds on all lakes—principles that depend on the differing interactions of thermal and gradient winds with a lake's near-shore topography.

Principle 1: Seek the stronger wind near the shore—one shore or the other.

Local knowledge or previous experience may permit the recognition of the advantaged side in advance. One exists. Which side that is depends on the shape of the lake, the location of the course on the lake, and the direction and nature of the wind.

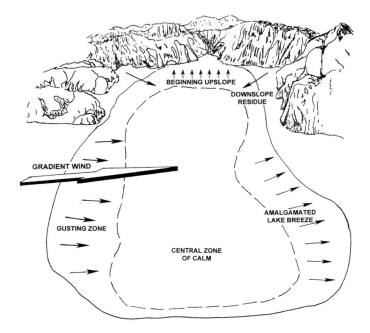

Figure 26.1. The wind along the shores of a small lake

Thermal winds composed of cold air that hugs the surface are particularly susceptible to lateral compression (channeling). Consequently, they accelerate and deviate as they round shoreline protuberances. Lake breezes emanate from the center of the lake and increase in strength as they approach the leeward shore (just beyond which the greatest pressure drop is occurring). Cool gradient winds, downslope winds, or offshore sea breezes, because of thermal turbulence over the land, are strongest near the windward shore. When two winds are present simultaneously, the gradient wind persists (in its downdrafts) longest and strongest near shore. Particularly when the wind is dying, "Go for the shore" (Figure 26.1).

This increase in the strength of the wind near shore is typical of summer. In winter, when the land is colder than the air (particularly when it is frozen or snow-covered), and whenever warm stable gradient winds flow above the surface in layers, vertical turbulence and the near-shore advantage are reduced. Such winds are strongest offshore (where blanketing is minimized) or near a low-lying leeward shore (where lifting is minimized), and require an offshore course. The effects of stability are most evident when the wind flows across the short axis of a lake; the effects of instability (typical of thermal winds) most evident when the wind aligns with its long axis.

Principle 2: Avoid the middle.

There is (almost) always less wind in the middle of a lake. The primary lake breeze begins there (over the coldest water, beneath the site of maximum subsidence), and all unstable winds are accelerated by shoreline effects. Even if the

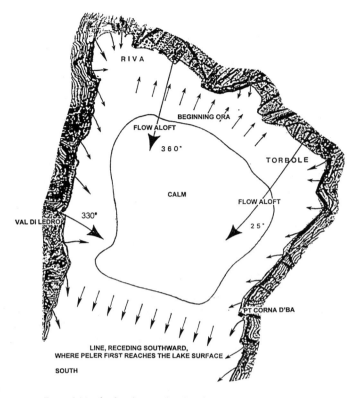

*Figure 26.2. The distribution of surface flow as the downslope
Peler is lifted from the surface by the beginning upslope Ora*

advantaged side (see above) is not obvious, avoid the middle; choose one side or
the other. In light air even the wrong side is better than the middle. When in doubt
select the side that lies closest to the mark ahead. Never cross the lake twice. If it
is necessary to cross the lake, stay on the near side until you reach the site that
permits the shortest and/or the fastest crossing (at the best sailing angle) (Figure
26.2).

*Principle 3: When sailing upwind (once the near-shore course has been selected), "Go for
the shift, not the wind velocity."*
    Within the near-shore zone of relatively strong wind or when you are tacking
toward a windward shore, the gains from wind shifts will outweigh the gains from
velocity increases. Keep to the lifted tack or headed jibe. Watch competitors at the
extremities of the course to detect shifts. Keep to the tack of the boats in a newly
arrived shift; don't let 'em cross you. But don't wander too far offshore. Hold headers
a little longer and tack out of lifts a little sooner so as to stay in the near-shore zone.

Principle 4: Keep to the intended course.

Don't tack or jibe away from the chosen course unless an advantage is obvious—i.e., near certain. (More light air races are lost because of a violation of this principle than any other.) Expect all shifts to be oscillating; hold lifts until the header (finally) appears (unless clearly leaving the near-shore wind zone). Beware of tacking too often—in lulls that appear to be headers or in transient oscillations—because the wind looks better "over there." Velocity variations are randomly distributed; beware moving toward the other fellow's gust and being absent when yours appears. Play the wind and the shifts that you have—not someone else's. If you keep changing course, you could be wrong all of the time; if you stick to the same course, you are bound to be right some of the time.

Principle 5: Look around constantly, but (except to keep clear air) ignore the nearby competition.

Look in the distance for the encroachment of a new wind (in late morning the thermal wind, in late afternoon the gradient wind) or for areas of persistence of the old wind. Dark patches of ruffled water indicate downdrafts of new wind; homogeneous areas, residues of old. Note the attitude of sailboats at a distance, the waving of flags, the deviation of rising smoke. When starting or rounding a mark, use this information to decide which side of the lake will be advantaged. Move immediately from the mark toward the advantaged side—and once committed to that side, continue on that side.

Beware of confusing stronger wind with a lifting shift and vice versa. Recognize that boats in stronger wind point higher and vice versa. Continue into the stronger air indicated by increased crew hiking, angle of heel, and higher pointing of boats on the (distant) leebow, instead of tacking away to get inside in a presumed "lift." Tack away (when certain) from the lighter air indicated by decreased crew hiking, angle of heel, and pointing of boats on the (distant) leebow, instead of continuing into a presumed "header." Sail around a zone in which other boats are clearly becalmed.

Principle 6: Approach the mark from its near-shore side—from above the layline if that course provides stronger wind.

Consider the approach to the mark well in advance. The strongest wind will usually be nearer the shore, beyond the mark and the laylines, and in many cases (due to thermal turbulence) the stronger wind will be veered. The overwater segment of the wind coming down the right side of the lake will diverge from its overland counterpart and accelerate. Thus an approach to the mark from the right on starboard (when this is the near-shore side) is often particularly beneficial. If there is a steep velocity gradient ascending toward the shore, don't hesitate to sail beyond the layline. Races are won (and lost) in Bermuda; at Starnberg, Germany; on Round Bay, Maryland; and on small bodies of water all over the world by boats that recognize this principle.

Principle 7: Keep in clear air when rounding marks. When in doubt, go out.

Come into marks with speed and escape their congestion in clear air. Decide in advance whether clear air is best obtained inside or outside (outside typically at windward marks, often at leeward marks, occasionally at jibe marks, and almost always in adverse current). In light air always pass astern and tack to windward of a group of boats on the starboard layline rather than tack under them. If clear air is to be obtained inside, hang back (if necessary) so as to obtain it. If outside, go wide and far beyond the congestion before jibing or rounding up. Consider holding a jibe beyond the jibe mark until 8 to 10 boat lengths to leeward of a mass of rounding boats (particularly if the second reach is broad), or holding the spinnaker until far beyond a mass of boats congealed at a leeward mark.

VII. *Thermal Winds: The Secondary Sea/Lake Breeze*

Alpena

Chesapeake Bay

Chicago

Long Island Sound

Marblehead

Massachusetts Bay

Milwaukee

Newport

Sarnia

Tampa Bay

Toronto

Anzio

Barcelona

Chichester Harbour

Hellerup

Kiel

Medemblik

Palamós

Punta Ala

Travemünde

Whitstable

27. The Secondary Sea Breeze: Long Island Sound and the Chesapeake

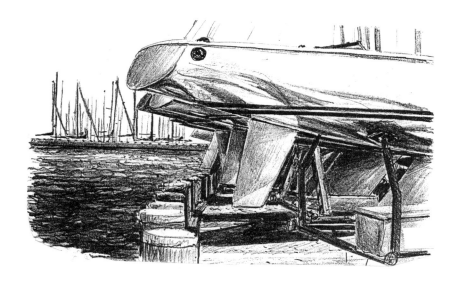

Northeast and clear, three days of sun.
Northwest and wet, three days of storm.

—TRADITIONAL

We have explored the typical circumstances and patterns of primary sea/lake breeze development. We have compared the ocean sea breezes (the Doctors) of Western Australia with the local sea breezes of Marblehead and Long Island Sound and with the lake breezes of small lakes. We should now look at the secondary sea/lake breezes—sea/lake breezes that develop beneath and with the support of offshore gradient winds.

Secondary sea/lake breezes develop offshore from an increasing ridge of subsidence, rather than near-shore from a fall in overland pressure (as do primary sea/lake breezes), and advance along a broad front toward the shore and the converging gradient wind.

Secondary sea/lake breezes are induced by the high lapse rate and deep turbulence created by insolation in the presence of unstable offshore gradient winds —

in the midlatitudes typically northwesterly, northerly, and northeasterly flows. The clear, dry, and relatively cold air facilitates separation and the great height of turbulence results in a major fall in overland surface pressure. The marine air is brought ashore by the strong thermal gradient—Phase I of sea breeze generation is achieved by the gradient wind itself—in the absence of a protective inversion. Indeed, a strong onshore flow may be generated in the absence of an overland sea breeze front. (See appendix 1—"The Differences between Primary and Secondary Sea/Lake Breezes.")

Secondary sea/lake breezes typically appear along south- and east-facing coasts on the second or third (in summer sometimes on the first) day after a cold front passage, when the unstable offshore gradient flow has become sufficiently warm and weak. *They appear only after the development of and beyond a zone of calm.* Never look for a shift from the gradient wind to a secondary sea breeze; look for the gradient wind to die—completely—and then in the calm look for the sea breeze to appear. (Only primary and amalgamated sea/lake breezes appear as shifts in the gradient wind.)

Long Island Sound

The strongest and most common sea breeze on the north shore of Long Island Sound (and at most sites in the midlatitudes) is the secondary sea breeze, the hallmark of which is its development after a period of dying offshore gradient flow and calm, followed by the pushing of both the calm and the residue of the gradient flow shoreward. Initially the secondary (like the primary) sea breeze seems to be a set of separate flows headed up-harbor into each of the indentations in the shoreline. However, the separate flows of a secondary sea breeze soon amalgamate to cover the general area between midsound and near shore, and flow homogeneously in a direction that varies with the general orientation of the nearest shoreline. At Noroton, Connecticut, this direction is approximately 190° to 200°, at Larchmont, New York, 210° to 220°.

Initially the secondary sea breeze creates the pattern of "two winds simultaneously": the sea breeze, a mile or more offshore, separated by a zone of calm, a few hundred yards to a half mile wide, from the offshore gradient wind in its near-shore gusting zone. If the gradient wind is strong and gusty and its advected air cold, as a northerly may be on the second day after a cold front passage, the secondary sea breeze will be unable to reach the shoreline. Downdrafts from the cold offshore flow will dominate the in-harbor surface throughout the day.

By 1300 to 1400, with insolation creating continuous liftoff and thermal turbulence extending to great heights, surface pressure over land falls to its lowest levels. Then, if the unstable gradient flow has become weak and warm, the sea breeze may lift even the gusts from the near-shore surface, cross the shoreline, and rush inland. The overwater flow will strengthen and veer, abruptly with the crossing of the shoreline and then more gradually, until insolation peaks at 1500 to 1600.

Secondary sea breezes, which develop in unstable, northerly gradient winds along "south-facing" shores, such as those of the Connecticut shore of Long Island Sound, are directed up-harbor and increase in strength when they cross the shoreline and invade low-lying near-shore land.

The Chesapeake

At Annapolis, Maryland, after the dying and receding of an unstable northerly gradient wind and a period of calm, the secondary sea breeze appears in late morning or early afternoon as a dark line extending northward from beyond Thomas Point. It spreads offshore and inshore so that much of the western portion of the bay is ultimately involved in the onshore movement. The secondary sea breeze flows toward the western shore, rather than the eastern, because gradient winds with high lapse rates and temperatures only slightly warmer than the water (i.e., northerlies) flow waterward off the western shore (Figure 27.1).

In spring (when all sea breezes are at their strongest) the initial secondary sea breeze flow, pushing across a zone of calm, may be from 165° to 175°, whereas the ultimate, fully developed flow, after incorporating a velocity veer and the bay sea breeze, may reach 205° or even 215°. It is essential to guard the right side of the course. However, later in the summer or in the fall, when secondary sea breezes are weak, one should not commit to the right corner (unless the wind is increasing in velocity and is still to the left of 190°).

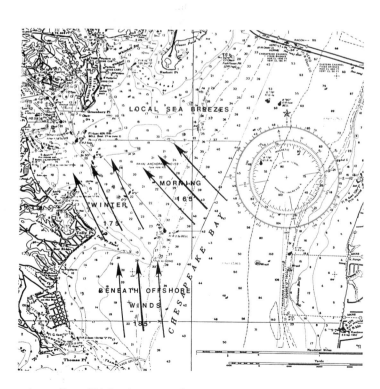

Figure 27.1. Local primary and secondary sea breezes at Annapolis

In summer, when a secondary sea breeze appears on the second or third day after cold front passage, the flow is typically limited to a zone between midbay and the near-shore gusting zone of the gradient wind. The intervening zone of calm often extends across a near-shore racecourse in Annapolis' outer harbor. It is important to remember that the sea breeze comes shoreward in a homogeneous front, whereas the gradient wind may appear in patches anywhere within the zone of calm. It is essential to select the wind that surrounds the mark ahead, to sail well into it, and to bear away for the mark only when well beyond the zone of calm. Boats attempting shortcuts are likely to be trapped for long periods in the calm zone while their competitors sail widely around them.

The Secondary Sea/Lake Breeze Front

The COAST Experiment evaluated (by the use of airplanes, radiosondes, and tower-mounted instruments) a day's invasion of the Dutch coast by a westerly secondary sea breeze front (in the presence of a weak offshore gradient flow) and gained valuable insight into the character and behavior of sea breeze fronts.

A computer simulation of the front, revealed that the maximum energy transfer (from heating land to overlying air) took place as the cold marine air made its initial contact with heated land in the immediate coastal zone. A low-pressure trough formed across the face of the front where the maximum temperature disparity between the cold overflowing air and the hot underlying land occurred. Here the sea breeze front moved at maximum speed, was the least deep, and produced the greatest subsidence. The marine layer, as it came onshore beneath the warmer air mass at 60°F, was but 1,200 feet deep and had an upper-level pressure of 28.76 inches. At about 12 miles from the coast the updrafts rising within the front reached the condensation level, and cumulus clouds made the sea breeze front visible. Thirty miles farther inland the pressure level of 28.76 inches and the suprajacent air temperature of 60°F were still at the top of the marine layer, but at an altitude of 8,000 feet.

Figure 27.2 shows the pattern of invasion of a sea breeze front beneath an offshore gradient wind in the Lower Murray River region of South Australia. This pattern is similar to that revealed in the COAST Experiment and is typical of midlatitude sea breezes. The section is take perpendicularly to the coast, at the moment when the front has reached the zero at the foot of the diagram. Distances from this point are shown in kilometers and miles. The streamlines demonstrate that as the marine air heats and expands, the front deepens and slows. The fast-moving 300- to 500-foot-deep flow of cool air that crossed the coast initially has been heated, expanded, and finally folded back upon itself so as to flow offshore beneath the gradient flow. Fifty miles from the coast the marine air is 4,000 feet deep and is flowing vertically, preparatory to being entrained in the offshore flow of the gradient wind above. Within 50 miles of the coast the gradient wind has been lifted 3,000 to 4,000 feet above the surface, and a 15- to 20-mile-wide band of calm (analogous to the calm recognized as the two winds initially meet over water) separates the gradient flow from the invading marine air.

This pattern of expansion and slowing of the sea breeze front and fixation of

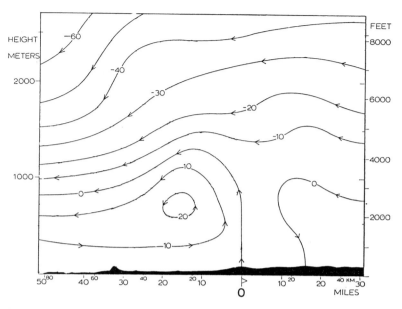

Figure 27.2. Streamlines in a secondary sea breeze front, Lower Murray River area, South Australia
(From Essenwanger, World Survey of Climatology; after R. H. Clarke, 1965.)

its maximal thermal gradient at the shoreline is typical of the secondary and primary sea breeze fronts in the midlatitudes, and is in stark contrast to the lack of expansion, persisting acceleration, and maintenance of a leading-edge trough when a sea breeze front invades across a desert in the Subtropics. In Western Australia the Esperance Doctor carries its cold marine air across the hot desert as it comes onshore—unexpanded and hurtling forward, none (or almost none) of it turned back toward the sea (See chapter 23, "Fremantle," and Figure 23.1, p.168)

Determinants of the Creation and Extent of the Secondary Sea/Lake Breeze

At about midday, if the gradient wind has induced a secondary sea/lake breeze and is similar in temperature to the marine air, the two flows will converge and the sea/lake breeze will endeavor to lift the gradient wind from the near-shore surface. The range of outcomes depends on the temperature, strength, instability, and direction of the gradient wind, and the strength of the thermal gradient. They include:

- a midday, near-shore diminution in the strength of the surface flow of the gradient wind, with no evident sea/lake breeze
- a diminution of surface flow to calm in a near-shore band from a few hundred yards to a few miles wide, but no evident sea/lake breeze
- the appearance of the sea/lake breeze offshore beyond a persistent zone of calm
- the shoreward spread of the sea/lake breeze halted near shore by the gusting zone of the gradient wind ("two winds simultaneously")

199

- the spread of the sea/lake breeze inland, crossing the shoreline and dramatically strengthening the overwater flow (the gradient wind completely displaced [until evening] from the near-shore surface)

The Temperature of the Gradient Wind

Alan Watts, writing about his experiences at Thorney Island on England's south coast, indicates that in the presence of a (sufficiently unstable) early-morning offshore flow, a sea breeze can be expected if the temperature of the near-shore surface water is less than the expected daytime air temperature. The sea breeze air (although typically about 2°F warmer than the water) should then be able to undermine the offshore gradient flow. If the offshore flow is colder than the water and/or very strong and unstable (two characteristics that tend to be associated), it will sweep the developing sea breeze from the surface.

In September 1995 the U.S. Laser Championships were held in Annapolis. A cold front went through the night before the first race, and I told John Torgerson, one of the competitors, that, with the bay water temperature at 76°F and the predicted air temperature at 76°F, the developing secondary sea breeze might diminish the expected offshore northwesterly to less than the predicted 15 to 20 knots, but that the gradient flow would persist and provide good racing throughout the day. Instead, shortly after the 1100 start, as the air temperature rose into the mid-80s, the northwesterly began to deteriorate. At 1230 the race had to be abandoned. Until 1600 the racecourse lay in the intervening zone of calm between the northwester's inshore gusting zone and the sea breeze.

The following day (the second day after the cold front passage) the air temperature was predicted to be "in the high 70s," the synoptic gradient was much reduced, and the gradient wind had shifted into the northeast. I told John that the northeaster with water on its left would be unlikely to persist and that with the temperature nearing 80°F, the secondary sea breeze, as it had done the day before, would undermine the gradient flow. But the air temperature never rose above the 75°F water temperature, the sea breeze never materialized, and two good races were conducted in a 12-knot northeaster.

The temperature and stability of an offshore flow are obviously more important than the strength of its gradient. The first-day northwester, although undoubtedly more unstable and presumably more likely to generate a sea breeze than the second-day northeaster, contained the residue of the warm prefront mTg air that it had pushed to the coast and was warmer than expected. The second day air, entirely derived from the cP air mass, was colder than the water—fully able to occupy the overwater surface.

The Strength of the Gradient Wind

Very strong offshore winds block sea/lake breeze development. Watts's "Rule of Thumb" for England's south coast is that if the offshore wind is at 7 to 10 knots by 0900, no sea breeze will develop. However, in late spring at Annapolis, with the water temperature in the 50s, I have occasionally seen a strong secondary sea breeze develop despite the northwester blowing at 12 knots prior to 0900. The temperature of the air and of the water are far more significant than the gradient wind velocity (unless it is very high or very low). Even strong northwesterlies are undermined in late spring or summer, but (almost) never in winter.

Downdraft Formation in the Gradient Wind

The strength of a gradient (or downslope) flow is not as important as its instability and gustiness. A secondary sea/lake breeze may push an intervening zone of calm shoreward; but near shore in the gusting zone, where overland thermal turbulence is operative, gusts, accelerated downward by gravity, often splash across the surface and sweep the marine air away. Violent downslope flows such as the Tramontana of Italy and the Santa Ana of Southern California, even though hot, extend a gusting zone 3 to 5 miles beyond the beach into a secondary sea/lake breeze.

At Marblehead and similar exposed coastal sites, the secondary sea breeze is composed of cold marine air—the coldest elements (nearest the sea, farthest from the suprajacent subsidence) at the bottom. On the other hand the temperature of the offshore gradient flow, characterized by instability (a high lapse rate), falls rapidly with increasing height above the surface. Into the convergence calm between the two winds the lowest layer of the colder sea breeze moves landward behind a well-defined band of ruffled water. The colder, denser elements of the offshore gradient wind, descending from far above the surface, are able to penetrate the calm only intermittently, and appear irregularly at the surface throughout the convergence zone. Unless the leading edge of the sea breeze has clearly reached the site, expect that any wind appearing in patches and puffs is the gradient wind— and, of course, expect to find more of that wind on approach to shore. (See Figure 4.2, p. 32.)

On Tampa Bay at St. Petersburg, by contrast, the lowest elements of the sea breeze, warmed by its overland passage, are its warmest. Here the warmed gradient wind is lifted uniformly from the surface by the only slightly cooler sea breeze, and dies and backs gradually and uniformly. The convergence zone is relatively free of gusts of either wind. Calm is complete until the gradient wind finally becomes so warmed as to be completely lifted from, or in late afternoon insolation is so diminished as to permit the gradient wind to return to, the surface.

A steady state of convergence calm, dependent on the temperature, strength, and instability of the offshore flow and on the temperature and temperature distribution within the sea/lake breeze, is often reached as the encroachment of the latter is halted beyond the periphery of the gusting zone.

Divergence and Convergence in the Gradient Flow

A fourth factor influencing the extent of secondary sea/lake breeze development is the orientation of the coast to the gradient wind. Strong sea/lake breezes (in the Northern Hemisphere) develop only when the gradient wind is veered— obliquely onshore, parallel to shore, or obliquely offshore—to a perpendicular to shore. In this orientation the gradient wind has water on its right, resulting in a supportive near-shore divergence between its overwater and overland segments. The strong parallel-to-shore northwesterly along the northern California coast and the famous parallel-to-shore "smoky southwester" in Buzzards Bay are examples.

From the Chesapeake Bay Bridge, on days when the secondary sea breeze is developing, one can see the strength of the southerly sea breeze flow along the western shore, where it flows with water on its right (veered to a perpendicular to shore), and its weakness along the Eastern Shore, where it flows with water on its left (backed to a perpendicular to shore). In the fall the strongest flow in the weak sea breeze is often found in a streak approximating the locus of the main bay buoys off the western shore, where the diverging overwater segment of the sea breeze is accelerated and strengthened. The boat that moves offshore beyond the headlands into the open bay reaches this streak and escapes from the disorganized mixture of backed overland gradient flow and veering sea breeze nearer shore.

When gradient winds flow alongshore with water on their right, sea breeze development is facilitated and the resultant surface flow is relatively strong and often strongest in a band a mile or so offshore. When gradient winds flow alongshore with water on their left, sea breeze development is impaired and the resultant surface flow is weak and confused.

28. Persistent Shifts in the Sea/Lake Breeze

Nothing is certain but the unforeseen.
—English proverb

It is the persistent shifts within sea/lake breezes—due to channeling, shoreline interference, divergence, and changes in velocity—not the oscillations, that determine the outcome of racing. Only local knowledge, experience at a particular site, will indicate the advantaged side at a particular time of the day, but in a sea/lake breeze there is likely to be an advantaged side.

Oscillating Shifts

In Primary and Secondary Sea/Lake Breezes

The initial flow in a primary or secondary sea/lake breeze approaching a shore is extremely steady and stable and remarkably free of oscillations. But once the leading edge of the sea breeze front crosses the shoreline, oscillating shifts become prominent. Thereafter, the surfaces encountered during its overland passage induce alterations in the speed and direction of the entrained overwater flow. The crossing of the shoreline by the front's leading edge will induce a sudden increase in velocity and a veer. Each strip or patch of particularly insolation-responsive surface subsequently encountered by the advancing front will also cause acceleration and veering.

The lowest levels of an onshore flow, slowed by friction, respond least to the Coriolis force, while the uppermost layers (500 to 1,500 feet above the surface), retarded only by the layers of air below them, respond most. Some small oscillating shifts and some velocity variations proportional to the velocity of flow are due to mechanical turbulence between these upper and lower layers. In offshore sea/lake breezes, oscillating shifts due to thermal turbulence over land are prominent.

In Amalgamated Sea/Lake Breezes

The gradient wind always dominates the upper levels of an amalgamated sea/lake breeze flow, but a few hundred feet above the surface over water and throughout the turbulent layer over land the two winds will, if of a similar temperature, combine to flow in a composite direction that can be determined by a vector analysis of their strength. On a seacoast (where the two winds are usually of similar temperature) with increasing insolation and a consequent increase in the thermal gradient, the *overwater surface air flow* typically shifts toward the primary sea/lake breeze direction until, when insolation is maximal, the near-shore flow *in the surface layer* is almost pure sea/lake breeze (and almost always closer to the primary sea/lake breeze direction than would be predicted by a vector analysis). However, the success with which an amalgamated sea/lake breeze amalgamates depends on the temperature disparity between the gradient wind and the marine air. If of a similar temperature, they amalgamate well; if the gradient wind is significantly warmer, however, they flow separately, the gradient wind above; if the gradient wind is colder, the two mix erratically. If their temperatures are disparate, oscillating shifts will occur continuously between the low-level layer of sea/lake breeze and the upper-level layer of gradient flow.

Persistent Shifts

Channeling

Straight, unvarying shorelines produce weak sea/lake breezes. The Coriolis force causes the marine air flowing onshore toward, and the heated air flowing offshore aloft from, such a shoreline to veer to the right of a perpendicular to the shoreline. The result is a poor correlation between the site of maximum heating and the upper-level outflow and the site of maximum cooling and the low-level inflow. By contrast, a sea/lake breeze becomes unusually strong when its entire circulation is confined (channeled) between the steep sides of a mountain lake (Lago di Garda, Italy), a river (the Columbia River Gorge), or a bay (San Francisco), and its upper-level outflow and lower-level inflow are precisely directed toward the sites of low pressure at that level (Table 10).

The onshore flow of a sea/lake breeze confined beneath a strong, low-level inversion is composed of the lowest, coldest, densest portion of the atmosphere and behaves like

TABLE 10: THE ADVANTAGED SIDE IN THE SEA/LAKE BREEZE

PORT (THE OFFSHORE) TACK FAVORED

Appearance	Time—back with appearance	Savannah
• Appearance of sea breeze in veered gradient wind		Long Island Sound
Fan effect	Zone—backed wind offshore	Rochester
• Early in a primary sea/lake breeze		
9H effect	Zone—less wind near shore	Acapulco
• Near-shore, steep elevations cause lifting		
Corner effect	Zone—accelerated wind	Garda
• Near-shore acceleration along promontories on left shore due to reinforcement by the Coriolis force		

STARBOARD (THE NEAR-SHORE) TACK FAVORED

Velocity veer	Time—veer with velocity	Alamitos Bay
• The effect of the Coriolis force on movement		
Appearance	Time—veer with appearance	St. Petersburg
• Appearance of sea breeze in backed gradient flow		
Windward-shore veer	Zone—veer near shore	Kingston
• Thermal turbulence incorporating veered upper-level air in offshore surface flow		
Divergence veer	Zone—veer near shore	Newport
• Divergence and acceleration along shore to right (looking upwind) in parallel-to-shore flow		

EITHER ONE OR THE OTHER TACK FAVORED

Successive sea breezes	Time—shift in progression	Annapolis
• Local sea/lake breeze incorporated into larger-scale coastal sea/lake breezes		
Channeling	Zone—back or veer	Northern California
• Deviation of cold, dense flow by topography		Chesapeake

Time = evident with time after onset   Zone = evident in localized zone

water. Unable to expand vertically, the flow adheres to the surface, creating waves at the interface with the lighter air above, deviating around the topographical elevations along the shore. If such a vertically confined flow is forced to enter a river or a high-sided cove, or to pass between an island and the shore, the space available to move the original volume of air is reduced. To maintain the same rate of flow, its direction must be altered and its speed increased. Dramatic differences in speed and direction are evident where the marine air runs inland in a river valley or an estuary, such as into the St. Lawrence River at Kingston, Ontario, into the estuaries along England's south coast, or into the tributaries of the Chesapeake. (See Figure 36.2, p.268)

The corner effect enhances or diminishes channeling. When a topographical feature (a "corner") intrudes into the air flow from its right (looking downwind), the flow turns in the direction of the Coriolis force and is accelerated. When a topographical feature intrudes into an air flow from its left, the flow turns in opposition to the Coriolis force and is diminished. A boat sailing to windward on a narrow water body, such as a river, will find a stronger channeled air flow around promontories on its left side (looking upwind) than on its right (Figure 28.1.)

Near-Shore/Offshore Effects

The sea/lake breeze, veered by the Coriolis force from its outset, comes onshore obliquely rather than perpendicularly. This effect varies with latitude from absence at the equator to extreme deviation near the poles. Therefore in the midlatitudes, port tack will be approximately parallel to shore (or heading inshore) and starboard tack will be directly offshore. *Any advantage offshore will be best reached on starboard and any advantage inshore best reached on port.* (See Figure 1.3, p. 8.)

Due to lifting and eddying, onshore flow is reduced within nine times the altitude of a near-shore elevation. At Acapulco, Mexico, a near-shore mountain to leeward requires an initial move left to escape the near-shore interference with

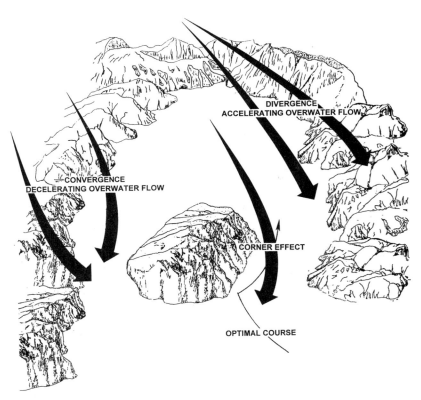

Figure 28.1. Acceleration due to the corner effect around an abrupt promontory on the right of the wind flow

and lifting of the sea breeze. This effect is evident wherever hills line a shore, but particularly in late summer and fall when the local sea breeze is weak and the "velocity veer" less prominent. The velocity on the left (more offshore) side of the course will be greater than it is inshore. Starboard tack, because it leads to greater boat speed and higher pointing in the increased pressure along the port tack lay-line, will be the initially advantaged tack.

The Local-to-Generalized Sea Breeze Shift

Every primary sea/lake breeze begins its flow aimed at the low pressure above a particular site of separation and liftoff ashore, i.e, perpendicular to the nearest shoreline. However, as it increases in depth and scope, it becomes integrated into a general onshore flow perpendicular to (and subsequently veered to) the general shoreline. *Each morning, the local in-harbor sea/lake breeze shifts toward a larger-scale flow.* A local sea/lake breeze that is blowing from the east onto a peninsula protruding from a west-facing coast will eventually be overwhelmed by a westerly onshore flow. Along the north shore of Long Island Sound, the shallow onshore flows within particular harbors gradually shift (back or veer) from morning to afternoon toward the general north-shore sea breeze direction. Primary sea breezes typically shift during the course of the afternoon by a combination of such amalgamation and by the veering due to their increase in velocity. (Secondary and amalgamated sea/lake breezes are oriented toward the general shoreline initially and do not [or only minimally] demonstrate this type of shift.)

The Velocity Veer

All air flows veer as they accelerate, and back as they decrease in velocity. *The velocity of sea/lake breeze flow increases so regularly with increasing insolation in late morning and early afternoon that it creates a predictable "velocity veer."* During this progressive veering the right side provides a shorter course, and at many venues becomes obviously advantaged.

The velocity veer is characteristic of the secondary sea/lake breeze and helps to distinguish it from the primary sea/lake breeze. The initial direction of the secondary sea/lake breeze is related to the general shoreline and is not subject to later incorporation in a larger-scale flow. In a secondary sea/lake breeze, velocity may build from 4 to 6 knots at onset to 15 to 18 knots after the front crosses the shoreline in late afternoon, and this velocity increase is regularly associated with a 10° to 15° veer. Although a velocity veer may be evident in a primary sea/lake breeze under a strong subsidence inversion, it is usually obscured by the shift to a larger-scale flow. The velocity veer is also obscured in an amalgamated sea/lake breeze, in this case by the shift between the sea/lake breeze and the gradient wind.

The shift in degrees is usually a little more than the increase in speed in knots; a 5-knot increase in wind speed from 10 to 15 knots will typically cause a shift of 5° to 8°. Although the total veer for the day (proportional to the total increase in velocity) may be only 20°, in early afternoon when the breeze is building, it may, in a single 30-minute beat, exceed 5°. On several of the courses at Kingston, an initial tack to port and its continuance to near the starboard layline is required because of the combination of a velocity veer with channeling.

In the absence of such channeling, a general rule (with many exceptions) for the management of a secondary sea/lake breeze during its building period is as follows: *Go right in the lulls (usually associated with oscillating backs) and hold port tack into the next header (the subsequent velocity increase) a little longer than usual. Keep to the right of the rhumb line—but, except at those venues where local knowledge requires such a move, avoid the corner.*

The Fan Effect

Early in the development of a primary or secondary sea/lake breeze, an important factor mitigating against the usual right-sided advantage (due to the velocity veer) is the "fan effect." In the morning as a sea/lake breeze is developing, the racecourse is likely to include a near-shore zone, where flow is accelerating onto the shoreline and is relatively veered, and an offshore zone, where flow is just beginning and is relatively backed. If the weather mark is in the second zone and the leeward mark in the first, as it often is off Newport Harbor and Annapolis, *a boat sailing to windward will experience a progressive back as it sails from a zone of higher-velocity veered air into a zone of lower-velocity backed air* (Figure 28.2).

Starboard tack will take the boat to the left, to a position half or two-thirds the way to the port layline, from which a crossing tack on port will provide a progressive lift above the fleet to the right. A "fan" develops as, in proportion to their distances offshore, boats on port tack lift away from one another, with the boat farthest to the left, farthest offshore, lifting and gaining the most. After the sea/lake

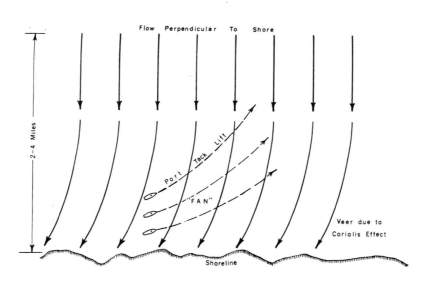

Figure 28.2. The fan effect

breeze has reached full generation, the fan effect disappears or moves sufficiently far offshore that it is no longer evident on a near-shore racecourse.

Divergence

When a sea/lake breeze is flowing parallel to shore, the surface friction encountered and the speed and direction of the overland and overwater segments of the flow differ (in the northern hemisphere). If water is on the left, the two segments converge; if water is on the right, the two segments diverge (Figure 28.3).

Convergence rarely occurs within sea/lake breezes, as they always flow veered to a perpendicular to the general coast with water on their right. However, on one side of an island or a peninsula intruding into a parallel-to-shore flow, water is on the left. A boat sailing along such a coast should, if possible, choose the left side (looking upwind) of the island or peninsula so as to avoid the convergence on the right.

Divergence occurs regularly, particularly where topographic features increase the veering of the onshore flow, deviating it more nearly parallel to shore. The overland and overwater segments of the flow separate from one another, lateral friction is reduced, and a trough—a pressure drop—develops along the shoreline. The thermal pressure gradient is increased, the net onshore flow is accelerated, and the near-shore portion of the overwater flow becomes (relatively) stronger and veered. If, as in the Chesapeake, the coast along which a sea/lake breeze is flowing with water on its right is deeply indented, a boat emerging from an indentation may experience a dramatic transition from the light, gusty, backed overland flow within a tributary to a band of strong, homogeneous, veered overwater flow

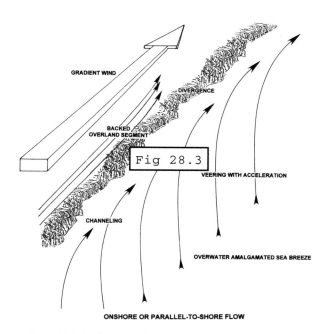

Figure 28.3. Acceleration and veering due to divergence and channeling

in the open bay (see Figure 31.3, p. 229). The effects of divergence are most prominent in early afternoon, when the temperature disparity between the overland and the overwater segments is maximal and the warm overland segment is most readily lifted from the surface.

If you are sailing to windward on a river or other narrow water body with reasonably straight shores and it is necessary to choose the preferable shore, select the right (looking upwind), where divergence will accelerate the overwater flow. If, however, the water body has prominent bends or indentations that are likely to deviate the flow, select the left, where the corner effect will increase the channeled shift. Strengthening due to divergence is most evident along the coasts of northern California and Western Australia where velocity shifts eventually cause the onshore flow to become parallel to the shore.

Near-Shore Veering in the Offshore Sea/Lake Breeze

The offshore flow of a sea/lake breeze that has transited land is entirely different from its original onshore flow: deeper, far more turbulent, and often so warmed that it sometimes flows above the marine air at the surface of an inland water body or only penetrates in gusts. The transit of heated land by cold marine air facilitates separation and thermal liftoff and brings higher-velocity veered upper-level flow to the near-shore surface.

Consequently, an offshore sea/lake breeze veers progressively with approach to shore, advantages the right side of the windward leg, and typically requires an early port tack approach to the starboard layline. At Annapolis in winter and spring the bay sea breeze comes offshore along the southern side of the outer harbor, creating a condition in which one side of the course is obviously advantaged (Category II; see Table 7, p. 130). If the racecourse is close to that shore, a move right to reach the near-shore veer is usually essential. Similar advantages are provided by a move right into the near-shore veer of the offshore sea breeze at St. Petersburg, to leeward of Kingston's islands, and within the north-shore harbors of Martha's Vineyard. (See Figure 15.4, p. 110)

29. Will a Sea/Lake Breeze Develop?

In the morning an easterly glin
Is a sure sign of a wet skin.
—AMERICAN PROVERB

Two different winds—a gradient wind and a thermal wind—are potentially present at every racing venue in the midlatitudes. Sailors need to know which of the two is present as they sail out to the start, and whether the other will develop and displace the first. They need to be able to predict the strength of the thermal gradient and to estimate whether or not its interaction with the synoptic gradient will result in the appearance of a thermal wind. The typical question for the sailor is whether or not a primary or a secondary sea/lake breeze will develop. Although the primary sea breezes of the midlatitudes develop only when the gradient wind is warm enough to be isolated above an inversion, they share the same facilitating circumstances as secondary sea breezes.

Perhaps this chapter should focus on the failure of a sea/lake breeze to develop —because in the midlatitudes this is the most frequent outcome of the interaction between the two winds. "Waiting for the sea/lake breeze" while drifting near a starting line or sitting on the yacht club porch is a major occupation of sailors throughout the world. The initial stage in the transition from one wind to the other is always convergence calm—and if the sea breeze generating factors (indicated below) are weak and/or the two winds are of similar temperature and strength (see chapter 27, "The Secondary Sea Breeze"), that transition may be incomplete and the calm protracted (see Table 11).

Thermal winds such as primary and secondary sea/lake breezes, in contrast to weather-system gradient winds, derive from an almost unvarying pressure gradient and a fixed topography, and are consequently characterized by a predictable time and rate of development, range of velocity, and range of direction. Their likelihood of appearance, distribution, and variation are the stuff of "local knowledge," with which the racing sailor is greatly advantaged and without which he is greatly handicapped.

TABLE II: DETERMINANTS OF SEA/LAKE BREEZE DEVELOPMENT

POTENTIAL FACTORS	Present	Absent
Geography		
Near-shore land—barren, dry	———	———
Water body—cold, deep, large	———	———
Topography		
River or other low-level access	———	———
Flow through narrow channel	———	———
Low near-shore land	———	———
Upslope flow to mountains	———	———

If the majority of these factors are present, the potential for a strong sea/lake breeze is high.

DETERMINING FACTORS	Present	Absent
Gradient wind		
Onshore, veered to perpendicular to shore	———	———
Gradient wind		
Offshore, warmer than marine air	———	———
Advected air		
Low moisture content	———	———
Unstable—high lapse rate	———	———
Temperatures		
Near-surface air temperature over land: 3°–12°F		
greater than water	———	———
Near-surface lapse rate—high	———	———

If the majority of these factors are also present (in the right season and at the right time of the day), a sea/lake breeze will develop.

	Present	Absent
SEASON: Spring/Summer	———	———
TIME OF DAY: Midday	———	———

Fixed Phenomena

- Temperature (degree of coldness) of the near-shore water
- Responsiveness to insolation of the near-shore land
- Topography of the near-shore land (height above the water and presence or absence of indentations)
- Presence of inland elevation

The essential element—resulting in a significant difference in surface pressure—is the disparity between the temperature of the water and the temperature of the midday land (not completely revealed by the disparity between the temperature of the overwater air and the overland air because these are measured at varied, but significant, heights above the surface). A practical simplification is the disparity between the minimally varying temperature of the water and the expected midday temperature of the overland near-surface air. A body of water tends to be colder if it is large and deep and frequently changed by tidal or river current. Land tends to be hotter (responds to insolation with a greater increase in temperature) if it is barren, dry, and flat. Land that is forested, wet, and/or uneven has a far greater surface area and is far more able to absorb heat without a change in temperature.

Once a thermal pressure gradient has been established, a large expanse of low-level near-shore land facilitates the inland movement of the marine air. Near-shore elevations prevent the cold, dense marine air from crossing the shoreline and reaching the heating sites. But elevations inland, by generating upslope flow—beyond a near-shore marsh, beach, or plain—support the invasion of the marine air. An estuary, a river mouth, or a series of inlets into the land will not only provide ready water-level access for the sea breeze front, but will also channel the onshore movement into one or more strong, concentrated flows.

Periodic Elements

- Seasonal changes
- Diurnal changes

In winter cold water is associated with cold land. Snow or ice covering the land will negate all types of sea/lake breeze generation, but often in winter under dry, clear skies the land heats readily and a significant onshore flow develops. In spring in the midlatitudes the water remains cold while the land heats, so that late spring is the optimal time for sea/lake breeze generation. The diminished temperature disparity and typically warm, moist tropical air of summer with its low near-surface lapse rate impair sea/lake breeze generation. Despite the reappearance of cold, dry air, sea/lake breeze generation is poorest in fall, when the water is warm while the land is cooling.

Diurnal variations in insolation determine the sea/lake breeze's characteristic onset in late morning or early afternoon (by which time, even after the dissipation of a radiation inversion, the heating of the surface elevates the critical near-surface lapse rate sufficiently to permit generalized separation), its increase in velocity and veering in early afternoon, and its dying and backing in late afternoon. However,

213

sea/lake breezes that must travel long distances to reach an inland sailing venue may not arrive until late afternoon. In spring off Annapolis in the Chesapeake, a light primary sea breeze may flow from 150° to 165° in the morning, a moderate overland ocean sea breeze from 180° to 190° at midday, and a strong overwater bay sea breeze at 200° to 210° in late afternoon.

Variable Elements

- Land temperature relative to air temperature
- Characteristics of the overlying air
  - moisture content—maritime or continental air
  - near-surface lapse rate
  - stability or instability
  - depth of the turbulent layer
- Presence of a nocturnal radiation inversion

No primary or secondary sea/lake breeze will develop unless the temperature of the water is at least 3°F less than the expected midday near surface air temperature, and no primary or secondary sea/lake breeze will develop unless the land temperature is at least 10°F greater than the overlying midday air temperature. With insolation the midday surface land temperature is (almost) always higher than the overlying air temperature, but it must be significantly higher, so that the near-surface lapse rate (the difference between the temperature of the air in contact with the surface and the suprajacent air) is 3.5 times the adiabatic lapse rate. An optimal sea/lake breeze generating condition develops when the water is at 75°F (or less), the overwater air at 77°F, the overland air at 80°F, and the land surface at 100°F. The land surface is most likely to rise to such a temperature and produce the necessarily high near-surface lapse rate in the clear, dry air of a cP air mass.

It is the instability or buoyancy of the advected air mass that ultimately determines whether a sea/lake breeze will develop. The advected air should be cold enough to create a high near-surface lapse rate and maintain this buoyancy (instability) to high levels (as well as be at least slightly warmer than the water). The hot, stable, muggy air of the usual summer day in the mid-latitudes (because it reduces the near-surface lapse rate) will diminish or negate sea/lake breeze generation. (An air temperature of 90°F or above will negate secondary sea/lake breeze generation along the usual forested shores of the midlatitudes). The advected air should be dry; a high water vapor content will, by absorbing shortwave incoming radiation, diminish surface heating while heating the overlying air itself, thereby diminishing the lapse rate.

When the advected air has a high lapse rate to high altitudes, heated surface air rising within it and cooling at the lesser adiabatic rate will become progressively hotter than its surroundings and will rise to the top of the deep turbulent layer. The higher the thermal columns rise, the greater the drop in surface pressure and the greater the inflow velocity of the marine air. It is not merely instability, but the height to which that instability extends, that determines whether the onshore flow of a primary sea/lake breeze will cross the shore and whether a secondary sea/lake breeze will develop.

Two circumstances in advance of the invasion of a sea breeze front provide deep instability:

1. Continental polar air flowing offshore behind a cold front provides the maximum possible depth of instability (to 10 or even 15,000 feet).
2. An onshore gradient flow of approximately the same temperature as the marine air (a gradient flow whose long traverse of the water has brought it to an equal temperature).

A radiation inversion, developing consequent to longwave heat loss from the land surface during a clear night, particularly by providing a high near-surface lapse rate, facilitates the development of a morning sea/lake breeze and (if an advection or subsidence inversion is also present) promotes the subsequent development of a large-scale primary or secondary sea/lake breeze in early afternoon. In the midlatitudes sea/lake breezes develop in the absence of nocturnal/morning radiation inversions, but to compensate for their absence, other generating factors, particularly the response to insolation, must be far more intense.

The Direction and Temperature of the Gradient Wind

The final and most important determinant of secondary sea/lake breeze generation is the temperature and direction of the gradient flow. If the circumstances (*vide ut supra*) are appropriate to sea/lake breeze generation, four general interactions occur:

1. If the gradient flow, warmer than the marine air, is isolated above a radiation, advection, or subsidence inversion, a primary sea/lake breeze will be generated.
2. If the gradient wind is offshore, unstable, and only slightly warmer than the marine air, a secondary sea/lake breeze will develop; two winds, the gradient wind near shore and the secondary sea/lake breeze offshore, may be present simultaneously.
3. If the gradient wind is onshore in the quadrant veered to a perpendicular to shore, the sea/lake breeze will amalgamate readily, and divergence between the overwater and overland segments of the gradient wind will facilitate the development of a strong onshore flow.
4. If the gradient wind is onshore in the quadrant backed to a perpendicular to shore, the convergence between the overwater and overland segments of the gradient wind will negate or obstruct sea/lake breeze development.

VIII. *Thermal Winds: The Amalgamated Sea/Lake Breeze*

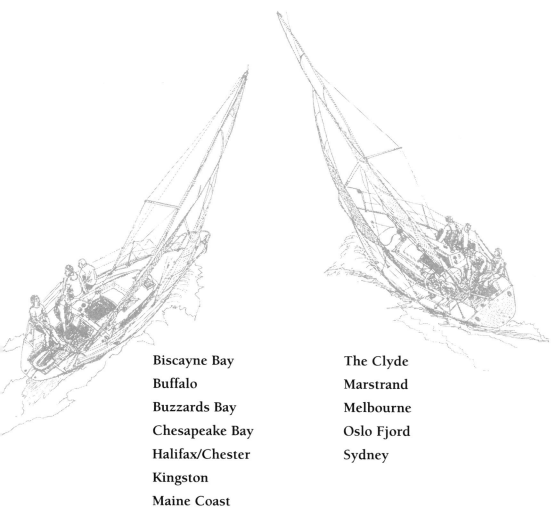

Biscayne Bay

Buffalo

Buzzards Bay

Chesapeake Bay

Halifax/Chester

Kingston

Maine Coast

Narragansett Bay

New Haven

The Clyde

Marstrand

Melbourne

Oslo Fjord

Sydney

30. Kingston

Pitch, pitch, Goddam your soul,
The more you pitch, the less you'll roll.
　　　　　　　　　　—SEA CHANTEY

The third form—the strongest and the most distinctive—of the sea/lake breeze is the amalgamated sea/lake breeze. Sea/lake breezes can amalgamate with any aligned gradient wind that has come onshore after a considerable passage over water and has acquired the temperature of the marine air. But the notable amalgamated sea/lake breezes are those that are aligned with the prevailing gradient wind of summer, so that the gradient wind with which they amalgamate is at its peak strength when the thermal gradient is at its peak strength. This is the situation at Kingston, whose summer southwester will be studied next, at Buzzards Bay, at Great South Bay, and in the lower Chesapeake. All of these famous breezes acquire their strength in part by the thermal turbulence they induce during passage over low-lying barrier land.

Geography

The northward movement of the Bermuda High in summer centers high pressure off the mid-Atlantic coast so that over the northeastern United States and eastern Canada the gradient flow is from the southwest, and inland—in the absence of the subsidence inversion—penetrates to the surface. The pressure gradient is greatest at the periphery of high pressure, particularly where that periphery is confined by the polar front, as at Kingston, Ontario. The strongest southwesters occur as the tropical air is compressed immediately ahead of an advancing low or in the warm sector, just ahead of an advancing cold front.

Kingston Bay is part of a south-facing coast—the north shore of Lake Ontario—and is therefore poised to develop sea/lake breeze flow beneath offshore northerly gradient winds as secondary lake breezes or, in association with southwest gradient winds, as amalgamated lake breezes. The southwester is strong because the gradient wind, veered to a perpendicular to shore, with water on its right, supports lake breeze generation; because its lower levels are suffi-

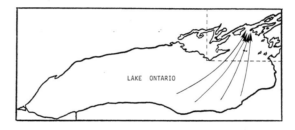

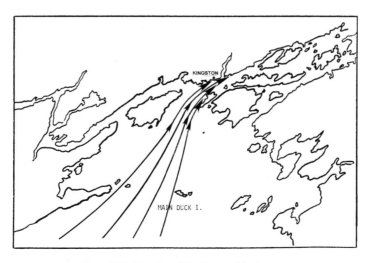

Figure 30.1. Funneling of the Kingston lake breeze

220

ciently cooled by their transit of Lake Ontario to amalgamate readily with the southwest lake breeze; and because the St. Lawrence River provides water-level access for the cold marine air to a vast area of readily heated low-level farmland (Figure 30.1).

The Southwester: An Amalgamated Lake Breeze

The strength of the amalgamated lake breeze is chiefly dependent on the coldness of the lake water. The strongest southwesters appear in May and June, when the water temperature is in the 50s, and the weakest in August and September, when the water temperature is in the 70s. The summer of '95, when the temperature of the lake rose to the high 70s, was notorious for the weakness of its lake breezes. But even then the occasionally precise alignment of a strong synoptic gradient with the thermal gradient (at about 210°) produced strong southwesters.

Amalgamated sea/lake breezes weaken on successive days because the temperature disparity that determines their thermal component progressively diminishes. The Kingston lake breeze is usually strongest immediately after the gradient flow has swung into the southwestern quadrant on the first day of a period of lake breeze days. Thereafter the gradient flow, by bringing cool air ashore—day and night—diminishes the heating of the land surface, and by bringing moist air ashore, diminishes the lapse rate and the ease of separation.

The strength of an amalgamated sea breeze, like the strength of a primary or secondary sea breeze, depends on the creation of a high near-surface lapse rate and continuous separation as the leading edge of the cold marine air invades the heated land.

Shifts between the Gradient Wind and the Lake Breeze

Amalgamation in a sea/lake breeze varies with the disparity between the temperature of the marine air and that of the gradient flow. In winter and early spring, when the gradient wind is cold, amalgamation is incomplete and 5° to 10° oscillating shifts between the two winds are prominent. In spring, when the gradient wind is warmer but still cool, amalgamation is almost complete, the surface flow is strong, and there are few oscillating shifts. In early summer, when the lake is still cold but the gradient wind is hot, amalgamation is again incomplete, the surface flow is weaker, and oscillating shifts, although smaller than in early spring, are again evident.

When the gradient wind direction is approximately the lake breeze median (210° at Snake Island), it amalgamates more readily with the lake breeze, and the perceived surface wind is usually strong and homogeneous. However, when the gradient flow has come more over land than over lake en route to Kingston, and particularly when it is warmer than usual, it amalgamates less well and one recognizes major variations in the strength and direction of the surface flow. These variations represent the intermittent appearance at the surface of elements of the deviant overflowing gradient wind, brought to the surface by overland thermal turbulence, and may be either backed or veered to the lake breeze.

If the gradient wind is veered to the sea/lake breeze, the combined wind is strengthened as the building thermal flow veers in response to the Coriolis force, and better aligned with the gradient flow and with the north-coast shoreline, develops an accelerating divergence. If the gradient wind is backed to the sea/lake breeze, the combined wind is likely to be diminished as the veering sea/lake breeze becomes increasingly misaligned and the overland and overwater segments of the gradient wind converge.

Near-Shore Thermal Turbulence

In midbay and when the southwester is near its median (190° to 210°), because of its long fetch over open water, the surface flow is almost entirely lake breeze with few oscillations and few persistent shifts. When the southwester is backed to the median, the upper-level flow from the southern side of the bay is traversing Simcoe Island. Near the island's shore, thermal turbulence brings down elements of backed, unamalgamated gradient flow, and on CORK's (Canadian Olympic Regatta Kingston) Alpha Course and Foxtrot Course often justifies a move to the left. The same effect may be evident in westerly gradient flow when thermal turbulence over Amherst Island brings down veered high-velocity upper-level flow, and on Bravo Course often justifies a move to the right. At CORK '92, in the presence of a southerly gradient wind, a line of strong backed flow (gusts of the upper-level southerly gradient wind brought to the surface by thermal turbulence) was present near Simcoe Island along the port tack layline and required a move to or above that line. Boats 100 yards below the layline were regularly overridden.

The gusting zone along a windward shore usually brings down veered upper-level elements of the surface flow and necessitates a move right, and an approach to a near-shore weather mark along the starboard layline. When, however, an overflowing gradient wind is backed to a sea/lake breeze, backed gusts of the gradient flow may be brought to the surface in the near-shore gusting zone and require a move left.

Channeling

As the cold, dense lower layers of a sea/lake breeze, unable to expand vertically, are squeezed horizontally into an ever-narrowing channel, they accelerate. At Kingston the funneling begins as the marine air flows from midlake between the 50-mile-apart pincers to either side of Main Duck Island, continues as it enters the 10-mile-wide passage between Amherst and Wolfe Islands, and reaches its maximum as it flows between Four Mile Point on Simcoe Island and Carruthers Point at the entrance to Kingston Harbour. The strongest flow in a median southwester is inside the harbor on CORK's Alpha Course.

In addition to increasing in speed, the lake breeze veers progressively as it bends from the open lake into the mouth of the St. Lawrence. On the outer limits of Foxtrot Course an average heading may be 200°, while at the inner limits of Charlie it is 235°, a net 35° veer! Thus, on each of the CORK courses a net back from the starting line to the windward mark is to be expected (Figure 30.2).

However, because the water surface of Kingston Bay narrows with distance to leeward, the streamlines representing the wind direction are converging. In such conditions, as at Lago di Garda, either side is advantaged, whereas going up the middle is usually disastrous. A header is available as each shore is approached, and on the opposite tack, a lift into the mark. The most advantaged shore is the

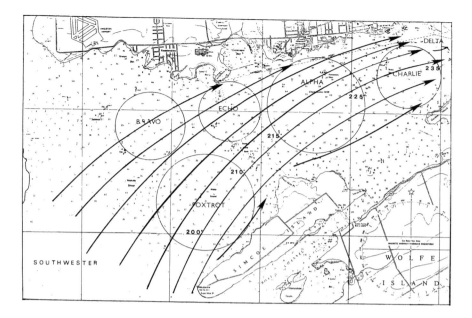

Figure 30.2. Channeled veer in the Kingston lake breeze

one that bends the wind most and/or the one nearest the weather mark, and that does not require a recrossing of the bay.

At the head of the bay, Alpha Course narrows with distance to windward (between Four Mile Point and Carruthers Point), and here the streamlines diverge. On this course a lift may occur with distance toward shore, and the farther one sails from the rhumb line, the longer the beat becomes.

Channeling, because it is so predictable, is the most important persistent shift that a sailor encounters. Its significance varies with the coldness of the water and the coldness of the onshore flow.

Err on moving toward the general channeled back, the near-shore thermal turbulence, the converging shoreline, or the channeled shift around the tip of an island, but recognize that oscillating shifts due to thermal turbulence and general changes in velocity and amalgamation may completely obscure the expected persistent shift during any 30-minute period.

Summary

1. As the lake breeze develops, it deviates the surface wind toward the lake breeze median—205° to 220°. If the early gradient wind direction is 185° to 190°, expect an intermittent but progressive veer to 205°. If the early wind is 235° to 245°, expect intermittent oscillations rather than a single progressive shift, with a trend toward 225°. If the early wind is 205° to 225°, expect oscillations within this range (usually 210° to 220°).

2. If land lies close to windward, expect more frequent and larger oscillations near shore with the gusts backed, if the gradient wind is backed to 210° (typical of Alpha Course and Foxtrot Course in a southerly); or veered, if the gradient wind is veered to 225° (typical of Bravo Course in a westerly).
3. If sailing where the bay is narrowing or widening with distance to windward, the surface air flow will diverge or converge across the entire course. If it is narrowing, avoid the shores (unless 2. [above] is considered more applicable). If widening (which it typically is), avoid the middle; tack toward the shore that converges more sharply and/or that will not require recrossing the middle. Expect a net back with distance to windward, but recognize that this effect is commonly obscured by oscillations.
4. Consider the ranges indicated in 1. (above; for the three basic patterns) and recognize that with few exceptions, oscillations are typical of the southwester, and progressive shifts persisting for an entire beat are improbable. Presume that a shift will persist in only one of the specified situations where channeling and/or thermal turbulence is prominent (such as near Simcoe Island).

31. The Chesapeake's Amalgamated Sea Breeze

Rain on the flood, only a scud.
Rain on the ebb, sailors to bed.
—ENGLISH PROVERB

A portion of the Atlantic coast's ocean sea breeze flows into the Chesapeake Bay and joins local onshore flows and the gradient southwesterly to create a bay sea breeze. This flow becomes prominent in spring and diminishes in summer as the bay gradually heats. Because the ocean remains cooler than the bay, the combined ocean/bay sea breeze of the lower bay and the ocean sea breeze coming directly from the ocean coast across the Eastern Shore to the upper bay persist through the summer. In early fall these may be the only sea breezes to appear. Local primary and secondary sea breezes are evident in winter and in spring, when the bay water is cold compared with the land, but are rare in summer and fall, when the bay is almost as warm as the land. The sea breeze likely to be present, and its behavior, differ with the season. One should not attempt to apply in the spring the lesson learned in the fall.

Sea/lake breezes vary in strength and direction with the seasonal changes in the temperature of the water and the amount of insolation.

The Bay Sea Breeze

In summer, beneath the subsidence inversion of the Bermuda High, the Atlantic coast's ocean sea breeze flows into the Chesapeake Bay at its sea-level access site between the Virginia Capes. However, thermal turbulence over the bay's extensive shoreline soon destroys the inversion, and the cool marine air emerging from under it into the warm southwesterly gradient flow forms a new inversion. Confined beneath the advection inversion produced by the warm overflowing air, the sea breeze front accelerates toward the upper bay and its tributaries (Figure 31.1).

In the lower bay the interface between the cold ocean air and the gradient wind is sharply defined. Farther north the marine air has become warmer and both mechanical and thermal turbulence have increased. Here the interface has disappeared and the flow has become a continuum whose character and direction vary with height from almost all sea/lake breeze at the bottom, through veered sea/lake breeze admixed with gradient flow at moderate elevation, to all gradient wind aloft.

The Lower Bay Sea Breeze

As the ocean sea breeze heads inland between the Capes toward the heating sites, it flows to the northwest into the major rivers of the western shore and turns

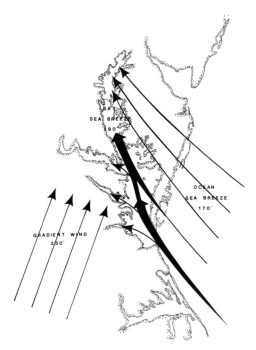

Figure 31.1. The Chesapeake ocean sea breeze

northward into the largest "river" of all, the Chesapeake Bay. It deviates in concordance with the bay's shorelines and even more markedly into its tributary rivers and creeks.

In the lower bay the direct access of the sea breeze to the large rivers of the western shore, the confinement afforded by the subsidence inversion (over the ocean and the open lower bay), and the low-level advection inversion farther inland result in a high-velocity southeast inflow aligned with and composed largely of marine air. But farther north (where the sea breeze and the gradient wind are partially amalgamated) the surface flow attains a high velocity only in those tributaries aligned with the gradient flow (approximately southwest/northeast).

The Upper Bay Sea Breeze

Early in the day the upper bay sea breeze is composed of air that has lain in the estuary and has been gradually heated during the morning. Later in the day, after this heated air has been pushed inland, the sea breeze is composed of ocean air drawn in through the Virginia Capes, far colder and denser than the morning air. In late afternoon it acts like water, channeling around promontories and into tributaries, deviating to become a westerly in some Eastern Shore rivers and an easterly in some western shore rivers (Figure 31.2).

In late morning the bay sea breeze may appear in midbay off Bloody Point from 210°, deviate into Eastern Bay at 235°, and be flowing from 270° at Tilghman's Point inside Eastern Bay. It flows across some of the low-lying peninsulas of the Eastern Shore onto its inland waters as a strong flow veered to 260°. It accelerates and veers as it channels through the narrow segments of the bay, such as those opposite Cove Point and opposite Sandy Point, just north of Annapolis.

The greater mass of heating land, and therefore higher average temperature toward the west and north, exert a constant pressure gradient to the west (in excess of the gradient to the east) and cause the surface flow to turn more readily and with greater velocity into the rivers of the western shore. The bay sea breeze is also strengthened along much of the western shore as the overwater and overland segments of the parallel-to-shore southerly amalgamated flow diverge and is diminished along the Eastern Shore as the near-shore segments converge.

Along the western shore the diverging segments create a significant difference between inshore and offshore surface flow (Figure 31.3). Within the harbors and rivers the backed overland segment amalgamates poorly with the gradient wind and consequently diminishes the progressively veering sea breeze. Offshore, along the main shoreline and the tips of the protruding peninsulas, the veered overwater segment amalgamates well and strengthens the veering sea breeze. The strongest, steadiest wind is typically found in the western portion of the bay, but offshore along the line of the main-channel buoys. Only in late afternoon, when thermal turbulence brings down gusts of the overland ocean sea breeze, is the flow stronger near the Eastern Shore.

Channeling and divergence (as an amalgamated sea breeze flows parallel to shore with water on its right) produce major changes in the strength and direction of the onshore flow of an amalgamated sea/lake breeze.

227

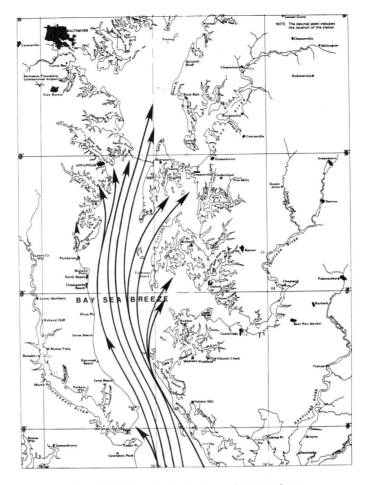

Figure 31.2. Channeling in the Chesapeake Bay sea breeze

The Bay Sea Breeze at Annapolis

• CHANNELING AND DIVERGENCE NEAR SHORE

At the mouth of the Severn River the bay sea breeze turns from its veered-to-up-bay trajectory of 200° to 210° and backs as it turns into the Severn (veers with distance down the Severn). The farther into the harbor and the closer to the southern shore of the Severn the flow extends, the more backed it becomes. An amalgamated sea breeze that flows from 210° in midbay may flow from 165° as it heads up the Severn past the Naval Academy. Late in the day, with the greater incorporation of ocean air, the sea breeze becomes increasingly cold and dense and this channeled shift becomes increasingly prominent (Figure 31.4).

In summer, in Severn Sailing Association's Area "A," due to channeling around Tolley Point and to divergence of the overwater segment of the gradient wind, the

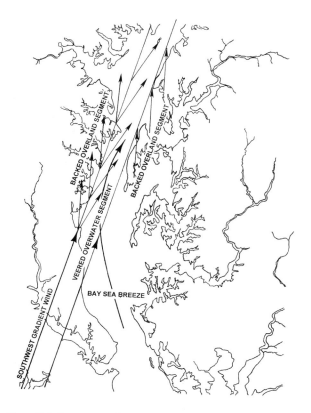

Figure 31.3. Divergence and convergence along the shores of the Chesapeake

bay sea breeze veers with distance sailed offshore on starboard tack and backs with distance sailed on port tack (as the boat moves across the axis of the Severn). In the lee of Tolley Point, where the overland segment intermixes, it is often lighter. The farther to the west ("up-harbor") one crosses on port, the more backed and lighter will be the wind encountered.

In summer and fall (when the bay water is too warm for the local sea breeze to be operative) starboard tack from the start or the leeward mark is usually preferred, chiefly because it avoids the detrimental channeled back to the right. An initial move left also takes the boat toward the stronger divergent air of the overwater segment in which it can point higher. The only time that this plan is clearly wrong is in the presence of a strong flood tide, when a move offshore takes the boat into stronger adverse current.

• CHANNELING OFFSHORE

Farther offshore at Annapolis the racing area is characterized by shorelines converging with distance to windward (the bay narrows opposite Tolley and Thomas Points). The bay sea breeze in summer and the ocean sea breeze in fall are therefore diverging with distance to leeward, and a boat sailing toward either

229

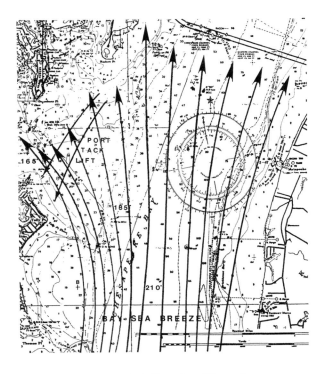

Figure 31.4. Channeling off Annapolis

shore will find, with distance from the rhumb line, a progressive lift on each tack.

The rule for shorelines converging to windward is "Stick to the rhumb line, avoid the course-lengthening lifts near the laylines (see Figure 15.3, p. 110)." At Annapolis, because the course is far closer to the western shore, this means one should go out (left) on starboard (just as it does on the inshore course) so as to stay closer to the bay's centerline and to avoid the lift inside Annapolis Roads. It is impressive that this channeled shift and the need to go left become progressively more evident as the afternoon progresses and the bay sea breeze becomes increasingly composed of cold, dense ocean air.

The Ocean Sea Breeze

In addition to entering the bay between the Virginia Capes at sea level, the ocean sea breeze crosses the Eastern Shore peninsula as a sea breeze front and comes offshore onto the upper bay. The speed of advance of a sea breeze front across flat, insolated land into the low-pressure trough across its leading edge is far greater than that of the same front advancing over water. Because of this rapid advance, and because the distance across the Eastern Shore is less than half the distance from the southern to the northern bay, the overland ocean sea breeze often arrives in the northern Chesapeake several hours ahead of the bay sea breeze (Figure 31.5).

At Annapolis in spring and early summer the morning local primary sea breeze typically flows from 165°. At about noon or slightly later, a veer to 185° with an increase in velocity heralds the arrival of the ocean sea breeze coming offshore onto the bay from the Eastern Shore. Later (between 1300 and 1500) the bay sea breeze comes up the bay, and the surface wind increases in speed and veers farther, to 210° or even 215°. During the Spring Soling Bowl of 1993 in late April, it paid to go right on every one of six beats, as the 10-knot local sea breeze at 165° was intermittently but progressively replaced by the 14- to 15-knot ocean sea breeze at 185° that, with the incorporation of the bay sea breeze, veered intermittently but progressively to 215° thereafter. Veering is always proportional to velocity and so is greater in spring, when the ocean and bay are cold, and less in summer and fall.

Due to thermal turbulence over land, the ocean sea breeze is typically strongest within the rivers of the Eastern Shore and stronger on the eastern side of the bay than on the western side. In spring and fall in buoyant cP air, the ocean sea breeze front may appear as a gusty 8- to 12-knot flow from 140° to 160° as early as noon on the rivers of the Eastern Shore, whereas the Chesapeake Bay is still a glassy calm. In summer in moist, stable mTg air, advancing at a slow 10 to 12 knots, the front often does not come offshore onto the Chesapeake and cross to Annapolis until 1600. Then it is often recognized as an "anchor breeze," appearing in late afternoon immediately after the race committee, for lack of wind, cancels racing. From the gusting zone off the Eastern Shore, it backs with distance toward the western shore (veers with distance to windward).

An offshore sea breeze is strongest, most veered, most subject to channeling, and most variable in strength and direction in the gusting zone near the windward shore.

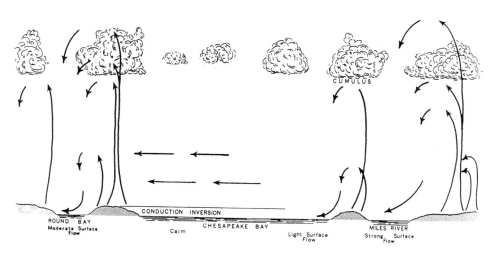

Figure 31.5. The progress of the ocean sea breeze front

IX. Thermal Winds: The Offshore Sea/Lake Breeze

32. Long Island Sound's Ocean Sea Breeze

When the wind is in the east,
The weather's not fit for man nor beast.
—ENGLISH PROVERB

Sea/lake breezes are onshore flows, and the sailor typically meets them prior to their reaching shore. However, because their sea breeze fronts are able to invade so far inland, they are often found on inland waters as offshore sea breezes. Here they are extremely turbulent, gusty, and shifty flows much more akin to offshore northerly gradient winds than to typical sea/lake breezes.

We now turn to one of the most famous of all yachting breezes, the ocean sea breeze, which, after transiting Long Island, comes offshore onto Long Island Sound, without which Long Island Sound would be an impossible sailing venue and within which some of the world's most famous sailors have learned their skills.

On Long Island's south coast, the strongest sea breezes occur in spring and summer in association with the subsidence inversion and southwesterly winds in the northwest periphery of the Bermuda High. Most are primary sea breezes facilitated by the protective overlap of the subsidence and nocturnal radiation inversions.

But along the south shore of Long Island, gradient winds over a range of 175° to 200° approach from over water, are relatively cool, and often amalgamate with the ocean sea breeze.

Long Island Sound's ocean sea breeze is the sea breeze front of Long Island's south coast sea breeze, a deep mass of cool, moist marine air that has traversed, in 3 to 4 hours, 20 to 30 miles of heated Long Island before sliding off its north shore onto the sound. In many respects it behaves more like an offshore gradient wind than a sea breeze. As it comes offshore onto the sound, it is a strong, turbulent mixture of upper and lower-level marine air, much stronger than the onshore portion of the Atlantic Ocean sea breeze, much warmer than the ocean, and as much as 2,000 feet deep.

The Transit of the Island

The best summer sailing on the U.S. East Coast is available in places like Buzzards Bay, where inshore of the Elizabeth Islands the afternoon sea breeze is typically 8 to 10 knots stronger and as much as 20° veered to the wind over the ocean outside. Enhancement of surface flow by interposed land is characteristic of most of the great sea breeze venues—Barnegat Bay, San Francisco Bay, Galveston Bay—and strong, veered flow is characteristic of many sheltered harbors along ocean coasts—Marblehead Harbor, Newport Harbor, Boothbay Harbor, Edgartown, Hampton Roads.

The low, sandy barrier islands interposed in the onshore air flow produce a similar enhancement of sea breeze flow on Great South Bay and other inshore waters along the ocean coast of Long Island. The barren, sandy strips extend the radiation inversion offshore, and the inland bays extend the subsidence inversion inshore. Protected by the overlapping inversions, the cold ocean air flows readily across the barrier beaches. Once the sea breeze surmounts those heated surfaces, updrafts rise into the marine air and induce the descent of strong, veered gusts onto the south-shore bays. This mixed flow accelerates across the inland waters, and because of its acquired instability, rises more readily onto the main Long Island shore.

Within a few minutes of the marine air's crossing the shoreline (usually between 0900 and 1000), the sea breeze front is marching inland. In summer and fall it is coming offshore onto the harbors that cut deeply into the north shore of Long Island by 1130, and by 1400 it is offshore on the sound (Figure 32.1).

As the sea breeze front overflows rolling vegetated hills rather than a hot desert, updrafts—cooler at the time of separation—rise only to the top of and accumulate within the marine layer. The sea breeze front warms and expands and the inversion level rises. The entire front slows, its lowest levels in contact with the irregular surface slow most of all, and its upper levels pile up and bulge forward.

As the front comes off the Long Island shore, its low-level flow is slowed and backed relative to the flow that came onshore from Great South Bay, but 2,000 feet up and several miles ahead of its surface flow, its higher-velocity leading elements are stronger and veered. Updrafts rising into the bulging leading edge bring strong veered downdrafts splashing across the surface long before the backed surface

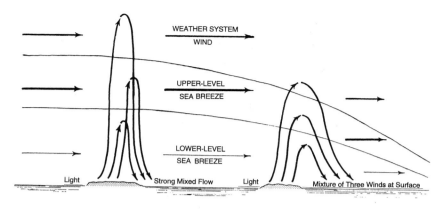

WEATHER SYSTEM
WIND

UPPER-LEVEL
SEA BREEZE

LOWER-LEVEL
SEA BREEZE

Light   Strong Mixed Flow   Light   Mixture of Three Winds at Surface

Figure 32.1. The effects of thermal turbulence

flow arrives. The initial veered gusting phase that heralds the ocean sea breeze's appearance on the sound may precede the arrival of the (relatively) steady backed surface flow by 10 or more minutes.

The passage over land (other than a desert) of a sea breeze front typically converts it from a shallow, relatively homogeneous, stable flow into a deep, turbulent, unstable one. As it comes offshore onto an inland water body, it creates a gusting zone where veered downdrafts impact the surface and produce marked variations in wind speed and direction.

The Transit of the Sound: Three Possible Outcomes

1. If the gradient wind is opposed or perpendicular to, and cooler and stronger than, the heated ocean sea breeze, it may dominate the central sound and may prevent the sea breeze from spreading beyond the near-Long Island shore surface (resulting in "two winds simultaneously"). This pattern may include a zone of calm or markedly diminished flow persistently separating the two winds, the ocean sea breeze extending a mile or two north of Long Island and the gradient wind present at the surface farther offshore.

2. If the typical southwesterly or westerly gradient wind is approximately aligned with, but weaker and warmer than, the ocean sea breeze, the gradient flow will be lifted from the surface of the sound as the sea breeze comes offshore. Then the momentum of the ocean sea breeze front carries it to midsound, where it may amalgamate with the local marine air and strengthen the north-shore sea breeze. The resultant pattern is a zone of gusty and veered ocean sea breeze near the Long Island shore, a midsound zone of backed and diminished ocean sea breeze, and along the Connecticut shore, a zone of strong and veered combined (local and ocean) sea breeze.

Secondary ocean (and local north-shore) sea breezes associated with northerly gradient winds create a variation of this pattern. If the opposing gradient flow is strong and almost as cold as the ocean water, the ocean sea breeze may be excluded from all but its gusting zone along the Long Island shore. A separate north-shore secondary sea breeze may also develop from midsound northward but be excluded from a near-north shore gusting zone by the gradient flow. While the boats near Buoy 32A in the middle of the sound drift and slat, those within Oyster Bay (on the northwest shore of Long Island) may be roaring along in a 15-knot ocean sea breeze. Simultaneously, boats off the Connecticut shore may be enjoying good racing in a local north-shore sea breeze, while others within the Connecticut harbors are sailing in the gusts of an offshore northerly gradient!

3. When the gradient wind is southerly and well amalgamated with the ocean sea breeze, the flow marches across the sound, amalgamates with the diverging north-shore sea breeze, and a strong homogeneous amalgamated flow occupies the entire sound. But even then the strongest flow is found near either shore, the least in the middle.

Long Island Sound acts like a huge lake, over which the ocean sea breeze behaves like a cool, unstable gradient wind. A gusting zone typically extends several miles off the "windward" Long Island shore into a band of reduced wind (or calm) in midsound, while near the "leeward" Connecticut shore the local and the ocean sea breeze may amalgamate to produce a strong homogeneous flow.

The Spread of the Ocean Sea Breeze

In the Harbors of Long Island's North Shore

Within Oyster Bay and the other north-shore harbors, the surface flow is composed entirely of ocean sea breeze—veered gusts from the upper levels and backed lulls from the lower—all of which is channeled by the high surrounding banks. Air flowing northward up Oyster Bay itself is channeled into a general flow from about 185°. As this air accelerates out from the bay into the sound, it produces a localized back in the usual midsound 200° to 210° ocean sea breeze flow. When the racecourse approaches the south shore in this vicinity, a zone of stronger backed wind at about 185° may be encountered. As one sails home from a midsound race, the wind backs with distance toward and into Oyster Bay and then veers abruptly as the cold, dense surface flow emerging around Centre Island is encountered.

In the Sound along the Long Island Shore

Off Oyster Bay when the gradient wind is southwesterly or westerly, the first gusts of the ocean sea breeze appear at approximately 220°. These downdrafts of upper-level flow are veered to the later-arriving lower-level flow, but are typically backed to the preexisting gradient wind. They spread out from the Long Island shore and appear initially (at about 1500) near or beyond the port tack layline (Figure 32.2).

Isolated gusts are soon replaced by surges of increasingly backed surface air. Patches of stronger air and protracted "holes" associated with oscillating shifts, often veered in the let-ups (the original gradient wind), backed in the surges (the sea breeze gusts), persist until the leading edge of the relatively homogeneous surface

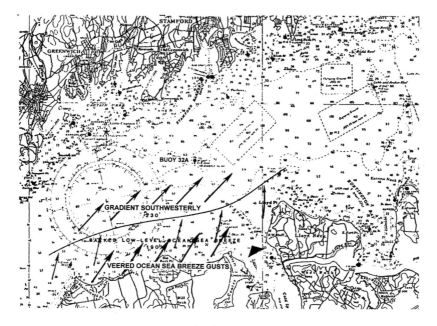

Figure 32.2. The offshore ocean sea breeze

sea breeze flow finally arrives. This flow, retarded by the friction of the Long Island land surface, is backed even more (up to 30°). During the first 30 minutes after the first appearance of the sea breeze gusts, it pays to keep moving left, each succeeding line of new wind being progressively further backed—often to as far left as 190°.

In spring or during a flood tide the ocean sea breeze, heated by its transit of Long Island, may be unable to penetrate the cold, dense air at the sound's surface. Despite the presence of a strong gusty flow above both shores and within the harbors, the ocean sea breeze will cross the calm sound above a low-level conduction inversion. Sometimes the surface flow will come and go with the tide, increasing on the Connecticut shore as the cold flood enhances the local sea breeze and diminishing on the Long Island shore as it prevents the warmed ocean sea breeze from reaching the surface.

Along the Connecticut Shore

Once the ocean sea breeze leaves the Long Island shore, only its momentum forces it onward and beyond the gusting zone. Its lower levels, warmed by passage across Long Island and devoid of downdraft gusts, penetrate the sound's dense marine air with difficulty. Consequently the strength of the surface flow decreases with distance from the Long Island shore and in midsound is always much reduced. However, if its momentum carries it across midsound, it will be entrained within the north-shore sea breeze as that flow accelerates (diverges) onto the north shore.

Off the Connecticut shore, the ocean sea breeze (if it is able to cross the sound) will appear at about 1500 to 1530 as an abrupt shift in a local sea breeze or a westerly gradient wind toward 190° to 200°. This shift may be heralded by a diminution of the preexisting wind flow and appear as a sharp line of new wind approaching from the south or as a more gradual, but progressive, back in a strong wind flow. The former pattern is more common in fall and with an ebb tide (when the sound is warmer), the latter in spring and with a flood tide (when the sound is colder).

As the sea breeze front moves beyond its gusting zone, the warmed flow reaches the cold surface of the sound with increasing difficulty until, beyond midsound, it is entrained within the local north-shore sea breeze.

33. The Offshore Sea Breeze at St. Petersburg and Charlotte Harbor

When inland fly the gulls,
Onshore flows the storm.
—TRADITIONAL

Winter, with its cold water and relatively hot land, is associated with strong sea breezes at many sites along Florida's coasts. Amalgamated sea breezes develop along the east coast, where the onshore flow aligns with the common southerly gradient flows, whereas along the west coast, where onshore flow lifts unstable easterlies from the surface, secondary sea breezes are common.

Behind a cold front, as it sweeps south to cross the Florida peninsula, the sea breeze reinforces the northwesterlies along the west coast and diminishes them along the east coast. A day or so after cold front passage, northerlies on the east coast, with water on their left, are a fluky mixture of their overland and overwater segments; but on the west coast, with water on their right, they are strong and persistent. Once the gradient wind is in the northeast or east, secondary sea breezes are common on both coasts. By the time the gradient has shifted to the southeast or south, secondary sea breezes are a certainty on the west coast, and amalgamated ones on the east coast. On Biscayne Bay a southwesterly readily amalgamates with the sea breeze and produces the strongest of its winter winds; on Tampa Bay the same flow will be lifted from the surface and replaced by a secondary sea breeze.

A secondary sea breeze requires that a gradient wind blow from land to sea, that it be unstable enough to create a high near-surface lapse rate, and that it be (or become) warmer than the offshore water and the marine air. Secondary sea breezes do not appear along Florida's west coast, at St. Petersburg and Charlotte Harbor, until the gradient wind shifts into the northeast (to come offshore) and is so warmed (at least late in the day) after crossing Florida that it exceeds the 50° to 60°F winter temperature of the gulf.

During daylight hours when a gradient wind is flowing offshore, three zones develop. The strongest surface wind is in a zone beginning 5 to 20 miles offshore. The next strongest is in a zone several miles inland, where its near-surface flow is diminished by friction. Between these two zones the sea breeze reduces or replaces the gradient flow. On bays and sounds inshore of the barrier islands, the gradient wind is always diminished and in early afternoon is regularly replaced by an offshore secondary sea breeze. When the secondary sea breeze develops, it extends only a few miles into the gulf (where it is separated from the gradient wind by a narrow zone of calm or fluky offshore flow paralleling the coast). As it flows over the low-lying barrier islands, it accelerates and reaches its maximum velocity on the inland bays.

The west coast of Florida illustrates three important characteristics of the offshore secondary sea breeze:
1. Its pattern of convergence is dependent on the surface over which it meets the gradient wind.
2. The portion(s) that comes over land accelerate, veer, and appear at inland sites earlier than the portion(s) that comes over water.
3. The overwater mixing of its overland and overwater portions cause its strength and direction to vary with proximity to shore.

Tampa Bay

Sea Breeze Invasion

The secondary sea breeze will appear on Tampa Bay if the sky to the east (over the mainland) is clear except for low cumulus, the air temperature exceeds the water temperature (but not by too much), and the strength of the gradient flow is less than 10 to 12 knots. Cumulus clouds forming in the unstable gradient wind over the peninsula to the west usually indicate that an insolation-induced reduction in overland pressure will soon draw a sea breeze onto the gulf beaches. (See appendix 2, "The Sea/Lake Breeze Front.")

The sea breeze front, as it comes onshore over the lower peninsula, accelerates, causes divergence and subsidence, and melts the preexistent cumuli in the gradient flow. Behind the front, updrafts—limited by the inversion lid confining the marine air—cease to form cumulus cloud. A sharp demarcation between clear sky and cumulus formation develops. Dave Ellis says that the movement of the cumuli (ahead of the advancing front) to the north of the downtown Hilton Hotel indicates that the sea breeze, coming across low land just to the south of town, will soon appear on Tampa Bay.

After a period of markedly diminished, backed, and fluky gradient flow and/or a period of calm, signs that indicate the imminent arrival of the sea breeze are very clear skies above the peninsula, the presence of small nonbiting flies and other insects (forced offshore by the advancing sea breeze front and caught between it and the gradient flow), and sea birds rising. Next, flags, the windsock at the St. Petersburg airport, and sailboats near shore demonstrate the actual presence of wind—and within minutes the breeze spreads across the bay.

Convergence

The temperatures of both the secondary sea breeze, as it transits the St. Petersburg peninsula en route from the gulf to Tampa Bay, and the gradient flow, as it transits the Florida peninsula, are increased to varying degrees by the insolation of the underlying land. Consequent to this varied heating (as well as their initial differences), the sea breeze may emerge onto Tampa Bay cooler, at the same temperature, or warmer than the offshore gradient wind that it opposes. If overland warming raises the temperature of the marine air to that of the gradient wind, Tampa Bay will be the scene of a convergence calm that may persist all afternoon.

Usually (by late morning or early afternoon), the offshore gradient wind has been so warmed by its overland passage that it begins to separate from the cool surface of Tampa Bay. The upper levels of the gradient wind (from a few hundred to a thousand feet above the surface) rise above the cooler bay air and continue their trajectory above the sea breeze front. But the gulf sea breeze approaching Tampa Bay across the St. Petersburg peninsula has also been warmed by its transit of land, and its lowest layers are its warmest. Instead of the marine air undermining the warmed gradient wind, the two surface flows converge for a protracted period over a wide area of the bay. The gradient wind gradually recedes eastward as its veered upper levels are displaced aloft. The residual surface flow is now composed exclusively of lower-velocity lower-level gradient wind, and backs (in response to the Coriolis force) often abruptly and homogeneously (Figure 33.1).

On Long Island Sound the same phenomenon is often observed: An easterly gradient wind backs to the northeast before dying ahead of an advancing offshore ocean sea breeze (at 190°). At St. Petersburg a northeasterly or an easterly typically backs to the north-northeast (shifting approximately 20°) ahead of the advancing offshore sea breeze. This back will usually be followed by a period of complete calm and finally (although not necessarily) by the appearance of the sea breeze in a dark line along the "leeward" shore. Until the calm appears, seek the left side of the course in the gradient wind, expecting a back—not the right side of the course, expecting the sea breeze.

Patterns of Convergence

The formation of a wide zone of convergence calm is dependent on the sea/lake breeze and the gradient wind's meeting over "open" water beyond the

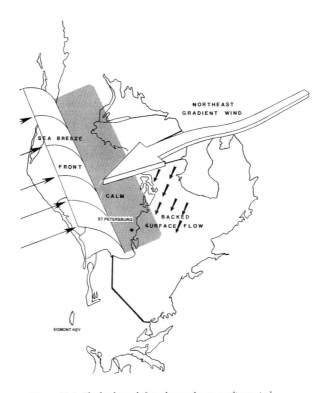

Figure 33.1. The backing shift in the northeast gradient wind

gusting zone. When convergence develops over land (after the sea/lake breeze front crosses the shoreline) or above marshes such as those at Savannah, or where sea and islands are interspersed in equal quantities as they are along the south coast of Finland, no convergence calm develops. Instead, the wind shifts abruptly (within a few yards) from an only slightly diminished offshore gradient wind to a sea breeze. Thermal turbulence brings the upper levels of both winds to the surface and obviates either a zone of calm or a zone of backed surface flow.

When a secondary sea/lake breeze approaches its initial landfall and lifts the gradient wind from the sea or lake surface, the sea/lake breeze air is cold (and coldest at the surface) and advances into the intervening zone of convergence calm in a fairly straight frontal line. The gradient wind is warmer than the marine air, but colder with height above the surface. Its colder upper elements are often able to penetrate the intervening zone of convergence calm to produce evanescent patches of surface flow veered to the initial gradient wind direction. No backing is evident (see Figure 4.2, p. 33).

When a secondary sea/lake breeze comes over land and offshore onto large inland water bodies such as Tampa Bay or the Chesapeake, successive bands of modified surface flow develop: nearest the windward shore a band of unaffected gradient wind (that in the gusting zone includes gusts); farther offshore a wide band of light, homogeneous, backed gradient wind; still farther out a wide band of calm; and farthest from the "windward" shore, a band of advancing sea/lake breeze. At the bay surface above a particular site, the morning gradient wind dies, backs as it dies, persists as a light flow from the backed direction (often in fitful puffs and lulls) for approximately 30 to 60 minutes, dies completely, and is replaced by a brief or prolonged period of calm, and finally, if the marine air is sufficiently cool, is replaced by the rapidly strengthening sea/lake breeze.

Charlotte Harbor: Overland and Overwater Flow

The Charlotte Harbor sea breeze, accelerated by its transit of heated land, develops in conditions—cloud cover, high moisture content, strong offshore gradient winds—that ordinarily hinder sea/lake breeze generation. Because it is strengthened by its overland passage, the sea breeze is likely to appear whenever the gradient flow is offshore and warm.

However, a strong, cool northeasterly will deter sea breeze formation. Flowing parallel to shore with water on its right, it will diminish at midday and begin to shift over a range of 20° to 40°, producing a split pattern. The overland overbay segment backed to the overgulf segment gradually dies (to 2 to 4 knots) and backs (to approximately 360°). No sea breeze appears.

An easterly, a warmer flow, is more likely to be replaced by the sea breeze. First, the easterly diminishes, backs, and becomes patchy; farther to leeward a zone of calm spreads across the entire harbor. An hour or two later the portion of the sea breeze coming over land (at 310° to 330° and 6 to 12 knots) ruffles the water along the shore of the peninsula that separates Charlotte Harbor from the gulf. This flow may reach its maximum velocity within a few minutes of its appearance and, associated with 10° to 5° oscillating shifts, spread to Charlotte Harbor's eastern shore. In late afternoon in the final phase, the sea breeze dies and the gradient wind reappears. The more northeasterly is the gradient flow, the more likely, if a sea breeze appears, will the overland sea breeze appear alone. The more southeasterly (or southerly) is the gradient wind, the more likely will the overwater portion of the sea breeze follow the appearance of the overland portion. If the gradient wind is from south of east, and if the overland sea breeze at 310° to 330° appears in early afternoon (before 1400), the overwater portion of the sea breeze at 240° to 270° will usually appear an hour or so later (Figure 33.2).

The overwater flow, a portion of the general west-coast onshore flow, channels through the open passages between the barrier islands and up Charlotte Harbor. In the racing area off Punta Gorda this flow gradually (over a period of 30 to 45 minutes) amalgamates with and backs the previously established, veered overland flow in a series of jumps—from 310° to 290° to 280° to 260° to 240°—until with occasional reversals, all the surface flow is moving in the basic overwater direction at 220° to 245°. As the overwater flow joins the overland flow, the surface wind strengthens to 14 to 16 knots. The midafternoon sea breeze may be an intermediate combination of overwater and overland flow, but if it is veered to 245° initially (which means that it is at least partially composed of overland flow), it will back, not veer, with increasing velocity thereafter. Once it reaches the 220° to

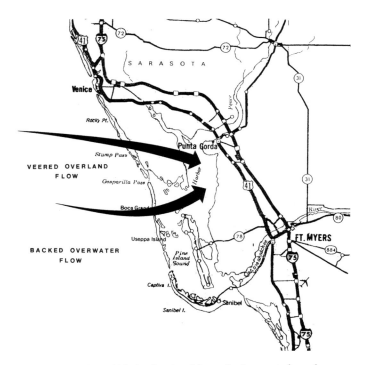

Figure 33.2. Acceleration of the overland segment of a sea breeze

245° range (which is the overwater direction), it will only oscillate.

At St. Petersburg the gusty overland flow (at 240° to 250°) is less veered to the overwater flow (at 200° to 210°), but its appearance may precede the latter by an hour or more. An ocean sea breeze accelerating across Maryland's Eastern Shore will sometimes bring 20-knot air to Annapolis 2 hours before its overwater elements, coming up the Chesapeake from the Virginia Capes, arrive. The Esperance Doctor in Western Australia comes ashore at 18 knots, crosses the desert, and reaches Kalgoorlie, 330 kilometers inland, 6 hours later—at an average speed of 30 knots!

The portion of a secondary sea/lake breeze front that transits flat, barren islands and peninsulas accelerates as it advances into reduced pressure and induces thermal turbulence (which brings higher-velocity upper level flow to the surface), whereas the portion that comes over water is exposed to no accelerating fall in pressure and is subjected to no thermal turbulence. If a sea/lake breeze comes partially across and partially around low-lying islands or peninsulas onto inland waters, the overland portion will come offshore onto the inland waters separate from and in advance of the overwater portion and will be stronger and more veered. When sailing on waters (bays or lakes) partially separated from the sea by an island or a peninsula or by low-level land, expect the secondary sea/lake breeze to appear first from a veered direction along the shore closest to the sea, to spread across the sailing area up to an hour prior to the appearance of any overwater flow, and then (if the overwater flow arrives) to back to the "basic" sea breeze direction.

Tampa Bay—Near-Shore and Midbay Variations

That portion of the secondary sea breeze coming over land at St. Petersburg—usually the first to appear—is an oscillating mixture of gusts moving at the speed and direction of the sea breeze's upper-level flow, and lulls—the basic overland flow. Because it includes downdrafts of higher-velocity air, the near-shore sea breeze is veered to the wind in midbay.

Beyond the gusting zone, 1 to 2 miles offshore, little of the overland upper-level flow is present at the surface, the velocity is reduced, and the wind is backed. Farther out, the surface wind is composed almost entirely of low-level flow coming over water up Tampa Bay from its entrance at Egmont Key. This cold, dense flow is channeled as the gulf sea breeze enters and turns up the bay, backing from 280° to 300° on the gulf coast beaches, to 230° to 240° in the lower bay, and to 200° to 210° as the flow comes abreast of St. Petersburg (Figure 33.3).

Early in the development of the St. Petersburg sea breeze, because it is then composed entirely of overland flow, the surface wind is relatively veered (220° to 230°) and increasingly veered with approach to shore (often to 240° or 250°, or

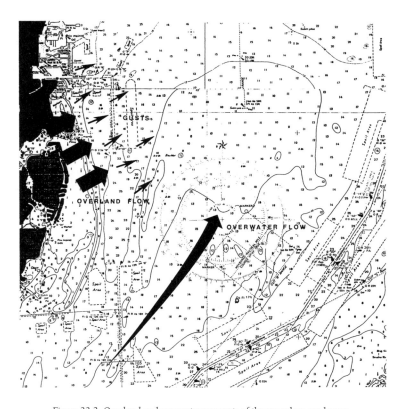

Figure 33.3. Overland and overwater segments of the secondary sea breeze

247

even 280° within the harbor). An additional progressive velocity veer also develops in late morning (or early afternoon). But at around 1330 to 1400 the velocity veer ceases, and in midbay is reversed by a gradual back as the surface flow becomes increasingly derived from the upbay overwater flow.

A beat (depending on its proximity to shore) conducted immediately after the appearance of the sea breeze should be managed by an initial port tack into the peninsula shore, expecting a veer. Subsequent beats are best managed in relation to the location of the weather mark: If it is close to shore go right, expecting some near-shore veer; if it is offshore go left, expecting the midbay back. I have seen (in midafternoon on a 2-mile course) the wind on the port layline to be 205° when, on the preceding beat on the starboard layline, it had been 235°.

Such persistent shifts must be managed in relation to the superimposition of a 10° to 15° range of oscillating shifts. Near shore the range will be greater, and oscillations are typically between 220° and 240°. Offshore they will be between 210° and 220°, the entire range backed to the near-shore flow. The advantage of being all the way in the correct corner can easily be negated by a 15° oscillation to the opposite side. This is particularly likely to happen when approaching the starboard (near-shore) layline.

Amalgamated Sea Breezes on the West Coast

Although along the gulf beaches the sea breeze is diminished by the perpendicular flow, in the entrance channels of Tampa Bay and Charlotte Harbor, a southwesterly gradient wind at 210° to 250° is aligned with the overwater sea breeze. At these sites the two winds will amalgamate and the surface flow will increase in strength to 14 to 18 knots and veer progressively to 240° to 270°. No late-morning zone of diminished wind nor patchiness intervenes. Only moderate 5° to 10° oscillations are evident (in contrast to the marked oscillations seen with the secondary sea breezes).

X. *Thermal Winds: Upslope Winds*

34. Lago di Garda

They have sown the wind
And they shall reap the whirlwind.
*—*Hosea

M ost sailors are content to sail in gradient winds or sea/lake breezes or some combination of the two. Most sailors are content to depend on the polar front and variations in insolation, temperature, and moisture content to obtain a decent sailing breeze. A fortunate few live near mountains where they have far more dependable air flows in which to sail.

On lakes such as Lago di Garda, strong winds blow upslope or downslope on almost every day of the year. Most of these winds depend on variations in insolation, and because they are cold air flows moving along the surface in response to local thermal gradients, are called thermal winds. In some cases—analogous to amalgamated sea/lake breezes—synoptic gradients align with thermal gradients to produce a third form of slope wind, the gradient-induced downslope wind. Lago di Garda boasts all three varieties—a thermal upslope wind, a thermal downslope wind, and a gradient-induced downslope wind.

Geography and Topography

Lago di Garda, like the other large northern Italian lakes, fills the southern portion of a 2- to 3-mile-wide U-shaped valley carved by an ice-age glacier. The mountains, which tower 1,500 to 4,000 feet above the northern third of the lake and whose slopes were cut away by the ice, appear to rise vertically from the lake's surface. On looking south from its northern end, one can see a tiny segment of horizon framed by the sheer cliffs and the Italian cypresses that line its shores. To the right of that distant line, beyond the pinnacles of Monti Rocchetta, towers the headland of Tignale; to the left, a mere mile away, the great silver cliff of Pt. Corna d'Ba hides the green slopes of Monte Baldo. In the opposite direction, 70 miles to the north, spanning the valley of the Sarca, stand the snow-capped mountains of the Brenta massif, the westernmost segment of the Dolomites and the birthplace of the glacier that created the lake.

In the northwest corner of the lake, plastered against the mountain side, is the largest town in the valley, Riva del Garda, and similarly sited, to the northeast, Torbole sul Garda. The 32-mile-long lake is but a few feet below the plain of the Po, into which its southern third protrudes, and but a few feet above the Adriatic. It is drained by a quiet stream, the Mincio, which, as a series of placid lakes, surrounds Mantova before emptying into the Po. At the southern end of Garda, baking in the summer heat, lie the castle-crowned promontory of Sirmione and, 20 miles to the southeast, Verona. To the west, between the lake and the next populated area around Lago d'Iseo, lie many miles of mountain wilderness. To the east only a narrow 5,000-foot-high ridge separates Garda from the valley of the Adige and the traffic on the Brenner Pass superhighway.

The northern portion of the lake is now recognized as the finest sailing site in Europe—perhaps in the world. Each year the yacht clubs at Torbole and Riva conduct world and European championship regattas. On a typical summer day thousands of boardsailors charge across the lake's enclosed northern end, and a hundred (or more) Olympic racing sailboats sweep around its buoys.

The Winds of Lago di Garda

All lakes develop "lake breezes," a daytime movement of cool air from above their cold water toward their heated shores. But Garda's lake breeze is special and deserves a special name, the Ora. To the north of the lake in the moraine-filled valley of the Sarca, a dramatic drop in pressure develops when heated air moves up the alpine slopes and separates at their peaks (Figure 34.1). Each afternoon in summer, when most other European lakes are calm, the upslope Ora blows from the south at 18 knots.

Sailors flock to Garda because of the Ora, but an often stronger, northerly downslope flow, the Peler, appears as regularly each morning. This mountain wind, a flow of cold air from the alpine peaks to the heated plains to the south, accelerates during its confinement between the lake's precipitous side walls. From dawn until about 0900, when the temperature disparity between the hot valley

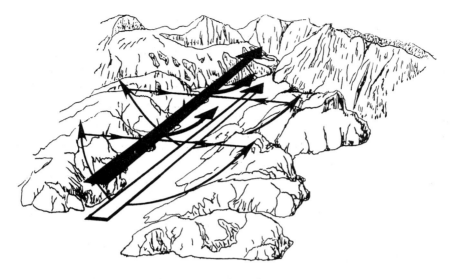

Figure 34.1. Upslope valley wind

and the alpine peaks reaches its zenith, the world's finest boardsailors reach back and forth across the lake at 20 to 30 knots.

As upper-slope flow ceases and the valley floor begins to heat in the sunlight, the Peler becomes intermittent. Pools of cold air accumulated above rocky constrictions during the night drain sequentially. The onshore Ora begins to move the marine air to the north, and where the flows converge the colder lifts the warmer from the surface. Usually by 1100 the pools have drained completely and the entire lake is calm.

The Ora

An hour or two later, the Ora, flowing initially a few meters above the surface, suddenly darkens the water to the south and begins to drag the cold surface air toward the heating sites in the Sarca Valley. Now colder than the downslope flow, it undermines the Peler all the way from Gargnano, halfway down the lake, to Torbole.

South of Gargnano the hot, homogeneous plain and the cold lake generate only a weak onshore flow that diffuses in multiple and often opposing directions from a central zone of calm. But at the northern end of the lake the only low-level near-shore land is the plain of the narrow Sarca Valley, which provides a precisely focused upslope flow into which the lake breeze can entrain and leads the marine air into continuous stream separation above the peaks of the Brenta massif. To this powerful gradient is added the acceleration due to channeling as the mass of air entrained from the open midlake zone is forced between the high rock walls that line Garda's northern third. (See appendix 3, "The Basis for Upslope Flow.")

The Ora is a secondary lake breeze developing beneath an offshore wind, but in this case the offshore wind is a downslope flow. As the morning advances, the overlake outflow of the Peler becomes so warmed (by the adiabatic heating associated with descent and the insolated surfaces over which it flows) that the Ora is able to lift it from the surface. Farther aloft, above the Ora, the warmed Peler continues its downward flow, subsiding to restore the overwater high pressure and creating a low-level inversion lid. This vertical confinement keeps the invading front cool and shallow, accelerates its flow inland and upslope, and accounts for the remarkable strength of the Ora over water.

Channeling of the Ora

At about 1300, as the sailors rest or finish their lunch in warm sunlight and complete calm, someone shouts, "There she comes!"—and the black line of the Ora sweeps up the lake. Within minutes, as the flow crosses the shoreline, an 18-knot wind is whistling through the rigging, sails are slatting, and the first boats are heeled over on their way to the starting line. The Ora increases in velocity for the first 20 minutes and veers slightly as it does.

The dominant characteristic of the cool lake breeze is its deviation and acceleration due to channeling—particularly its turn to the left (as it flows north) around Cap Reamol on the western shore and its turn to the right around Pt. Corna d'Ba on the eastern shore. The widening of the lake and the diverging of the flow with distance to windward permit a shorter course to the weather mark to be sailed along either shore—and cause the middle to be always wrong. But on the western side of the lake, because the flow is parallel to shore with water on its right, divergence accelerates and veers the channeled flow. Garda provides the world's most dramatic examples of channeling, because—in both the Ora and the Peler—the air flow is unusually cold, is confined by a low-level inversion lid and by the near-vertical mountainous sides of the lake, and is aligned with the long axis of the lake (Figure 34.2).

Channeling on the Torbole Course

In the '70s, the course along the eastern shore that took advantage of the big back at Pt. Corna d'Ba was considered to be the proper Ho Chi Minh Trail. But (perhaps in response to the evidence that there was but one way to go) the Circolo Vela Torbole's race committee decided to move the weather mark farther upwind (downlake). The local sailors made it a practice to drive along the corniche road and determine how far upwind the mark was being set. The farther upwind was the mark, the more it departed from the zone of backed air immediately south of Pt. Corna d'Ba (accelerated by the corner effect) and the more it entered the mid-lake zone of wind veered by both the channeling and the divergence around Cap Reamol. For the big Soling regattas the mark is now being set so far south that boats emerging from the big port tack lift at Corna d'Ba are faced with traversing a large area of progressive veer before they reach the mark—which typically negates all their eastern-shore gains (Figure 34.3).

When racing on a Circolo Vela Torbole course on the eastern side of the lake

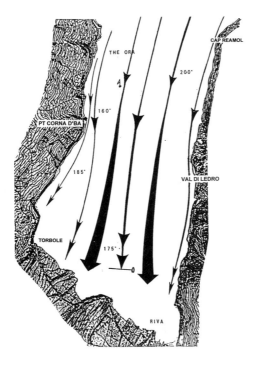

Figure 34.2. The Ora

in an Ora, standard practice today is to tack to port either immediately or after a short hitch on starboard—in any case before the eastern-shore veer (starboard tack lift) to leeward of Pt. Corna d'Ba is encountered—so as to be among the first to reach the big veer north of Cap Reamol. This results in passing through a transition zone where the wind backs modestly (a port tack lift) to a zone in which it veers progressively. One must be careful not to tack in the header too soon, as it progresses even beyond the starboard layline. Tactical considerations (and modest oscillations) may dictate a series of tacks, but the ultimate intent is to get to or above the starboard layline before one's competitors. The veer may be particularly pronounced just at the layline, and boats tacking below it may find a fan effect in which the boats farthest to the right lift (on starboard) the most, and everyone else, in proportion to their position to the left, lifts less.

Occasionally, in light air when the Ora is just beginning, it is backed, and then its deviation around Pt. Corna d'Ba is pronounced. If the heading at the starting line shows a wind to the left of 170°, the boats emerging from under Corna d'Ba may be far ahead of those coming in from the right—but don't count on it and only dare it on the first beat. If you do try this course, come away from the rocks early—at least 200 yards below Pt. Corna d'Ba; never go into the left shore to the south of the point. It is essential to be ahead and to leeward of your competitors as you approach midlake and enter the Cap Reamol veer. On several occasions I've lifted in the Corna d'Ba backing wind and been convinced that I was far

255

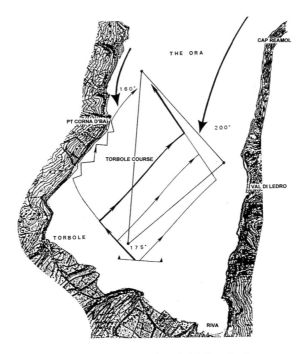

Figure 34.3. Channeled shifts in the Ora

in the lead—and each time, as I traversed the progressive veer, lost at least six or eight boats from the right.

On the first reach the boats experience a gradual heading veer as they cross the lake to the jibe mark close under the high wall below Pregasina. But close to the rocks the wind is backed, facilitating the jibe. The optimal course in a strong Ora is above the layline so that one can bear away in the strong veered gusts and jibe with some degree of control. In a lighter Ora it may pay to come in low, catching those who have gone too high and thus have to bear away for the mark in the back. The second reach ends with a velocity increase, an effective back, in the wind funneling over Torbole, and requires heading high initially so as to avoid being caught later below the spinnaker layline.

On the second beat it is again evident that a short starboard hitch in toward shore to clear one's air is not harmful—and is often advantageous. But an hour or more after the commencement of the Ora, on the second beat, it almost never pays to continue into the rocks to the left. As the entire uplake flow strengthens and veers, it becomes more parallel to the eastern shore, less deviated by Pt. Corna d'Ba and the corner effect. Carry port to the starboard layline and expect an even larger veer (greater divergence along the shore to the right) in the fully developed Ora.

On the run, an immediate jibe to starboard will carry the boat into a progressive header in the back near Pt. Corna d'Ba. The optimal course thereafter is close to shore in the strengthening induced by the point's intrusion in the wind flow. A

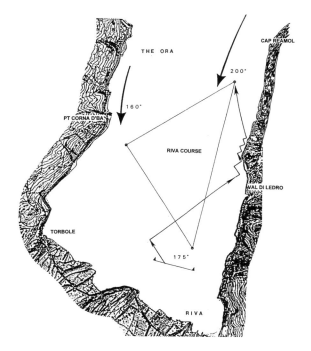

Figure 34.4. Channeled shifts in the Ora

final jibe slightly above the port jibe layline to the leeward mark should take the boat across the progressive veer associated with the flow into the valley above Torbole. The final beat should be managed just like the second. It may sometimes pay to go left on the first beat, but never on the final one.

Channeling on the Riva Course

The Riva Course on the western side of the lake, although only a mile away from the Torbole Course, must be managed quite differently. The main channeling around the headland below Pregasina on the western shore and the eddying in the indentation at the entrance of the Val di Ledro determine the management of the beat. Standard practice is to take port tack so as to reach the western shore at the point that protrudes just south of the Val di Ledro (but to avoid the inshore eddying to the north of that point). Thereafter, as the wind continues to veer along the western wall, it is necessary to keep right by short-tacking along the shore. The final tack for the mark, in the veer (which progresses with distance offshore) must be made precisely on the curving, lifting layline (Figure 34.4).

As the boats cross the lake on the first reach, the wind lightens, but the stronger backed air near the mark off Pt. Corna d'Ba warrants a deviation to windward. On the second reach they should sail high in a zone of backed air before entering a zone of veered flow directed into the valley above Riva. Because, as the leeward mark is approached, this latter flow lifts from the surface (aiming for the top of the near-shore ridge) and lightens, a course to leeward is usually advantaged. The same considerations apply on the run. Although in the backing air a starboard jibe takes the boat (undesirably) toward the immediate shift, it leads into stronger air (but avoid going too far offshore, where its strength diminishes). The final port jibe into the mark is headed as it takes the boat out of the midlake back and into the veered air channeling over Riva.

35. The Brunn Wind

It's a warm wind, the west wind,
Full of bird's cries.
—JOHN MASEFIELD

T he famous Brunn wind that attracts sailors to Austria's Wolfgangsee combines almost every one of the many forces that are involved in the creation of upslope flow—and comes downslope onto the Wolfgangsee! This long, narrow lake lies within the northern foothills of the Austrian Alps, 30 miles from the Dachstein massif. To its north lie Austria's hilly "lowlands" (altitude 1,200 to 2,000 feet) and nearby, at the base of the foothills, two large lakes—the Mondsee and the Attersee. To its south the long line of the Alps stretches east-west from Hungary to France. The Wolfgangsee nestles in a branch of the Traun River Valley immediately to the south of a portion of the long Höllen-Gebirge, a pre-alpine ridge that rises abruptly 1,500 to 4,000 feet from the northern lowlands. Except for the Wolfgangsee, which lies 190 feet above the Mondsee, and the remainder of the narrow Traun River Valley, the land to the south of the Höllen-Gebirge is a mountainous upland 300 to 8,000 feet above the rolling plains to the north.

The relatively barren surfaces to the north of the Höllen-Gebirge respond to insolation far more readily than the tree-covered, mountainous surfaces to its south. There, the mountainous surface area is inclined, often at an acute angle, to the sun and often, at any given hour, in the shade. It is vegetated by large trees (which dissipate insolation) or is covered with snow or ice (which reflect insolation) or water (which absorbs and distributes insolation rapidly). Over the mountains heated air is readily drawn off and dissipated through peak separation. Over the lowlands it lies trapped, unable to lift off until and unless the lapse rate rises significantly. Consequently, for a given amount of insolation the air to the north of the Höllen-Gebirge is heated far more than the air to the south.

In addition, the average depth (the volume) of air below any given altitude over the lowlands to the north of the Höllen-Gebirge is considerably greater than over the uplands to its south. Therefore, for any given amount of surface heating, the air to the north expands more than the air to the south (Figure 35.1).

A greater response to insolation—producing greater heating of the surface and the overlying air—and greater expansion of the deeper overlying air for a given amount of heating combine to produce a far greater expansion of the air to the

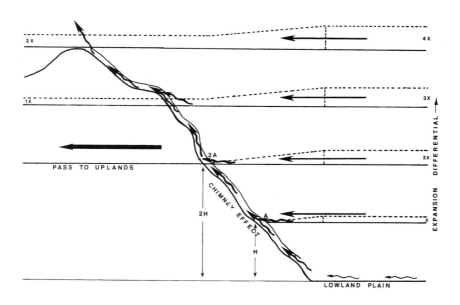

Figure 35.1. Onslope and upslope flow

north and therefore a large and widespread thermal pressure gradient from the northern lowlands across the Höllen-Gebirge toward the southern uplands. (See appendix 3, "The Basis for Upslope Flow.")

The Expansion Differential

The difference in expansion across the Höllen-Gebirge is but a portion of a large-scale expansion differential that results from the lower altitude of the mid-Austrian lowlands (average altitude 1,600 feet) to the north of the Alps vis-à-vis the Enns Valley (average altitude 2,500 to 4,000 feet) to the south of the Alps. With insolation the greater expansion of the larger volume of air above the northern lowlands creates a major pressure gradient and a massive daytime movement of air from the northern plains toward the vast uplands of the Enns Valley. Simultaneously, on the south side of the Alps, a similar expansion differential moves air upslope from the Po Valley and the Adriatic toward the Enns. These near-surface flows are counterbalanced each day by upper-level reverse flows (either above an inversion or within a gradient flow) and each night by surface downslope flows.

The general transridge horizontal gradient forcing air from the northern low-lands toward the Enns uplands is abetted by a vertical upslope and onslope pressure gradient (producing a chimney effect) along the steep north face of the Höllen-Gebirge. During insolation, free air is forced onslope, and surface air is forced upslope toward continuous stream separation at the 3,300-plus-foot ridgetop and through the passes toward the lower pressure in the Enns Valley. (See appendix 3, "The Basis for Upslope Flow.")

The Scharfling Pass

There are but two passes through the Höllen-Gebirge into the Traun Valley— the low-level primary valley (by way of the Traunsee, past Bad Ischl to the Hallstättersee and the Dachstein) and the higher-level Scharfling Pass at the southern tip of the Mondsee. The 3-mile-long Scharfling Pass, at 1,930 feet, separates the Mondsee, at 1,580 feet, from the Wolfgangsee, at 1,770 feet. The portion of the massive flow headed for the Dachstein and the Enns Valley that comes through the Scharfling Pass and spills down into the sailing layer above the Wolfgangsee is known as the Brunn wind (Figure 35.2).

In clear weather moderate insolation initiates a lake breeze from the Mondsee toward the Höllen-Gebirge that entrains within the general upslope flow. A portion of this flow rises 350 feet to enter the Scharfling Pass, breaks through the Höllen-Gebirge, and escapes, compressed and accelerated, downslope onto the western end of the Wolfgangsee 190 feet below. The Wolfgangsee lake breeze, responding primarily to a gradient toward the heating flatlands of the Ischl Valley at its eastern end, provides a near lake-level outlet for the flow descending from the Scharfling. Valley wind circulations (lateral upslope flow with central subsidence) within the Wolfgangsee/Ischl/Traun River Valley reinforce this cross-lake surface flow.

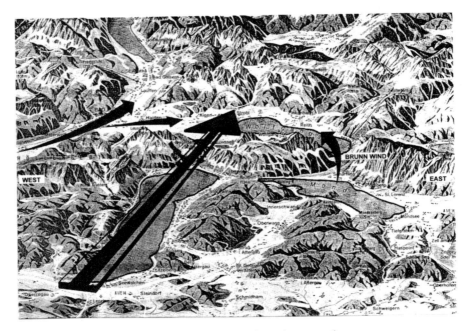

Figure 35.2. Upslope flow to the Dachstein massif

The Development of the Brunn Wind

The outflow from the Scharfling Pass to the Wolfgangsee, the Brunn wind, appears on a clear summer day shortly after noon (sometimes not until midafternoon) following a period of complete calm. Whatever gradient wind has been present must first be warmed and lifted from the surface by the cold lake's conduction inversion. The Brunn wind comes onto the lake from over Brunnwinkl, the corner of the lake just below the Scharfling Pass, in surges and gusts of cold, dense air. At the nearby Union Yacht Club, sailors await the first movement of leaves in the treetops. Within minutes after their first ruffling, the flow descends to the lake, stirring its surface into dark patches.

The early elements of the flow are so highly variable in strength and contain such huge oscillating shifts that it is difficult to detect evidence of channeling. In approximately 20 minutes, however, as the flow spreads south and east toward the flatlands on the far shore and draws in the warmer local air and the smoother upper-level air of the general southgoing flow, it becomes less gusty, more homogeneous. Thereafter channeling becomes prominent.

Channeling in the Brunn Wind

Near Brunnwinkl, as the flow comes out from the Scharfling Pass, its direction ranges between 360° and 030°. As it flows across the lake toward the low-level outlet of the Ischl/Traun Valley and is deflected by the mountain wall along the lake's southern shore and channeled around the major bend of the northern shore near the Ochsenkreuz, it backs progressively. At the leeward end of the main lake near the typical starting line off Farchen, the median direction is 330°; near the Ochsenkreuz it is about 350°; and at the weather mark, a quarter-mile farther to windward, gusts will often be veered beyond 360°. Oscillations are evident throughout the lake and throughout the afternoon but are especially prominent near Brunnwinkl and early in the wind's development. The speed of the Brunn wind averages 14 knots when fully developed, but gusts up to 18 knots are occasionally seen. The usual oscillating shift is only 10° to 15°, but during any one race winds backed to 330° or veered to 10° (or even 20°) may be seen (Figure 35.3).

Because the wind veers with distance to windward, standard practice is to start on starboard tack at the starboard end of the line, in the expectation of a gradual lift. However, as most of the channeled veer does not appear until the bend near the Ochsenkreuz is reached, oscillations regularly offset this effect. It is always dangerous to move too far right into the shadow of Falkenstein Cliff (where the wind backs and dies). In a veer, a start on the leebow of the fleet is best. In a back, down the line on its weather quarter, prepared to tack to port, is safest. Thereafter, until close to the Ochsenkreuz, where the median wind direction is 350°, one should play the oscillations, working shift by shift to the right.

Figure 35.3. The Brunn wind

263

One should hold starboard in any wind direction above 350° but tack away from port whenever the heading indicates a wind above 345°. When heading toward the cliff on a port tack lift, one should fear getting too close and should thus take the leebow of the most windward group of starboard tack boats, expecting that at least one more back will permit one's crossing them before they come abreast of the Ochsenkreuz. Finally, so as to be inside at the bend beyond which the big veer will appear, one must (usually) move right and inside.

Occasionally, however, the expected veer is obscured by big gusts, calm patches, and backing oscillations (particularly late in the day). The compass must be watched as the Ochsenkreuz is approached—if a big veer (beyond 350°) is already present, it is better to continue left rather than to risk being caught in the right corner in a big oscillating back. If a back (below 345°) is already present, one should go right into the rocks below the point as closely as possible.

Particularly on the first round before warmer air is incorporated into the flow, the wind at the windward end of the lake is gusty and veered. On the first reach the temptation is to defend one's quarter from boats riding up in gusts and to stray far to windward of the rhumb line. Usually, however, it is better to work down and inside in what will become a progressive veer. A particularly veered oscillation may sometimes permit a jibe. An inside position can be very valuable in the usual melee created by boats surging up in short-lived gusts.

On the second reach, which parallels the southern shore, the strongest wind is sometimes near shore, accelerated as it turns along the face of the Gahberg. In light air, a longer, curving course nearer shore may be faster than a straight one. But in stronger winds, because the gusts are both stronger and more prolonged in midlake, a sharp and immediate move left to prevent boats from riding over is usually correct. For the same reason, stronger wind may advantage the right side of the run (nearer the middle of the lake). It is important to keep away from the Falkenstein Cliff, particularly if the general velocity is decreasing.

The South Wind

A portion of the general upslope movement flowing south over the Traunsee and up the Traun Valley turns into the Ischl Valley and flows from the southeast upslope toward the western end of the valley, the outlet of the Wolfgangsee. In some conditions this southeasterly flow collides with the northwesterly Brunn wind above the lake. Because the Brunn wind derives from air cooled by rising 350 feet to surmount the Scharfling Pass (and only falling 190 feet) and the "south wind" comes across the level Traunsee and up the warm, gradually rising Ischl Valley, the Brunn wind is usually the denser and the more dominant of the two.

But the Brunn wind is actually a mixture of air coming over the pass, and local air drawn into its movement. If it arrives late and emerges beneath overheated air trapped for hours in the cul-de-sac at the lake's western end, it may gradually, as the day progresses, warm to a temperature above that of the south wind. On the second or third round, boats coming down the run in a Brunn wind may find themselves running out of air, and the cooler south wind, spreading out from the leeward shore, undermining and lifting the Brunn wind from the surface.

One should seek the shortest course across the intervening zone of calm when approaching or departing the "leeward" mark. A straight course down the run is the most likely to be halted by the calm. A wide approach to the "leeward" mark from either side is better, but a move right, as it takes the boat across the calm and into the new wind most directly, is usually best.

Because the weather mark always remains in the Brunn wind, cold enough as it flows out onto the lake from the Scharfling Pass to dominate the western end of the lake, the problem after rounding the leeward mark is to find the fastest route back into it. The quickest crossing of the zone of calm is never up the middle but always to one side or the other. And the acceleration induced in both flows by the steep southern shore often advantages a course to the south.

The West Wind

When low pressure lies over the Baltic, bringing cold, rain, and westerly gradient flow to the valley of the Danube, the wind on the Wolfgangsee may be from a direction similar to that of the Brunn wind. This "west wind" (usually backed 10° to 20° from the Brunn) is often strong and comes onto the lake from the northwest through the pass from Fuschl am See. Oscillations, which are frequent and often large, are the most important consideration. The warmer, less stable "west wind" shows little of the channeling around the Ochsenkreuz so characteristic of the Brunn wind and therefore requires no move to the right near this point. Indeed, a course near the cliffs is risky, often stranding the boat in patches of light air. The best approach to the weather mark is often from the left corner along the port tack layline, where the wind is backed by its course along the face of the Gahberg.

36. The Determinants of Channeling

And the wheel's kick and the wind's song
And the white sail's shaking,
And a gray mist on the sea's face
And a gray dawn breaking.
— JOHN MASEFIELD

Because channeling causes predictable, persistent shifts in the near-surface air flow, it is, to the sailor, the most important effect of topography. Three factors influence channeling:
1. The height and rate of rise of the topographical barriers
2. The temperature and stability of the air flow
3. The alignment of the air flow with the topographical barriers

The Height and Rate of Rise of the Barriers

Bluffs, hills, or mountains that rise abruptly to confine air flows overlying lakes, rivers, and harbors induce channeling. Lago di Garda, in northern Italy, where the surrounding mountains rise abruptly to thousands of feet, is renowned for the channeling of its upslope and downslope winds. "Never go up the middle," it is said—always seek the channeled shifts along Garda's shores. The banks of the Severn River are much more modest in height, but in many areas rise no less abruptly than those of Garda. Channeling is equally evident—which demonstrates that the height of the barrier above the sailing layer (above the height of the masts of the boats involved) is of little moment. It is the degree of confinement of the layer in which the boats sail that matters (Figure 36.1).

The momentum of each portion of a moving mass of air requires it to keep pace with the remainder by moving at the average speed of the whole. The surface layer, of unchanging volume but varying lateral confinement, must accelerate and decelerate to move at the average speed of the flow suprajacent to its confinement.

Figure 36.1. Channeling in a cross-river flow

267

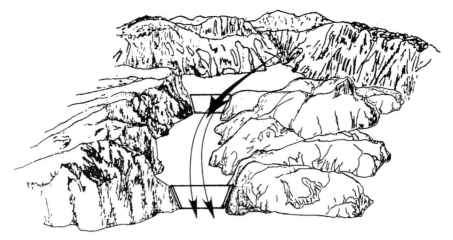

Figure 36.2. Relationship of velocity to vertical cross section

If a lake, river, or harbor narrows between confining banks, the area of the vertical plane available for the passage of air flow is reduced, and the flow of the surface layer through the gap must accelerate. If the water body widens and/or its banks slope away more gently, the area of the vertical plane is increased and the flow of the surface layer must decelerate (Figure 36.2).

Flow will also be channeled around a promontory protruding from a single shore. If the topography near shore is of mast height or above, a more-or-less parallel-to-shore surface flow will tend to align with deviations of the shoreline, turning waterward on reaching the windward face of a promontory, accelerating around its tip, and turning shoreward beyond the promontory, on its leeward side.

The Temperature and Stability of the Air Flow

When the surface air is cold and dense, when it is devoid of thermal turbulence—such as it is in an onshore sea/lake breeze—it behaves like water, flowing along the surface, deviated by every obstacle in its path. Capped by an inversion lid, sea/lake breezes run into and out of water-level openings and change direction and velocity dramatically to flow around intrusions. A typical example is the Chesapeake's bay sea breeze which enters the Chesapeake from the ocean between the Virginia Capes and turns to enter each of the Chesapeake's hundreds of tributaries, aligning itself with the long axis of each. The bay sea breeze is an easterly in the James River, a southeasterly in the York and the Potomac, a southerly in midbay, and a southwesterly in Eastern Bay on the Eastern Shore.

The degree to which a sea/lake breeze is channeled varies with its temperature, and its temperature varies with time. At onset a sea/lake breeze is composed of a relatively warm mass of air that has lain for a protracted period above shallow near-shore water. Later it is composed of cool air drawn in from offshore, from above a deeper, colder ocean or lake. In summer on the Chesapeake the morning bay sea breeze, composed of air from within the estuary, is but slightly cooler than the nearby land. Later in the day as ocean air is drawn inland and the temperature of the sea breeze falls, channeling becomes progressively more prominent. On an estuary on the final beat of an afternoon race one must be particularly concerned to respond to the channeled shifts.

Channeling is even more evident in the heavy surface layer of a gust splash than it is in the cold, stable air of an onshore sea breeze. Mechanical turbulence can readily cause some elements of a 500- to 1,000-foot-deep onshore sea breeze to rise above an obstacle. But the dramatic difference between the density of a downdraft and that of the air 50 to 60 feet above the surface means that all of a downdraft flows along the surface, that all of its violence is transmitted in a very shallow layer, and that, unable to rise, it must channel around any obstacles in its path.

The Alignment of the Topography with the Air Flow

A cold, dense air flow approximately aligned with the long axis of a water body will maintain its basic strength and direction over open water. But it will be deviated waterward and accelerated where the lateral shoreline rises abruptly to obstruct its passage inland, and deviated landward at low-level gaps in the lateral shoreline that permit its passage inland.

A cold, dense air flow crossing the main axis of a water body will tend to turn and align with that axis as it approaches the leeward shore. The air flow will be strongest and least deviated to leeward of gaps, and weakest to leeward of elevations in the windward shoreline. It will be deviated and accelerated along elevated segments of the leeward shoreline. It will maintain its original perpendicular trajectory where the leeward shore is low or a cove or tributary provides an escape route. Here its speed may be increased if the opening is isolated and the shoreline low, or decreased if the opening is but one of many and its shoreline elevated (Figure 36.1, p. 267).

The Corner Effect

The direction that the wind turns to round an obstacle influences its acceleration. Studies of the "corner effect" on the downslope Mistral as it rounds the Massif Central, in France, demonstrate that the veering caused by the intrusion of topography into the right side of a flow (looking downflow) causes a greater acceleration than expected. The same effect may be seen in a gradient wind turning to the right around a sharply delineated atmospheric ridge. Intrusion of an obstacle from the left side causes backing and a reduction in the expected acceleration.

The veering associated with turning around a right-side protrusion increases the alignment of the flow with the Coriolis force so that the net force acting in the direction of flow is significantly increased. The surface layer of the flow confined by the protrusion accelerates and diverges beneath the unconfined upper layers. Backing around a left-side protrusion opposes the Coriolis force so that the net force acting in the direction of flow is decreased. The surface flow decelerates and converges beneath the unconfined upper layers. (See Figure 28.1, p. 206.)

The Effects of Channeling

Variations in wind direction may be used to significantly shorten the course of a boat sailing to windward and are far more important than variations in wind speed (which only affect boat speed and then only in a modest manner). Downwind, where shortening the course is improbable, variations in wind speed and sailing angle produce significant differences in boat speed and are far more important than variations in wind direction. ("To windward, go for the shift; downwind, go for the increased velocity.")

Upwind

When you are sailing to windward, channeled shifts should be managed as persistent shifts. The boat should be sailed toward the expected shift (toward the shore from which the expected shift will emanate) in a relative lift, expecting to find a heading shift near that shore. Such a tack should be continued into the header until its maximum effect is reached, beyond the "median wind" heading (or until the boat is about to run aground or be blanketed), and then tacked to the lifted tack (Figure 36.3).

The location of the maximum heading shift is on the downwind side of and close to the tip of a protruding promontory, at a bend proximal to a segment of deviating shoreline

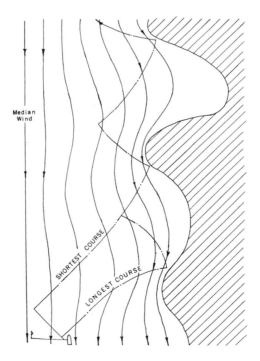

Figure 36.3. Management of channeled flow

(including a cove or other tributary); where a water body diverges into a broader sur-
face; or where a leeward shore begins to rise abruptly. When sailing to windward, "Be
inside at the bends"; be closer than the competition to the side of the course and the site
where the channeled deviation begins.

Ordinarily a water body and its suprajacent air flow will turn relative to only one promontory on one side at a time—but if protrusions appear on both sides of a narrow water body and are similar, one should usually seek the promontory along the left shore (looking upwind), as here the corner effect will produce a greater acceleration and a greater change in direction than on the right side. However, two caveats must be kept in mind:

1. Unless the water body is very narrow one should not cross it twice, should not leave the typical near-shore advantage more often than necessary.
2. Divergence between the overland and the overwater segments of a parallel-to-shore flow increases the speed of flow along the right shore (looking upwind). (See Figure 28.3, p. 209.)

Go left if there is a protrusion; go right if the shoreline is straight.

When sailing upwind on a small body of water whose shores are converging (and the air flow is diverging) with distance to windward, the shortest course, which avoids the course-lengthening lifts that become increasingly severe near either shore, is close to the rhumb line. When sailing upwind where the shores are diverging (and the air flow is converging), the shortest course is close to one of the laylines, en route to which one finds a progressive header and along which one finds a near-shore lift. As there is always some asymmetry in the shorelines, the practical rule is to move out toward the side that diverges the most. (See Figures 15.4, p. 110, and 28.1, p. 206.)

Channeled shifts, deviating the wind flow in a predictable manner, provide opportu-
nities for greater and more certain gains (by shortening the course to be sailed) than any
other variation in wind speed or direction.

Downwind

When you are sailing downwind, wind speed is typically more important than direction. The course that provides the strongest wind and the best sailing angle should be sought. On a run the boat should be "tacked downwind," jibing to remain in the stronger air and at the better sailing angle provided by the varia-tion in wind direction and speed on each segment of the course. If the sailing angle does not justify jibing, one must choose between a course nearer or farther from shore on the same jibe. An elevated obliquely leeward shore should be approached more closely as the nearby air flow will usually be compressed and accelerated along it.

Where the leeward shore is low or where tributaries to leeward make away from the main water body, the air flow is expanded and decelerated. Where both shores of a narrow water body are elevated the wind shifts aft so as to align with its long axis. When sailing downwind, the boat should be positioned so as to enter segments of diminished or aft-shifted air flow near the leeward shore so that they may be crossed at a higher sailing angle. This may require sailing at a lower sailing angle or on the opposite jibe in the stronger air of a prior, more open segment.

XI. *Thermal Winds: Downslope Winds*

37. Mountain Winds on New York's Finger Lakes

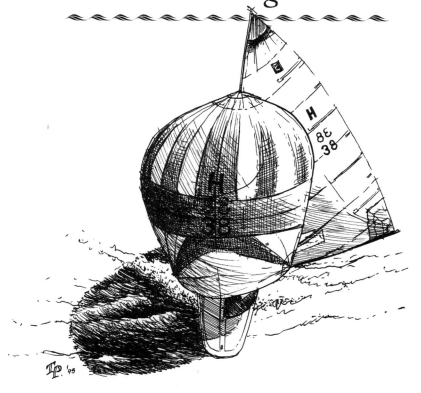

Friday dawns clear as a bell,
Rain on Saturday, sure as hell.
—ENGLISH PROVERB

The high Alps that rise adjacent to Lago di Garda and the Wolfgangsee create large differences in the response to insolation of neighboring surfaces and generate strong upslope winds each day. The previous chapters have demonstrated that these flows regularly provide excellent sailing. The small mountains that surround the Finger Lakes create only minimal differences in the response to insolation of neighboring surfaces. The weak upslope winds that result are overwhelmed by the usual daytime gradient winds. At night, however, downslope flows are protected from the interference of the gradient winds by the radiation inversion. Nocturnal downslope flows often begin sufficiently early in the evening and sometimes persist sufficiently late in the morning to be used by the racing sailor.

Geography, Topography, and Thermal Winds

The Finger Lakes of western New York lie in valleys extending northward from the mountains of the Southern Tier. The peaks at the southern ends of these lakes rise to approximately 1,800 to 2,000 feet, whereas the lakes themselves lie at an altitude of 400 to 800 feet. The northern ends of the lakes emerge from confining ridges onto a plain that extends 50 or more miles to Lake Ontario.

This geographical relationship resembles that of Lago di Garda at the foot of the Italian Alps and results in the formation of similar local winds. Late afternoon, nocturnal, and early-morning downslope flow from the mountains of the Southern Tier to the southern ends of the Finger Lakes is encouraged by the steep drop from the mountains to the lake surfaces, by the mountain wind circulation in the narrow valleys that confine the lakes, and by the open outlets (near lake level) and diurnal lake breezes that develop at the northern ends of the lakes. However, as the height of the peaks above the lakes and the steepness of their confining valley walls are not nearly so great as at Garda, the downslope flows of the Finger Lakes are far lighter and evident only in the absence of strong gradient winds.

Although their deepwater temperature remains at about 40°F, the surface temperature of the Finger Lakes typically reaches 70°F in summer. Smaller in volume than Garda, they heat much more readily. Consequently, except when the deep water is brought to the surface by strong southerly gradient winds, lake breezes are weak.

Because the insolation-responsive plains to the north heat rapidly, while much of the hilly surface to the south remains in shadow, the morning lake breeze gradient is directed to the north and reinforces the southerly downslope flows, accelerating them northward between the steep, confining hillsides. This reinforcement of downslope flow by onshore lake breeze flow is most evident when the lake surface is cold—in spring and after strong southerlies (Figure 37.1).

Upslope/lake breeze flow to the south is rarely evident. In contrast to Garda, where the relatively flat Sarca Valley facilitates the crossing of the shoreline by the lake breeze front, the mountains at the ends of the Finger Lakes rise steeply from the lake shore to prevent the cool lake air from rising to reach any significant heating surfaces. Indeed, because the opposing upslope flow is so weak, downslope flow often begins in late afternoon as soon as the east-facing upper mountain slopes fall into shade. On some lakes, such as Cayuga, late-afternoon racing takes place in downslope flow emanating from particularly well-shaded valleys.

Downslope flow on mountain lakes is more frequent and stronger than upslope flow because cold upper slope air sinks readily in response to gravity, and steep near-shore slopes prevent an incipient lake breeze from crossing the shore to reinforce upslope movement.

Downslope Flow on Skaneateles Lake

Sailboat racing is conducted on Canandaigua, Skaneateles, Cayuga, and Seneca Lakes. The latter two are the largest and therefore the coolest, have the high-

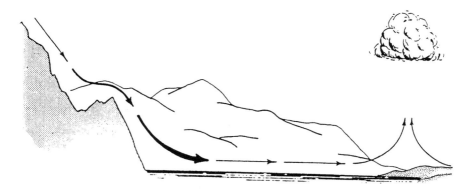

Figure 37.1. Downslope flow leading into a cross-lake breeze

est mountains at their southern extremities, and the greatest disparity between the altitude of the nearby mountains and that of the lake surface—and therefore the best downslope winds.

I observed the southerly downslope wind of Skaneateles Lake one morning in August. The lake lay ahead of an advancing cold front to the northwest of a cP High centered over Pennsylvania. That afternoon at Kingston, to the north, the southwest gradient flow amalgamated with the Ontario lake breeze to blow onshore at 20 knots. On Skaneateles, at 0600, a downslope wind was blowing from the south straight up the lake at 5 knots. By 0800 it had increased to a peak of 8 knots. By 0900 it had decreased to about 6 knots, and by 1000, following the appearance of patches of calm, had disappeared. Thereafter it was gradually replaced by the southwesterly gradient wind, which strengthened and persisted for the remainder of the day.

Above a mountain lake, cold air trapped beneath a radiation and/or an advection inversion may protect downslope winds from the gradient flow until midday, when thermal turbulence destroys the inversion.

Downslope Flow on Cayuga Lake

On Cayuga, in the midst of the summer doldrums, the Ithaca Yacht Club often prefers to arrange racing to take advantage of the morning downslope wind—rather than to await the protracted calm of a typical "motorboat day." As at Garda they sometimes roust out the competitors for a 0700 start and have two hours of good racing in smooth water and 8 knots of southerly (Figure 37.2).

Summertime racing (under the "settled" conditions accompanying the northward displacement of the Bermuda High) may also take place in a late-afternoon downslope flow. As the sun sinks, the high east-facing mountains on the west side of the valleys that extend south from the lake begin to shade the valley floors. By late afternoon from over the village of Newfield and out onto the calm lake comes a southerly downslope flow called the Newfield drift. And simultaneously, from

277

Figure 37.2. Downslope flow on Cayuga and Seneca Lakes (Courtesy Ernest Hauser, Ithaca, N.Y.)

the valley of the Salmon Creek, a short distance north of Ithaca, a similar, north-easterly flow emerges.

Ernest Hauser, an experienced observer of the local air flows, describes a dramatic incident that reveals the pattern of development of the Newfield drift. One summer afternoon in a light southerly gradient wind he was leading a group of boats approaching a windward mark at the southern end of Cayuga Lake. As patches of calm were becoming widespread, Hauser attempted to approach the mark from above the layline on a wide inshore swing, ran out of wind—and stopped. Among the trailing boats were several with 40- to 50-foot masts, and these continued to move forward on the layline. And behind these, directly to leeward of them, a group of shorter-masted boats appeared to have a wind of similar strength, and despite the ever-encroaching calm, approached the mark at almost the same speed. However, as soon as the taller-masted boats rounded the mark and headed downwind to the north, the shorter-masted boats stopped, as unable to round the mark as was Hauser.

The subsequent retreat of the gradient wind to the north and its replacement by a 3- to 4-knot southeasterly surface flow that, a few minutes after the rounding, ruffled the near-shore water, demonstrated that the circumstances described were associated with the initial appearance of the Newfield drift. The cold downslope flow, hugging the surface as it left the shoreline, lifted the warmer gradient wind from the surface as the two winds converged. However, 50 feet above the surface and above the halted layer of cold downslope flow, the gradient wind continued, and it was this wind that the taller-masted boats were using to round the mark.

And directly to leeward of these masts, and apparently brought to the surface by the mechanical turbulence they had induced, a band of gradient wind moved a group of shorter-masted boats toward the mark until the cause of the turbulence—the tall masts—rounded the mark and headed downwind!

When flows of differing temperature meet, the colder will occupy the surface and displace the other to a suprajacent layer. A zone of convergence calm will develop between the two winds, but the warmer will continue to flow above the colder and, when the colder is shallow (as is a typical downslope wind), may be reachable by a sufficiently tall mast.

Mountain-Wind Generation

Downslope winds develop because temperature typically decreases with altitude (the higher the site on a slope, the colder the air) and because, after the cessation of insolation, the land (by radiation) and its suprajacent air (by conduction) cool more rapidly than the free air at the same level. Each evening the colder, denser air accumulating on a slope will eventually break through the frictional resistance and begin to slide toward the less dense air below. Depending on the steepness and smoothness of the slope and the rate of radiational cooling, large segments of the surface air will move downslope. Warmer free air at the same level will move down the pressure isolines toward the slope (will move "onslope") and will be entrained in the downslope flow. On sufficiently steep slopes, intermittent flow will become (almost) continuous (Figure 37.3).

The downslope flows on either side of a valley combine to produce a downvalley ("mountain wind"), and each small valley adds its mountain wind to a combined large valley downflow. At the large valley outlet onto the sea or lake, such combined flows are intermittent because the tributary flows, prevented from entering the main valley until a critical mass accumulates, periodically obstruct the main valley flow. However, if a smooth, almost friction-free water surface lies below, the air rushes toward and across it, heading for its lowest-level outlet. The near-lake-level outlet onto the plains to the north of the Finger Lakes minimizes the trapping of cold air in the mountain valleys and facilitates a near-continuous outflow. (See appendix 4, "The Basis for Downslope Flow.")

Morning Downslope Flow on the Finger Lakes

Throughout the night the lake surfaces remain considerably warmer than the air in the upper valleys and at the mountain summits. Although flow from the heights is down in all directions, in the mountains of the Southern Tier it acquires greater velocity northward, because in this direction the declination is steepest

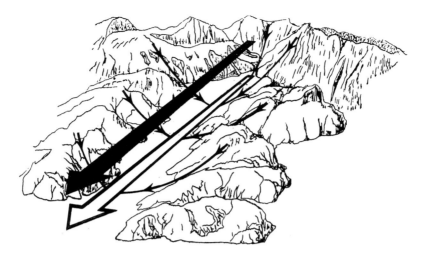

Figure 37.3. Downslope mountain wind

and the surfaces (the lakes) downslope the warmest. Dense downslope flows seek the lower overlake pressure, readily lift the warm lake air, and, retaining their downslope momentum, surge across the lake surfaces.

All southerly downslope flows are well established by midnight and persist at a steady strength until daybreak. When the vast plain to the north begins to heat and generate convection, the overlying surface pressure falls. Onshore flow from the high pressure over the lakes develops at their northern ends and reinforces the southerly downslope gradients at their southern ends. At about 0800 the acceleration induced as the lake breeze front crosses the shoreline into the overland pressure trough often converts the weak downslope flow into a translake sailing breeze.

The mountain wind is most evident on the third or fourth day after the passage of a cold front (when the synoptic gradient is least and the ambient air is warmest) and typically foretells (according to Dick Besse, a local expert) a "motorboat day"—a late morning and afternoon of glassy calm or variable winds less than 5 knots. Under high pressure in clear cP air, cooling of the upper mountain slopes by longwave radiation is enhanced, the upper-slope air becomes colder and denser than usual, and the nocturnal and early-morning radiation inversion is strong. The warm lid protects the lower few hundred feet of the atmosphere from even strong gradient winds, and on lakes such as Skaneateles permits 6 or 8 hours of downslope flow between 0200 and 1000.

By midmorning, when rising columns of heated air break through and destroy the inversion, the downslope southerly dies and a generalized midday calm develops. A few minutes (to several hours) later, thermal turbulence may bring the suprajacent gradient wind to the surface. On some lakes, after an afternoon of calm or light gradient wind, downslope flow may return early enough to support evening sailing.

Mountain (thermally induced downslope) winds become strong enough to provide satisfactory sailing under radiation or advection inversions when they are aligned with the long axes of valley lakes.

Evening Downslope Flow on the Finger Lakes

The Newfield drift and other late-afternoon downslope flows require two preconditions: a high and extensive east-facing slope that falls into shade in midafternoon, and a low-lying flatland that remains insolated until near sundown between the slope and the lake. Onslope and downslope flow begin on high mountain slopes as soon as they are shaded. If the intervening slopes remain heated, generating liftoff and retaining low pressure, such flows will carry to and out onto the lake below. The Newfield drift comes across a valley from east-facing slopes in shade to west-facing slopes in sun, down to insolated lowlands in the Newfield Valley and along the lake shore, and out onto the lake. As no thermal gradient (no lake breeze on the opposite shore) is available to carry such evening downslope flows onward, they rely entirely on momentum, and ordinarily do not extend more than a mile or two from shore.

38. The Peler

The Peler, Lago di Garda's downslope wind, is dependent on the temperature/density difference between the cold air surrounding the 10,000-foot peaks of the Brenta massif to its north and the warm air over the lake and the Po Valley to its south. It is a portion of the nocturnal downslope phase of an alternating Alps to Adriatic and return surface flow. It is strengthened by its confinement between the mountains lining the Sarca Valley and the northern portion of the lake, and accelerated each morning by the heating of the plains of the Po. The Peler typically appears after midnight, blows at 12 to 15 knots until dawn, builds to a peak speed of 18 to 25 knots at 0830 (when the disparity between the temperature at the icy alpine peaks and the hot flatlands reaches a maximum), and gradually dies until at about 1100, lifted by the upslope Ora (see chapter 34, "Lago di Garda"), it leaves the lake in complete calm (see Table 12).

For its first 70 miles down the valley of the Sarca River, the Peler is a mountain

282

TABLE 12: DOWNSLOPE WINDS

FIXED DRAINAGE (FALL) WINDS
- a. Cause—cold air fall from glacier, snow, waterfalls
- b. Typical venues—Thunersee, Vierwaldstättersee, New Zealand lakes, Lake of Geneva

DIURNAL DRAINAGE WINDS
1. Nocturnal and morning downslope (mountain) winds
   - a. Cause—cold air accumulation at high altitude
   - b. Typical venues—Finger Lakes, California coast, Norwegian fjords, Lago di Garda
2. Shade-induced, evening downslope winds
   - a. Cause—cold-air accumulation in shade
   - b. Typical venues—Finger Lakes, Lake of Geneva
3. Combined upslope/downslope winds
   - a. Cause—overflow of an upslope flow across a ridge
   - b. Typical venues—Wolfgangsee (Brunn wind), Maloja Pass

GRADIENT-INDUCED DRAINAGE WINDS
1. Transmountain flows—Föhn, Santa Ana, Chinook
   - a. Cause—transmountain synoptic pressure gradient
   - b. Typical venues—Thunersee, Bodensee, Palma de Mallorca
2. High-pressure drainage—Mistral, La Bise, Tramontana, Bora
   - a. Cause—accumulation of cold air on upland plateau
   - b. Typical venues—Lake of Geneva, Riviera, Adriatic

---

wind; then, for its next 35 miles down Lake Garda, a translake wind; and finally, for many miles inland from the lake's southern shore, a lake breeze. Thus it usually depends, as does the afternoon lake breeze/upslope Ora, on clear, dry air to facilitate radiational heat loss from the mountain peaks during the night, and on the insolation of the low-lying lands around the lake during the day. Clear, dry air in which the lapse rate is high also facilitates descent and ensures that the downflow, despite adiabatic heating, emerges at the lake surface denser than the surrounding air. (See appendix 4, "The Basis for Downslope Flow.")

A strong Ora typically follows a strong Peler—the thermal gradient merely reversing with insolation. But the Peler, a far more extensive wind than the Ora, is much more affected by the synoptic pressure gradient. When low pressure to the south of the Alps combines with high pressure to the north of the Alps, the Peler may spill over the mountains as a north Föhn and appear on the lake as a gradient-induced downslope flow (resembling the Mistral).

The Effect of the Synoptic Gradient

The thermal gradient that induces the Peler operates over hundreds of miles (from the Brenta massif to the Po) and is greatly affected by the synoptic gradient. If the synoptic gradient is northward and upslope (up the valley of the Sarca), unless the air is clear and dry (optimal for thermal generation), the Peler will be weak and short-lived. If the synoptic gradient is downslope but the ambient air is hot and moist, the Peler will also be weak, but in this case persistent. If the mountains are barely visible in the haze of a hot, maritime air mass, the Peler will be weaker than the Ora. Cloud cover and water vapor during the night (the greenhouse effect) severely diminish the longwave radiational cooling of the mountain peaks on which the Peler depends, whereas shortwave insolation during the day penetrates to the surface readily, melts the haze and the cloud cover, and creates the thermal turbulence on which the Ora depends. If the synoptic gradient is downslope and the skies clear, the Peler will be strong and persistent.

A downslope thermal gradient operates only during nocturnal and early-morning hours, whereas a synoptic gradient operates continuously. A Peler induced by thermal factors alone will die by 1100; a Peler induced by synoptic factors may persist until midafternoon (or even later). Whereas a glance at the sky will indicate the likelihood of a strong Ora, one needs to look at the weather map to predict the Peler. Gradient-aided Pelers behave similarly to thermal Pelers and provide good racing on "bad" (cloudy or rainy) days. Because the Peler occurs in such a variety of circumstances, racing is more often conducted in Pelers than in Oras.

Strength

The strength of the Peler is largely due to thermal factors: the tremendous pressure head created by the accumulation of cold, dense air on the surface of glaciers 10,000 feet above the surface of the lake, the confinement of the cold, dense flow vertically by an inversion a few hundred feet above the surface and laterally by the steep sides of the Sarca Valley and the northern end of the lake, and the low pressure developing each morning over the heated plains beyond the lake-level outlet at its southern end.

The 25- to 30-knot Pelers with the high gusts (due to avalanches of cold air hurtling over precipices onto the lake) occur after clear, dry nights during which longwave radiation from the upper mountain slopes has caused the ground surface and the air above to cool maximally. In late spring the combination of very cold air and maximum insolation through air with a very high lapse rate produces the strongest downslope flows; rarely, in the absence of insolation, do even wintertime synoptic pressure gradients produce a Peler of similar strength.

Direction and Distribution

Downslope flows composed of cold, dense air are more affected by channeling than any other type of air flow. They are typically only a few hundred feet deep, and confined by a strong inversion of their own creation are unable to expand vertically. They rush along the surface directly down the steepest slopes and are channeled around obstacles in their path.

The 600-foot escarpment that rises between Torbole and Riva divides the flow coming down the valley of the Sarca into the Riva flow (reinforced by drainage from the side valley above Tenno), at 360° to 10°, and the Torbole flow, at 20° to 30°. In addition, a major downflow emerges on the western side of the lake from the Val di Ledro (a tributary valley elevated a thousand feet above Garda) that splashes onto the lake from approximately 330° and intermittently adds 30- to 40-knot cascades, backed 30° to the Riva flow. The Torbole flow affects only the northeast corner of the lake north of Pt. Corna d'Ba. Most of the midlake is in the Riva flow (Figure 38.1).

Near the Circolo Vela Torbole's starting line to the south of Pt. Corna d'Ba, the amalgamated wind, combining all three flows, varies (with medium and short oscillations) over a range of 20°, between 360° and 20°. Farther north the flows are more obviously separated. Because of channeling along both shores of the widening lake (diverging from the starting line with distance to windward), a course along either side provides course-shortening shifts. Boats that opt to go up the eastern (right) shore find, as they emerge from below Pt. Corna d'Ba, a 10° to 20° veer associated with the intrusion of the point into the Torbole flow (at 20° to 30°). Boats that opt to go up the western (left) shore find, as they close the abrupt western wall, a 10° back associated with the channeling of the Riva flow. As these boats pass the Val di Ledro a half mile from the weather mark, they experience an even greater back as the Val di Ledro flow deviates the surface wind. But the convergence

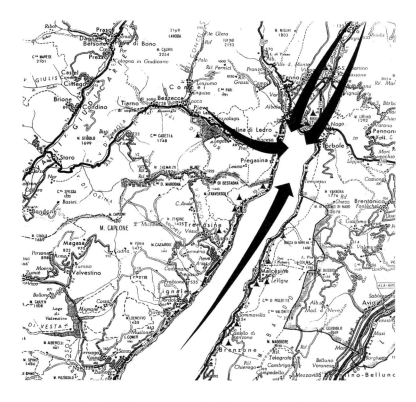

Figure 38.1. Three segments of the Peler converging with the Ora

285

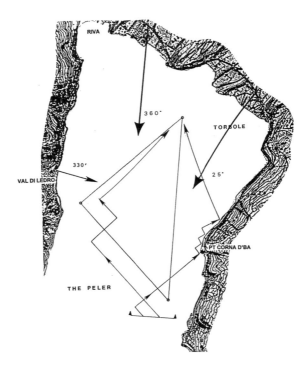

Figure 38.2. Channeled shifts in the Peler

of the three air flows in the lake's center may produce course-lengthening headers on either layline; boats emerging from either corner may lose all they have gained inshore (Figure 38.2).

Divergence between the overwater and overland segments of the flow along the east shore should produce some near-shore acceleration. That this is not evident may be due to the opposition of the Coriolis force as the flow makes a sharp left turn around Pt. Corna d'Ba (the reverse corner effect). Typically, boats holding left nearer the western shore do better, particularly when, on the port layline, they reach the Val di Ledro back.

The Dying Peler

During a race the Peler (weak or strong) is always dying. It has usually reached its peak velocity before and diminishes progressively after 0830. The thermal gradient has usually reversed by 1100 to 1130 (although occasionally, when the synoptic gradient is strong, downvalley flow will continue until midafternoon). Strong Pelers are more likely to be immediately supplanted by strong Oras—the Peler scarcely disappearing from the surface before the Ora is seen racing up the lake. Typical Pelers, disappearing at 1100, are followed by 1 to 2 hours of nearly complete calm before insolation is sufficient to generate a recognizable Ora.

The Midlake Calm

Although the Peler is (at least) three winds, it flows from the shore, from all shores—down a long, narrow lake with but two sides. And in a dying wind on a lake, the sides are always favored. In a dying Peler (as in most winds at Garda) one must avoid the middle; always seek one shore or the other. (See Figure 26.2, p. 189.)

The main flow down the Sarca Valley, already divided by the escarpment between Riva and Torbole, becomes increasingly segregated, compressed, and accelerated along each shore. In some conditions the most prolonged flow is from the Val di Ledro, pools of cold air continuing to drop down the 1,000-foot cliff for up to an hour after the last remnants of the flow down the Sarca Valley have disappeared.

The Convergence Calm

As the slopes heat in the sunlight and separation begins at the peaks, the warming downslope flow becomes less and less able to penetrate the pool of cold air at the bottom of the valley and over the lake. A low-level upslope flow begins to lift the downslope flow from the surface of the land. Entrained by this upslope movement, the near-shore lake air begins to move toward the shore and lifts the downslope flow from the near-shore lake. Soon only gusts of very cold high-velocity upper-level downslope flow are able to break through the cold, dense overlake air, and only at greater and greater distances from the northern shore.

In late morning the progressively enlarging calm at the northern end of the lake may be associated with a distinct line of dark ruffled water to the south (that is often misread as the advancing Ora) where, beyond the near-shore zone of low-level opposition, the Peler still reaches the surface. At this time boats but a few hundred feet farther south (in the better-penetrating air) often move at twice the speed of their more northerly competitors. Finally the warmed downslope flow is everywhere displaced above the cold surface layer and the calm is pervasive. (See Figure 26.2, p 189.)

The two simultaneous influences—the segregation of the flow to the sides of the lake and the southward recession of its surface penetration—produce the characteristic distribution of a dying Peler:

- The least wind—the earliest calm—is in the middle, farthest from the lateral shores.
- The strongest wind is along one shore or the other.
- The calm is progressively more complete with distance north and the flow progressively stronger with distance south.

The Principles of Managing a Dying Wind on a Lake

1. Early in the morning (during the first round of a race) the wind is homogeneous and its direction is far more important than its strength. Take the side of the course that will provide the most advantageous shift(s). In early morning the wind is stronger along the west wall and backs 15° (a lift) as one approaches the mark along the port layline. Although boats on the east side gain from the veer beyond Pt. Corna d'Ba, they are headed in the backed Val

di Ledro flow, as they approach the mark on the starboard layline.

2. As the wind begins to die, keep to the side of the lake on which the marks beginning and ending the leg lie. If they lie on opposite sides, cross the lake as directly as possible to reach the side on which the next mark lies.

   a. Do not cross the lake twice on any one leg.

   b. When crossing the lake, cross it as far to the south as possible—the surface wind is stronger with distance south.

3. When the wind has died and calm patches are present, the residual wind will persist on only one side of the lake. (It may be flowing at 5 to 8 knots there, whereas the other side is in nearly complete calm). Tack or jibe immediately from the rounding mark toward that side (which is readily recognizable by the persistently ruffled water), where the residual wind still exists. When the typical downslope wind develops under strong combined thermal and synoptic gradients, the major Riva flow on the west side of the lake will persist longest. When the Peler is weak (having developed with little thermal support), the minor Torbole flow on the east side of the lake will persist longest.

39. The Lake of Geneva

When the wind's before the rain,
Shake 'em out and go again.
—AMERICAN PROVERB

T
he Lake of Geneva (or Lac Léman) constitutes a vast open space surrounded by mountains: the French Alps, including Mt. Blanc, range
along its southern shore; the Swiss Alps mass at its eastern end; and the
long escarpment of the Jura slants down to its western end. The lake induces air
to flow through, up, down, and over those mountains and across its waters in
response to a wide variety of thermal and synoptic gradients and consequently, has
more distinctive, repetitive, and therefore named winds than any other site in the
world. Rarely, if ever, does a wind appear on the lake that a local sailor is unable
to recognize and name (rightly or wrongly). (See Table 13 and Figure 39.1.)

It may be the immense vineyard-covered slopes along its northern shore that
are most responsible for this naming. For it is from these slopes (upon which most
of the local inhabitants live) that one can observe the wind and the entire 60-mile-
long sweep of the lake. From almost any elevation in this vast amphitheater one

TABLE 13: THE WINDS OF THE LAKE OF GENEVA (LAC LÉMAN)

UNDER THE AZORES HIGH

The Rebat (the lake breeze)	Midday	2 – 8 knots
The Morget (downslope NW)	Evening	6 – 14 knots
The Fraidieu (downslope S)	Evening	6 – 10 knots
The Jurasson, the Bisoton, the Jaman	Morning	4 – 6 knots
The Séchard (gradient NE)	All day	8 – 10 knots

LOW PRESSURE APPROACHING TO THE NORTH

The Vent (gradient SW)	All day	20 – 25 knots
The Vent-blanc (gradient W)	All day	20 – 30 knots
The Vaudaire (induced Föhn)	All day	25 – 30 knots
(in the Haut Lac and Grand Lac only)		

AFTER WARM FRONT PASSAGE

The Maurabia (gradient SW)	All day	20 – 30 knots

AFTER COLD FRONT PASSAGE

The Joran (gradient NW-N)	Brief	25 – 30 knots

AFTER THE JORAN

The Bise (induced downslope NE)	Many days	10 – 40 knots
The Bise Noir (gradient NE)	All day	15 – 20 knots

can see the distinctive pattern that each wind makes as it plays upon the surface of the water. There are few places in the world from which one can see winds so well and over so large an area.

Geography

The Lake of Geneva, at the western end of Switzerland, is a dilatation of the Rhône River, created as its flow across the Swiss Plateau is blocked by the Jura Mountains. The Rhône flows from a glacier in eastern Switzerland and down a long valley between two major alpine ridges before emptying into the portion of the lake known as the Haut Lac near Montreux. Sixty miles to the west the largest (in volume) lake in Europe spills out from its narrowest portion (known as the Petit Lac), through the Jura Mountains at Geneva, and begins its long journey down France's Rhône Valley to the Mediterranean at Marseille. The most frequent and strongest winds of the lake develop in its confined ends, the Petit Lac and the Haut Lac.

The low-pressure systems of the polar front, sweeping into Europe from across the Atlantic, provide gradient winds as they pass either to the north and into the Baltic or to the south and into the Mediterranean. Two major gradient-induced downslope flows (and some less frequent variants) are generated by the passage of low pressure nearby: La Bise, when the low pressure is to the south of the Alps, and the Vaudaire, when the low pressure is to the north of the Alps.

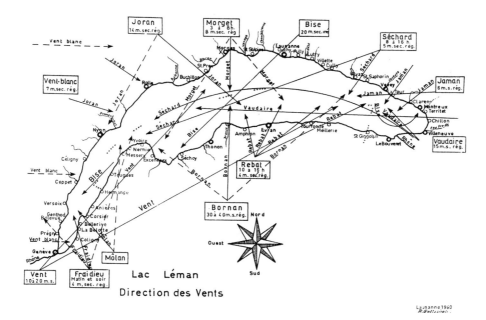

Figure 39.1. The winds of the Lake of Geneva (Lac Léman) (Courtesy E. Gottschall, Lausanne, 1960.)

Consequent to its unique geography and surrounding mountains the Lake of Geneva develops, in addition to the gradient-induced flows, a full range of thermal winds. A lake breeze and a variety of upslope, downslope, valley, and mountain winds appear regularly at appropriate sites along the lake.

Regime 1: The High-Pressure Winds of Summer

In summer the inversion, created as air within the eastern margin of the Azores High subsides (on a continental west coast) over the cold north Atlantic, is stronger and extends much farther inland than does the inversion created as air within the western margin of the Bermuda High subsides over the warm Gulf Stream. Over Europe the polar front is blocked and unable to move south of the Baltic for prolonged periods. The subsiding air in the Azores High, heating as it sinks, may form a protective subsidence/advection inversion over almost all of western Europe, including Scandinavia. When it settles over the Léman, it protects a whole galaxy of winds that develop in accordance with diurnal variations in insolation.

The Rebat

When the gradient winds are excluded by the inversion, the winds of the Léman are light—but distinctive. Each of the thermal winds that appears develops from calm and provides an air flow for a particular segment of the lake, leaving the remainder either in calm or in the sway of another local thermal wind.

291

Into the calm of these conditions, at about 1000, comes the Rebat—the lake breeze. Because both the surrounding mountains and the flattest, most insolation-responsive surfaces are uniformly distributed, the Rebat is weak, unfocused, and spreads in all directions from a central zone of calm. It is rarely stronger than 8 knots and then only when it combines with a local upslope flow. It is often so light that the calm is barely disturbed.

The Rebat is strongest along shores that slope gently up from the lake, permitting the cold lake air to reach a large area of heating lowland across a low-lying shoreline. It is weakest along those shores (such as the French southern shore) from which the mountains rise steeply and block the access of the marine air. The Rebat always leaves the majority of the Grand Lac (its deepest, coldest central portions) in complete calm, flowing with increasing force near shore (particularly the north shore) and into the narrow lake ends. Its increased strength in the Petit Lac at the lake's western end (where it is called, and is not distinguishable from, the Séchard) and in the Haut Lac at its eastern end depends on its confinement in these narrow segments and on its combination with upslope flows across near-shore flatlands toward the Jura and the French Alps.

Unless a lake breeze has a focus toward a particularly well-insolated, low-lying, near-shore surface or an isolated group of mountains at one end of a lake, it will be weak, absent from the lake's center, and evident only within a mile or two of shore.

The Morget and Evening Downslope Flows

The Rebat begins to die at about 1400 because it is weak, because cold air flows down far more readily than up, and because, with so much of the mountainous terrain falling into shadow, its upslope flow component weakens early. By 1600 the Rebat is gone (except where well-insolated flatlands lead to a mountain slope that is still in sun) and is followed between 1700 and 1800 by a set of named downslope flows. Three of these are consequent to the southeastern face of the Jura falling into shade while the slopes between the Jura and the lake remain in sun: the Morget, the strongest and most famous (which flows out onto the lake from over Morges); the Jurasson from over Nyon; and the Bisoton (or Dezaley) from the steeper slopes to the east of Lausanne. One, the Jaman, is due to the cooling of the upper slopes of a mountain named Jaman, near Montreux. All are typical afternoon downslope flows—cold air sliding down shaded, often ice-covered, upper slopes toward low pressure engendered over still-insolated lower slopes that "draw" the flow onward and out onto the lake. The momentum of these flows is usually insufficient to carry them beyond the center of the lake (despite the still-sunlit slopes on the opposite shore), and they typically subside in late evening after insolation ceases (Figure 39.2).

The Morget, the strongest *thermic* of the Léman, displaces the Rebat (or a dead calm) at about 1700 on sunny summer days and sometimes persists throughout the night and occasionally into the morning. It appears first alongshore and gradually spreads offshore. So regular and repetitive is the Morget that the yacht club at Morges schedules its summer racing for 1800 and starts the fleets between a set of fixed posts across its expected northwesterly direction. After a brief beat toward the land, the fleet reaches or runs offshore to a long beat home. Construction

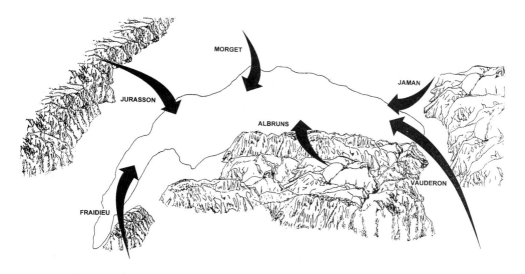

Figure 39.2. Downslope winds of the Lake of Geneva

along the coast has diminished the heating of the lower slopes, and the Morget, which once blew at 20 knots and crossed the lake to Yvoire, now rarely exceeds 14 to 16 knots and ordinarily does not extend beyond the lake's center.

Evening downslope flows are light to moderate near-shore flows that respond to a thermal gradient created by the simultaneous cooling of mountain slopes and the insolation of intervening lowlands.

The Vauderon, the Fraidieu, and the Albruns

Three downslope flows, the Vauderon, the Albruns, and the Fraidieu, begin in late evening and strengthen in early morning and behave more like typical nocturnal downslope flows. The Vauderon is a mountain wind, an amalgamation of downslope flows from the Alps on both sides of the Upper Rhône Valley. After a long, straight passage the flow turns right (creating a corner effect) near Martigny, and is confined in a narrow pass where its 25-knot velocity in midmorning attracts local boardsailors to a tiny lake. A few miles beyond, it spreads out onto the wide Haut Lac, and its speed diminishes to 12 knots.

The Albruns is a widespread but very light downslope flow that may be detected on clear, quiet nights along the mountainous southern Léman shore. Because the Albruns slides down steep slopes and gains heat rapidly by adiabatic compression, it has difficulty penetrating the layer of dense air above the deep, cold water and is never found more than a mile or two offshore.

The Fraidieu descends from the French Alps onto the lowlands that lie to the east of the city of Geneva, and confined by the steep shores may accelerate to 12 knots as it flows from the south across the entire Petit Lac. It typically continues throughout the night and reaches its peak velocity as the vineyards of Vaud on the lake's north shore heat in the morning sun.

Typical downslope flows begin after nightfall, continue throughout the night, and often accelerate in early morning as the insolation of near-shore or far-shore lowlands begins.

The Séchard

When the subsidence inversion is strong, sailors sit ashore watching the glassy calm and waiting—in the Petit Lac for the Rebat, elsewhere for one of the late-afternoon downslope flows. Sometimes, however, in these same warm, sunny conditions, there is another wind, the Séchard. When the inversion is weak or absent, the gradient wind of the southeast quadrant of the Azores High reaches the surface. This gradient flow is deviated so as to come onto the lake parallel to the Jura from the northeast.

As it comes offshore in the Grand Lac, although rarely stronger than 8 to 10 knots, it occasionally overwhelms the onshore southerly Rebat and spreads across the entire lake. In most cases, however, the Séchard is limited to the Petit Lac, where it combines with the local Rebat (flowing toward the southwest tip of the lake) to produce an amalgamated lake breeze. The increase in velocity to 15 (or more) knots produced by this amalgamation justifies its being called the Little Bise. The Haut Lac rarely has wind in these conditions because there the Rebat is westerly and opposes the easterly Séchard.

In summer, because the rest of the lake so often languishes in calm, major championships are conducted in the Petit Lac at Versoix or at Geneva. Off Versoix the amalgamated northeasterly Séchard/Rebat flows parallel to the Swiss shore with water on its left, and gusts of its backed, more northerly, converging overland segment are brought to the surface by thermal turbulence. One typically needs to go inshore to the left to get into the stronger wind, but must beware of getting too far left in the veering overwater segment.

Because lake breezes and upslope and downslope winds respond to thermal gradients, which are created by insolation and easily overwhelmed by strong synoptic gradients, they typically appear in association with high pressure and beneath inversions.

Regime 2: The Low-Pressure Winds

If, as often happens, low pressure spawned in the North Atlantic halts over Scandinavia, a persistent gradient flow ahead of the trailing fronts affects Switzerland. If this flow is from the southwest, it is called the Vent (the wind); if the low has moved farther east and the gradient flow is from the west, it is called the Vent-blanc. If the low itself is close by to the north, high pressure over the Mediterranean may cause a gradient-induced downslope flow over the Alps, a "south Föhn" called the Vaudaire.

If a warm front has passed and Switzerland lies in the warm sector to the south of the low, the gradient wind will be south-southwesterly (from Spain): the Maurabia. This is a hot wind of good weather. After the cold front trailing the low has passed, the gradient flow is from the northwest. Although this flow, known on the lake as the Joran, advects maritime rather than continental, polar air over western Europe, it is cool and clear with a high lapse rate and produces much thermal turbulence.

The Vent

The Vent is a wind of "bad" weather associated with rain and dark cumulonimbus over Geneva and the Jura. The flow from the southwest appears gradually ahead of an advancing Atlantic depression. Condensation occurs as the warm (in summer), wet airstream is lifted over the Jura. The wind seems to come in waves: a 20- to 30-knot gale followed by several hours of lighter wind and then another period of strength. Because the homogeneous flow is warm and stable, it is little affected by channeling or thermal turbulence, oscillates minimally, and appears everywhere to be from the same direction. However, the Dents du Midi along the southern shore displace the flow upward, so that even when the wind is howling in the Grand Lac, the Haut Lac may be calm.

The stable air remains elevated as it comes off the windward shore and lifts as it approaches the leeward shore and the waves diminish. When racing at Rolle in the southwesterly, port tack will take the boat into smoother water inshore. The first boat to reach the starboard, near-shore layline often wins.

The Vent-blanc

The Vent-blanc is due to the same circumstances as the Vent, except that the low pressure is stronger and halts over Norway or Denmark. Its name derives from the likelihood that the lake will be white with breaking waves. There may be multiple small depressions and successive warm or occluded fronts passing across the region. The wind is from the west, is cooler and more unstable than the Vent, and is strong. It seems to come directly from the Jura, is gusty and shifty—producing oscillating wind conditions. Rain and clouds may persist for one or two days, clear, and then return for periods of up to a week. When a cold front finally appears and clears away the rain and clouds, the wind shifts to the north—the Joran—and is very strong, producing big waves at the eastern end of the lake, where it has its longest fetch.

The Vaudaire

Low pressure passing across northern Europe, particularly if it passes farther south (closer to the Léman) than usual, will create, in the presence of high pressure over the Mediterranean, a gradient forcing air northward over the Alps. If the gradient is sufficiently strong, it will generate a strong Föhn down the north faces of the southern Alps and out onto the lake in direct opposition to the gradient wind. The Vent, the Vent-blanc, or the Joran may be blowing from the west or northwest across the remainder of Europe, but just north of the Alps the Vaudaire lifts the gradient wind from the surface. The flow has lost its moisture in its ascent of the south slopes of the Alps and brings a strong, hot, dry wind to the Upper Rhône Valley and the eastern portions of the lake (Figure 39.3).

The Vaudaire appears suddenly (usually in the midst of the Vent or Vent-blanc) and produces a dramatic shift and an increase in strength to 25 to 30 knots. It flows from the south to the southeast in the Haut Lac, from the southeast to east in the Grand Lac, and rarely reaches as far west as Morges. A zone of calm protected by the Dents du Midi extends along the Savoy coast. The Haut Lac and part of the Grand Lac lie in the gusting zone, where its downslope momentum carries

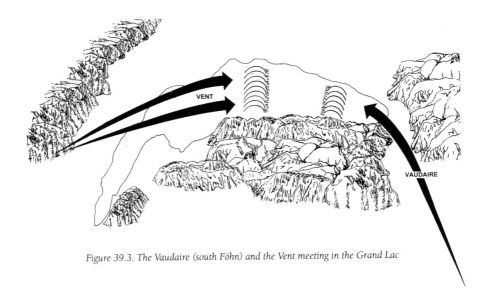

Figure 39.3. The Vaudaire (south Föhn) and the Vent meeting in the Grand Lac

the wind through the pool of cold air to the lake surface. In the Petit Lac and the western portion of the Grand Lac, however, the Vent often persists, lifting the warm Vaudaire from the surface. In the center of the Grand Lac the two winds may meet in a zone of violent shifts, gusts, and huge waves.

The Vaudaire usually appears about 12 times each year, typically in the spring or fall, as a typical Föhn, gaining heat rapidly as it descends through stable air. The required relationship between low and high pressure to either side of the Mt. Blanc massif rarely persists for more than one day, so the Vaudaire is soon gone. In winter, cold air stagnating in the bottom of the Rhône Valley usually prevents the Vaudaire from reaching the lake surface.

The Maurabia

Maurabia means to "make the wheat ripe," and this wind appears in July or August in the warm sector between the trailing fronts of a low-pressure system passing over Scandinavia. Because the gradient flow is from the south or southwest, immediately ahead of an approaching cold front, it is strong and produces big waves. The first sign of its approach is the sky turning gray without obvious clouds. It is said to blow only at the surface, "*without making the poplars move!*"

The Joran

The *Joran* is the name given to the northwesterly (and sometimes northerly or northeasterly) flow behind a cold front. It follows the Vent or Vent-blanc (and/or the Vaudaire) and appears suddenly as the rain disappears and the sky clears. It is dreaded at Morges, where one often sees round black clouds at the top of the Jura just before the wind swoops down to the lake. The initial blast often arriving with the sun is usually the strongest, blowing at 25 to 35 knots for 5 to 6 minutes. Thereafter, the cold, gusty flow gradually diminishes and veers to the north as the barometer rises.

The Joran ordinarily lasts but a few hours and is often followed by La Bise—"*it takes the Bise's hand.*" The increase in pressure north of the Alps consequent to the passage of the cold front, if combined with low pressure in the Gulf of Lyons, creates the downslope Bise.

Regime 3: La Bise

This regime, consequent to low pressure forming in the Mediterranean or passing into the Mediterranean from the Bay of Biscay, produces a gradient-induced downslope wind, known on the Léman as La Bise. La Bise is a portion of a widespread downslope movement from the entire alpine region toward low pressure in the Gulf of Lyons. In the Lower Rhône Valley and along the French Riviera, this flow is known as the Mistral, in Italy as the Tramontana, in the Adriatic as the Bora. La Bise is the most important branch of the Mistral; the Swiss Plateau contributes much of the air that flows down the Rhône Valley to the Mediterranean. It is the most common wind of the Léman, occurring on about 100 days each year. (See chapter 40, "La Bise.")

XII. Gradient-Induced Downslope Winds

40. La Bise

Blow, winds, and crack your cheeks!
Rage!, Blow!

—SHAKESPEARE

We have seen the power of diurnal upslope and nocturnal downslope flows. When we add a synoptic gradient to such a thermal gradient, particularly to a strong, downslope thermal gradient, a persistent wind is created. The Mistral, for instance, is far more common in France, northern Spain, Switzerland, and northern Italy than any other wind flow. It is produced when a synoptic pressure gradient develops between high pressure in northern Europe—a common occurrence—and low pressure in the western Mediterranean—an even more common occurrence. This gradient—the northeast flow to the southeast of the high and the northeast flow to the northwest of the low—causes air to flow downslope from the Swiss Alps to the Mediterranean. The thermal gradient strengthens the flow each night and each morning. On the Lake of Geneva the flow, which makes for great sailing, is called La Bise.

A Race in La Bise

From our little hotel up in the vineyards above Rolle, the entire surface of Lake Geneva appeared to be covered with whitecaps and so, as we arrived at the club at about 0800, I worried that the wind might be too strong for racing. My crew, Jean Pierre ("JP") Marmier, reminded me that La Bise, a gradient-induced downslope wind, was aided by thermal effects. It was always at its strongest in early morning and typically diminished with the heating of the day. He thought that during the afternoon it might even die away and be replaced by the Rebat (the lake breeze), but that it would reappear during the night and the following morning.

I walked out to the end of the breakwater, staggering in the gusts. La Bise was highly variable; some of the gusts were at 20 to 25 knots, but there were lulls of less than 10 knots. The main sweep of the wind was parallel to the shore, which at Rolle was about north-northeast, and was coming over a bulge in the coastline about 3 miles to the east. Many of the gusts were markedly backed to the basic flow; some seemed to be coming off the immediate shore.

As we sailed south toward the start, I asked JP about the strategy of racing in La Bise at Rolle. "Keep to the left, toward shore," he said. "Don't let anyone else get farther left." I reasoned that this would position us farther into those backed gusts coming off the shore—and probably meant that the wind generally backed with distance toward shore. We luffed to check the wind several times before reaching the starting line and several times thereafter, and confirmed our presumptions: both the range and the median wind direction were backed with distance toward shore.

With the weather mark set close to shore, but directly upwind in the relatively veered offshore flow, we made an excellent port-end start, and on the lee-bow of the fleet, headed toward shore. "Where's Roger?" "He's tacked." I looked back and was amazed to see about half the fleet, including the local ace, Roger Guignard, off on port from the middle of the line. I mused: *They can't be right— but that's okay with me—we'll have them all easily.* In an abrupt header the boat on our weather quarter tacked, we tacked—and we were laying the mark! *Uh, oh!* But we had them all—we couldn't lose. Not until we lifted—and lifted—above any heading we'd seen before the start—cracked sheets, and rode the last big gust into the mark astern of that other half of the fleet. How had they known that they would be able to lay the mark from the middle of the line?

The first reach was a lulu; we were barely able to lay the mark with the pole on the headstay, were blown over in the gusts, broached, and finally forced to drop the chute and beat to the near-shore jibe mark—but we had gained. And on the subsequent beats, with a little more care to avoid overstanding, eventually finished fourth.

By the time the second race was started at about 1130, the wind was down to a gentlemanly 12 to 15 knots and the weather mark had been shifted left to provide a good, balanced beat in the average wind—but the oscillations were even bigger. In a veer we again made an excellent port-end start, but this time played the oscillations and came into the weather mark with a 100-foot lead over those who had gone right initially. We pulled away on the reaches as those astern, in the lulls, luffed one another far above the rhumb line. Up the middle of the second beat we hit a series of shifts just right, and as we rounded the second weather mark were nearly a half mile ahead. But on the run, when a little to the left of the rhumb line, we ran almost completely out of wind and watched the entire fleet surge up in a 15-knot gust that never quite reached us. We struggled to finish second.

The final race of the day was started about 1400, after La Bise had died completely. We were expecting the Rebat, the lake breeze, from the southeast; it eventually appeared from the east-southeast, straight down the center of the lake. This wind, coming over water rather than over land, showed only minimal oscillations but was extremely patchy. On the first beat we went left, looked to be able to cross everyone, and then stopped as the fleet came in with a good breeze on the starboard layline. We reversed the situation on the second beat, but as we approached the finish our principal opponent came out of the left corner with a little more wind, the lead, the race, and the series.

Characteristics of La Bise

La Bise is the Swiss portion of the Mistral, the northeasterly outflow from high pressure induced by subsidence in a cold polar air mass over the British Isles or Scandinavia. This outflow moves southwest toward low pressure over the Mediterranean, channels across the Swiss Plateau between the Jura and the Bernese Alps, crosses the Lake of Geneva parallel to its north shore, and spills down the Rhône Valley en route to the Gulf of Lyons. At Lausanne it appears on 94 days per year, with a maximum frequency in March. Its average speed is only about 8 knots, but it reaches gale force 10 percent of the time. Due to the forced uplift, it brings clouds and rain to the mountains of the Bernese Oberland, but having deposited its moisture over these mountains, flows cold, dry, and clear down the open, sunlit slopes of Vaud and onto the Lake of Geneva. The high lapse rate and resultant thermal turbulence over these heating slopes facilitates La Bize's descent, the cold air accelerating downslope as it becomes progressively denser than its surroundings (Figure 40.1).

La Bise is at its coldest and strongest in early morning. At this time the lapse rate between the heating surface and the cold overflow is at its highest, facilitating the descent of the cold air. At the same time the lowland surfaces to the west of the lake and down the Rhône Valley toward the Mediterranean are heating rapidly, the air at the peaks is at its coldest, and a large thermal pressure head is being added to the synoptic pressure gradient.

Adiabatic heating from the descent, and heat uptake from the warming slopes, soon overcome the initial coldness of the downslope flow—and La Bise begins to lift above the cold lake air. If, as it was in May when we sailed at Rolle, the lake is colder than the warmed midday La Bise, its surface air will ultimately respond to the overland heating and begin to flow shoreward under the descending Bise as the Rebat—the lake breeze. *Our day of racing had been typical of gradient-induced downslope wind behavior: in the early-morning strong, cold, turbulent downslope flow; in late morning the gradual dying of that flow; at midday calm; in midafternoon the appearance of an onshore sea/lake breeze; and during the night the reappearance of the downslope wind.*

303

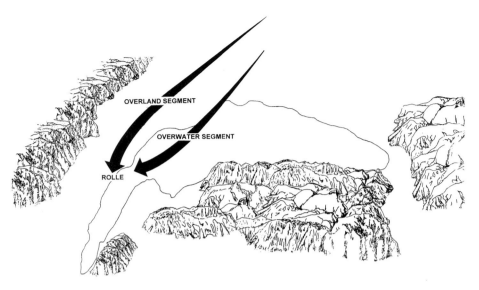

Figure 40.1. Splitting of La Bize at Rolle

Convergence along Shore

The difference in surface friction encountered as the overland and overwater segments of La Bise flow parallel to the Lake of Geneva's north shore causes them to separate into two flows: the overland, slowed and backed; the overwater, accelerated and veered. In the racing area within a mile or two of shore, these flows converge (the faster overwater flow veering into the slower overland flow), resulting in dramatic gusts, marked and prolonged reductions in wind flow, and huge oscillations of as much as 50° between the backed overland flow (brought to the near-shore surface by thermal turbulence) and the veered overwater flow. The farther offshore (near the starting line and the leeward marks) one sailed, the more dominant became the more homogeneous, veered overwater flow. The farther inshore one sailed, the more dominant became the backed and turbulent overland flow.

It had been necessary to move from the veered offshore flow, the overwater segment of La Bise, operative at the starting line into the flow extant at the weather mark. On our first beat we had overdone the effort—had moved into a wind that was backed 30° to 40° from the original—and overstood the mark. We had sailed the entire first reach in this gusty, backed overland segment. During the second race the distinction between the direction of the inshore and offshore flows had diminished as the overland flow became warmed and lifted from the surface. Near shore the variation in strength was paramount, as the warmed air was brought down to the surface only in prolonged oscillations.

41. Cold Gradient-Induced Downslope Winds

Mackeral skies and mare's tails
Make tall ships carry low sails.
—ENGLISH PROVERB

A Bora in the Adriatic

When we cruised the Dalmatian coast in 1985, my Austrian shipmates constantly reminded me of the Bora. We must sail with a "weather eye" to the northeast; we must always anchor in a harbor protected from the northeast; if low pressure develops in the Mediterranean, we must not venture far from shelter. Such are the concerns of those who sail along mountainous coasts where cold drainage winds periodically appear—the Pontias at Nyons, the Breva of Lago di Como, the Inverna of Lago di Maggiore, the Tehuantepecer along the west coast of Mexico, the Pampero of Argentina, the Williwaw of Chile, or the Norte of Central America.

One day in a dead calm we motored north from Mljet. As we reached Korčula and moored stern-to the massive Venetian key on the north side of the ancient city, the Peljašec Maestral (the classic afternoon sea breeze) appeared. But we were no sooner ashore and wandering the lovely streets of the romantic port than my shipmates began discussing (in German) the risks of a mooring so exposed to the Bora—and eventually demanded that we leave to spend the night in a very unromantic but protected harbor 10 miles to the north. The Bora failed to materialize.

Several days later as we slipped northward in a warm, light northwesterly sea breeze, a cold blast of markedly veered strong air suddenly hit us and we were forced to tack to starboard. Although we spent the rest of the afternoon wrapped in sweaters and foul-weather gear instead of the T-shirts and bathing suits to which we had become accustomed, the wind never exceeded 20 knots, and coming off the nearby shore scarcely disturbed the smooth water. In the Mediterranean (to our south) a low-pressure system was moving past and, near Trogir, close to the Dinaric Alps, the conditions were right for a Bora. But the cold downslope wind—the little Bora—in which we had sailed was never a threat; we spent a quiet night in a lovely little island harbor, not more than 100 feet in diameter—and wakened to the usual morning calm.

The Bora and the Mistral result from the same synoptic situation: high pressure inland to the north of the Alps (typically advecting cool, dry air with a high lapse rate) and low pressure over the Mediterranean. The resultant northeasterly flow is downslope from cold uplands toward warm water, in the case of the Bora from over the Karst and Dinaric Alps of Slovenia and Croatia to the Adriatic. Because the Alps are close to the sea, lessening the amount of friction, and the final overland passage is down steep near-shore hills, the Bora is often both stronger and more treacherous than the Mistral. But it is less frequent, appearing on perhaps 30 days per year and rarely in summer (Figure 41.1).

The negative buoyancy of the cold air and the precipitous drop sometimes cause the classic Bora to rush downslope with the velocity of a thermal downdraft. It is said to appear as an icy blast from the northeast out of a clear blue sky and to increase to 50 knots in 15 minutes! But the Bora may also appear as a Föhn-type flow through air with a low lapse rate, warming as it descends, while retaining some of its original high altitude coldness. Even then, because in many locations the slopes are so steep and its descent so rapid (an "aerial cascade"), it is often able to penetrate the dense overwater air in the near-shore gusting zone.

The Mistral

The name *Mistral* is given to that portion of a general trans- and interalpine flow resulting when high pressure centered over the British Isles or Scandinavia creates in its southeast quadrant clockwise flow from the north or northeast and, simultaneously, when low pressure in the Gulf of Lyons or the Gulf of Genoa creates in its northwest quadrant counterclockwise flow from the north or northeast. The Gulf of Lyons (French for "lion") derives its name from the frequency with which the Mistral develops and blows across it—about 100 days per year! Once initiated it may blow for days (or weeks) and is capable of blowing completely across the Mediterranean, producing the Tramontana of the Balearics and the northerly storms of Corsica and Sardinia en route.

The same high pressure that produces the Mistral causes flow across Switzerland

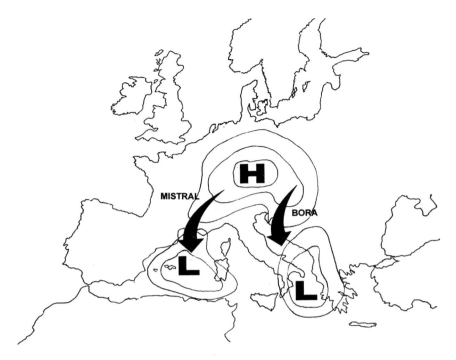

Figure 41.1. The Mistral and the Bora

as La Bise; flow to the west of France's Massif Central, bending around the eastern end of the Cantabrian Mountains to emerge on the Mediterranean coast as a Tramontane; flow around the eastern end of the Pyrenees near Perpignan as a Maestral, or Cers; and flow through the gaps in the Maritime Alps along the Italian Riviera as a Tramontana.

The Mistral may develop at any time of the year but is particularly common in winter, when the greatest temperature disparity exists between the air over the cold uplands and the air over the warm Mediterranean and when the lapse rate in the surrounding clear, cold air is likely to be high. Its maximum strength is evident at dawn in association with the maximum temperature disparity between the Alps and the sea and the highest lapse rate in the intervening air.

The Mistral, descending through air with a high lapse rate, becomes progressively denser, colder, and dryer than the surrounding free air. In winter at least, the descending air, despite adiabatic heating, remains colder than its surroundings all the way to the French coast, where it is often bitterly cold. The farther downslope and the more rapidly it descends, as in certain steep portions of the Rhône Valley and the Maritime Alps, the stronger and gustier it becomes.

The cold Mistral air hugs the ground, channeled downward by every vale and valley, so that it emerges on the coast as a mixture of many flows, alternating and often interfering with one another. Over the coast, sea breeze formation, encouraged

307

by the high lapse rate, regularly diminishes the Mistral in early afternoon. Over near-shore water the strength of the Mistral peaks at 1000 in summer (noon in winter), diminishes in early afternoon, and revives in late evening.

The confinement of this massive cold flow, both vertically beneath its created inversion and horizontally as it passes through the relatively narrow gaps in the obstructing mountain ranges, causes significant local acceleration. To this stimulus is added the corner effect, first described in relation to the Mistral's deformation as it bends around the eastern end of the Massif Central and the Pyrenees. The imposition of these mountains in the stream, forcing the wind left, sets up an intensified pressure gradient to leeward of the mountains, where the wind returns right, strengthening the Coriolis force. The corner effect accounts for much of the local increase in velocity in the Rhône Valley and for the unusually strong Mistral or Cers at Perpignan (Figure 41.2).

In May of 1988 the Mistral of the Italian Maritime Alps (the Tramontana) blew so hard for three days that it almost prevented the completion of the Soling European Championship. At Alassio, as the northeast flow came down through clear air almost parallel to the coast, we watched ferocious downdrafts flatten the surface of the water and drive great circular arcs of foam downwind at 40 to 50 knots.

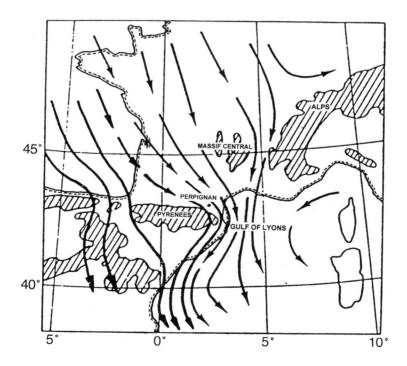

Figure 41.2. The corner effect in the Mistral (From Willett and Sanders, Descriptive Meteorology; after Cruette, 1976)

308

Determinants of Cold Gradient-Induced Downslope Flow

Cold, synoptic gradient-induced downslope flows drain down steep slopes that separate high snow-covered plateaus or ranges from relatively warm water. They are strengthened by and vary in intensity with the thermal gradients of the local diurnal downslope (mountain) winds. They are typically stronger, often far stronger, and gustier—often characterized by dramatic changes in velocity and direction— and typically colder. They are the most feared winds in their zone of influence, often, as in the Rhone Valley, causing the inhabitants to build their homes down-slope and to the south of sheltering topography, or, as along the Dalmatian coast, necessitating the construction of special harbors.

A low-level inversion forms above the sliding air and confines these cold flows to the lowest hundreds of feet of the troposphere, where they are typically channeled into relatively narrow streams by topographical features. The characteristically high velocity of the Mistral and the Bora and their ilk are consequent to the combined effects of the pressure gradient force (the least significant), the confinement of the flow into narrow, shallow streams by the topography and the inversion, the formation of lee waves (see chapter 42, "The Föhn"), and the progressively rising relative density of the descending air.

When the lapse rate in the surrounding air is greater than the adiabatic descending air, gaining heat at the lower adiabatic rate becomes, relative to the surrounding free air, progressively more dense. With a progressively increasing pressure head, it falls at a progressively increasing velocity. Even in surrounding air with a low lapse rate, air derived from very cold uplands may, despite adiabatic heating, retain enough of its initial coldness so as to arrive at the base of the slope colder than its surroundings.

Downslope flows, aided by gravity, acquire momentum and cannot be halted abruptly. Once set in motion—even though heating and losing density in air with a low lapse rate, even when encountering colder air—such flows typically slide onward until their momentum is dissipated, often far out to sea. (The Mistral occasionally crosses the Mediterranean!) Because the pressure gradient operates far beyond the slope, gradient-induced downslope winds are not limited (as are thermally induced downslope flows) by entrance into a pool of colder, denser air accumulating at the slope's base. Instead, as the flow comes offshore onto the water, over an area of reduced friction, it typically accelerates.

Mechanical turbulence introduced by friction, chiefly at the interface above, and thermal turbulence induced by the flow of cold air over warm land cause these flows to become extremely gusty. In addition, the periodic obstruction of flow channeled down one tributary valley by another or the obstruction of the main valley flow by the flow from a tributary valley often creates large-scale intermittence at the base of a slope or over water. At Palma de Mallorca several passes direct the flows of a Tramontana through the Balearic Mountains, and the multiple flows periodically diverge to augment one another, or converge to diminish one another. They emerge on the water as strong, cool, gusty winds, shifting dramatically (as much as 50°) between the separate outflows of the coastal valleys. We learned that in these "big shift" conditions it was necessary on every beat to go for one layline or the other.

42. The Föhn

Every wind has its weather.
—FRANCIS BACON

We were admiring the Eiger, the Monsch, and the Jungfrau from the club lawn, more than satisfied with a one-race day on the Lake of Thun in Switzerland (on 35 percent of summer days the wind is insufficient to permit any racing on the Thunersee). The morning had dawned cloudy, and with low pressure spreading eastward from the North Sea, we had thought that this might be one of those days. But after we had waited several hours, the sun had broken through and the standard northwesterly, an upslope wind directed toward the alpine peaks, began to ruffle the surface of the lake. The one race we did sail had been a long and exciting one. My wife, Frances, sailed as middleman (after my regular crew failed to appear), the lead changed on every leg, and in the last fitful gasps of the upslope wind, we pulled ahead to win.

At 1830, while the sailors lounged about drinking beer, rehashing the day's race, and wondering about tomorrow's, a huge wall of cloud began to build above the alpine peaks and overhead there appeared a patch of blue. "The Föhn is coming," someone shouted. As the race committee huddled, we were suddenly hit by a blast of hot air. Within minutes the calm lake was converted into a mass of whitecaps, the trees were swaying in a 20-knot southerly, and the committee boat horn was whirring, whirring! "They can't intend to start another race at 1900, can they?" asked Frances. They can—and they did. Without her, in the hot 20-knot gusts, we managed a seventh, which, coupled with another first in Sunday's light air, was sufficient to win the regatta. Engraved on the Jungfrau Trophy is "1986—US 725—Walker, Walker, Seemann."

The Föhn

The Föhn is far more than a mere hot downslope wind; it is a respected and feared climatological event. It alters the growth of vegetation and the behavior of humans and animals. It appears in overcast or rainy conditions from a patch of blue sky as a fierce and erratic blast of hot wind. Previously obscured mountaintops and a huge bank of dark clouds (the "Föhn wall") are suddenly revealed. Near the foot of the mountains dry, dust-laden air rushes down at 20 to 30 (sometimes 50 to 80) knots and raises the temperature 20° to 50°F in a matter of minutes. A few miles farther to leeward (farther from the mountains) there is either little or no wind or only the original gradient flow. Along a coast or lake the strong, gusty flow may continue for hours or days, extending offshore as the temperature rises and retreating as it falls (Figure 42.1). (See appendix 4, "The Basis for Downslope Flow.")

Wherever winds of this character occur, they receive names. In Europe there is the Föhn, the classic south Föhn—air flowing down the north face of the Alps onto the Thunersee, the Vierwaldstättersee, or the Bodensee, or onto the Lake of Geneva as La Vaudaire—and the less frequent north Föhn. In the Andes, it is the Sondo; in Argentina, the Zonda; on the eastern face of the Rockies, the Chinook;

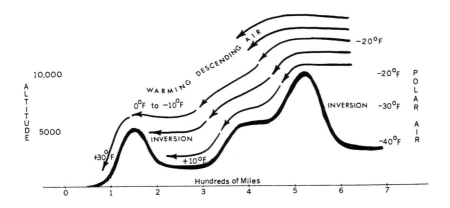

Figure 42.1. Gradient-induced downslope flow

on the Southern California coast, the Santa Ana. Föhn-type winds—suddenly appearing, strong, hot downslope winds—are common and occur wherever a significant mountain range intrudes in the path of weather features migrating along the polar front.

Föhn Generation

Typically the hot Föhn-type downslope winds derive from warm maritime air that has been induced by a synoptic gradient to move inland and over and down a mountain range, whereas the cold Bora-type downslope winds derive from cold continental air that has been induced by a synoptic gradient to move seaward and over and down a mountain range. Typically the hot downslope winds are deep, involving the whole troposphere (the inversion at the tropopause is just above them), whereas the cold downslope winds are shallow, involving only the near-surface layers and creating a low-level inversion as they go.

However, it is now recognized that these distinctions are incomplete, that intermediate types of all gradations occur. The same mountain range may produce a hot downslope flow in one condition and a cold one in another. A hot flow may develop toward the sea—the Santa Ana, for instance—or a cold flow may progress inland—the Vaudaire, for instance. The flow may appear gradually rather than abruptly; it may be cool one day and hot the next; it may be strong or weak, brief or persistent. A special set of circumstances is required for abrupt appearance, another for temperature elevation, a third for violence, a fourth for extent, a fifth for duration.

The Föhn was originally described as the consequence of a gradient operating to elevate moist air upslope in stable conditions. When the elevated air lost heat adiabatically, its contained water vapor would condense and release its "heat of condensation" in a Föhn wall cloud bank. When the flow descended to a similar level on the far side of the mountain ridge, gaining its lost heat adiabatically, the ambient temperature of the now dry air would be higher by the amount of the heat of condensation.

Until recently a number of facts that were inconsistent with or unexplained by this simple description were ignored:
- The addition of heat by condensation is inadequate to explain the often dramatic net temperature increase.
- The recognized temperature elevation and expansion should, but does not, prevent the descent of the flow to the foot of the mountain.
- The abrupt appearance and occasional violence of the air flow at the foot of the slope and out onto adjacent water are far in excess of the velocity of the gradient flow on the windward side of the mountain or at its summit.

The Effect of the Lapse Rate

Investigations in the 60s and 70s revealed that moist air and the release of latent heat accompanied only one type of Föhn—a cyclonic Föhn occurring in a stable atmosphere. Computer modeling demonstrated that in cold downslope flows the velocity is directly proportional to the lapse rate of the surrounding air (the higher the SLR, the more rapidly the flow gains in relative density) and inversely proportional to the slope angle (the steeper the slope, the less the friction and the more rapid the descent), but the extent to which this applied to hot flows was not certain.

Other studies showed that whenever the adiabatic lapse rate affecting the descending air was greater than the lapse rate in the surrounding air, downslope flows became progressively hotter than their surroundings as they descended—regardless of the release of the heat of condensation. (And still other studies demonstrated that whenever the ALR was less than the SLR, downslope flows [the Bora-type] became progressively cooler and denser and flowed downslope at progressively higher velocity.) "Dimmer Föhns" were recognized in which the flow started down the slope but never reached the bottom—flowed off instead at some upper level above the cold surface air. However, this discovery was not immediately accompanied by the recognition that partial descent was the norm and complete descent the exception.

The reason that hot Föhns were usually composed of maritime air and flowed inland, and Bora-type downslope flows were usually composed of continental air and flowed seaward, was clarified. Maritime air had a low lapse rate and continental air a high lapse rate! Until the last decade one question remained unanswered—why should a hot flow descend through colder air all the way to the bottom of a slope—and out onto nearby water—at far greater velocity than the flow from which it derived?

Lee Waves

It was belatedly recognized that when the hot flow struck the lower slope or the surfaces at the foot of a slope with great violence, belts of reduced velocity were present both above and beyond this zone of maximum effect. A distinctive cloud form, lenticular in shape, that remained in a fixed location as much as 12 to 19 miles to leeward of the transited mountain range was often noted. After striking the surface, sometimes at high velocity, the Föhn apparently rebounded to high levels, where this distinctive condensation occurred. These phenomena were ultimately recognized as wave activity, and the persisting lines of cloud across the wind flow as condensation at the sites of crests in lee waves (Figure 42.2).

Despite the absence of a clear-cut upper surface, it has now become apparent that downslope flows behave like water and obey hydraulic principles. Air transiting a mountain, like a stream encountering a submerged rock, dips and accelerates on its approach to the obstacle. Instead of elevating (in opposition to gravity) a deep mass at a low speed, it accelerates a shallow mass to a high speed—converts potential energy into kinetic energy.

Severe Downslope Flow

The startling characteristic of downslope flows, particularly of the Föhn type, is their occasional conversion from moderate winds on the upslope side of a

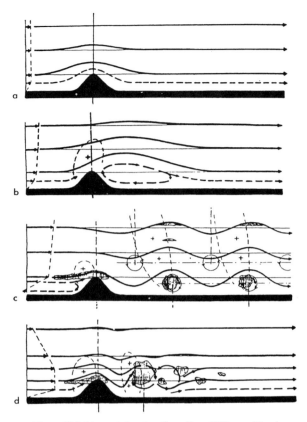

Figure 42.2. Mountain barrier effects (From Willett and Sanders,
Descriptive Meteorology; after Corby, 1954.)

mountain to roaring gales exceeding 125 miles per hour (200 kilometers per hour) on the downslope side. The National Center for Atmospheric Research (NCAR) was built in Boulder, Colorado, in time to study such a gale, the great Boulder Windstorm of 1972 (Figure 42.3). Research aircraft flying within the 125 mph (200 kph) storm discovered that the 6-mile-deep (10 km) westerly flow had been squeezed into a surface layer only 1.2 miles (2 km) deep as it began its acceleration downslope. The depth of the flowing mass dramatically decreased on the crest approach, and as it contracted beneath the stagnant wedge of warmer turbulent air, its velocity increased and its lateral pressure decreased. This was clearly the beginning of wave activity.

The problems remaining after the 1972 studies were to explain the failure of the wave phenomena to persist and the failure of the energies involved to dissipate themselves in a cyclic motion that would return the flow to its preencounter state. It is evident that in some circumstances (whether Föhn-type or Bora-type) the downslope windstorm is different from mere wave activity. In order to achieve the speeds involved, the moving surface flow must "decouple" from the atmosphere above.

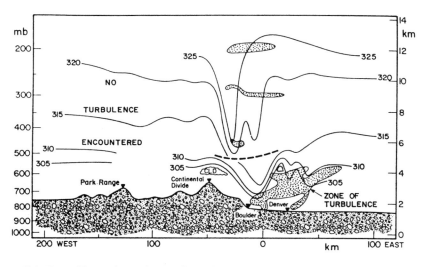

Figure 42.3. The Boulder Windstorm (From Willett and Sanders, Descriptive Meteorology; after Lilly, 1978.)

Wave-Breaking, Hydraulic Jumps, and Pulsations

Two theses have been advanced to explain this decoupling and the violence of the occasional Föhn. One presented by scientists at the University of Toronto and the NCAR is that the wave of accelerated flow "breaks" (as does an ocean wave), leaving the moving air free to fall away and accelerate further. The Alpex experiment appeared to confirm that wave-breaking accounted for the violence of the Bora winds that shoot out onto the Adriatic from the steep Dinaric Alps (Figure 42.4).

This study and others have emphasized the development of supercritical flow and a "hydraulic jump" in the high-velocity thin layer that transits the mountain crest. The jump permits the wave to blow downstream and the decoupled air to accelerate downslope the way flowing water accelerates, clings, and drops down on the back side of a submerged rock. According to this thesis, the downslope flow—water or air—returns to its preexistent state through an abrupt jump upward in a turbulent zone beyond the foot of the slope. And, of course, it is close to the foot of the slope, just proximal to the jump, that sailors often sail and are exposed to the worst of downslope flows.

A second thesis is that within severe downslope winds pulsations sometimes appear that abruptly increase their velocity. Colorado's Boulder Windstorms are thought to be characterized by an intense pulsation in the subinversion flow with a period of approximately 10 minutes. Such pulsations seem to result when internal waves develop within high-velocity stratified flow (associated with transition into a high-drag, supercritical state), are forced to critical steepness, and, consequently, "break."

As the lowest layer of the flow decelerates in the lee of an obstacle or below the edge of a precipice, secondary instability is superimposed upon the primary instability of the upper layers. The cross section of the "jet" flow is abruptly reduced

315

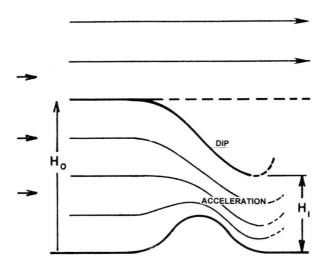

Figure 42.4. Acceleration of downslope flow in a wave to leeward of an obstacle (From Smith, "On Severe Downslope Winds," Journal of the Atmospheric Sciences.)

and its velocity abruptly increased when the overlying mixed layer decelerates and its upper surface retracts just beyond the obstacle. Such instability tends to recur at the same location, indicating that its major determinant is the topography.

The appearance of the Föhn at Thun was, of course, dependent on an increase in the transmountain synoptic gradient and was not related to the strength of the preexisting upslope wind. Once the gradient flow crossed the alpine ridge and started down, it would displace any thermal wind regardless of its strength or temperature. Despite its high temperature the downslope flow descended to the lake in response to wave influences and affected different parts of the lake differently. Far less wind was evident at Interlaken, at the "foot of the slope," nearer the mountains, than was evident at Thun 10 miles to the north, and far more at Thun than on the plains beyond. We apparently sailed in a zone of maximum velocity increase beyond the foot of the slope, but proximal to the "hydraulic jump."

The Differences between Primary and Secondary Sea/Lake Breezes

I use the term *secondary* to indicate that sea/lake breezes developing under unstable offshore winds are closely related to, but distinct from, primary sea breezes developing under inversions. Meteorologists make no such distinction, but sailors should. The circumstances in which these winds develop, the likelihood of their completely displacing the gradient wind, and their ability to produce the condition of "two winds simultaneously" are quite different.

In both primary and secondary sea breezes, the initial onshore movement of the marine air is dependent on convection induced over land. But the secondary sea/lake breeze is created by convection within an unstable gradient flow. The primary sea breeze must rely on the protection of an inversion to bring its tenuous onshore flow across the shoreline, and on its own sea breeze front to create the necessarily high near-surface lapse rate over land. Initially its upper-level waterward flow is autonomous, separated from whatever gradient wind is blowing by a preexisting inversion. The secondary sea breeze, on the other hand, may never cross the shoreline and never develop an upper-level waterward flow of its own. It is secondary to the gradient flow. It relies on that flow to provide both the necessarily high overland lapse rate and the subsidence offshore that replenishes the overwater high pressure.

THE PRIMARY (OR PURE) SEA/LAKE BREEZE

Primary Source of the Thermal Gradient:
> The localized fall in surface pressure, or trough, created as the cold leading edge of its self-created sea breeze front invades across hot land.

Determinants of Strength:
> The coldness of the offshore water, the heat of the inland land, and the overland near surface lapse rate.

Sea Breeze Front (essential):
> Rapidly invasive, shallow, containing relatively stable cold air.

Gradient Flow:
> Warm to hot, from any direction (as long as it is isolated above an inversion).

Inversion (essential):
> Protects the sea breeze from the interference of the gradient wind (at least initially) and isolates the gradient wind above the inversion.

Circulation:
> Cold marine air flowing in the sea breeze front over the surface of heated land facilitates separation and convection; heated air rises to the preexistent inversion, then moves offshore toward and subsides into the upper-level trough above the water.

THE SECONDARY (OR "PURE") SEA/LAKE BREEZE

Although the secondary sea/lake breeze is an imitation of the primary, the differences are distinct. Compare these salient characteristics of the secondary with those of the primary *(vide ut supra)*:

Thermal Gradient (primary source):
The generalized fall in surface pressure overland induced by a cool, deep, unstable gradient wind (independent of a sea breeze front).

Determinants of Strength:
The instability, coldness, and direction of the gradient flow.

Sea Breeze Front (nonessential, though beneficial):
Even if the onshore flow crosses the shoreline, it will usually be slowed and deepened by the opposition of the gradient flow.

Gradient Flow:
Cool and unstable; flowing offshore.

Inversion:
Nonexistent (except at the tropopause) until the marine air begins to flow in a sea breeze front beneath the warmer gradient wind; initially the two winds meet at the surface.

Circulation:
When exposed to the high lapse rate and instability of the cool gradient wind, heated surface air over the land separates, rises to the tropopause, is entrained in the gradient wind, and moves offshore toward and subsides into the upper-level trough above the water. This addition to the overwater high pressure initiates and maintains an onshore flow that may be halted short of the shoreline by the gusting zone of the gradient wind.

In the midlatitudes, secondary sea/lake breezes develop in association with cool, unstable, offshore gradient winds (typically northerlies on "south-facing" coasts) and are dependent on them for their strength and extent. Primary sea/lake breezes require the protection of an inversion to bring their fronts onshore (a radiation inversion for morning local sea breezes, an advection inversion for most lake breezes, and a subsidence inversion for the primary sea breezes of the ocean coasts).

Once a sea breeze front is established, however, its progress, the convection within it, and its effect on the overwater onshore flow are the same. Thermal turbulence within the sea breeze front of a primary sea/lake breeze developing under an inversion may break through that inversion, and the upper-level outflow, which earlier in the day had been autonomous, may become embedded within the offshore flow of the gradient wind. Then a primary sea/lake breeze can be said to have become a secondary sea/lake breeze.

APPENDIX 2

The Sea/Lake Breeze Front

Prior to a primary or secondary sea breeze front's crossing the shoreline, the development of a sea/lake breeze at a given site and—if it develops—the strength of its overwater onshore flow are dependent on external factors such as the presence of protective inversions, the instability of the ambient air, the accessibility and insolation responsiveness of the inshore land, and the overland near-surface lapse rate. (See chapters 24, "The Sea/Lake Breeze: Initiation," and 29, "Will a Sea/Lake Breeze Develop?") Once the sea breeze front has crossed the shoreline, however, its internal near-surface lapse rate determines the thermal pressure gradient, and its speed of advance determines the speed of the onshore flow. Thereafter the speed of the onshore flow is directly proportional to the ease of separation at the shoreline, within the front, and at its leading edge. The ease of separation is directly proportional to the initial coldness of the marine air and the responsiveness of the underlying surfaces to insolation, and inversely proportional to the rate of heating and expansion of the marine layer.

The Crossing of the Shoreline

The initial crossing of the shoreline, which is essential to the establishment of a sea/lake breeze front and the maintenance of a primary sea breeze depends on:
• sufficient contraction and subsidence to raise (or maintain) pressure over cold water
• sufficient separation and convection to diminish pressure over heated land
• an inversion or series of inversions above the onshore flow of cold marine air

A primary sea/lake breeze must utilize, in the absence of the dramatic reduction in overland pressure created by the instability of the secondary sea/lake breeze's gradient flow, an inversion or a combination of inversions to protect the nascent onshore flow. Depending on the inversion or inversions available, the primary sea/lake breeze will be a light, transient, localized flow or become a strong, persistent, large-scale flow.

The marine air will, of course, cross the shoreline more readily if and where that shoreline is low and if and where the air's crossing is aligned with another synoptic or thermal (upslope, onslope, downslope, or expansion differential) pressure gradient. But regardless of the presence of such an advantage, the beginning flow of a primary sea breeze needs an inversion. Inversions provide cold surface air to facilitate the development of a high near-surface lapse rate and protect the surface from the interference of the gradient wind—until such time as the sea/lake breeze front creates an appropriate environment autonomously.

A radiation inversion provides an accumulation of cold surface air temporally associated with the beginning of insolation: an increase in overwater pressure and a high near-surface lapse rate in association with the facilitation of insolation by clear, dry air. A low-level onshore flow—a local primary morning sea/lake breeze—and a subinversion offshore flow will commence beneath a radiation inversion and persist until heating of the subinversion air causes the near-surface lapse rate to fall below the critical level.

A subsidence inversion that overlaps the near-shore land and the radiation inversion will preserve the necessarily high near-surface lapse rate and will permit the sea/lake breeze to maintain or reestablish both a low-level onshore flow and an upper-level subinversion flow. Usually by early afternoon, insolation and the thermal pressure gradient (in otherwise appropriate conditions) are great enough that the marine air can cross the shoreline in the absence of a preexistent inversion. Now the formation of a large-scale afternoon sea/lake breeze requires only that the marine air be colder than the ambient air, so that an advection inversion can form between them.

The Formation of the Shoreline Trough

As the leading edge of an invading sea/lake breeze front crosses the shoreline, cold marine air encounters hot land, and large volumes of air separate from the surface, rise through the marine layer, and surge upward to the preexistent inversion or into the gradient flow above. A band of maximum separation and expansion, a low-pressure trough, forms beneath the leading edge of the front, and the onshore flow rushes into it. Typically the maximum energy transfer takes place in this shoreline trough, where the cold marine air first encounters the hot land. The crossing of the shoreline has a dramatic enhancing effect on the onshore flow, which abruptly accelerates and veers and thereafter flows at maximum velocity just proximal to the site of formation of the trough, over the water to windward of a (low-lying) shoreline.

When an air flow meets a dramatic pressure transition, it is forced either to decelerate (converge)—when low pressure meets high—or to accelerate (diverge)—when high pressure meets low. When the cold, dense air of a sea/lake breeze front crosses onto heated land and encounters the dramatic drop in pressure at the shoreline low/trough, it accelerates and diverges. The pressure gradient force (acting toward the center of low pressure) attempts (in the Northern Hemisphere) to back the accelerating inflow. But the sudden acceleration exceeds the pressure gradient effect (the combination of centrifugal and Coriolis force overwhelms the pressure gradient force) and some of the air, instead of backing (turning left), escapes to the right, and the air loss intensifies the low. This continuous intensification of the low-pressure trough at the shoreline accelerates the invasion of the sea/lake breeze front and accounts for the surprising strength of some sea/lake breezes.

Near-Shore Divergence

The dramatic acceleration of the flow as it crosses the shoreline has two major effects on the overwater flow. To accommodate the acceleration, the cross-sectional area (the height) of the frontal mass is reduced and the inversion lid lowered. This vertical divergence (which is evidenced by clearing of low-level cloud and lucency in the Doppler radar image) increases near-shore subsidence over water and elevates near-shore pressure, thereby enhancing the thermal gradient and adding to the acceleration.

The zone of acceleration immediately beyond the shoreline is well demarcated in a secondary sea breeze. The cumulus cloud streets in an offshore gradient flow disappear abruptly a few miles inland along a line that roughly approximates the indentations in the shoreline. Subsidence above the accelerating sea/lake breeze front melts the cumuli as if they had been cut with a knife. This zone of clear sky overlying the near-shore trough remains fixed throughout the afternoon while the sea/lake breeze front slowly extends inland beneath the overflowing cumulus. At first, convection deriving from the cooler surfaces within the front halts (at the top of the marine layer) below the condensation level, and the overflowing cumuli (if any) are the shreds of those clouds produced farther inland in the gradient wind. Eventually, however, the front deepens, convection reaches the condensation level before reaching the inversion, and cumuli develop within the front itself.

The acceleration into the near-shore trough elicits an increase in Coriolis force, which causes the overwater flow to veer abruptly and remain veered. This veering is translated back offshore, but is always maximal just proximal to the shoreline at the site of maximal acceleration. Thus the overwater flow backs with distance to windward, and this shift is particularly evident early in sea/lake breeze development when the onshore flow first crosses the shoreline (the fan effect).

Frontal Warming

As the front moves inland, updrafts of heated air are typically trapped beneath its lid inversion, and the marine layer heats and expands. Never again is the frontal air so cold, nor is the disparity between its temperature and the heated surfaces it encounters inland so great. The greatest temperature contrast, the highest near-surface lapse rate, persists in a band along the shoreline (the shoreline trough) where the marine air retains its over-water coldness, and to a lesser degree at the leading edge where, although the marine air becomes progressively warmed, the underlying land retains its hotness.

Where the overflowing gradient wind is very hot and forms a strong low-level advection inversion, as it does in Southern California and/or where the underlying sur-face is very hot as it is in Western Australia, the marine air retains its coldness, the leading-edge trough persists, and the front—racing across the intensely hot surfaces ahead—remains shallow. The marine air is so cold relative to the hot surface that updrafts pass clear through the cold layer without expanding it, and the marine air arrives 100 miles inland at almost the temperature and depth at which it came ashore. On the Chesapeake "the best sea breezes of the year" appear in spring, when cold water and hot westerlies in the warm sector combine to produce shallow sea breeze fronts that race inland beneath strong inversion lids.

In the midlatitudes, however, the front usually becomes progressively warmer, more expanded, and deeper; the height of its leading edge rises to many thousands of feet above the surface. Throughout the front the near-surface lapse rate and separation diminish both because the marine air becomes warmer and because the underlying land becomes cooler. Separating updrafts become progressively warmer and cease to rise at lesser and lesser heights. The front slows, its frontal cross section enlarges, and the marine air mass becomes a huge wedge—its greatest depth at its leading edge, its least at the shoreline, where acceleration and divergence draw down the inversion lid.

However, as the front moves inland it affects a progressively larger area, permits the generation of a fall in pressure over a progressively larger surface, and results in the trans-port inland of increasingly large amounts of marine air. Despite the reduction in the rate of separation, the vast expansion of the marine layer over an ever-increasing area typi-cally results in a progressive increase in volume and a relatively steady velocity of onshore flow.

The Speed of Advance

The Insolation Responsiveness of the Overland Surfaces

A sea/lake breeze front coming ashore over an extremely hot, flat desert will accel-erate, draw down its confining lid (the inversion), extend far inland, and induce a strong onshore air flow. A sea/lake breeze front coming ashore over marshes and inlets will accelerate less (and over patches of water will decelerate) and expand vertically, but, exposed to minimal friction, retain its momentum, extend moderately far inland, and induce a moderate onshore air flow. A sea/lake breeze front coming ashore over hilly vege-tated land will decelerate, expand rapidly, and exposed to marked friction, lose its momentum, extend but minimally inland, and induce a weak onshore air flow.

Over a zone of improved separation and/or reduced friction (smooth, barren deserts and fields, and gradually rising near-shore slopes), the front accelerates (diverges) and its depth diminishes. Over a zone of diminished separation (bodies of water, extensive forestation, abrupt elevations, an urban center that heats readily but traps the heat), the front decelerates (converges) and its depth increases.

Where an indentation or a low-lying marsh facilitates the crossing of the shoreline, the overwater flow accelerates and deviates toward that site. When acceleration or deceleration occur as the front subsequently encounters insolation-responsive or insolation-resistant sites, the effect is reflected backward into changes in speed and oscillating shifts within the entrained overwater onshore flow.

A special contrast in the speed of advance is evident where a sea/lake breeze comes inshore partially over water and partially over land. Although hot stable gradient flows accelerate as they emerge onto water and are characterized by the more rapid flow of their overwater segments, cold sea/lake breeze fronts are characterized by a reverse relationship. Unless the land surface is unusually hilly and heavily vegetated, the overland flow, because it accelerates into the shoreline and leading-edge troughs, invades far more rapidly than the overwater flow. At sites like St. Petersburg and in the upper Chesapeake, where the sea breeze flows both directly up the bay and across intervening land, the overland flow may arrive on inland waters 1 or more hours before the overwater flow.

The Size and Latitude of the Landmass

An optimal sea breeze is created by the invasion of a landmass approximately 60 to 90 miles in width. A lesser width provides a smaller heating surface and the possibility of a sea/lake breeze from the opposite side of the landmass meeting and opposing the flow. Small islands generate much vertical liftoff but very little horizontal onshore flow.

A number of modeling studies have demonstrated the dependence of sea/lake breeze strength on latitude. At the equator, because of the near absence of the Coriolis force, sea/lake breezes are weak even though their flow, perpendicular to shore, is aligned with the thermal gradient. In the high latitudes they are also weak, because the extremely high Coriolis force causes them to flow almost parallel to shore, perpendicular to the thermal gradient. They theoretically reach a maximum strength and their greatest inland penetration at approximately 30° latitude, where the thermal gradient and the Coriolis effect are best aligned. The Western Australian sea breezes at this latitude are amongst the world's strongest and most rapidly invasive.

The Height of the Preexistent Inversion

Primary sea/lake breezes that develop under low-level radiation and advection inversions that extend over and limit the height of turbulence above the near-shore land are weak. Primary sea/lake breezes that develop under the higher subsidence inversions of the subtropical highs may exceed 18 knots. Secondary sea/lake breezes (in the midlatitudes) are stronger than primary sea/lake breezes because the height of updraft ascent in the unstable air ahead of the front is limited only by the tropopause.

Extent Inland

The sea/lake breeze front and its entrained overwater onshore flow usually reach their maximum velocity and maximum volume/depth over land by midafternoon, but continue to extend for many hours thereafter. The extent of the sea/lake breeze offshore, which is rarely more than 12 miles, is limited chiefly by the distance required for the heated air from over the land to cool to the temperature of the air above the water, and on the volume of marine air entrained in the onshore flow. The extent of the sea breeze front inshore (which may be as much as 200 or more miles) is dependent on the same factors that determine its speed of advance (its internal near-surface lapse rate and the resultant thermal gradient, and the persisting coldness and shallowness of its leading edge). (See chapter 23, "Fremantle: The Primary Subtropical Sea Breeze.")

The front will continue to extend inland until the warming of the marine air or the cooling of the land causes the near-surface lapse rate to fall below the critical level, the leading-edge trough to fill in, and the momentum of the onshore flow to be insufficient to overcome surface friction.

SEA/LAKE BREEZE FRONT SEGMENTS

Segment I: Over Water

a. Offshore
- INVERSION LEVEL—300 to 3,000 feet
- TEMPERATURE—3°F greater than water temperature
- THERMAL TURBULENCE—None
- SPEED—4 to 6 knots (until front crosses shore)
- DIRECTION—Perpendicular to coast

b. Near shore
- INVERSION LEVEL—300 to 1,200 feet (at top of marine layer) diminishing as front crosses shore
- TEMPERATURE—3°F greater than water temperature
- THERMAL TURBULENCE—None
- SPEED—6 to 8 knots (until front crosses shore)
- DIRECTION—Veered 10° from a perpendicular to shore

Segment II: Crossing the Shoreline
- INVERSION LEVEL—600 to 2,500 feet (at top of marine layer)
- TEMPERATURE—4°F greater water temperature
- THERMAL TURBULENCE—
    In shoreline trough—through marine layer and aloft to inversion (if any)
    In leading-edge trough and within front—to top of marine layer
- SPEED—Acceleration of the overwater flow when the front crosses the shoreline
    8 to 20 knots near surface (12 to 25 knots aloft)—maximum speed at the shoreline
- DIRECTION—Veers the overwater flow 20° to 30° from a perpendicular to shore

Segment III: Inland

a. In warm stable ambient air
- INVERSION LEVEL—2,500 to 10,000 feet
    Top of sea breeze front blends with inversion
- TEMPERATURE—5° to 10°F greater than water temperature
- THERMAL TURBULENCE—
    Ahead of leading edge—6,000 to 10,000 feet
    Within marine layer—2,500 to 10,000 feet
- SPEED—Deceleration over land (convergence)
    6 to 10 knots at surface (12 to 18 aloft)
- DIRECTION—Backed (slightly)

b. Over hot, barren land (deserts)
- INVERSION LEVEL—200 to 1,200 feet (at top of marine layer)

(Continued next page)

- TEMPERATURE—
    10°F greater than water temperature
    10°F less than ambient air
- THERMAL TURBULENCE—
    Ahead of leading edge—3,000 to 6,000 feet
    Above marine layer—3,000 to 6,000 feet
- SPEED—20 to 30 knots at surface (25 to 35 aloft)
    Acceleration over land and over water
- DIRECTION—Veered 50° to 90° from perpendicular

c. In cold unstable air (in a secondary sea/lake breeze)
- INVERSION LEVEL—1,500 to 3,000 feet (at top of marine layer)
- TEMPERATURE—3° to 5°F greater than water temperature
- THERMAL TURBULENCE—
    Ahead of leading edge—6,000 to 15,000 feet
    Within marine layer—1,500 to 3,000 feet
- SPEED—Acceleration over water (deceleration over land)
    12 to 16 knots at surface (16 to 20 aloft)
- DIRECTION—Veered 30° to 50° to perpendicular

APPENDIX 3

The Basis for Upslope Flow

Upslope flow, whether rising to the summit of a high mountain or gliding across a gently sloping beach, is a major contributor to sea/lake breeze generation. Following the insolation of a flat surface or a slope, air—heated by conduction—seeks to expand but is compressed from above and from all sides by surrounding denser air. Because it cannot separate and escape upward until its temperature exceeds 3.5 times the temperature of the suprajacent air, it initially moves along the surface toward a site of lower pressure. Because pressure falls with altitude, on a slope the nearest site of lower pressure is upslope. Therefore, insolation will initiate an upslope movement of surface air in mid- or late morning of almost every (at least, every sunny) day and—inasmuch as the higher the position of a site along a slope, the lower its pressure—once initiated, this flow will continue to the top of the slope.

That pressure falls with altitude is a basic principle underlying all mechanisms of upslope flow. But large-scale upslope winds that contribute to sea/lake breeze generation depend on five additional phenomena:
1. Local differences in insolation that create *upslope flows* such as the "valley wind"
2. The chimney effect
3. Differences in the expansion of air at varying distances from a slope that create *onslope flows*
4. The effect of *slope angle*
5. Differences in the expansion of air (*expansion differentials*) on either side of a ridge that create flows through mountain passes

The Gudbrandsdalen

Studies performed along the Gudbrandsdalen—a set of valleys and a pass that transect, from the Atlantic Ocean to the Oslo Fjord, the mountainous ridge of southern Norway— provide insight into the development of slope winds (Figure A3.1).

Early Morning

At 0600, as the eastern, more gradual slopes of the Gudbrandsdalen begin to heat with exposure to the rising sun, the nocturnal downslope flow reverses, and in many eastern valleys a shallow *upslope* flow begins. Because the lower slopes lie at a large angle of inclination to the insolation and because the very cold, dense air that has accumulated along the valley floor is under the highest pressure, flow is first evident at the bottom of valleys. A shallow layer of cold air with a strong inversion lid begins to move upslope along the surface toward sites of lower pressure.

As the air overlying the heated surfaces expands with insolation, levels of equal pressure rise relative to the volume of expansion. Because the turbulent layer is deeper and

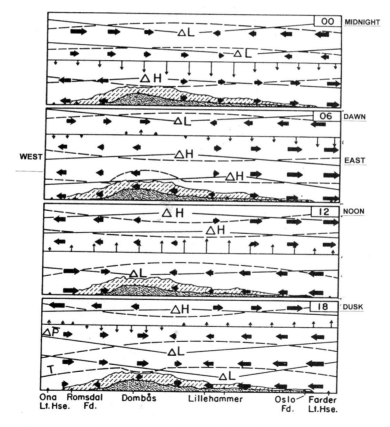

Figure A3.1. Upslope and downslope flow across the Gudbrandsdalen (From Willett and Sanders, Descriptive Meteorology; *after Sterten and Knutsen.*)

its volume greater over the near-shore plains, the pressure levels rise higher there than over the uplands. An *onslope* pressure gradient forms from above the plains toward the uplands. Flow down this gradient persists because free air moving toward and accumulating on the slope is carried away upslope by the *upslope* flow. At 0600 the eastern *upslope* flow carries over the ridge into the persisting downslope flow on the shaded west face. At the highest elevations continuous stream separation begins to expand the overlying air.

Noon

By noon both the *onslope* and the *upslope* gradients are producing a strong, relatively deep upslope wind from both bodies of water toward the ridge. Velocity (at least above the friction in the near-surface layer) is evenly distributed throughout the depth of the turbulent layer, but is maximal at the shorelines and gradually diminishes to zero at the ridge, where the two opposing flows converge. With an increase in time and insolation the turbulent layer expands and the inversion level at the top of the *upslope* flow rises. Expansion is negligible over the water and reaches a maximum midway between the two water bodies (rather than at the ridge).

Aloft, above the expanded turbulent layer, a compensating downslope flow, outward from the ridge in both directions toward the two water bodies, begins in midmorning and is fully developed by noon. This upper-level flow reverses before midnight and is upslope thereafter (until midmorning) from both water bodies toward the ridge.

Evening

By 1800 subsidence over the cooling ridge and downslope flow at the surface of the upper valleys begin. *Upslope* flow continues in the upper portion of the turbulent layer, on the lower slopes, and over the shorelines. By late evening the *upslope* flow is completely reversed; all flow in the turbulent layer is downslope in both directions from the ridge to the water.

Analysis

The *upslope* and *onslope* gradients are entirely determined by insolation, are modified both by cloud cover and by the angle of incidence of the sun, and are twice as strong in summer as in winter. Early in the morning, when downslope flow persists on the west face, *upslope* flow begins on the east face. Because the west slope of the Gudbrandsdalen is steeper, the deep air mass on that side expands (with insolation) more than the shallow air mass over a comparable surface area of the uplands to the east. The result at midday is a greater *onslope* gradient and a higher-velocity *upslope* flow from the west coast to the ridge than from the eastern uplands to the ridge.

The steep near-shore western slopes facilitate separation and create an *expansion differential* that results in a strong midday *upslope* and *onslope* flow. But the west coast sea breeze, less able to invade the steep coast, begins later and ceases sooner (shortly after 1800, when expansion ceases) than the east coast sea breeze. On the more gradual eastern slopes, insolation and radiational cooling act on a far larger, less steeply inclined surface, and the dense marine air of the sea breeze front is able to invade much farther inland. Consequently, over water on the Oslo Fjord, both the onshore sea breeze/*upslope* wind and the offshore downslope wind are stronger and more durable than are their ocean counterparts.

Upslope Flow: The Valley Wind

Insolation of flat, barren rock or cultivated fields creates a thermal gradient relative to less responsive forested or cloud-covered mountain surfaces. But the major effect of topography is the markedly reduced insolation and absorption of heat on surfaces inclined to the sun at angles less than 75°, down to and including those in the shade. The insolation of one side of a valley while the other is in the shade creates a difference in overlying expansion and surface pressure and a flow analogous to that recognizable in the movement of dust and trash between the shaded and the sunlit side of a city street.

Organization of upslope flow into a "valley wind" is usually required before a significant breeze results. A valley, by protecting the surface air from disturbance by gradient overflow and by providing a large heat-radiating surface, enhances the heating of the air within its confines. A shallow low-velocity flow up the walls of a valley—from the well-insolated, gradually rising lower slopes toward the poorly insolated, steep upper slopes—is the first *upslope* movement of the day (Figure A3.2).

Separate *upslope* flows soon become organized into a general valley circulation: at the surface from the center of the valley *upslope* on each side, at the ridge level horizontally from the ridges toward the center of the valley, and from the center of the valley vertically downward to the valley floor—and repeat. As the air rising along and heated by the slopes separates from the ridges, it cools and moves horizontally toward the valley center, where subsidence of the coldest air has formed a trough (analogous to the upper-level overwater trough of a sea/lake breeze). As the cooling air subsides over the valley center, it increases the pressure gradient toward the lateral slopes and completes the circulation.

Slightly later in the morning, consequent to the enhanced heating of the less inclined, more confined floor and the greater expansion of the larger volume of overlying air, a consolidated, deep, higher-velocity, upvalley flow begins (the noon upslope winds of the eastern slopes of the Gudbrandsdalen). Some of this flow fuels the lateral *upslope* flows, but most of it continues along the valley floor toward the higher plateau that typically lies ahead. This low-level upvalley flow is replenished by the midvalley subsidence of air drawn in from the lateral ridges. As the upvalley flow entrains additional air, a large-scale surface flow commences from across the plain, lake, or sea that lies downslope.

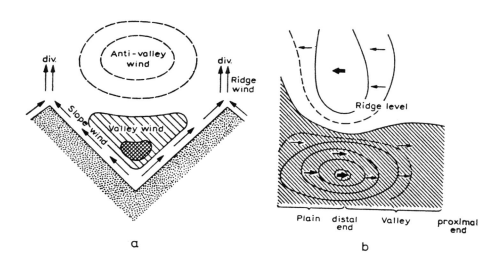

Figure A3.2. The valley wind (From Barry and Chorley, Atmosphere, Weather, and Climate; after Buettner and Thyer, 1965.)

The initiation, volume, and velocity of upvalley flow (the valley wind) depend on the orientation of the valley to the sun and to the surrounding plain. Nocturnal downslope flow continues until insolation begins each morning. In valleys whose axis is north/south cross-valley surface flow from east to west may be evident from the time the sun rises and insolates the east-facing slope until late morning, when the west-facing slope is first insolated. Such cross-valley flows interfere with and delay the formation of general upvalley flow.

The Chimney Effect

Rising air loses heat and gains density at the adiabatic rate, whether it is flowing upward along a slope (unseparated) or free. But during insolation, air rising along a slope is constantly rewarmed by contact with the surface. Thus the free air in the turbulent layer, mixing randomly, cools with height at a rate equal to or higher than the adiabatic rate, whereas at every level, air in contact with a heating slope remains warmer. A boundary develops between the cold free air and the warm near-surface air, below which the surface air flows toward lower pressure farther up the slope. Because the warm air, flowing up the slope, is everywhere held against the slope by the colder, denser free air, a wide, flattened "chimney" forms and this chimney extends along the heated slope all the way to the ridge where, at high altitude in cold air, separation occurs readily.

Because the weight of a column of rising heated air is less than the weight of a similarly dimensioned column of surrounding air, a pressure head develops. Cool, dense air surrounding the chimney sinks down and into the area of lower pressure below the warm expanded air, is warmed by contact with the surface, and is forced up the stack to the ridge or to the inversion level. The higher the peak or ridge at the top of the slope, the greater the difference (the pressure head) between the weight of air in the heated slope air and in the cooler, denser free air. Whether the chimney lies at an angle to the vertical, or is vertical, is of little significance; what matters is the difference in height between its top and its bottom.

Chiefly because of the chimney effect, thermal wind flow develops more readily and becomes stronger in mountainous terrain. Where mountains rise above the turbulent layer (or, more accurately, carry the turbulent layer with them), the height to which a column of heated air can rise is typically increased. The pressure head provided by an *upslope* flow to the top of a 10,000-foot mountain is 10 times the pressure head provided by vertical liftoff to an inversion level at 1,000 feet.

Onslope Flow

The lateral expansion of a heated mass of air is limited by the higher pressure in the air over surrounding less well-insolated surfaces, and therefore expansion is largely upward. Total expansion is a percentage of the total original volume, and the final height of an expanded mass of air is a percentage of its original height. For a given change in temperature a larger volume will expand more, rise higher, than a smaller one. However, because the total mass (weight) of air above an expanded volume remains the same, the level of a given pressure rises with and in proportion to the degree of expansion. Differences in the original volume of air above different sites will cause the levels of equal pressure to differ even when insolation is equal.

Isobaric pressure levels rise higher in the free air above a heated site on a low-lying plain than at a site on an elevated slope, and the steeper the slope, the greater the disparity. For example, at some altitude A and height of air mass H above a site at the base of a slope, expansion will cause the pressure level to rise by a factor X. At $2H$ above that site the pressure level, about twice the volume of expanding air, will rise by a factor $2X$, and so on. But at altitude $2A$ on the slope, the height of the air mass H will be zero and no expansion can occur. Consequently, pressure at $2H$ aloft in the free air above the base of the slope will be at a level $2X$ higher than the equal pressure on the slope. (See Figure 1.4, p. 10.)

The locus of equal pressure (the isoline) will slope downward from the free air toward the slope, creating a gradient down which air will flow. This *onslope* flow contributes a far greater volume into the rising surface air than does the *upslope* flow. *Onslope* flow will be greater along a steep slope, greater in proportion to the height of the summit (above its base), and greatest (relative to its base) near the summit, where the difference in the height of the isobaric levels is most magnified. In a valley the onslope flow creates the trough over the valley's centerline toward which the upper circulation of the valley wind is directed.

The Effect of Slope Angle on On- and Upslope Flow

The angle of a slope modifies insolation and therefore the time of initiation and the velocity of an *upslope* wind. An angle of less than 15° (from the horizontal) scarcely diminishes the projected area of exposure, but provides only a minimal increase in the lateral pressure gradient and the *onslope* flow. An angle greater than 45° significantly diminishes the area of exposure and thereby diminishes the *upslope* flow, but provides a markedly increased lateral pressure gradient and *onslope* flow. Therefore, slope angles between 15° and 45° provide maximum total upslope wind generation. As is clearly demonstrated by the Gudbrandsdalen studies (and explaining the greater horizontal flow on the eastern slope), optimal flow is achieved when a large area of lower slope at a readily heatable angle of 15° to 25° creates *upslope* flow and leads to an upper slope attracting *onslope* flow at an angle of 35° to 45°.

Differential Expansion

If on one side of a mountain range insolation is greater, or the surface heats more readily with insolation, or, most commonly, if the altitude of the land and consequently the volume of air below a given altitude is greater, during insolation the air on that side will expand more than on the other and will create an *expansion differential* and a transmountain pressure gradient.

During insolation a transmountain pressure gradient will develop (in proportion to the degree of disparity in the altitude of the two surfaces) between a lower heated plain and an upland plateau and will produce a flow through the passes of a mountain barrier from the plain toward the upland. This is the mechanism for the famous wind of the Columbia River Gorge; for the Maloja wind, which flows up the Maloja Pass in eastern Switzerland; and for Austria's Brunn wind, a daytime flow from the lower Mondsee through the Scharfling Pass onto the higher Wolfgangsee. (See chapter 35, "The Brunn Wind.")

APPENDIX 4

The Basis for Downslope Flow

~~~~~~~~~~~~~~~~~~

The temperature of free air changes minimally with variations in insolation, whereas the temperature of the land surface and the air in immediate contact with it changes greatly. Free air typically diminishes in temperature with altitude, each level being colder than the one immediately below. Each night the surface air on a slope, all along a slope—by conduction from the cooling land beneath it—becomes colder and denser than the free air at the same level, and therefore colder than the surface air immediately below (which had been at the warmer temperature of the lower-level free air).

Consequently, as the air on a slope becomes colder and denser than the air immediately below, it begins to slide downward. Such sliding flows—downslope winds—are common, occurring wherever topographical features cause surface air to cool below the temperature of the free air at the same elevation. Downslope flow is also instigated by inherently cold surfaces (ice and snow), by evaporation, by a pressure gradient's advection of air over a mountain range, and by drainage of cold air accumulated in an upland basin. Downslope winds can be shallow barely moving trickles, such as may be found in the early morning along any elevated coast, or massive flows of hurricane force such as when the entire troposphere, condensed into a layer but 1 mile deep, forms the Boulder Windstorm (of the Colorado Rockies).

The Initiation of Downslope Flow

Surface air is cooled chiefly by conduction, and conduction is facilitated by the lack of turbulence characteristic of nocturnal and other thermostable conditions (in which the coldest air is at the bottom). Air cooled by conduction sinks from the surface of elevated vegetation and protrusions to accumulate in depressions and breaks in the surface. The lessened insolation and the lack of turbulence in depressions enhance the cooling induced by cold air accumulation and counteract the heating induced by the enlarged surrounding surface.

Once all nearby depressions are filled, cold air begins to pile up in circumscribed puddles. Friction retards the lateral movement of such puddles until a mass of sufficient height accumulates and its upper layers begin to slide free of the trapped lowest layers.

Sliding will begin earlier in proportion to the steepness of a slope, and to its smoothness. In alpine regions where the slope is steep and the upper surfaces covered with ice or snow, downslope flow may be strong and appear early in the evening, whereas in the Tropics it may be weak and delayed until after sunrise. Relatively friction-free surfaces like ice and snow permit movement after minimal accumulation (glacier winds are typically continuous and homogeneous), whereas vegetation prevents movement until the cold air mass becomes deep. Shallow downslope flow is continuous over snow and ice because their high reflective capacity (*albedo*) causes them to remain colder than the free air even during insolation.

Characteristics of the Overland Flow

Cold air flows downslope more like porridge or thick syrup than like water. On a slope, air accumulates in puddles with flat upper surfaces and leading edges that bulge downslope.

More quickly on steep slopes, belatedly on plateaus along the slope or where trees or other obstacles obstruct or where the valley constricts, the rising edge of the accumulating puddle reaches a critical height, topples forward, and spills the cold air downslope.

Once set in motion (because sliding friction is much less than starting friction), the entire upper portion of the thick puddle entrains behind the initial spill, slips over the lowest layer (which remains fixed to the surface), and slides downslope to the next obstruction. Free air entrained by the movement, but warmer (less dense) than the air it replaces, accumulates above the original site. The bottom layer, trapped at the site by surface friction, conducts its coldness into the new, warmer air above, and the cycle repeats itself.

In alpine valleys, downslope flow typically begins in late evening and ceases at sunrise or shortly thereafter (later on shaded slopes than sunlit) and is most evident in winter. Cooling of the upper slopes and downslope flow is maximal in clear, dry air, which facilitates longwave (infrared) radiation, and least in cloudy, rainy weather, which markedly reduces the heat loss (the greenhouse effect). The cooler the upper slopes, the greater the density change in the suprajacent air and the sooner downslope flow is initiated. And the cooler the upper slopes the greater the initial density advantage and the farther downslope the flow will slide before adiabatic heating neutralizes that advantage.

As it flows downslope, the slope air increases in temperature adiabatically in proportion to its rate of descent and decreases in temperature in proportion to its time of residence above a particular cooling surface. Its rate of descent slows as it approaches dense air in the bottom of a valley or sinkhole. It will cease to flow when it meets air that is colder and denser.

The coldest surface air in a given area will be found at the bottom of a basin or sinkhole, where the absence of turbulence permits the temperature of the air to drop to that of the underlying radiating surface. When finally, in response to additional inflow or a pressure gradient, the accumulation spills over the lip of the sinkhole or basin, its density is often so great that it falls as an aerial cataract upon the slopes below.

Constrictions or belts of forest in a valley will dam the sliding cold air into a series of "lakes." If so, outflow onto a downslope water surface will be intermittent, a series of massive lulls and gusts as each dammed-up "lake" alternately accumulates cold air, and at a critical height spills downslope (Figure A4.1).

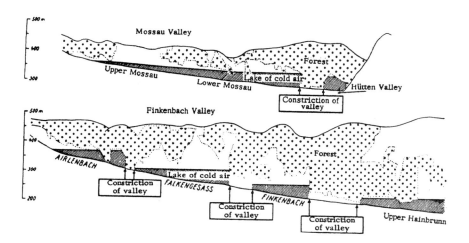

Figure A4.1. Downslope flow in two Odenwald valleys (From Geiger,
The Climate near the Ground; *after Schnelle, 1961.)*

The Anatomy of a Downslope Flow

A downslope flow on an upper slope is typically separated into five layers:
1. An immobile layer of very cold air fixed to the surface of the slope
2. Next, above a layer flowing downslope (intermittently or continuously), the downslope wind
3. A turbulent inversion layer between the cold, downslope flow and the warmer free air above
4. A layer of warmer upslope flow that compensates for and replenishes the downslope outflow
5. Above all, the unaffected free air moving in response to the synoptic pressure gradient force
   Significant shears are present within and between each of these layers that contribute to the directional variations and gustiness of the outflow.

A fully developed single downslope wind is typically about 150 feet deep. Sliding always takes place in layers, the lowest layer fixed to the surface, the upper layers (in a fully developed downslope flow) sliding progressively faster to a maximum velocity at 60 to 120 feet above the surface. It has been shown that fully developed downslope flow, sliding on its lowest layer, is almost free of surface friction; retardation is largely consequent to mixing at the upper inversion surface.

Mountain Winds

Downslope flow sufficient to provide a good sailing breeze requires
- a large pressure head due to a large disparity in temperature and altitude between the surface air over the peaks and over the water
- the amalgamation of many slope flows into a single combined downvalley flow, thereby increasing the velocity and smoothing out the intermittency characteristic of flow down a single slope
- the amalgamation of many tributary valley flows into a single main valley flow—a mountain wind
- a linear valley opening onto a plain, sea, or lake toward which the accumulated air can pour and beyond which it can exit

The larger and higher the catchment area and the less restricted the outflow, the greater will be the volume of cold air entrained, the easier it will be discharged, and the greater will be the velocity and duration of the resultant flow.

The "mountain wind"—the combination of many nocturnal downslope flows into a single wind directed down the long axis of a valley—is the opposite of the upslope valley wind. The flow in a mountain wind is intermittent in part because downslope flow is intermittent, but chiefly because the flows from the tributary valleys alternately block and reinforce one another. The coldest air at the bottom of the deepest (the main) valley will obstruct flow out from the tributaries until a large enough mass of a sufficient coldness has accumulated. And once this tributary flow begins, it blocks the main valley flow until it in turn accumulates a sufficient mass and spills downvalley once again.

The volume and velocity of a mountain wind depend on the distance it falls (which determines its pressure head) and on the initial temperature disparity between the air at the top of the slope and at the bottom. At night descending air will always heat more rapidly than the surrounding air (the lapse rate in the surrounding air is always low—the coldest air is at the bottom). Therefore the excess density of the downslope flow depends entirely on its initial advantage. A mountain wind can fall 1,800 feet, heating at the adiabatic rate, 0.6°F per 100 feet, as long as it begins 10°F colder than the air at the bottom of the slope.

Near the base of the slope the cold air accumulates, the downflowing layer becomes thicker—very thick if the outflow is restricted, less thick if it is unrestricted. Before accelerating out onto water (if present), the downslope flow is slowed by the dense air accumulating at the bottom of the slope. Above a completely enclosed lake a thick pool of cold air may approach the slope several hundreds of feet above its base and prevent any flow from reaching the surface. A thermal belt, above which the descending air is heating and accelerating, below which it is cooling and slowing, forms and moves up and down the slope in a seesaw motion as the pool of cold air accumulates and dissipates.

Characteristics of the Overwater Flow

The strength of the overwater flow depends on the strength of the overland flow and the degree of obstruction to water-level outflow. If the water body is large (the sea) or a low-lying plain exists on the far side of the lake, flow will continue from the slope to the far side at nearly the slope speed. If, however, the lake is enclosed, the overwater surface flow will diminish progressively as the sliding air runs out above an ever-deepening pool of cold air.

Nocturnal and Early-Morning Downslope Flow

A mass of air flowing downslope is cold and dense relative to its surroundings, and limited by a strong inversion lid a few hundred feet above the surface. Such a flow is highly susceptible to channeling and emerges onto a water body along the trajectory of the final valley. Over water it appears in a set of distinct flows dominating the surface adjacent to the opening of a valley, and spreading fanlike until halted by another flow. A boat sailing alongshore will meet a series of oscillating shifts and dramatic variations in wind speed as it enters and departs from these zones of influence.

The overwater portion of a downslope wind begins to diminish at sunrise or whenever the slope is first exposed to the sun. In the upper valley the mountain wind may continue—often for several hours—as the accumulated pools of cold air gradually deplete. But on a lake at the foot of a slope, the warming pool from above is less and less able to penetrate the cold pool below, and the surface flow soon disappears. Only where a preexistent nocturnal flow is drawn onward across a lake into a morning sea/lake breeze (as it is on Lago di Garda and on New York's Finger Lakes) will its strength persist or increase into the morning hours. As a warming morning flow dies, its surface flow, less and less able to penetrate the near-shore pool of accumulated cold air, recedes from the shoreline. The final evidence of residual flow is typically brought to the surface by mechanical turbulence a mile or more from the shore.

Initial single-slope downflow is tranquil, though intermittent; each shallow mass of sliding air is free of dramatic changes in velocity or direction. But after the amalgamation of tributary flows, when a cushion of cold barely moving air covers the surface obstacles, flow in the middle layers can reach "shooting" velocity. Confined beneath an inversion above, and sliding on, a mat of absolutely smooth cold air below, the stream may develop wave characteristics. When then it encounters a major constriction or falls from a precipice, it may manifest a "jump" (a dramatic alteration in velocity associated with altered confinement in the vertical plane) and may be associated with a violent and sustained gust impact splash on a lake below.

Evening Downslope Flow

Downslope flow may appear on a lake in early evening as the afternoon lake breeze dies. Such flows occur below (usually steep) slopes that face more or less east and fall into shade in late afternoon. If a large area of flat (or less steeply inclined) insolation-responsive land intervenes between the slope and the lake, the immature downslope flow will be drawn into a thermal circulation. Low pressure induced by the continued heating of the sunlit lower slopes creates a thermal gradient relative to the shaded slopes above, and the reinforced downslope flow, spreading across the insolated area, will flow out onto the lake beyond. The overlake flow is merely the consequence of the momentum induced in the moving air. No thermal gradient draws it onward, and it usually dissipates within a mile or two of shore.

Evening downslope flows usually disappear at nightfall as the lower slopes fall into shade, but in some cases, if the upper slopes form a large catchment area, are the forerunners of persistent nocturnal downslope flow.

Glossary

~~~~~~~~~~~~~~~~~~~~~~~~

Adiabatic: The change induced by vertical movement in the character (temperature, moisture content, etc.) of the air.

Adiabatic lapse rate (ALR): The rate of change in temperature with altitude in a mass of lifting or sinking air, associated with the expansion or contraction of that air mass during vertical movement (0.6°F/100 feet, or 1°C/100 meters).

Advected air: The air (its temperature, lapse rate, humidity, etc.) transported horizontally in an air flow.

Advection: The transport of heat, humidity, and similar characteristics by the horizontal movement of air.

Air mass: A large segment of the atmosphere possessing the same weather properties, temperature, humidity, and stability throughout.

Amalgamated sea/lake breeze: The type of sea/lake breeze in which the surface onshore flow is amalgamated with an onshore gradient wind (in the absence of an upper-level offshore flow).

Atmosphere: The body of air that envelops the earth.

Axial flow: Surface air flow channeled parallel to the long axis of an enclosed body of water.

Back: A counterclockwise shift in wind direction.

Barrier: An obstruction to wind flow that may (depending on the direction and stability of the air flow) result in blanketing, lifting, or channeling.

Bermuda High: The semipermanent subtropical high situated over the North Atlantic from early spring until late summer.

Bernouli's principle: Pressure decreases lateral to a moving gas or fluid in proportion to the velocity of the flow.

Bise (la): The northeasterly portion (that flows across the Swiss Plateau) of a widespread gradient-induced downslope flow from the Alps to the Mediterranean.

Blanketing: The reduction and disturbance in wind flow to leeward of a barrier.

Bora: A gradient-induced downslope flow from the Dinaric Alps to the Adriatic.

Boundary layer: The layer closest to the surface (usually the earth's surface) within which convection begins and all motion is vertical.

Boyle's law: A gas expands or contracts in proportion to its temperature.

Breakthrough: The dissolution of an inversion by the convection and accumulation of heated air from below.

Bubble: The focal accumulation and expansion of air above a heated surface prior to the air's separation.

Buoyancy: The net excess of pressure acting upward (in opposition to gravity) consequent to the greater density of air below, compared with above, a given level.

Calm: The absence of wind flow at the surface.

Centripetal force: The theoretical force causing air to flow in an intermediate direction between perpendicular to the pressure gradient, in response to the Coriolis force, and parallel to the pressure gradient, in response to the pressure gradient force.

Channeling: The altered speed and deviation (so as to flow more parallel to the contours of the topography) of a stable air flow produced by its encounter with a topographical feature.

Chimney effect: The pressure decrease along an insolated slope that forces air onslope and upslope beneath and overlying layer of cooler free air.

Circulation: The movement (vertical or horizontal) of air or water that maintains a pressure gradient, producing flow toward the depleting high pressure and away from the accumulation at the site of low pressure.

Cold front: A deviation of the polar front that results in cold air undermining and lifting warm air as it advances to the east.

Compression: The increase in density of a mass of air consequent to its sinking, associated with an increase in temperature.

Condensation: Cloud formation. The process by which water vapor is converted to its liquid form, associated with the release of heat (the "latent heat of condensation") and the enhancement of convection.

Conduction: The transmission of heat by direct contact.

Confinement: The vertical or horizontal restriction of an air flow by an inversion, a topographical feature, or a pressure ridge.

Continental polar (cP) air: Dry, cold sinking air derived from a high-pressure air mass that has accumulated over northern continental plains.

Contraction: The reduction in volume and increase in density and heat associated with compression (usually due to sinking).

Convection: The transport of heat, humidity, and similar characteristics by the vertical movement (accompanied by expansion and cooling) of parcels of air heated as a result of contact with an insolated surface.

Convergence: The approach and impact of one air flow (or segment of an air flow) with another, resulting in slowing and lifting.

Converging shoreline: A shoreline that with distance downwind causes the water body to narrow.

Coriolis (Geostrophic) force: The force, due to differences in the speed of rotation of the earth at different latitudes, that causes the trajectory of all flow to be deviated (in the Northern Hemisphere to veer, and in the Southern Hemisphere to back) in proportion to its speed and vertical separation from the earth's surface.

Corner effect: The reinforcement of the pressure gradient force by the Coriolis force when an air flow is turned right (veered) by topography or by a pressure ridge.

"Crossing the shoreline": The dramatic alteration in surface pressure, in the thermal gradient, and in the velocity of the onshore flow induced when the cool marine air in a sea/lake breeze crosses the shoreline.

Cumulus: Fluffy white cotton wool clouds that form at low and midlevel when condensation occurs in updrafts.

Divergence: The separation of one air flow (or segment of an air flow) from another, resulting in acceleration and sinking.

Diverging shoreline: A shoreline that with distance downwind causes the water body to widen.

Doppler radar: The imaging of echoes created by radar transmission that demonstrates the water-droplet content of a given air mass; used to detect convergence and divergence.

Downburst: The amalgamation of many downdrafts into a large cylindrical mass of descending air; the generic name for all downdrafts regardless of size.

Downdraft: A column of descending air (the amalgamation of multiple falling parcels) associated with an updraft (a column of ascending air) that brings veered higher-velocity air to the surface and results in a gust.

Downslope wind: The movement of cold air down a slope, associated with adiabatic compression and heating.

Drainage wind: A cold surface flow that drains downslope from high pressure above an upland plateau.

Elevation: The upward movement of a layer of air, associated with expansion, decrease in density, and cooling.

Equatorial Convergence Zone: The zone to either side of the equator, characterized by convergence, uplift, and condensation and containing the Equatorial Heat Lows.

Evaporation: The process by which liquid water is converted to its gaseous form (water vapor), associated with the acquisition of heat by the water and the cooling of the surrounding air.

Expansion: The decrease in density and the cooling of a mass of air consequent to its lifting.

Expansion differential: The pressure gradient created by differences in insolation-induced expansion on either side of a mountain barrier.

Fan effect: The backing of a developing sea/lake breeze that produces a progressive lift (a "fan") on port tack with distance to windward and away from land.

Flow (or Air flow): The persistent movement in response to a pressure gradient of a mass of air, characterized by direction, speed, depth, and extent.

Föhn: A downslope wind that due to compression becomes progressively warmer with descent.

Free air: The air unattached to and separated from the earth's surface.

Friction: The resistance to the movement of an air flow, associated with contact with an adjacent surface.

Front: The boundary between two air masses of different density.

Glacier wind: A wind composed of cold, dense air flowing downslope from the surface of a glacier toward non-ice-covered surrounding land.

Gradient (pressure gradient): The difference in pressure between two sites at the same altitude; usually induced by either thermal or synoptic influences.

Gradient wind: The horizontal movement of air in response to a large-scale, or synoptic, pressure gradient.

Gravity: The net excess of pressure acting downward (in opposition to buoyancy) consequent to the basic force attracting one mass to another (specifically to the surface of the earth).

Greenhouse effect: The effect (similar to that of a greenhouse) of cloud cover in permitting incoming ultraviolet radiation but blocking outgoing infrared radiation.

Gust: The horizontal translation of the vertical impact of a downdraft with the earth's surface.

Gusting zone: The near-shore, overwater zone within which downdrafts induced by, and displaced downwind from, overland updrafts reach the surface.

Header (Heading Shift): A shift that requires the boat to head farther away from the median wind.

Heat: The energy involved in the motion of molecules that, in air, is transmitted chiefly by convection.

Heat low: A low-pressure system formed over a large area of barren heated land in summer.

High (High-Pressure Area): A mass of sinking air that is denser than its surroundings, from which air flows outward.

Horizontal convective roll (HCR): The organization of convection in unstable airstreams into sheets of rising air that form adjacent, counterrotating helices and (presumably) account for the formation of cumulus cloud streets and medium oscillations in the surface wind.

Humidity: The concentration of water vapor in the air.

Inertia: The resistance of a stationary mass to the initiation of motion.

Inflow: The surface flow inward toward a center of low pressure.

Infrared radiation: The longwave radiation associated with the cooling of land and of water droplets; most evident nocturnally.

Inshore (or Near-Shore): An area of a water body lying close to shore or in the direction toward shore.

Insolation: The heating of the earth's surface by shortwave radiation from the sun. *Insolation responsiveness* is the degree to which the temperature of a surface is raised by insolation.

Instability: The facilitation of convection by relatively cold, buoyant air in which the lapse rate is greater than the adiabatic.

Inversion: A level or layer in the atmosphere at which the normal lapse rate reverses and the temperature rises with increasing elevation. A *conduction inversion* is an inversion induced by the cooling of the air in contact with a cool surface and the accumulation of the cooled air over low-lying surfaces. A *radiation inversion* is an inversion induced by the cooling of the land surface by longwave (infrared) radiation and of the near-surface air by conduction. A *subsidence inversion* is an inversion induced by the sinking and heating (by compression) of upper-level air above a cold surface (usually water). An *advection inversion* is an inversion induced by the advection of warm air across a cold surface (usually water).

Isobar: The locus of points of equal pressure in a horizontal plane, drawn on a weather map around centers of high and low pressure.

Isoline: The locus of points of equal pressure in a vertical plane, drawn as slopes down which air flows from high pressure toward low pressure.

Jet stream: A narrow band of strong winds at the level of the tropopause (above 30,000 feet), the position of which determines the position of the polar front and the intensity of the low-pressure systems that form along the front.

Lake breeze: See *Sea/lake breeze.*

Laminar flow: Flow characterized by a lack of turbulence, attachment to adjacent surfaces, and a major shear (increase in speed and veering) with distance above the surface (typical of light air).

Lapse rate: The rate of change with altitude of the temperature of the atmosphere, typically a decrease with distance from the earth's surface. See also *Surrounding air lapse rate, Adiabatic lapse rate,* and *Near-surface lapse rate.*

Latent heat of condensation: The heat released when water vapor condenses into liquid water, typically in cloud formation.

Latitude: The distance north or south of the equator; a determinant of the strength of the Coriolis force and of sea/lake breeze generation.

Layer: A horizontal segment or stratum of air or of an air flow that differs from the supra-

and subjacent segments. Layering is characteristic of stable conditions (e.g., down-flows) in which the coldest air is at the bottom.

Layline: The course that permits a close-hauled or running boat to fetch the mark ahead.

Lift (Lifting Shift): A shift that permits the boat to head closer to the median wind (the opposite of header).

Lifting: The elevation of a layer of air when it encounters cold air *(frontal lift)*, a mountain *(orographic lift)*, another air mass *(convergence)*, or consequent to convection *(thermal lift)*.

Liftoff: The elevation, after separation, of heated air in the form of an updraft.

Local sea/lake breeze: A sea/lake breeze limited to a confined near-shore zone; usually light and transient.

Longwave radiation: The infrared radiation associated with the cooling of the land and of water droplets; most evident nocturnally.

Low (Low-Pressure Area): A mass of rising air that is less dense than its surroundings, toward which surrounding air flows.

Low level: The segment of the troposphere (its winds and clouds) lying closest to the earth's surface, usually below an altitude of 6,500 feet; the lower portion of an air flow, such as a sea/lake breeze.

Lull: A transient decrease in surface air flow consequent to convergence or the impaired penetration of an overflowing wind, an intergust period.

Marine air: Air that has lain above the water surface and has acquired the temperature and other characteristics of the water.

Marine layer: The lowest layer (usually the lowest 1,000 to 2,000 feet) of the troposphere overlying the ocean that moves ashore in a sea breeze front.

Maritime tropical gulf (mTg) air: The moist, warm air derived from a high-pressure air mass that has accumulated over the Gulf of Mexico.

Median wind: The wind direction midway between the extreme shifts (backs and veers) in an oscillating air flow.

Medium oscillations: Persisting large-scale variations in the speed and direction of an air flow, occurring every 3 to 20 minutes and induced by horizontal convective rolls (HCRs) developed over land.

Meltemi: A strong northerly air flow in the Aegean, due to the proximity of high pressure to the west and the Arabian Heat Low to the east.

Microburst (Misoburst): A large and violent downburst from 100 to 1,000 yards in diameter, accelerated during descent from the upper level of the atmosphere by the evaporation of ice crystals.

Midlevel: The segment of the troposphere, its winds and clouds (alto), that are typically present between 6,500 and 20,000 feet.

Mistral: The gradient-induced downslope wind descending the Rhône Valley from high pressure over the Swiss Plateau toward low pressure in the Gulf of Lyons.

Momentum: The resistance of a moving mass to slowing.

Near-shore (Inshore): An area of a water body lying close to shore and characterized by a modified air flow; in an offshore wind, a gusting zone.

Near-surface lapse rate: The difference in temperature between the surface of a bubble of heated surface air and the suprajacent ambient air; separation occurs when the near-surface lapse rate reaches a critically high level (3.5 times greater than the ALR).

New wind: A wind from a new source that displaces or replaces a calm or an existing wind.

Nucleation sites: Sites highly responsive to insolation, where bubbles of heated air form and subsequently separate into continuous stream convection.

Occlusion (Occluded Front): The result of a cold front overtaking a warm front and (often) becoming stationary.

Ocean sea breeze: A sea breeze that comes from an ocean across an ocean shoreline, that may extend far inland and come offshore onto an inland water body.

Offshore sea/lake breeze: A sea/lake breeze that crosses intervening land and comes offshore onto a second water body.

Offshore wind: An overland air flow that is directed toward and comes off a shoreline.

Onshore wind: An overwater air flow that is directed toward and crosses a shoreline.

Orographic: Induced in an airstream by mountains, as orographic lift, fog, cloud, etc.

Oscillating shift: A shift in wind direction that is followed within minutes (prior to the completion of a leg of a sailing race) by a return shift toward the original direction; characteristic of unstable air flows.

Outflow: The surface flow outward from a center of high pressure.

Parallel-to-shore air flow: An air flow that during some portion of its trajectory flows parallel to a shoreline and is characterized by the differing speeds and directions of its overwater and overland segments.

Persistent shift: A shift in wind direction that is not followed (prior to the completion of a leg of a sailing race) by a return shift toward the original direction.

Phase: The weather and wind direction characteristic of a given position of the polar front and its attendant low-pressure centers.

Polar front: The line beneath the jet stream along which polar air masses meet tropical air masses and along which low-pressure centers form and migrate.

Pressure: The force downward of a column of air; equal to the total weight of the column of air above a given surface or level in the atmosphere (density × volume [height × area]).

Pressure gradient: The difference in pressure between two sites at the same level that produces the pressure gradient force and results in horizontal air flow; the difference between the weight of a column of heavy (contracted, dense, colder) air and an adjacent column of light (expanded, less dense, warmer) air.

Pressure gradient force: The force produced by a pressure gradient that causes air to move down the gradient.

Pressure head: A stable, continuous pressure differential created by a difference in altitude, in surface temperature (such as a glacier or a waterfall), in heat production, etc.

Pressure level: The level in the atmosphere at which a certain pressure exists.

Primary sea/lake breeze: The type of simple sea/lake breeze in which the entire circulation (onshore surface and offshore upper level flows), developing beneath an inversion, is independent of the gradient wind.

Progressive shift: A persistent shift that progresses in the same direction.

Radiation: The transmission of energy in waves (infrared, ultraviolet, etc.).

Radiational cooling: The cooling of the earth's surface and the layer of air in contact with it due to the loss of heat in infrared radiation; most evident nocturnally.

Resistance: The force engendered by movement and acting in opposition to that movement; chiefly friction.

Rhumb line: The straightline course between two marks.

Ridge: An elevation of the isobars along a track extending away from a center of high pressure; a locus of sites at which the pressure is higher than at adjacent sites to either side.

Roll cloud: The low, black, cigar-shaped cloud that forms in the vortex or rotor near the surface in the outflow of a thunderstorm or line squall.

Rotor: A horizontal vortex, forming in rapidly flowing air, that persists at a given site or position.

Santa Ana wind: A hot gradient-induced downslope wind developing in the Los Angeles area that flows from the Sierra Madre Mountains toward the Pacific Ocean.

Sea/lake breeze: A thermal wind system responding to a pressure gradient caused by the insolation and heating of land in the presence of cold water. See *Primary sea/lake breeze, Secondary sea/lake breeze,* and *Amalgamated sea/lake breeze.*

Secondary sea/lake breeze: The type sea/lake breeze that is induced by the reduction in overland pressure created by an unstable offshore gradient wind and whose upper-level (offshore) circulation is provided by that gradient wind.

Separation: The detachment and vertical movement of a bubble of heated air accumulating on an insolated surface consequent to the creation of a near-surface lapse rate 3.5 times the adiabatic lapse rate.

Shear (Wind Shear): The rate of change in wind direction with altitude and/or with distance in another plane. Shear is pronounced at the surface of rapidly moving layers of air, as in downslope flows.

Shortwave radiation: The ultraviolet radiation from the sun that is the principal component of insolation.

Sinkhole: A depression in the surface of the land that allows cold air in downslope flow to accumulate and from which the cold air cannot escape until the depression is filled.

Slope air: The air, attached to a slope, that moves up- or downslope without separating from the surface in response to a pressure gradient; distinguished from free air by its attachment.

Speed (Wind Speed): The rate of movement (of an air flow) horizontally. (Distinguish velocity.)

Splitting: The separation of segments of a single air flow that (as they flow over surfaces inducing differing friction, usually to either side of a shoreline) vary in speed and consequently in direction.

Squall: A brief, violent downburst system typically located in a line ahead of an advancing cold front.

Stability: The diminution of convection in air characterized by a low lapse rate, the layering of cold air beneath warm, and one or more low-level inversions.

Stream (Continuous Stream Separation): A form of convection resulting in the continuous vertical movement of parcels of air.

Streamlines: Lines indicating the direction of the wind, usually representing a composite of recorded wind flows for a given period.

Subsidence (Sinking): The downward movement of a layer of air (in response to subjacent contraction), resulting in the contraction, compression, increase in density, and heating of the subsiding air. See also *Inversion.*

Subtropical high: A high-pressure system formed over one of the major oceans, in which air that has risen in the Equatorial Convergence Zone subsides, heats, and forms a subsidence inversion.

Surface wind: The air flow that is nearest the surface (beneath the upper-level surface air flow) and that would affect a sailboat.

Surrounding air lapse rate (SLR): The rate of change of temperature with altitude in the ambient air, as in the air surrounding an updraft or a downdraft.

341

Synoptic pressure gradient: The pressure gradient associated with large-scale differences in atmospheric pressure consequent to the global air circulation (called *synoptic* because it is the pressure gradient indicated on synoptic weather maps: synopses of meteorological data for a particular time).

Thermal wind: The horizontal movement of air in response to a small-scale (meso or miso) pressure gradient created by differences in surface temperature.

Thunderstorm: A major convection cell into which heated updrafts are drawn and their moisture condensed into cumulonimbus cloud, which in turn induces violent downdraft flow (frequently associated with rain and hail).

Topography: The shape of the land surface, particularly the variations in the height of the land.

Trade winds: Relatively constant easterly (southeasterly to northeasterly) winds produced by the flow of air from the equatorward sides of the subtropical highs toward the adjacent equatorial lows.

Trajectory: The direction (in three dimensions) in which the momentum of an air flow causes the air to flow.

Transmountain wind: An air flow induced by a pressure gradient to rise above and transit a mountain range.

Tropopause: The top of the troposphere, where temperature ceases to fall with height, creating an inversion.

Troposphere: The lower 30,000 to 50,000 feet of the atmosphere, which contains almost all the water vapor and weather systems and which is bounded aloft by the tropopause (a layer above which temperature ceases to fall with altitude).

Trough: A dip in the isobars along a track extending away from a center of low pressure; a locus of sites at which the pressure is lower than at adjacent sites to either side.

Turbulence, *Thermal*: The vertical movement of parcels of air (updrafts and downdrafts) in response to insolation. *Mechanical*: The movement, in all directions, of parcels of air in response to the interaction between the flow and the obstacles it encounters (the surface topography, other air flows, or other segments of the same air flow).

Turbulent layer: The layer within which all turbulence takes place, between the surface boundary layer and an inversion, or the tropopause.

Two winds simultaneously: The simultaneous presence at the surface of two winds of different origin, usually a secondary sea/lake breeze and a gradient wind.

Ultraviolet radiation: The shortwave radiation from the sun that is the principal component of insolation.

Unstable air flow: A cold air flow, the temperature of which rapidly falls with height (characterized by a high lapse rate) and within which, overland and in the near-shore gusting zone, thermal turbulence is marked.

Updraft: A column of ascending air (the amalgamation of multiple rising parcels) induced by separation from an insolated surface.

Upper level: the upper portion of an air flow that is less affected by surface friction, is veered, and moves at a higher velocity than the lower surface portion.

Upslope flow: The movement of heated air up a slope in response to a pressure gradient. Typically associated with adiabatic expansion and cooling.

Upwelling: The elevation of cold bottom water to the surface in response to the divergence of a surface current away from a coast.

Valley wind: The organized upslope flow of air in a valley in response to the insolation of its sides and ridges.

Veer: A clockwise change in wind direction.

Velocity: The rate of movement (of an air flow) in a given direction, usually represented by a vector.

Velocity veer: The veering of an air flow due to the Coriolis force, in response to an increase in velocity.

Virga: The vertical streams of water droplets trailing beneath a cumulonimbus cloud, indicating rain that evaporates before reaching the earth.

Warm front: A deviation of the polar front that results in the elevation of a warm air mass over a cold air mass, typically ahead of and/or to the equatorward side of a low-pressure center.

Warm sector: The segment of the troposphere between a warm front and a cold front, characterized by vertical instability and westerly winds.

Warmth: The presence of heat; a state of high molecular movement.

Water droplets: Water in its visible, liquid state, which constitutes a cloud; following condensation, prior to evaporation.

Water vapor: Water in its gaseous state, following evaporation and prior to condensation.

Weather system: A high- or low-pressure system and its associated gradient winds.

Wind: Horizontal air flow in response to a pressure gradient (thermal or synoptic).

Bibliography

I. Simple Onshore Winds

DE LA RUE, E. A. *Man and the Winds.* New York: Philosophical Library, 1955.

DUTTON, J. A. *The Ceaseless Wind.* New York: McGraw-Hill, 1976.

HUMPHREYS, W. J. *Physics of the Air.* Philadelphia: J. P. Lippincott, 1920.

JOHNSON, M. E., J. D. KALMA, and D. PEDERSON. "A Study of the Dependence of Surface Wind Direction on the Gradient Wind." *Monthly Weather Review* 114 (1986): 257.

ZHONG, S., and E. S. TAKLE. "The Effects of Large-Scale Winds on the Sea-Land-Breeze Circulations in an Area of Complex Coastal Heating." *Journal of Applied Meteorology* 32 (1993): 1181.

II. Gradient Winds: Diurnal Variations

BARRY, R. G., and R. J. CHORLEY. *Atmosphere, Weather, and Climate.* London: Methuen and Co., 1968.

BETHWAITE, F., *High Performance Sailing.* Camden, Me.: International Marine (A division of the McGraw-Hill Companies), 1993.

BLACKADAR, A. "The Wind above the Willows." *Weatherwise* 43 (1990): 103.

DONN, W. L. *Meteorology.* New York: McGraw-Hill, 1965.

GODSKE, O. L., T. BERGERAN, J. BJERKNES, and R. C. BUNGAARD. *Dynamic Meteorology and Weather Forecasting.* American Meteorological Society and the Carnegie Institute of Washington. Baltimore: Waverly Press, 1957.

GOSSARD, E. E., and W. H. HOOKE. *Waves in the Atmosphere.* Amsterdam-New York: Elsevier, 1975.

HSU, S. A. *Coastal Meteorology.* San Diego: Academic Press, 1988.

POWELL, M. D. *Wind Forecasting for the Sailing Events of the 1996 Olympics.* NOAA Hurricane Research Division, AOML. Miami, 1996.

SMITH, R. K. "Traveling Waves and Bores in the Lower Atmosphere." *Earth-Science Reviews* 25 (1988): 267.

WILLETT, H. C. *Descriptive Meteorology.* New York: Academic Press, 1950.

III. Gradient Winds: Weekly and Seasonal Variations

ESSENWANGER, O. M. *World Survey of Climatology.* Vols. 5, 11, 13. Amsterdam-New York: Elsevier, 1985.

Hammond Universal World Atlas. Maplewood, N.J.: Hammond, Inc., 1988.

WHELPLEY, D. A. *Weather, Water, and Boating.* Cambridge, Md.: Cornell Maritime Press, 1961.

IV. Gradient Winds: Offshore Flow

EPPINGER, J. "The Deadly Dynamics of the Microburst." *Science Digest* 94 (1986): 52.

FALLER, A. J. "Large Eddies in the Atmospheric Boundary Layer and Their Possible Role in the Formation of Cloud Rows." *Journal of the Atmospheric Sciences* 22 (1965): 176.

FUJITA, T. T. "The Downburst: Microburst and Microburst." Satellite and Mesometeorology Research Project Res. Pap. #210, University of Chicago, 122 pp., 1985.

FUJITA, T. T. "Tornadoes and Downbursts in the Context of Generalized Planetary Scales." *Journal of the Atmospheric Sciences* 38 (1981): 1511.

HJELMFELT, M. R. "The Microbursts of 22 June 1982 in JAWS." *Journal of the Atmospheric Sciences* 44 (1987): 1646.

KELLY, R. D. "Horizontal Roll and Boundary-Layer Interrelationships Observed over Lake Michigan." *Journal of the Atmospheric Sciences* 41 (1984): 1816.

KUETTNER, J. P. "Cloud Bands in the Earth's Atmosphere." *Tellus* 23 (1971): 404.

LINDEN, P. F., and J. E. SIMPSON. "Microbursts: A Hazard to Aircraft." *Nature* 317 (1985): 601.

MIURA, Y. "Aspect Ratios of Longitudinal Rolls and Convection Cells Observed during Cold Air Outbreaks." *Journal of the Atmospheric Sciences* 43 (1986): 26.

PARSONS, D. B., and R. KROPFLI. "Dynamics and Fine Structure of a Microburst." *Journal of the Atmospheric Sciences* 47 (1990): 1674.

PLANK, V. G. "Wind Conditions in Situations of Pattern-form and Non-Pattern-Form Cumulus Convection." *Tellus* 18 (1966): 2.

THORPE, A. "Meteorology: Watery Model for Microbursts." *Nature* 317 (1985): 572.

WILLETT, H. G., and F. SANDERS. *Descriptive Meteorology*. New York: Academic Press, 1944.

V. Gradient Winds: Parallel-to-Shore Flow

BERNOT, J-Y. *Bernot on Breezes*. Shrewsbury, England: Waterline Books, 1993.

GRAHAM, N. E., and T. P. BARNETT. "Sea Surface Temperature, Surface Wind Divergence, and Convection over Tropical Oceans." *Science* 238 (1987): 657.

WINANT, C. D., C. E. DORMAN, and C. A. FRIEHE. "The Marine Layer off Northern California: An Example of Supercritical Channel Flow." *Journal of the Atmospheric Sciences* 45 (1988): 3588.

VI. Thermal Winds: The Primary Sea/Lake Breeze

BANTA, R. M., L. D. OLIVIER, and D. H. LEVINSON. "Evolution of the Monterey Bay Sea Breeze Layer." *Journal of the Atmospheric Sciences* 50 (1993): 3959.

BRUBAKER, J. M. "Similarity Structure in the Convective Boundary Layer of a Lake." *Nature* 330 (1987):742.

HOUNAM, C. E. "The Sea Breeze at Perth." *Weather Development Research Bulletin* 3 (1945): 20.

KEPERT, J. D., and R. K. SMITH. "A Simple Model of the Australian West Coast Trough." *Monthly Weather Review* 120 (1992): 2042.

MAHRER, Y., and M. SEGAL. "On the Effects of an Island's Geometry and Size on Inducing Sea Breeze Circulation." *Monthly Weather Review* 113 (1985): 170.

SIMPSON, J. E. *Sea Breeze and Local Wind*. Cambridge: Cambridge University Press, 1994.

WATTS, A. J. *Instant Weather Forecasting*. New York: Dodd, Mead & Co., 1968.

WYATT, R. A. "The Sea Breeze at Hobart." Australia, Bureau of Meteorology, Working Papers (1963): 62.

YOSHIKADO, H. "Numerical Study of the Daytime Urban Effect and Its Interaction with the Sea Breeze." *Journal of Applied Meteorology* 31 (1992): 1146.

VII. Thermal Winds: The Secondary Sea/Lake Breeze

DALU, G. A., and R. A. PIELKE. "An Analytical Study of the Sea Breeze." *Journal of the Atmospheric Sciences* 46 (1989): 1815.

DURAND, P., S. BRIERE, and A. DRUILHET. "A Sea-Land Transition Observed during the COAST Experiment." *Journal of the Atmospheric Sciences* 46 (1989): 96.

FELIKS, Y. "An Analytical Model of the Diurnal Oscillation of the Inversion Base Due to the Sea Breeze." *Journal of the Atmospheric Sciences* 51 (1994): 991.

FELIKS, Y. "A Numerical Model for the Estimation of the Diurnal Fluctuation of the Inversion Height Due to the Breeze." *Boundary-Layer Meteorology* 62 (1993): 151.

FETT, R. W., and P. M. TAG. "The Sea Breeze-Induced Coastal Calm Zone as Revealed by Satellite Data and Simulated by a Numerical Model." *Monthly Weather Review* 112 (1984): 1226.

GERBER, H., S. CHANG, and T. HOLT. "Evolution of a Marine Boundary Layer Jet." *Journal of the Atmospheric Sciences* 46 (1989): 1312.

HONG, Y., and R. A. ANTHES. "The Effect of Latitude on the Sea Breeze." *Monthly Weather Review* 115 (1987): 936.

LU, R., and R. P. TURCO. "Air Pollutant Transport in a Coastal Environment, Part I: Two-Dimensional Simulations of Sea-Breeze and Mountain Effects." *Journal of the Atmospheric Sciences* 51 (1994): 2285.

SHA, W., T. KAWAMURA, and H. UEDA. "A Numerical Study of Sea/Land Breezes as a Gravity Current." *Journal of the Atmospheric Sciences* 50 (1991): 1649.

SIMPSON, J. E., D. A. MANSFIELD, and J. R. MILFORD. "Inland Penetration of the Sea Breeze Front." *Quarterly Journal of the Royal Meteorological Society* 103 (1977): 47.

WAKIMOTO, R. M., and N. T. ATKINS. "Observations of the Sea Breeze Front during CaPE." *Marine Weather Review* 122 (1994): 1092.

ZHONG, S., J. M. LEONE, JR., and E. S. TAKLE. "Interaction of the Sea Breeze with a River Breeze in an Area of Complex Coastal Heating." *Boundary-Layer Meteorology* 56 (1991): 101.

VIII. Thermal Winds: The Amalgamated Sea/Lake Breeze

ABBS, D. "Sea Breeze Interactions along a Concave Coastline in Southern Australia." *Marine Weather Review* 114 (1986): 831.

ARRITT, R. W. "Effects of the Large Scale Flow on Characteristic Features of the Sea Breeze." *Journal of Applied Meteorology* 32 (1993): 116.

IX. Thermal Winds: The Offshore Sea/Lake Breeze

JASPERSON, W. H., G. D. NASTROM, and D. C. FRITTS. "Further Study of Terrain Effects on the Mesoscale Spectrum of Atmospheric Motions." *Journal of the Atmospheric Sciences* 46 (1990): 979.

NICHOLIS, M. E., R. A. PIELKE, and W. R. COTTON. "A Two-Dimensional Numerical Investigation of the Interaction between Sea Breezes and Deep Convection over the Florida Peninsula." *Monthly Weather Review* 119 (1991): 298.

X. Thermal Winds: Upslope Winds

GEIGER, RUDOLF. *The Climate near the Ground.* Cambridge: Harvard University Press, 1965.

HAUSER, ERNEST. Personal communication with chart. Ithaca, New York, USA.

PORCH, W. M., W. E. CLEMENTS, and R. L. COULTER. "Nightime Valley Waves." *Journal of Applied Meteorology* 30 (1991): 145.

SEGAL, M., J. F. W. PURDOM, and J. L. SONG. "Evaluation of Cloud-Shading Effects on the

Generation and Modification of Mesoscale Circulations." *Monthly Weather Review* 114 (1986): 1201.

XI. Thermal Winds: Downslope Winds

HORST, T. W., and J. C. DORAN. "The Turbulent Structure of Nocturnal Slope Flow." *Journal of the Atmospheric Sciences* 45 (1988): 605.

PELTIER, W. R., and J. F. SCINOCCA. "The Origin of Severe Downslope Windstorm Pulsations." *Journal of the Atmospheric Sciences* 47 (1990): 2853.

SMITH, R. B. "On Severe Downslope Winds." *Journal of the Atmospheric Sciences* 42 (1985): 2597.

VERGEINER, I., E. DREISEITL, and C. D. WHITEMAN. "Dynamics of Katabatic Winds in Colorado's Brush Creek Valley." *Journal of the Atmospheric Sciences* 44 (1987): 148.

XU, QIN. "A Theoretical Study of Cold Air Damming." *Journal of the Atmospheric Sciences* 47 (1990): 2969.

XII. Gradient-Induced Downslope Winds

DURRAN, D. R., and J. B. KLEMP. "Another Look at Downslope Winds: Non-Linear Amplification beneath Wave-Overturning Layers." *Journal of the Atmospheric Sciences* 44 (1987): 3402.

KERR, R. A. "Chinook Winds Resemble Water Flowing over a Rock." *Science* 231 (1986): 1244.

LESSARD, A. G. "The Santa Ana Wind of Southern California." *Weatherwise* 41 (1988): 100.

SMITH, R. B. "Aerial Observations of the Yugoslavian Bora." *Journal of the Atmospheric Sciences* 44 (1987): 269.

Index